ETHNIC CHINESE in SINGAPORE and MALAYSIA

A Dialogue between Tradition and Modernity

CONTRIBUTORS

- **Wang Gungwu**, PhD, Professor and Director, East Asian Institute, National University of Singapore
- **Chiew Seen Kong**, PhD, former Senior Lecturer, Department of Sociology, National University of Singapore
- **Tey Nai Peng**, PhD, Associate Professor, Department of Economics, University of Malaya, Kuala Lumpur, Malaysia
- **Yong Ching Fatt (CF Yong)**, PhD, former Reader, Department of History, Faculty of Social Sciences, Flinders University of South Australia
- **Leo Suryadinata**, PhD, Professor, Department of Political Science, National University of Singapore
- **Eugene KB Tan**, Lecturer, Department of Law, School of Business, Singapore Management University; former Senior Tutor, Department of Political Science, National University of Singapore
- **Ho Khai Leong**, PhD, Senior Lecturer, Department of Political Science, National University of Singapore
- **Tan Liok Ee**, PhD, former Associate Professor, School of Humanities, Universiti Sains Malaysia, Penang, Malaysia
- **Jamie Mackie**, Emeritus Professor, Department of Economics, Australian National University
- **Yen Ching-hwang**, PhD, Reader, Department of History, Adelaide University, Australia; formerly Chair Professor in History, University of Hong Kong
- **Lee Kam Hing**, PhD, former Professor, Department of History, University of Malaya; currently Senior Editor, *The Star*, Kuala Lumpur, Malaysia
- **Ng Beoy Kui**, PhD, Associate Professor, Nanyang Business School, Nanyang Technological University, Singapore
- **Thomas Menkhoff**, PhD, Practice Associate Professor of Management, School of Business, Singapore Management University
- **Benjamin Loh**, Researcher, School of Business, Singapore Management University
- **Jean DeBernardi**, PhD, Associate Professor, Department of Anthropology, University of Alberta, Canada
- **Choong Chee Pang**, PhD, former Dean of Trinity Theological College, Singapore; currently Visiting Professor at Peking University
- **Philip Yuen-sang Leung**, PhD, Professor, Department of History, Chinese University of Hong Kong
- **Koh Tai Ann**, PhD, Professor and Academic Dean, National Institute of Education, Nanyang Technological University, Singapore
- **Quah Sy Ren**, PhD, Assistant Professor, Chinese Language and Culture Division, National Institute of Education, Nanyang Technological University, Singapore
- **Koh Hock Kiat**, PhD, Assistant Professor, Chinese Language and Culture Division, National Institute of Education, Nanyang Technological University, Singapore

ETHNIC CHINESE in SINGAPORE and MALAYSIA

A Dialogue between Tradition and Modernity

LEO SURYADINATA (ed.)

TIMES ACADEMIC PRESS

© 2002 Times Media Private Limited

First published 2002 by Times International Publishing
under the imprint **Times Academic Press**
Times Media Academic Publishing
Times Centre, 1 New Industrial Road, Singapore 536196
Fax: (65) 6 2889 254   E-mail: tap@tpl.com.sg
Online Book Store: http://www.timesone.com.sg/tap

All rights reserved. No part of this publication may be reproduced, stored in a retrieval system, or transmitted, in any form or by any means, electronic, mechanical, photocopying, recording or otherwise, without the prior permission of the publishers.

Printed by CMO Image Printing Enterprise, Singapore

National Library Board (Singapore) Cataloguing in Publication Data

Ethnic Chinese in Singapore and Malaysia: A Dialogue Between Tradition and Modernity / [edited by] Leo Suryadinata. – Singapore : Times Academic Press, c2002.
   p. cm.

   ISBN : 981-210-186-1

1. Chinese – Singapore.   2. Chinese – Malaysia.
I. Suryadinata, Leo, 1941-

   DS610.25
   305.895105957 — dc21   SLS2002023920

Contents

Preface   *vii*

Introduction   *viii*

1 Local and National: A Dialogue between Tradition and Modernity, *Wang Gungwu*   *1*

Part I: Population and Society

2 Chinese Singaporeans: Three Decades of Progress and Changes, *Chiew Seen Kong*   *11*

3 The Changing Demographic Situation of Malaysian Chinese, *Tey Nai Peng*   *45*

Part II: Politics, Identity and Education

4 Peranakan Chinese Identities in Singapore and Malaysia: A Re-examination, *Leo Suryadinata*   *69*

5 Modern Transformation of Chinese Political Leadership in Colonial Singapore, *CF Yong*   *85*

6 Reconceptualizing Chinese Identity: The Politics of Chineseness in Singapore, *Eugene KB Tan*   *109*

7 Bureaucratic Participation and Political Mobilization: Comparing Pre- and Post-1970 Malaysian Chinese Politics, *Ho Khai Leong*   *137*

8 Baggage from the Past, Eyes on the Future: Chinese Education in Malaysia Today, *Tan Liok Ee*   *155*

Part III: Culture and Entrepreneurship

9   Chinese Entrepreneurs in Malaysia: Traditional and Modern, *Jamie Mackie*   175

10   Traditional Ethnic Chinese Business Organizations in Singapore and Malaysia, *Yen Ching-hwang*   195

11   The Emergence of Modern Chinese Business in Malaya: The Case of the Straits Chinese and Oversea-Chinese Banking Corporation, *Lee Kam Hing*   219

12   The Changing Role of Ethnic Chinese SMEs in Economic Restructuring in Singapore: From "Two-legged" Policy to "Three-legged" Strategy, *Ng Beoy Kui*   255

13   Champions of Change or Petty Dinosaurs? A Survey of Organizational Change Management Practices of Chinese SMEs in Singapore, *Thomas Menkhoff and Benjamin Loh*   277

Part IV: Religion

14   Malaysian Chinese Religious Culture: Past and Present, *Jean DeBernardi*   301

15   Religious Composition of the Chinese in Singapore: Some Comments on the Census 2000, *Choong Chee Pang*   325

16   The Moses of China: Huang Naishang and the Christian Commune in Sibu, *Philip Yuen-sang Leung*   337

Part V: Literature

17   Tradition and Modernity in the Fiction of Lee Kok Liang and Catherine Lim: Malaysian and Singaporean Chinese Perspectives, *Koh Tai Ann*   355

18   Evolving Multilingual Theatre in Singapore: The Case of Kuo Pao Kun, *Quah Sy Ren*   377

19   Singapore Poetry in English and Chinese: A Comparison between Simon Tay and Chia Hwee Pheng, *Koh Hock Kiat*   389

Index   401

Preface

The Centre for Chinese Language and Culture at Nanyang Technological University (NTU), the Association of Nanyang University Graduates and Singapore Society of Asian Studies jointly organized an international conference on "Ethnic Chinese in Singapore and Malaysia: A Dialogue between Tradition and Modernity", on 30 June and 1 July 2001 in Singapore. In order to make the conference truly international, the Institute of Modern History, Academia Sinica (Taipei), the Centre for Malaysian Chinese Studies (Kuala Lumpur) and Overseas Chinese Archives of the Chinese University of Hong Kong were invited to be associate organizers.

The conference was conducted in both English and Chinese. There were more than 40 papers, of which half were in English and the other half in Chinese. The English papers, after revision, have been collected in this volume, while the Chinese papers are published by the Centre for Chinese Language and Culture at NTU. We would like to take this opportunity to thank the paper contributors again for their kind co-operation and Times Academic Press for agreeing to publish this book.

The Organizing Committee of the International Conference
on Ethnic Chinese in Singapore and Malaysia

26 December 2001

Introduction

ETHNIC CHINESE IN SINGAPORE AND MALAYSIA: A DIALOGUE BETWEEN TRADITION AND MODERNITY

Leo Suryadinata

There have been many studies on the ethnic Chinese communities in Singapore and Malaysia but most concentrate on the two countries individually. In 2001 three Singapore associations/institutions organized an international conference on both the countries with the focus on tradition and modernity. The contributors were encouraged to undertake a study of Singapore or Malaysia or a comparative study of the two countries. The studies should have a comparative perspective, especially a comparison between the traditional past and the modern present. This book is a product of the conference. However, as the subtitle of the conference indicates, we have adopted the terms "tradition" and "modernity" instead of "the traditional" and "the modern".

Tradition and Modernity

There have been debates on the meanings of tradition and modernity, but there has been no general agreement on these two concepts. Some argue that anything old is tradition while anything new is modernity. Some even maintain that tradition is outdated and, hence, inferior, while modernity is up to date and, therefore, superior.[1]

However, many academics maintain that "Modernity implies modernization, a continuous process of improvement in the capacity of humanity to manage and control its physical, social and cultural environment for its own benefit".[2] It is "a belief in the rational and scientific control of

---

1 "General Commentary: The Meaning of Modernity", in *Modernity: Critical Concepts*, edited by Malcolm Waters, vol 1 (Modernization), London and New York: Routledge, 1999, pp i–ii.
2 Ibid, p iii.

man's physical and social environment and the application of technology to that end".[3] This rational and scientific attitude is supposed to differentiate a modern man from a traditional man, who is superstitious and irrational.

Although academics do not agree with the value judgement on tradition and modernity, many of them agree that modernity is a process of change as a result of "the impact of more upon less 'advanced societies'".[4] From my observation, the authors of this volume use the term "modernity" to mean a process of change, especially economic, social and cultural change, from simplicity to complexity, from the agricultural to the industrial, from the rural to the urban, from the local to the national. These changes are the results of the challenge of rapid industrialization and globalization.

Wang Gungwu in his article addresses the issue of the local (tradition) and the national (modernity) with special reference to the ethnic Chinese identities in Singapore and Malaysia. Ethnic Chinese, as an immigrant community, are naturally oriented towards their original locality. However, after being in the region for some time and confronted with the modern concept of "nation-state" they have also been compelled to change. Nevertheless, the transformation has been different between those ethnic Chinese in Singapore and the ones in Malaysia. In Singapore, the ethnic Chinese are the majority group and as they are "local" as well as "national" in circumstances, they have abandoned the ethnic Chinese tradition to become fully "national" to meet the challenge of globalization. In Malaysia, however, the Chinese continue to rely on tradition in coping with both national and global challenges.

Chinese Societies and Population

Although during the historical period, Singapore and Peninsular Malaya were both ruled by the British, and had similar, if not identical, colonial experiences, they eventually parted and developed separate identities, as Singapore is now a multi-ethnic society with a Chinese dominance, while Malaysia is a multi-ethnic society with a Malay dominance. In the last 30 years or so, these two societies have developed their own characteristics. Chiew Seen Kong analyses the structural and cultural changes of resident

---

3   John H Kautsky, *The Political Consequences of Modernization*, New York and London: John Wiley and Sons, 1972, p 19.

4   Fred Riggs, *Thailand: The Modernization of Bureaucratic Polity*, Honolulu: East-West Center Press, 1966, pp 368–69. Perhaps, a better term is either "economically developed societies" or "industrialized societies".

Singaporeans of Chinese origin over the last three decades (1970–2000) based on available census and survey data. Owing to data limitation, when referring to structural changes, Chiew focuses on the progress in social class attainment; while for cultural changes, he deals with the changes in religion, language usage patterns, fertility, inter-ethnic marriage, ethnic and national identity. He highlights the importance of the impact of China's economic and cultural development on the Singaporean Chinese identity, arguing that this will be the greatest challenge that the Singapore Chinese population has to face.

Tey Nai Peng, on the other hand, addresses the changing demographic situation of the Malaysian Chinese since 1970. He presents very interesting findings: the Chinese population in Malaysia increased from 419,355 persons in 1901 to 3.7 million in 1970 and about 5.6 million in 2001. It has been growing at around 1 per cent per annum in the last two decades, down from 1.7 per cent in the 1970s and 2.5 per cent prior to 1970. During the last decade, the proportionate share of the Chinese population declined steadily from 35.6 per cent to 24.5 per cent. In the 1980s, an estimated 10 per cent emigrated from the country.

Chinese Identities, Politics and Education

The Chinese in Singapore and Malaysia have been heterogeneous groups. They have been divided by class, culture and nationality. However, the cultural, and consequently political, divide appears to be significant. Those Chinese who came earlier and have been partially assimilated into the local society, often known as Baba or Peranakan, and the more recently arrived Chinese, often popularly called Sinkeh (*xinke* or newcomers), constitute two subgroups within the Chinese community. Leo Suryadinata examines the Peranakan Chinese in both Malaysia and Singapore, by looking at the various terms used to refer to this subgroup by outsiders or by themselves. This group is also known as the "Straits Chinese" or "Straits-born Chinese". Suryadinata focuses on the evolution of various Peranakan Chinese identities as reflected in the use of several "equivalent terms", starting from the colonial era and continuing to the present. While "Peranakan" and "Baba" are sociocultural identities, which were first others-given identities and later developed into self-identity, "Straits Chinese" is basically a political and historical identity, which has become anachronistic following the demise of British colonialism, while "Straits-born Chinese" refers to birthplace rather than politics or culture. Post-independent Malaya/Malaysia and

Singapore have both witnessed the revival of such Peranakan/Baba identity but in a weakened form. Instead, the division between different kinds of education, that is, English and Chinese or Malay/English and Chinese, has become more important politically.

Focusing on the Chinese in colonial Singapore, CF Yong, in his article, examines the transformation of the Chinese political leadership in the late 19th century and the first half of the 20th century. Initially, there were two major sources of political leadership, one was the Straits Chinese, which was recognized by the British, while the other came from the Chinese secret societies, mainly from the Sinkeh group. However, at the end of the 19th century, there was a rise of Chinese nationalism, which affected the Chinese in both Singapore and Malaysia. At the turn of the 20th century, the Straits Chinese formed their first organization, the Straits Chinese British Association (SCBA), which became a major political organization in British Malaya. Sinkeh or newly arrived immigrants were also involved in the Kuomintang and later the Malayan Communist Party (MCP). These were, however, modern rather than traditional political organizations. The Japanese rule, which generated a mass-based movement, contributed to the ending of colonial rule much faster than the colonial power would have wanted. The English-educated Chinese leadership in Singapore, especially the Straits Chinese, eventually hurriedly established a party (the People's Action Party) and led Singapore to self-government and eventual independence. In fact, we can certainly argue that this was also the case in peninsular Malaya.

Although Singapore's independence was led by the English-educated, the masses remained Chinese-educated or received little education. There was a division between the English-educated and Chinese-educated leaders, both in Singapore and in Malaya. However, after Singapore achieved independence in 1965, Singapore political identity became separated from that of Malaysia. Eugene Tan's article examines the management of Chinese identity and culture since Singapore attained independence. Due to the 'delicate' environment, ethnic Chinese identity has been closely managed by the ruling elite, which has been dominated by English-educated Chinese. In Tan's view, there has been an evolution from a deliberate policy of maintaining a low-key ethnic Chinese profile to the recent effort to "resinicize" the majority ethnic group. He argues that this landmark change in reconceptualizing the Chinese-Singaporean identity can be attributed to the needs of regime maintenance, buttressed by Confucian ethos as well as the security demands of nation-building. He also maintains that such a move derives from a misplaced sense of the progress of nation-building in Singapore.

On the other hand, the ethnic Chinese in Peninsular Malaysia have had to come to terms with the dominant Malay groups. The Chinese have always been a junior partner in the political equation. With the progress of time, ethnic Chinese political power has been eroded, even marginalized. Ho Khai Leong's paper addresses the issue of political participation in Peninsular Malaysia, especially after 1970. He maintains that Chinese participation can be conceptualized as "political mobilization and bureaucratic participation": Chinese electorates, mobilized at the mass level, are generally sympathetic to the political opposition while the Chinese political elite shares power with the Malay political class in the form of bureaucratic involvement. Ho does not deny that the Chinese are politically marginalized as he admits that they have been relatively deprived of power in the major decision-making processes, or "encapsulated" in the Malaysian political process, despite the fact that they are "represented" in the government by Chinese-based political parties. Nevertheless, Ho suggests that in addition to the above argument, there is a countercurrent, which is equally intense and forceful, occurring at the mass level, that has been making ethnic Chinese political participation in the Malaysian political process a complex and multifaceted phenomenon.

If Chinese education in Singapore has declined and been replaced by national education, in Malaysia Chinese-medium schools remain strong, a fact which poses a challenge to the so-called nation-building process in Malaysia. Tan Liok Ee's paper discusses Chinese education today and its likely future development. Tan argues that Chinese education in Malaysia, in comparison with that in other Southeast Asian countries, has an exceptionally long, continuous and resilient history. A unique mix of interrelated demographic, sociocultural, economic and political factors has enabled the Chinese schools to negotiate the terms for their survival through different phases of their history. Nevertheless, this has also left many unresolved anomalies and recurrent problems, including the survival of Chinese schools. Tan attempts to review the sources of resilience in the past of Chinese education in Malaysia in the light of vulnerabilities in the present and the challenges it must face in the future—all as part of a continuing dialogue between the past and the present, tradition and modernity, in the lives of Malaysians of Chinese descent.

Chinese Culture and Entrepreneurship

Jamie Mackie's paper addresses the issue of tradition and modernity in Malaysian Chinese business, arguing that the two concepts often form a wide spectrum rather than a dichotomy. However, he agrees that some Chinese businesses have more traditional characteristics while others have more modern features. In fact, big businesses, especially MNCs, are by definition modern. Nevertheless, even modern Chinese businesses are not completely free of traditional elements such as familial involvement, *guanxi* (connection) and *xinyong* (trust). For an example of traditional tycoons he uses Loke Yew (1846–1917), while Lee Kong Chian (1894–1967) serves as an example of modern tycoons and Robert Kuok, Lim Goh Tong and Lo Boon Siew as "some later variants of the modern tycoon".

Yen Ching-hwang's paper focuses on traditional ethnic Chinese business organizations such as Chinese craft guilds, business guilds, mutual-aid societies and business clubs. He maintains that these organizations used to provide important instrumental support for ethnic Chinese business by monopolizing certain lines of trade and serving as training ground for prospective entrepreneurs. In Yen's view, these organizations were also used by the *bang* (dialect and geographical entity) as a mechanism through which it perpetuated its control over certain business lines. He finally argues that these traditional business organizations prepared the Chinese for entry into the modern business world.

Unlike Yen Ching-hwang, Lee Kam Hing concentrates on the Straits Chinese rather than the Sinkeh (newcomer) Chinese entrepreneurs. Lee traces the rise of a group of Chinese entrepreneurs in Malacca and Singapore who were involved in the establishment of the Straits Steamship, Straits Trading, Oversea-Chinese Banking Corporation (OCBC) and Great Eastern Life Insurance. He maintains that a Western-based educational background, acceptance by colonial power and business ties with Western entrepreneurs were important factors that led to the success of their ventures. He briefly compared this group with another Chinese group (more recently arrived) centred largely in Penang who made efforts in similar business ventures but had only limited success.

Two papers focus on small-medium enterprises (SMEs) in Singapore. Ng Beoy Kui's article examines ethnic Chinese SMEs, which are large in number, but have not been in the mainstream of economic development in the country. He attributes this to the government's "two-legged" policy, which, until recently, placed emphasis on multinational corporations (MNCs) and government-linked companies (GLCs) as the main instruments for economic development. Ethnic Chinese SMEs were totally left out of policy consideration. However, after the 1997 financial crisis, there was a change in government policy, which now includes these SMEs. Ng argues that the government intends to nurture SMEs to become the "third leg" of

Singapore, so that they can collaborate closely with the MNCs and GLCs for further economic development.

The article by Thomas Menkhoff and Benjamin Loh sets out to examine the organizational change management practices of Chinese SMEs in Singapore. It looks into the adaptability and change readiness of these enterprises *vis-à-vis* the rapidly changing external business environment. A total of 101 companies responded to a survey which reveals some surprising findings: these companies' managers-owners (averaging 42 years in age and English-educated) are risk-takers and are ready to change. Nevertheless, the authors conclude that they need relevant skill upgrading and awareness-building measures in order to survive in the present rapidly changing economy.

Religion

Jean DeBernardi addresses the issue of Malaysian Chinese religious culture and investigates the ways in which the Chinese have reworked their religious culture in both colonial and contemporary Malaysia. In considering Chinese religious culture, she focuses on the political and social dimensions of that culture. She argues that religion defines the boundaries of community and its subcultural groupings. She shows that Chinese sacred sites became sites that defined cultural authenticity and autonomy, and symbols of traditional China for a community undergoing social change. At present, the antiquity of Malaysian Chinese temples offers tangible proof of the depth of Chinese roots that stand against the stereotype that they are merely sojourners and birds of passage.

In his article, Choong Chee Pang uses the 2000 population census to analyse the religious composition of the Chinese in Singapore. He notes that the religious composition of residents in Singapore has remained relatively stable in the last ten years. However, there are also some significant changes and trends among the Chinese in regard to Buddhism, Taoism (Daoism) and Christianity. While the followers of Islam have decreased numerically (from 15.7% in 1980 to 14.9% in 2000), the greatest decline has been in the number of Taoists (from 30% in 1980 to 8.5% in 2000). However, the Buddhists have increased in number (from 27% in 1980 to 42.5% in 2000), as have the Christians (although more moderately from 14.3% in 1980 to 16.5% in 2000). The increase in the number of Buddhists among the Chinese is particularly "impressive", from 34.3 per cent in 1980 to 53.6 per cent in 2000. Choong also discusses the relationship between religion and education, and that between religion and class/language background.

Philip Leung has made a study of Huang Naishang (Wong Nai Siong), the Chinese Methodist church leader who led a migration movement from a northern Fujian province to Sibu in Sarawak, East Malaysia, and the development of the settlement there. His article is focused on two aspects: firstly, the vision, role and leadership of Huang Naishang in the migration movement and in the building of the Chinese community in Sibu; and secondly, the strong influence of the Christian religion in the development of the settlement in Sibu, in terms of community structure, social life and education. Leung argues that its communal characteristics in many ways resemble but predate those of the People's Commune in the PRC in the 1960s.

Literature

Tradition and modernity have also been the concern of ethnic Chinese writers. Their views on tradition and modernity differ in accordance with their educational background, generation and life experiences. Nevertheless, ethnic Chinese writers in Singapore and Malaysia, regardless of their language backgrounds, inevitably address the issues of tradition and modernity.

Koh Tai Ann selects the fiction of two ethnic Chinese writers in English— Lee Kok Liang and Catherine Lim—for comparison. She maintains that while the early works of both writers expose the hypocrisies and corruptions of "tradition" among both the immigrant poor and the wealthy who made good, the later works of both novelists search for alternative moral centres of authority, negotiating between the two potent forces of tradition and modernity, spiritualism and materialism, and a social order which is not predicated on the repression of human individuality and identity.

Unlike Koh Tai Ann, who studies the English writings, Koh Hock Kiat focuses on two young Singapore Chinese writers, one (Simon Tay) who writes in English and the other (Chia Hwee Pheng), in Chinese. The author discovers that these two poets have differences in their outlooks and themes. Both are concerned with the Singapore society, but Simon Tay is more optimistic and cares more about the "gains" after changes, while Chia Hwee Pheng is more pessimistic and worries about the "losses" after changes. Tay is concerned with the value of life, upgrading individual life quality and beautifying one's life; while Chia is concerned with the disappearance of Chinese culture and tradition.

There is no doubt that both Simon Tay and Chia Hwee Pheng are the products of a multilingual Singapore. Kuo Pao Kun, the founder of Singapore Performing Art School and, later, Practice Theatre Ensemble, has also been shaped by Singapore's multilingual society. But unlike Tay and Chia, Kuo is equally at home in two languages and has produced plays in both Chinese and English with multilingual dialogues. Quah Sy Ren's article is about this extraordinary playwright/director and his works. According to Quah, Kuo started producing plays in the 1960s, first in Chinese, later in English. Nevertheless, he was ignored initially by the English theatre circle as well as its observers, probably due to prejudice. However, with the passing of time, Kuo has developed Singapore theatre from bilingual to multilingual. In his plays, several languages are spoken during the performance, including English, Tamil, Malay, Hokkien, Cantonese and Teochew. Quah Sy Ren argues that this unprecedented experiment has been a great success and has earned him a leading status in Singapore theatre in both the Mandarin- and English-speaking communities.

Concluding Remarks

The 19 articles in this volume examine the ethnic Chinese in Singapore and Malaysia from various perspectives. Although some articles do address the issues of tradition and modernity, others trace the process of change in terms of ethnic Chinese society, politics, identity, education, business and literature in these two countries. Nevertheless, one can certainly argue that these articles also deal with the traditional and the modern, depending on how one defines tradition and modernity. The comparison between the past and the present is always interesting, and cross-country comparison is equally fascinating. Yet, not many articles in this volume focus on the latter. Only in those articles by Wang Gungwu, Leo Suryadinata and Koh Tai Ann has an attempt been made. By conducting comparative studies, one will get a different perspective. Nevertheless, detailed comparison between the Chinese in Singapore and those in Malaysia can be a topic for further investigation.

Chapter 1

LOCAL AND NATIONAL: A DIALOGUE BETWEEN TRADITION AND MODERNITY

Wang Gungwu

You will be familiar with the idea that, despite all the talk about national politics, all politics is ultimately local. Something analogous but not about politics can be said of the idea of tradition. From the study of the ethnic Chinese in Singapore and Malaysia, I suggest that, while there are modern national traditions, living traditions are ultimately local, especially among peoples of immigrant origins.

Let me begin with a comparison of the people of Chinese descent in the two countries. Today, they both strive to be modern but have different responses towards tradition. Those in Malaysia are community-centred, with a strong sense of locality, because what is national for them does not provide them with equality. Thus, although they are modernizing themselves through outreach to other communities and to the world outside, their local identities have allowed them to keep many of their own older traditions alive. Those in Singapore, however, had the chance to take a different course and have established a clear national identity with reference to a globalizing world. They no longer live with a sense of what is local and have not had to depend on Chinese-based traditions.

The changes to their respective ways of life have created a significant difference between the Chinese in the two countries. This difference raises questions about how the two communities within their different national frameworks will develop and how either will relate to the other. It makes it important for these Chinese to understand the nature of the divergence. It is a divergence that is especially relevant to the theme of tradition and modernity in this conference. However, before I turn to that theme, I should explain what I mean by the two key words here, "local" and "national", and also have them placed in historical context.

The word "local" here has at least two layers of meaning. Historically, it refers to the strong sense of locality, that is, identification with home district, clan and speech group, that the early Chinese immigrants brought with them from China. Today, it also describes the new sense of locality that has developed in various parts of a large country like Malaysia. For example, those who live in Johor have their own sense of locality when compared with those in Selangor and Perak, and there are significant differences among those who settled in Kelantan, or Kedah and Perlis, or Sarawak, or Sabah, or Penang. There is ample evidence to show that Chinese traditions, especially those belonging to the Little Tradition, have always been closely linked to locality, and that the local and the traditional remain connected in that way, whether these traditions are old or new.

The word "national", however, emphasizes the political good of the larger community, and places that ideal high above parochial interests. The nationalist cause, therefore, plays down the needs and traditions of the local, if not replacing them altogether with new symbols of the nation-state. The idea of the national among the overseas Chinese had begun with a new national consciousness in China. The impact of that on the *huaqiao* in British Malaya was considerable. After the independence of Singapore and Malaysia, however, the link with the Chinese nation had to be abandoned in favour of their respective nation-building efforts. In the enlarged and complex federation of Malaysia, the hopes for a new multicultural nation turned into anxiety for the Chinese, as they became concerned that they might not have equal rights in it. Until they could identify fully with that nationhood, the many local communities have turned to their own store of tradition. This has influenced the education they have provided for their children in support of their quest for modernity. Singapore, however, is a small nation-state seeking a modern and global security in a large, unstable and variegated region. Its nation-building policy since independence in 1965 has ensured that the local and the national are not distinguishable. In any case, the idea of the national is seen by many as being shaped by the ethnic Chinese majority.

Both what is local and what is national can also be modern. By "modern", I refer to those challenges to local traditions that have been brought to the region by industrial capitalism, colonialism, imperial expansion and social revolution. There is no contradiction between this modernity and both the local and the national. Local traditions can be modified to meet modern challenges. What is national, however, being directly related to the nation-state, has led to the independence of former colonies and confirmed the sovereignty of such states in a globalized world. Here are multidimensional challenges to the nation, and the interests of the national are always expected to take precedence over the local and the traditional.

Being Local

I need now to place these concepts in historical context. Early in the 19th century, only the word "local" really mattered. Whether Chinese immigrants passed through Singapore and moved on, or went directly to the Malay states of both West and East Malaysia, or came to Singapore and went no further, they all had a strong sense of the local. For some, that came from their place of origin in China; for others, it was shaped by their own local communities elsewhere in Southeast Asia. They carried with them their village and dialect group identities, and their distinctive variants of the Chinese Little Traditions from Guangdong and Fujian provinces. In time, most of them adapted themselves to local conditions in this part of the Malay world.

The one notable difference among the Chinese was that between the Baba Chinese who had settled in Malacca and its environs earlier on, and those who arrived from China during the 19th century. The former were localized in having distinctive traditions of their own that were developed in a Malay environment, while the latter held to the traditions of their home localities in China. The British found this difference convenient. For their purposes, it was advantageous to employ the Baba, the truly local, to help them establish their trading networks while encouraging some of the later arrivals to exercise their entrepreneurial talents, adapt to local conditions and perhaps settle down. With the establishment of the Straits Settlements, all the local-born were qualified to become Straits Chinese. When British rule was extended to the Malay peninsula, more localized Chinese were brought into the fold as protected subjects, the precursors of the Malayan Chinese the British came to recognize during the first half of the 20th century.

Under these circumstances, being local implied holding on to certain sets of traditions. For all except the Baba, these initially meant traditions originally from China. But, by the end of the 19th century, some Chinese had begun to acquire other local characteristics, for example, those who lived all their lives in Kelantan, Penang and Selangor were distinguishable from those in Singapore. They might have had common dialect origins and shared basic customs, but they had to deal with a different mix of Malays and other races in each place, and they had different experiences of the increasingly powerful British authorities. At this point, although all Chinese were still traditional, they could be divided into those who were primarily China-traditional and those who could be called local-traditional. The latter, local-born for at least one generation, and skilled in a range of local ways whether Malay or British, may be considered a new kind of Peranakan. They were distinguishable from the Baba by being Chinese-speaking and comfortable in either Malay or English or both. This was a group evolving most notably in Penang and Singapore early in the 20th century, and spreading along the west coast of the Malay peninsula. Both kinds of Chinese, whether China-oriented or local-oriented, could draw on distinctive living traditions.

The condition of being local was open to changes brought to the region by European colonial rulers. By the beginning of the 20th century, these were characterized by the dominance of capitalist economics and the pressures of social revolution that came to be identified with modernity. The impact of such transformations, however alien they first appeared, spared no one. There was, in any case, nothing to prevent the local from seeking to be modern if they wanted to. Depending on where the Chinese were localized in British Malaya (this included Singapore) and northern Borneo, they were becoming modern at different rates. Differences in access to modernizing environments, and the relative remoteness of some localities, separated those who modernized fast from those who did so gradually. Everywhere were those who were looking to modify, update, even upgrade, their respective traditions. For example, traditional organizations based on dialect and descent groups were intertwined with newer social and occupational clubs and societies. As long as they were established for Chinese, they followed recognizably traditional practices. The one growing difference was that between those who were oriented towards changes in China and those led by Chinese-speaking Peranakan whose sources of modernity were found locally or derived directly from Britain.

The Chance to Be National

But nation-building in the two countries, and the new power of the national, brought further changes. There came the chance for people of all races and communities to reach out for what many saw then as the ultimate in modernity, the nation-state. This was the secret of European power, the source of their economic and military success and, therefore, the critical institution for people living in colonies to regain their self-respect. The driving force was the humiliation of having been conquered and ruled by foreigners. As long as the Chinese were sojourners waiting to return to China, this was not a problem for them in their localities abroad. Their awareness of the national was raised only after the opening of the Treaty

Ports of coastal China, some of which were close to the very localities from where most of them had come. It was not surprising that these Chinese were moved by the chance to overthrow the weakened empire ruled by the Manchu and replace it with a Chinese nation. Thus, new leaders like Sun Yat-sen were given a hearing. The encounter with the ideas of race and nation as promoted by China's first modern politician was a riveting one for most overseas Chinese. Over the next three decades, Sun Yat-sen and his nationalist followers began to unite the young and the frustrated and overcome their local differences, no matter where they were and what dialect group they belonged to.

It was this force that brought the concept of *huaqiao* to the region. This was a call for the unity of all Chinese that placed the emphasis on what was national in China. It was a call that began to diminish the differences among the Chinese of various distinctive localities of British Malaya and elsewhere. The growth of the Chinese press that tied it directly to political, economic and cultural advances in Shanghai, and gave a new national perspective to developments in Guangzhou, Xiamen and Shantou, was a powerful factor for rapid change. The introduction of modern Chinese schools in all the territories quickly transplanted the idea of the national into the consciousness of local-born Chinese of all classes. Even some of the Baba who had looked up to the British, and were uneasy at the strong emotions aroused, found this national cause in China difficult to resist.

A similar national ideal awakened the Malays and other communities as well. During the 1930s, at least three competing national appeals were being made by various groups of Malays, Indians and Chinese. Despite the different sources of inspiration, the drive to nationalist mobilization was a serious barrier to local social harmony. Each set of national leaders sought support exclusively from their respective communities. The British wrestled with the implications for local order, and for the future of their authority in Malaya, until the Pacific War swept all their plans away. The Japanese further aggravated the nationalistic differences, and the War ended with three potential 'nations' for the British to pacify when they returned.

The outcome is familiar to us. Intricate negotiations had led to the creation of the Federation of Malaya, with the colony of Singapore detached. The Malayan Emergency drove a larger wedge between the Chinese and the Malays. This wedge led eventually to the formation of Malaysia and the failure to keep Singapore in the new federation. Outside, what pressed on both Malaysia and Singapore was the ideological hot war in the region and the efforts at an experimental regionalism with ASEAN. Underlying the whole process were the different degrees of success in nation-building among the neighbours. But there was no turning back on the need to modernize by being national through the nation-state.

The most important result for the Chinese who stayed on in Singapore and Malaysia and did not return to China was the double divide for them on both nationalist and ideological grounds. The rejection of Chinese nationality, with the abandonment of the idea of being *huaqiao*, was the first step. The disillusionment with Communism following the excesses of the Cultural Revolution in China was the second. Now was the time for the local Chinese in both countries to focus on the development of the national in their respective adopted countries.

Tradition and Modernity

I have suggested that the sense of locality can lead people to modernize the traditions that they have inherited, but the pressure to become national presses people to subsume their local traditions to new unifying symbols. Thus, the dialogue between tradition and modernity held in Singapore and Malaysia has bifurcated over the past three decades. Today, the differences deserve to be studied closely. What lies at the heart of the two separate dialogues?

Singapore has provided the Chinese with a majority status that has been played down by the stress on a multicultural nation-state. The country is, in any case, too small to have internal localities with any meaning. State policy has diluted the appeal of most traditional organizations. It has encouraged the minimizing of residual local differences by stressing the nation-state that has been defined by external pressures on a global scale, especially in economic competition. In that context, what is national has been real for the Chinese there. The nation-building process has been one in which they have participated equally, one in which traditions associated with a Chinese national identity are no longer appropriate. Instead, what have taken precedence are measures to meet global technological challenges that entail different attitudes towards the very idea of tradition itself.

Singapore's uniform national education has, in fact, all but eliminated local traditions. The policy of emphasizing English in order to facilitate nation-building, tap available international resources and globalize the economy, has been carried through. For the Chinese, the Speak Mandarin programme has reduced the value of the original mother tongues. The use of simplified characters and Pinyin has been justified for its practical value, but the emotional linking with China has been carefully avoided. The approach towards tradition has been redefined as one that starts afresh to build a new set of national values, of patriotism and loyalty directed primarily to Singapore. Such a tradition might be further enriched by customs and practices from other parts of the world that have been brought in to enhance the nation's chances for survival and sustained prosperity. All these would one day add up to a distinct national tradition, but that is not a priority and not sought for its own sake. To use the language prevalent today, the challenge is to keep up with the shifting demands of a modernity that is global and ever changing, and that calls for the "creative destruction" of all that stands in the way.

In Malaysia, multiple traditions have drawn sustenance from their different community origins, and from the mix of races and cultures in separate localities. They have survived a nation-building process that has been widely seen as discriminatory. Those of Chinese descent seem to have accepted the process as a temporary stage. In the mean time, they have reserved the right to preserve as many as possible of the organizations they have inherited, and also try to cultivate some modernized but distinctive traditions of their own. They have reacted in this way because they see themselves as targets of a nation-building process that is aimed at changing them to conform to something external to their traditions. They also feel that the struggle to contribute equally to a new nationality has been postponed again and again. Also, the prospect of such equality actually appears to have dimmed over time. The promise of becoming modern through what is national has thus been replaced by one that challenges the Chinese to be modern through adapting their local community traditions to the demands and opportunities of the world outside their country.

Thus, the urge to enhance the local has taken various forms. One has been that of a truly local identity which they could identify with wherever their new homes are actually located. I have mentioned variations among Chinese communities in localities like Johor, Selangor, Kelantan, Sarawak, Sabah and Penang. Some of the local Chinese in each place could, of course, still hope to influence national policy by making a subnational contribution, but when they turn to political action, their activities could be seen as communal and against national interests. Whether manifested locally or communally, that is the product of an incomplete national experience that allows, if not encourages, the Chinese to hold on to the traditions they already have and seek to modernize in their own distinctive ways. It also allows them to reach out beyond national borders to other Chinese who feel incompletely national in similar ways, and use modern communications technology to help them build overarching transnational networks. The proliferation of such networks wherever there are such Chinese may be an index of the resilience of tradition in each modernizing local community.

The two dialogues between tradition and modernity thus provide a contrast for the Chinese in both countries to learn from. They raise many important questions that deserve attention. Let me end with three of them:

1 Local community traditions have survived over long periods of time, and have ensured the vitality of the modern Chinese in Malaysia. Is there still a role for these traditions in the lives of the Chinese in Singapore?
2 The division created between the two groups came about because the Chinese had to choose between different national frameworks. What kind of framework would make it possible for the Chinese in both countries to share their traditions again?
3 The Chinese of the two countries have adapted creatively to a variety of adverse changes largely beyond their control. How can they ensure that future generations will be able and willing to go on doing so?

The history of the Chinese in Singapore and Malaysia suggests that, when what is national is found wanting or inadequate for one reason or another, the answers to these questions may be found in the idea that traditions are ultimately local.

Part I

Population and Society

Chapter 2

CHINESE SINGAPOREANS: THREE DECADES OF PROGRESS AND CHANGES

Chiew Seen Kong

The Research Focus

This article provides an update on the structural and cultural changes of resident Singaporeans of Chinese origin over the last three decades, 1970–2000, based on available census and survey data.

Due to data limitation, the structural changes refer mainly to the progress in social class attainment while the cultural changes refer to changes in religion, language usage patterns, fertility, inter-ethnic marriage, ethnic identity and national identity.

A theory will be proposed regarding the complex relationship between ethnic identity and national identity and the evolutionary change from the former to the latter. The impact of China's economic and cultural development on the Chinese Singaporeans' identity will also be discussed.

Data on Chinese Singaporeans

Since 1980, the annual Singapore Labour Force Survey does not publish data by race even though data on race and data by race have been collected. Thus scholars have to rely on the population census which is carried out only every ten years. Data on race are available from the published census reports for 1970, 1980 and 1990 and limited data have been published so far for 2000.

Censuses gather and report only on 'hard' data such as age, sex, education, occupation, income, type of dwelling, religion, language spoken at home and so forth but not 'soft' data such as ethnic identity, national identity, attitudes towards social and political issues, and so on, which are difficult to measure or scale and gather for a population census of millions of people.

Such soft or intangible data have been gathered by surveys. However, survey data on ethnic identity, national identity by race, ethnic prejudice, and suchlike are not easily assessable as they are often gathered by government ministries or other organizations which keep these data (collected at great cost to them) for internal use.

These data constraints limit the scope of this research to whatever published data which are available on the Chinese Singaporeans over the last three decades.

Radical Changes in Singapore Society and Their Impact on Chinese Singaporeans

Singapore is a multiracial society. About three-fourths of the population are Chinese in origin. Though the Chinese Singaporeans constitute a numerical majority and the dominant group, the government's policies of equal treatment of the races, meritocracy and nation-building are designed *not* to preserve the ethnic distinctiveness of the races but, instead, are designed to *reduce* if not eliminate their cultural and social distinctiveness in order to achieve more and more common ground among the races and greater racial harmony.

These policies of nation-building have changed Singaporeans of Chinese origin in many ways. This article focuses on some of the changes over the last three decades based on available data.

Brief Historical Background of the Chinese Population

Stamford Raffles colonized the island Singapore and the surrounding smaller islands in 1819. There were then only about 30 Chinese and 120 Malays. Raffles set Singapore up as a free trading port. The free port attracted Chinese immigration. By 1836 the Chinese had outnumbered the Malays (13,700 Chinese and 12,600 Malays) and become the largest ethnic group, though it was not yet the majority (46%). By 1849, the Chinese had become the majority (53%) in Singapore. Net immigration was the most important source of population increase until the worldwide economic depression of around 1930. The Depression led to immigration restriction. Thereafter, the sex ratio slowly normalized. Since then, natural increase (ie, births minus deaths) has become the main source of population growth for Singapore as a whole and for the Chinese as a community.

Today, 76.8 per cent of the resident population of 3,263,209 citizens and permanent residents, or 2,505,379 of the people, are Singaporeans of Chinese origin, bearing Chinese surnames and names. There are another 754,524 non-residents of various ethnic backgrounds working or living here.

The early Chinese immigrants were largely illiterate or semi-literate farmers, craftsmen, labourers and pedlars. About nine in ten were men from the southern provinces of Fujian and Guangdong and the island of Hainan. They were not bearers of Chinese literati culture or learning. They brought with them the Chinese folk traditions of these southern areas of China, speaking dialects such as Fujian *hua* (Hokkien), Chaozhou *hua* (Teochew), Guangdong *hua* (Cantonese), Hainan *hua* (Hainanese), Kejia *hua* (Khek) and other dialects and sub-dialects.

Overall, the Chinese immigrants who arrived here prior to 1930 or so were largely of humble social and cultural origins.

These early Chinese immigrants came with a very strong n Ach (need for achievement) or economic motivation. They worked very long hours and lived very frugally in order to save as much of what little they had. Most of them came from poverty-stricken families in China. They came here not to spread their culture or religion but in search of opportunities to make money. The goal was to return home to provide a better life for their families in southern China.

Singapore: A Land of Hope and Fulfilment for Chinese Singaporeans

When Singapore became independent in 1965, it was a Third World country with little natural resources. Commentators then did not think that Singapore had any future as an independent state. The unemployment rates in the 1960s stood at 9 to 12 per cent of the labour force. The population was small in size and the people were poor. The small domestic aggregate demand for goods and the hostility of its immediate neighbouring countries made Singapore an unattractive place for foreign investment to produce goods for the small domestic market. On 15 January 1968 the Labour Party government in Britain announced that it would close down the British military bases in Singapore in 1971, instead of 1974. Some 30 to 40 thousand base workers would soon be unemployed. The British bases contributed about 20 per cent of Singapore's GDP. Singapore's future looked bleak then.

The government under PM Lee Kuan Yew realized the urgency of developing the economy. It worked very hard and desperately to develop the economy. Many tax and other incentives were given to encourage foreign investment in labour-intensive industries and to encourage export to the world market. The industrial peace created with the co-operation of both labour unions and employers in the late 1960s, the political stability and the racial harmony which evolved all helped to attract foreign investment. Numerous jobs were created over the next decade. Full employment was achieved in 1972 and labour shortage appeared from the mid-1970s. By 1980, 10.8 per cent of the labour force was foreign. In 1978 the government announced the need to restructure the economy from one dependent on labour-intensive industries to one based on capital- and skill-intensive industries.

The unskilled and semi-skilled Chinese pinned their hopes on their children. They believed in education as the means of upward social mobility. Quite astutely, most of them believed that an English education in an ex-British colony and the presence of many MNCs would give their children a better chance for upward mobility than a Chinese education. When it came to choosing between cultural and linguistic loyalty on the one hand and English education for improving their life chances on the other, most Chinese parents chose the latter: they were not ethnic or cultural chauvinists. They were pragmatic, driven by a strong n Ach. After all, the Chinese came here not to promote their culture or religion but to achieve a higher standard of living for themselves and their children.

They pushed their children hard, to make sure that they succeeded in school. They did not want their children to inherit their low social status and income. An old Chinese primary school reader (*Wu Zi Jing* or Five-Character Line Reader) taught Chinese children, "All things are lowly. Only education is lofty!" (*Wan ban jie xia pin; wei you du shu gao!*). The Chinese students almost always performed better than the Malay and Indian students as Chinese parents 'implanted' their n Ach into their children's 'DNA' or value system. Their improving educational attainment eventually served the Chinese well as Singapore's economy grew and grew and created increasing demands for skilled labour, managers and professionals over the last three and a half decades. As Singapore's economy developed from a developing economy to a First World economy, the Chinese Singaporeans were busy acquiring diplomas, degrees and skills, and thus prospered.

Educational achievement

Table 1 shows that in 1970, 89 per cent had less than a secondary education. By 2000, only 42.1 per cent had only this low level of educational attainment. In 1980, only 2.4 per cent of Chinese adults (strictly, non-students aged 10 or 15 years or older, varying from census to census) had a university education. This rate rose to 5.1 per cent in 1990 and then 12.6 per cent in 2000.

Table 1: Highest qualifications attained, 1970–2000 (in percentages)

Highest qualification attained	1970	1980	1990	2000
No qualification		36.6	32.0	20.2
Primary		42.5	25.6	21.9
Below secondary	89.0	NA	NA	NA
Secondary & above	11.0	NA	NA	NA
Secondary		12.5	25.7	23.2
Upper secondary		6.0	7.6	15.0
Polytechnic		NA	4.1	7.0
University		2.4	5.1	12.6
Total	**100.0**	**100.0**	**100.0**	**100.0**

Sources: *Singapore Census of Population 1990: Economic Characteristics*, Singapore: Dept of Statistics, 1993, p xvi; Mary Tay Wan Joo, *Trends in Language, Literacy and Education in Singapore*, Census Monograph No 2, Singapore: Dept of Statistics, nd, p 77, Table 4.3; and *Singapore Census of Population 2000: Advance Data Release (ADR) #1*, Singapore: Dept of Statistics, p 2, Table 2.

However, part of this increase was due to the inflow of Chinese who, like earlier immigrants, were attracted here by the economic opportunities in a rapidly growing economy. Table 2 shows that in 1990, only 4.6 per cent of Chinese citizens had university degrees compared with 16.3 per cent of the Chinese permanent residents (PRs). By 2000, 10.8 per cent of the citizens while 29.7 per cent of the PRs were graduates. Chinese citizens who were graduates increased significantly during the last decade from 4.6 to 10.8 per cent. The Chinese community is reinforced by better qualified Chinese PRs, many of whom will eventually become citizens.

Table 2: University graduates by residential status, 1990–2000 (in percentages)

Residential status	1990	2000
Citizens	4.6	10.8
Permanent residents	16.3	29.7
Total	**5.1**	**12.6**

Source: *Singapore Census of Population 2000: ADR #1*, Singapore: Dept of Statistics, p 3, Table 3.

Occupational achievement

Education and occupational status are closely and positively correlated, though the correlation is not perfect. Given sustained economic growth during the last three and a half decades, the progress made in education was paralleled by occupational attainment. Table 3 shows that the proportion of Class 1 occupations (managers, professionals and technical workers) increased greatly among the Chinese Singaporeans from 10.1 per cent in 1970 to 19.0 per cent in 1980, 29.8 per cent in 1990 and, finally, to 46.2 per cent in 2000. Part of this increase was no doubt due to the immigration of some highly qualified Chinese.

Table 3: Occupational distribution, 1970–2000 (in percentages)

Occupational category	1970	1980	1990	2000
Administrative & managerial	1.7	6.8	11.0	15.9
Professional	NA	NA	5.8	10.7
Technical & related	NA	NA	13.0	19.6
Professional & technical	8.4	12.2	NA	NA
Subtotal: Class 1	**10.1**	**19.0**	**29.8**	**46.2**
Clerical	12.7	14.9	14.9	13.5
Sales & services	29.3	15.2	14.0	11.7
Subtotal: Class 2	**42.0**	**30.1**	**28.9**	**25.2**
Production & related	44.4	42.8	26.5	18.6
Cleaners & labourers	NA	NA	9.7	6.2
Subtotal: Class 3	**44.4**	**42.8**	**36.2**	**24.8**
Others/Not classifiable	3.5	6.3	5.3	3.8
Total	**100.0**	**100.0**	**100.0**	**100.0**

Sources: *Report on the Census of Population 1970 Singapore*, Vol II, Singapore: Dept of Statistics, 1973, p 90, Table 72; *Singapore Census of Population 1990: Economic Characteristics*, Singapore: Dept of Statistics, 1993, p xvii; and *ADR #4*, p 5, Table 4.

Conversely, the numbers of Chinese in Classes 2 and 3 occupations declined. In 1970, 42.0 per cent were clerks, sales and service workers. A decade later, their numbers decreased rapidly to 30.1 per cent, then 28.9 per cent in 1990 and, finally, dropped even further to 25.2 per cent in 2000. The numbers in Class 3 occupations (production workers and labourers) fell even more, from 44.4 per cent in 1970 to 24.8 per cent in 2000.

Thus, as the educational attainment of Chinese Singaporeans progressed, their occupational achievement also progressed.

The Chinese labour force showed structural change: in 1970, 23.9 per cent of the workers were involved in manufacturing activities, a proportion which declined eventually to 19.9 per cent in 2000 (see Table 4). The proportion of those who were engaged in construction remained more or less steady at around 6.7 to 7.0 per cent during the last three decades.

Table 4: Industrial distribution of labour force, 1970–2000 (in percentages)

Industry	1970	1980	1990	2000
Goods producing industries	35.9	38.5	33.4	27.3
Manufacturing	23.9	29.1	25.8	19.9
Construction	7.0	6.8	6.7	6.9
Other goods industries	5.0	2.6	0.8	0.6
Services producing industries	64.1	61.5	66.6	72.7
Wholesale & retail trade	NA	NA	19.7	18.5
Hotels & restaurants	NA	NA	7.4	6.5
Commerce	25.4	23.7	NA	NA
Transport & communications	11.4	10.8	10.2	11.0
Financial services	NA	NA	4.8	6.3
Business services	NA	NA	7.6	12.4
Financial & business services	3.5	7.3	NA	NA
Community, social & personal	23.8	19.7	16.9	18.0
Total	**100.0**	**100.0**	**100.0**	**100.0**

Sources: *Report on the Census of Population 1970 Singapore*, Vol II, Singapore: Dept of Statistics, 1973, p 90, Table 71; *Singapore Census of Population 1990: Economic Characteristics,* Singapore: Dept of Statistics, 1993, p xvii; and *ADR #4,* p 6, Table 6.

Many more Chinese were in the service industries, their numbers rising from a high 64.1 per cent in 1970 to 72.7 per cent in 2000. In 1970, a mere 3.5 per cent provided financial and business services, this percentage rising to 18.7 in 2000. On the other hand, 23.8 per cent provided community, social and personal services in 1970, but this percentage declined to 18.0 in 2000.

Economic dependency

The term "economic dependency" refers to the number of economically inactive persons (students, home makers, retirees) supported by every 100 economically active persons. Table 5 shows that in 1970, 113 economically inactive persons were supported by 100 economically active persons. This ratio declined rapidly to 59.8 in 1980. In 1972, full employment was achieved. Thereafter, labour demand exceeded supply, as a result of rapid and sustained economic growth. Labour shortages appeared: expanding companies imported foreign labour and professionals. In 1980, 10.8 per cent of the labour force comprised non-residents (ie, foreigners). By 2000, the economic dependency ratio had dropped further, but only slightly, to 56.2.

Table 5: Economic dependency ratio, 1970–2000

Census year	Economic dependency ratio
1970	113.0
1980	59.8
1990	57.8
2000	56.2

Note: Economic dependency ratio = economically inactive persons per 100 economically active persons.

Sources: *Report on the Census of Population 1970 Singapore*, Vol II, Singapore: Dept of Statistics, 1973, p 62, Table 44; *Singapore Census of Population 1990: Economic Characteristics,* Singapore: Dept of Statistics, 1993, p xvi; and *ADR #4,* p 11, Table 11.

Type of dwelling

Fertility rates were very high after the end of the Japanese Occupation. With the return of peace, people felt safe to form families. This resulted in increasing demand for housing as more and more families were formed through marriage. The Housing and Development Board (HDB) was set up in 1960 to solve the problem of housing shortage.

Table 6 shows that 36.1 per cent of the Chinese Singaporeans in 1970 were living in HDB flats. By 2000, 88.0 per cent of the Chinese Singaporeans were living in HDB flats and they lived in bigger and bigger flats. In 1980, only 15.3 per cent lived in 4-room and bigger flats. Two decades later, in 2000, 56.9 per cent were residing in these bigger flats. In 1970, 50.8 per cent lived in shophouses and attap- and zinc-roofed houses. By 2000, only a mere 0.9 per cent lived in such dwellings. In 1970, 13.1 per cent lived in private houses. As property values shot up during the last three decades, by 2000 only 5.1 per cent lived in landed properties while 6.0 per cent lived in private flats and condominium apartments (which had not existed previously). Many landed properties were demolished and the valuable land was used to construct condominium apartments.

Table 6: Type of dwelling, 1970–2000 (in percentages)

Type of dwelling	1970	1980	1990	2000
HDB flats	36.1	67.9	84.6	88.0
1- & 2-room	NA	17.3	8.2	5.0
3-room	NA	34.1	35.4	25.7
4-room	NA	NA	27.4	33.2
5-room/executive	NA	NA	13.0	23.7
4-room or more	NA	15.3	NA	NA
Others	NA	1.2	0.7	0.4
Condominiums & private flats	NA	2.1	4.1	6.0
Private houses	13.1	9.2	7.0	5.1
Others*	50.8	20.7	4.3	0.9
Total	**100.0**	**100.0**	**100.0**	**100.0**

*Includes non-HDB shophouses, attap/zinc-roofed houses and other public flats.
Sources: *Report on the Census of Population 1970 Singapore*, Vol II, Singapore: Dept of Statistics, 1973, p 215, Table 106; *Singapore Census of Population 1990: Economic Characteristics,* Singapore: Dept of Statistics, 1993, p xvi; and *ADR #6*, p 6, Table 7.

Home ownership

As incomes rose, instead of renting out flats, HDB encouraged home ownership. Home ownership was viewed by the government as a means of giving citizens a stake in the country as Singaporeans are very house-proud, as evidenced by the large outlay spent on renovating their HDB flats and private properties. Table 7 shows home ownership rose from 32.2 per cent in 1970 to 92.9 per cent in 2000. This is probably the highest rate of home ownership in the world.

Table 7: Home ownership, 1970–2000 (in percentages)

Tenancy	1970	1980	1990	2000
Owner occupied	32.2	61.9	87.5	92.9
Tenant	62.9	NA	11.9	6.0
Others	4.9	NA	0.6	1.1
Tenant/Others	NA	38.1	NA	NA
Total	**100.0**	**100.0**	**100.0**	**100.0**

Sources: *Report on the Census of Population 1970 Singapore,* Vol II, Singapore: Dept of Statistics, 1973, p 520, Table 254; *Singapore Census of Population 1990: Economic Characteristics,* Singapore: Dept of Statistics, 1993, p xiv; and *ADR #6,* p 7, Table 8.

Home ownership among Chinese Singaporeans is very high for large-size properties. Table 8 shows that in 2000, among those living in 1-room and 2-room HDB flats, only 20.2 per cent owned them, compared with 98.7 per cent who owned their 5-room and executive HDB flats, 98.2 per cent who owned their 4-room flats and 96.4 per cent who owned their 3-room flats. Among the 41,909 Chinese Singaporeans who lived in landed properties, 91.4 per cent owned them. Among the 48,985 who lived in condominiums and private apartments, 86.2 per cent owned them. Home ownership data index the progress in social class achievement of the Chinese Singaporeans during the last three decades.

Table 8: Home ownership by type of dwelling, 2000

Type of dwelling	Number				Per cent			
	Total	Owner	Tenant	Others	Total	Owner	Tenant	Others
Total	731496	679384	43935	8177	100.0	92.9	6.0	1.1
HDB dwellings	633330	592567	35595	5168	100.0	93.6	5.6	0.8
1-room/2-room	32896	6628	26031	236	100.0	20.2	79.1	0.7
3-room	187078	180357	4809	1913	100.0	96.4	2.6	1.0
4-room	235940	231726	2508	1706	100.0	98.2	1.1	0.7
5-room/executive	174274	171924	1259	1092	100.0	98.7	0.7	0.6
Others	3142	1932	988	221	100.0	61.5	31.5	7.0
Other public flats	6422	5871	447	103	100.0	91.4	7.0	1.6
Condo/private flats	48985	42209	5355	1421	100.0	86.2	10.9	2.9
Landed properties	41909	38319	2183	1406	100.0	91.4	5.2	3.4
Bungalows	6555	5989	241	325	100.0	91.4	3.7	4.9
Semi-detached	14702	13522	733	447	100.0	92.0	5.0	3.0
Terrace houses	20652	18808	1210	634	100.0	91.1	5.9	3.0
Others	851	414	354	79	100.0	49.1	41.6	9.3

Source: *Singapore Census of Population 2000: Advance Data Release,* Singapore: Dept of Statistics, May 2001, p 174, Table 38.

Income

Sustained and rapid economic growth led to rapidly rising money and real incomes as the inflation rates remained low at 2 to 3 per cent per year over the last three decades. Table 9 shows that in 1980, the average household income was S$1,240 per month. It rose to S$3,213 in 1990, and then went up further to S$5,219 in 2000. Incomes increased 4.2 times in just two decades. The median household monthly income also rose rapidly from S$2,400 in 1990 to S$3,848 in 2000, increasing 1.6 times in just one decade.

Table 9: Household monthly income from work, 1980–2000 (in Singapore dollars)

Household income	1980	1990	2000
Mean income	1240	3213	5219
Median income	NA	2400	3848

Sources: Stephen HK Yeh, *Households and Housing*, Singapore: Dept of Statistics, nd, p 37, Table 2.11; and *ADR #7*, p 3, Table 4.

Upward social mobility

The progress made in education, occupation, housing, home ownership and income over the last three decades indicates that the Chinese Singaporeans in general have benefited from economic development and its correlated processes of change such as educational expansion and housing development. Comprising some 77 per cent of the population, the achievements of Chinese Singaporeans reflect more or less national development as they form not only a numerical majority but constitute the dominant group in Singapore society. "Chinese are Singapore" is more real than "Metro is Singapore".

Cultural and Cognitive Changes

Changes in socioeconomic status achieved during the last three decades did not occur in isolation. There were parallel cultural and cognitive changes, such as changes in values, beliefs, norms, attitudes, lifestyles and identity. These intangible changes are hard to document in the form of fixed-time series, unlike the censuses taken every ten years. Fortunately, the censuses do provide some data on them.

Religion

As the first generation of Chinese immigrants were succeeded by subsequent generations of local-born Chinese or Chinese Singaporeans, the folk culture brought by the first generation of immigrants slowly lost its grip on the subsequent generations who largely went to English schools prior to 1966, and who since 1966 have been attending bilingual state-funded schools and increasingly exposed to the rapidly developing and then globalizing Singapore economy and society, thus becoming familiar with foreign goods (eg, Coca-Cola drinks, McDonald's hamburgers, Swatch watches), ideas (through foreign media and TV shows), values (democracy, human rights, animal rights, environment protection, gender equality, civic society), beliefs (Christianity) and norms (sexual mores, body piercing, Internet chats, WAP phone SMS). While these foreign influences can be found in almost every corner of Singapore society, exposure to them is often selective. People choose to expose themselves to what they like and avoid what they do not like. Thus, these affect different individuals and generations differently and to varying extents. These differential local (eg, Chinese schools versus bilingual schools) and foreign influences create intergenerational differences and changes among Chinese Singaporeans.

Table 10 shows that Daoism (Taoism) has lost its appeal, falling from 38.2 per cent in 1980 to only 10.8 per cent in 2000. The Daoism practised here is mainly the folk variety, instead of the scholarly variety (ie, the Daoism of Lao Zi and Zhuang Zi). Buddhism has gained greater adherence, particularly among the younger Chinese Singaporeans, rising from 34.3 per cent in 1980 to 53.6 per cent in 2000. More and more Buddhists monks here hold university degrees, lending prestige to their religion. This has not yet happened to Daoists and Daoism. Christianity has also made some gains, rising from 10.9 to 16.5 per cent during the two decades. Those who profess Christianity and those have no religion tend to be better educated while Daoists tend to be poorly educated and older. The Buddhists are somewhat in between them.

Table 10: Religion of residents aged 15 and over, 1980–2000 (in percentages)

Religion	1980	1990	2000
No religion	16.4	17.7	18.6
Buddhism	34.3	39.4	53.6
Daoism	38.2	28.4	10.8
Christianity	10.9	14.3	16.5
Other religions	0.2	0.3	0.5
Total	**100.0**	**100.0**	**100.0**

Source: *ADR #2,* p 4, Table 2.

Those who profess to have no religion tend to be younger. Table 11 shows that in 1990, 21.8 per cent of those aged 15–24 years and 20.6 per cent of those aged 25–34 years reported no religious beliefs compared with 17.4 per cent for all age groups, and only 10.6 per cent for those aged 55 years and older.

In 2000, the same pattern held true: 22.5 per cent of those aged 15–24 years and 23.0 per cent of those aged 25–34 years had no religion compared with 18.6 per cent for all age groups and 11.9 per cent for the old folks. The secular outlook in life seems to have become more and more prevalent among the young over the last two decades among Chinese Singaporeans.

Table 11: Persons reporting No Religion by age group, 1990 and 2000 (in percentages)

Age group	1990	2000
15–24	21.8	22.5
25–34	20.6	23.0
35–44	19.9	19.1
45–54	13.5	16.7
55 and older	10.6	11.9
Total	17.4	18.6

Source: *ADR #2*, p 5, Table 3.

Bilingualism in English and Mandarin

In 1966, bilingualism was made compulsory in school from Primary 1. Most parents of Chinese origin chose then, and today choose, a combination of English (as first language, EL1) and Chinese (as second language, CL2: written Chinese and oral Mandarin) for their children when registering for Primary 1 admission. The first generation of Chinese immigrants were largely illiterate or semi-literate. They spoke Chinese dialects. Some also spoke bazaar Malay. Some second-generation Chinese attended Chinese schools. But all state-funded schools became bilingual schools in 1966. Since then, few private schools have remained. These are mainly foreign schools such as the American School and the Japanese School.

In the 1970 to 2000 censuses, literacy was measured crudely as the ability to read a newspaper in any language with "understanding". There was no test conducted by census enumerators to verify the oral claims of such ability made by the people or their level of "understanding".

Table 12 shows that those who were literate only in (reading) Chinese comprised 54.2 per cent in 1970. By 2000, the percentage had declined to 32.0. The percentage of those who were literate only in (reading) English also fell rapidly from 31.6 in 1970 to 16.4 in 2000. On the other hand, the numbers of those who were literate in both Chinese and English rose rapidly from 11.8 to 48.3 per cent.

Table 12: Language literacy of residents aged 10 or 15 and over, 1970–2000 (in percentages)

Language literate in	1970	1980	1990	2000
Chinese only	54.2	47.6	40.6	32.0
English only	31.6	20.4	19.8	16.4
Chinese and English only	11.8	29.6	37.8	48.3
Others	2.4	2.4	1.9	3.3
Total	100.0	100.0	100.0	100.0

Note: Aged 10 years and over for censuses 1970 and 1980; and aged 15 years and over for 1990 and 2000.

Sources: Mary Tay Wan Joo, *Trends in Language, Literacy and Education in Singapore*, Singapore: Dept of Statistics, nd, p 64, Table 3.7; and *ADR #3*, p 1, Table 1.

From 1970 to 2000, Chinese Singaporeans who were literate in Chinese rose from 66.0 (54.2 + 11.8) to 80.3 (32.0 + 48.3) per cent. Those who were literate in English rose from 43.4 (31.6 + 11.8) to 64.7 (16.4 + 48.3) per cent. Thus, bilingualism did not "kill" the Chinese language but, instead, made it more widespread in terms of "basic" literacy among Chinese Singaporeans. Thus, among Chinese Singaporeans, more than 50 per cent had become literate in Chinese (80.3%) and English (64.7%) by 2000. They now have two common languages at their disposal. English has also become the lingua franca for all five major ethnic groups (Chinese, Malays, Indians, Eurasians and Europeans) in Singapore. It serves as a social bridge in bringing them together in their everyday life.

Dominant home languages

Chinese dialects were the dominant media spoken by the majority of the Chinese Singaporeans at home right up to 1990. Table 13 shows that 81.4 per cent spoke Chinese dialects most frequently at home in 1980. This percentage declined rapidly to 50.3 in 1990. By 2000, only 30.7 per cent spoke Chinese dialects most frequently at home. Mandarin gained importance over the last two decades. In 1980, only 10.2 per cent spoke Mandarin most frequently at home. A decade later, 30.1 per cent used it at home as the dominant language. By 2000, 45.1 per cent were speaking Mandarin most frequently at home. In the next decade, Mandarin is likely to be the common home language among Chinese Singaporeans.

Table 13: Languages most frequently spoken at home, 1980–2000 (in percentages)

Language	1980	1990	2000
Chinese dialects	81.4	50.3	30.7
Mandarin	10.2	30.1	45.1
English	7.9	19.3	23.9
Others	0.5	0.3	0.4
Total	**100.0**	**100.0**	**100.0**

Note: Aged 5 years and over for censuses 1970 and 1980; and aged 15 years and over for 1990 and 2000.

Sources: Mary Tay Wan Joo, *Trends in Language, Literacy and Education in Singapore*, Singapore: Dept of Statistics, nd, p 19, Table 2.5; and *ADR #3*, p 4, Table 3.

The increasing use of Mandarin is likely to be due to two major processes of change—one internal and the other external. The annual Speak Mandarin campaigns have finally registered in the minds of Chinese Singaporeans. These campaigns aim at making Mandarin a living language in everyday social life, so that students of Chinese origin use it more and more and consequently do better in school (after having mastered it), thereby reducing the much-feared attrition rates in school in human resource–conscious Singapore. The emergent Chinese market has been growing rapidly since 1978. Today, China is viewed by the Ministry of Trade and Industry as the "fourth growth engine" of Singapore's economy (*The Straits Times*, 19 May 2001, S16). Thus, mastery of Mandarin serves instrumental, if not also sentimental, functions among Chinese Singaporeans.

Table 14 shows that in 1990, only 18.9 per cent of those aged 5–14 years spoke Chinese dialects at home most frequently, compared with 58.8 to 87.7 per cent of those aged 40 years and older.

By 2000, only 4.3 to 30.7 per cent of those who spoke Chinese dialects at home were aged below 55 years while 71.8 per cent of those aged 55 or older spoke Chinese dialects. There is a positive correlation between age and speaking Chinese dialects frequently at home.

The pattern is reversed for Mandarin: there is an inverse relation between speaking Mandarin and age. In 1990, 57.6 per cent of those aged 5–14 years spoke Mandarin most frequently at home, while 6.1 per cent of those aged 55 years or older spoke Mandarin. A decade later, in 2000, 59.6 to 59.8 per cent of those who spoke Mandarin were aged 5–24 years while only 17.8 per cent of those aged 55 years or older spoke it at home. Thus, in the last two decades, the use of Mandarin has become more and more widespread among the young and the middle-aged Chinese Singaporeans.

Table 14: Languages most frequently spoken at home by age group, 1990–2000 (in percentages)

Language/Year		5–14	15–24	25–39	40–54	55 & older
Chinese dialects:	1990	18.9	51.5	44.8	58.8	87.8
	2000	4.3	18.4	28.0	30.7	71.8
Mandarin:	1990	57.6	28.5	30.4	24.8	6.1
	2000	59.6	59.8	46.5	43.9	17.8
English:	1990	23.3	19.9	24.6	16.1	5.3
	2000	35.8	21.5	25.2	25.1	9.9
Others:	1990	0.2	0.2	0.3	0.4	0.9
	2000	0.4	0.3	0.3	0.3	0.5
Total:	1990 & 2000	100.0	100.0	100.0	100.0	100.0

Source: *ADR #3*, p 6, Table 4.

In 1990, only 23.3 per cent of those aged 5–14 years spoke English most frequently at home: these were schoolchildren. A decade later, in 2000, 35.8 per cent of this cohort spoke English at home most frequently. Lower proportions of older cohorts used English at home frequently. English has not caught on as a dominant home language among young and old Chinese Singaporeans.

Table 15 shows that there is an inverse relation between educational qualifications and speaking Chinese dialects at home and a positive correlation between educational qualifications and speaking Mandarin as well as English. Among those with no educational qualification, 75.5 per cent spoke Chinese dialects, 22.8 per cent spoke Mandarin and a mere 1.3 per cent spoke English at home. Among university graduates, 17.5 per cent spoke Chinese dialects, 34.7 per cent spoke Mandarin and 47.1 per cent spoke English at home.

Similar patterns are found with regard to types of dwelling. Table 16 shows that 63.3 per cent of those living in 1-room and 2-room HDB flats spoke Chinese dialects. The percentage was 44.4 for those residing in 3-room HDB flats, and 32.8 for those living in 4-room HDB flats, and only 21.1 for those living in 5-room or executive HDB flats. Only 17.1 per cent of those living in private properties spoke Chinese dialects.

Table 15: Languages most frequently spoken at home by highest educational qualification, 2000 (in percentages)

Language	No qualification	Primary	Secondary	Post-secondary	University	Total
Chinese dialects	75.5	42.2	26.5	23.2	17.5	37.8
Mandarin	22.8	50.7	46.0	44.0	34.7	40.6
English	1.3	6.8	27.3	32.5	47.1	21.3
Others	0.4	0.4	0.2	0.2	0.6	0.4
Total	100.0	100.0	100.0	100.0	100.0	100.0

Note: Residents aged 15 years and older.
Source: *ADR #3*, p 6, Table 4.

Table 16: Languages most frequently spoken at home by type of dwelling, 2000 (in percentages)

Language	HDB 1-/2-rm	HDB 3-rm	HDB 4-rm	HDB 5-rm/ Executive	Pte flats & houses	Total
Chinese dialects	63.3	44.4	32.8	21.1	17.1	30.7
Mandarin	31.5	45.9	52.6	45.2	26.4	45.1
English	4.4	9.3	14.3	33.5	55.9	23.9
Others	0.8	0.4	0.3	0.2	0.6	0.4
Total	100.0	100.0	100.0	100.0	100.0	100.0

Note: Residents aged 5 years and older.
Source: *ADR #3*, p 8, Table 6.

The relation between the type of dwelling and speaking Mandarin is curvilinear in the form of an inverted-U. Those living in 4-room HDB flats had the highest rate (52.6%) of speaking Mandarin most frequently at home. The rates were lower for those residing in 3-room HDB flats (45.9%) or smaller flats (31.5%), and for those living in 5-room and executive HDB flats (45.2%) or private residences (26.4%).

There is a positive correlation between speaking English and type of dwelling. Only a mere 4.4 per cent of those living in 1- or 2-room flats spoke English most frequently at home to family members, with the percentage rising to 33.5 for residents of 5-room or executive HDB flats, and to 55.9 for residents of private properties.

These census data indicate that speech behaviour at home is a function of age and social class, as indexed by educational qualification and type of residence. Hence, progress made in SES or socioeconomic status by Chinese Singaporeans over the last three decades affected cultural change in the form of a switch from the real mother tongues of Hokkien, Teochew, Cantonese and Hainanese Singaporeans to Mandarin (a standardized form of Beijing tongue) and English (a foreign language to Chinese Singaporeans). The younger generation also switched away from their mother tongues or Chinese dialects to both Mandarin and English.

Deferred first marriage

As mentioned above, full employment was achieved in 1972. Labour shortage soon followed. This led to (1) more and more females joining the labour force as labour shortage bid up wages and salaries, (2) importation of foreign labour, and (3) automation and computerization. As more and more females work, they are torn between career and marriage.

With rapid and sustained economic growth, family incomes rose. As incomes rose, more and more parents sent both their sons and daughters to school and kept them longer in school. More and more daughters were sent to junior colleges and universities. With more and more female graduates, more and more women earned high salaries. Concerned about their careers, females married later and later. Table 17 shows this trend: the mean age at first marriage was only 20.7 for those who were married in 1960 or earlier. The mean age at first marriage steadily increased to 26.9 years for those who married during the last decade, 1991–2000.

It is thus clear that progress in SES affects private or personal behaviour as to when to marry.

Table 17: Mean age at first marriage by year of marriage of ever-married females

Year of marriage	Mean age at first marriage
1960 or earlier	20.7
1961–70	23.3
1971–80	24.3
1981–90	26.1
1991–2000	26.9

Source: *ADR #2,* p 56, Table 5.

Intermarriage

Since independence in 1965, overall, inter-ethnic marriage rates have increased steadily except in the decade after the 13 May 1969 riots in Kuala Lumpur (see Table 18). Intermarriages decreased from 5.5 per cent in 1965 to 4.4 per cent in 1970, then rose slowly to 5.2 per cent in 1980, and continued to rise steadily to 10.8 per cent in 1998. Steady structural and social integration and the racial harmony achieved during the last three decades probably accounted for the rise in intermarriages.

Table 18: Intermarriage rates, 1965–98 (in percentages)

Year	Inter-ethnic marriages/100 marriages
1966	5.5
1970*	4.4
1975	4.5
1980	5.2
1985	6.5
1990	7.6
1995	9.0
1998	10.8

*Race riots on 13 May 1969 in Kuala Lumpur.
Source: Annual reports on marriages.

Number of children born

Not only have women delayed marriage, they have also given birth to fewer children. Traditionally, the Chinese value children, especially sons who carry on their surnames. The probability of having a son is increased with more births. In Third World countries, infant mortality tends to be very high. Singapore was a Third World country in the 1950s and 1960s.

Married Chinese women aged 50 and over in 1970 gave birth to 4.3 children on average. Those aged 50 and over in 2000 bore 3.7 children (see Table 19). The mean number of children born of women aged 40–49 years declined steadily from 5.4 in 1970 to 2.1 in 2000. The mean number of children born of those aged 30–39 years likewise fell from 4.0 in 1970 to 1.6 in 2000. Among women aged below 30 years, the mean number of children born also fell from 1.8 in 1970 to 0.6 in 2000.

Each age cohort gave birth to fewer and fewer children during the last three decades. Overall, the mean number of children born of Chinese

Singaporean women declined from 3.9 in 1970 to 2.5 in 2000. In the face of labour shortage during the last 25 years or so, the diminishing number of births implies that local labour supply would shrink in the future.

Table 19: Mean number of children born by age group of ever-married females, 1970–2000

Age group	Year	Mean number of children born
Below 30:	1970	1.8
	1990	0.9
	2000	0.6
30–39:	1970	4.0
	1990	1.8
	2000	1.6
40–49:	1970	5.4
	1990	2.6
	2000	2.1
50 and over:	1970	4.3
	1990	4.5
	2000	3.7
Total:	**1970**	**3.9**
	1990	**2.8**
	2000	**2.5**

Sources: *Report on the Census of Population 1970 Singapore,* Vol II, Singapore: Dept of Statistics, 1973, p 500, Table 235; and *ADR #8,* p 7, Table 7.

In view of this trend, the Singapore government is encouraging citizens to have more children. Many incentives are given to encourage births. But babies born in 2001 cannot help solve the problem of labour shortage today. Assuming that on average they will complete 12 years of education (GCE 'A' level) at the age of 18 years, these baby girls born today will enter the labour force at age 18 in 2019 and the baby boys born today will enter the labour market in 2022, as they have to serve 2.5 years of National Service. As the maturing Singapore economy is expected to grow at a slower rate in the next two to three decades, with consequently lower demand for labour, encouraging births today may create future unemployment.

Singles

Not only have men and women delayed their first marriage and restricted births in favour of career development and maintenance of higher standards of living, more and more men and women have chosen to remain single. When more men and women remain single, fewer children will be born and the supply of labour will be reduced in the future. As the labour supply shrinks due to previous birth control or restraint, an expanding economy will lead to more foreign labour being imported. Foreigners bring with them their values, beliefs, lifestyles, norms and so on, some of which may conflict with the local values, beliefs and so forth. A depluralized society will become pluralized again. Years of effort to depluralize Singapore society will be wiped out by the increasing presence of foreign cultures. Further efforts and resources will have to be spent on depluralizing Singapore society continuously as foreigners are needed to sustain growth.

Table 20 shows that among female Chinese Singaporeans, the extremes, that is, those with below secondary and those with university education, had more singles between 1990 and 2000. Among the former, the proportion of singles increased from 9.6 to 10.8 per cent (an increase of 1.2 percentage points) and among the university graduates, it increased from 26.7 to 29.2 per cent (an increase of 2.5 percentage points). The percentage of singles decreased among those with secondary (19.5 down to 16.5) and post-secondary education (23.8 to 22.1).

Table 20: Percentages of singles among male and female citizens by highest qualification attained, 1990 and 2000

Highest qualification attained/Sex	1990	2000	1990–2000
Males			
Below secondary	18.3	28.2	9.9
Secondary	13.3	18.4	5.1
Post-secondary	11.3	13.9	2.6
University	9.4	13.5	4.1
Females			
Below secondary	9.6	10.8	1.2
Secondary	19.5	16.5	-3.0
Post-secondary	23.8	22.1	-1.7
University	26.7	29.2	2.5

Source: *ADR #8*, p 4, Table 4.

However, among male Chinese Singaporeans, the percentage of singles increased for all levels of educational achievement. Those with up to secondary education increased most: 9.9 percentage points for those with less than secondary education and 5.1 percentage points for those with secondary education. University graduates had the third largest increase: 4.1 percentage points. Those with post-secondary education had the lowest increase: 2.6 percentage points.

In terms of rates, female graduates had the highest percentage of singles in 2000 among females (29.2), while males below secondary education had the highest (28.2). Chinese males tend to marry women with SES lower than their own, while Chinese women tend to marry men with SES higher than theirs. Hence, it is statistically and socially harder for female graduates to find unmarried men who have superior SES, and men with less than secondary education to find unmarried women even less educated than they are.

Consistent with the above argument, among men, those with university education had the lowest percentage of singles in 2000 (13.5) while women with below secondary education had the lowest (10.8).

Ethnic and National Identity: A Proposed Theory

Ethnic identity

Have the above structural and cultural changes led to identity shifts? There are three different dimensions of ethnic identity. First, it refers to a psychological state or process. Some people identify or perceive themselves as Chinese. Some do not. For example, when Tan Ah Dee was asked, "Who are you?", he said that he was a Chinese. Ah Dee perceives himself to be a member of the Chinese community. The Chinese are an identifiable group or community with identifiable characteristics known as culture. This culture, which identifies a group, has evolved over a long period of time and become 'established' as that group's set of characteristics which differentiates this group from other groups.

However, Ah Dee does not tell people that he is Chinese all the time. Sometimes, he plays down his identity as a Chinese and, instead, emphasizes that he is a Singaporean, his *national* identity. At other times he prefers to project his Hokkien or sub-ethnic identity. Thus, ethnic identity as a psychological state or process is unstable. This is sometimes known as "situational ethnicity".

Second, Ah Dee may bear many Chinese characteristics which make him identify himself as a member of the Chinese community. For instance, he bears a Chinese name, "Tan". His name "Ah Dee" is also Chinese, specifically, Hokkien. A man named Tan Ah Dee cannot be an Indian, Malay or European. Ah Dee celebrates Chinese New Year, makes annual visits to his grandparents' graves during Qing Ming festival, celebrates the August moon festival on the 15th day of the eighth month in the Chinese calendar. He reads Chinese newspapers regularly and enjoys bean milk and Jin Yong's martial arts novels. However, Ah Dee's parents bear more Chinese characteristics than Ah Dee. If a scale of Chinese traits were constructed to range from, say, 0 to 100, his parents would score higher on this scale than Ah Dee on Chinese traits; that is, Ah Dee is *less* Chinese than his parents. To the scholar who studies people like Ah Dee and his parents, people of Chinese origin may be Chinese to *different* degrees. Their degrees of "Chineseness" vary. This Chineseness can theoretically be measured objectively based on people's verbal, behavioural, dress style, and other manifestations. People do not change their habits every day. Generally, people will get up at their usual time, go to the bathroom, brush their teeth, eat breakfast in the neighbourhood coffee shop, ordering it in Hokkien or another dialect, take a bus to work, arrive at the office at 9.00 am and so on. These are repeated day in and day out, every week, every month, and nearly every year. They do not change their cultural behaviour much. Thus people's Chineseness or ethnic Chinese identity is fairly stable, unlike situational ethnicity. To distinguish this from the above concept of situational ethnic identity, this may be termed "ethnic cultural identity".

Third, Tan Ah Dee would never be mistaken for an Indian, Malay or European when he is in Singapore even if he were to dye his hair yellow. People around him and even strangers identify him to be a Chinese. These people also identify his parents and other family members as Chinese, regardless of their different degrees of Chineseness. If, however, Ah Dee were to travel in Europe, some Europeans might take him for a Korean or a Japanese. This sort of ethnic identity is a social process and is better termed "ethnic labelling" or "labelled ethnicity". The ethnic label applied on people may or may not be accurate or correct. Every day in West Asia and East Europe, people shoot one another on the basis of visual ethnic identity. Many innocent lives are lost this way.

I will examine more carefully the first two dimensions or types of ethnic identity.

In general, the first-generation Chinese immigrants identified themselves as Chinese and as Hokkiens, Teochews, and so forth. They practised Chinese folk culture and did not know of any other cultures when they first arrived in this part of Nanyang (South Sea).

Some of them sent their children to Chinese schools and others sent theirs to English schools. Their Chinese-educated children practised Chinese culture in their daily life and they identified themselves strongly as Chinese. Their English-educated children were bicultural. They also practised Chinese culture as much as their Chinese-educated cousins but they also enjoyed Hollywood movies and Western music, and so on. Some of them identified themselves strongly as Chinese; some others also identified themselves as Chinese but not to the same extent as their Chinese-educated cousins.

These Chinese-educated and English-educated children of the first-generation Chinese immigrants were the first-generation local-born. Over subsequent generations, fewer and fewer parents sent their children to Chinese schools while more and more parents sent their children to English schools. From 1966 onwards, they all sent their children to bilingual schools. Almost all of them chose EL1 + CL2 while a minority (approximately 10%) chose CL1 + EL2 for their children, especially their daughters. These subsequent generations of local-born Chinese were increasingly more competent in English than in Mandarin. Given three decades of rapid and sustained economic growth, more and more parents sent their children to Britain, North America, Australia and New Zealand for tertiary education. These overseas educated were more exposed to Western influence than those who attended local universities.

Hence, it is proposed that in general, those who practise Chinese culture (ethnic cultural identity) in their everyday life tend to identify themselves more strongly as Chinese (situational ethnic identity). Conversely, those who practise Chinese culture less tend to express a weaker Chinese identity. There is a positive but not a perfect correlation between Chineseness and ethnic Chinese identity (see Figure 1). Under certain social circumstances, some people low in Chineseness may strongly proclaim that they are Chinese, such as students studying abroad who want to assert their ethnic identity in the face of foreigners or presence of ethnic Chinese from Taiwan or Hong Kong.

National or Singaporean identity

I pioneered an empirical study of national or Singaporean identity in a large-scale survey of 990 voters in 1969 (Chiew, 1971). Just as people identify themselves psychologically as Chinese, some people also identify themselves psychologically as Singaporeans. Many people call themselves

Figure 1: Practising Chinese culture and ethnic Chinese identity: A proposed positive relation

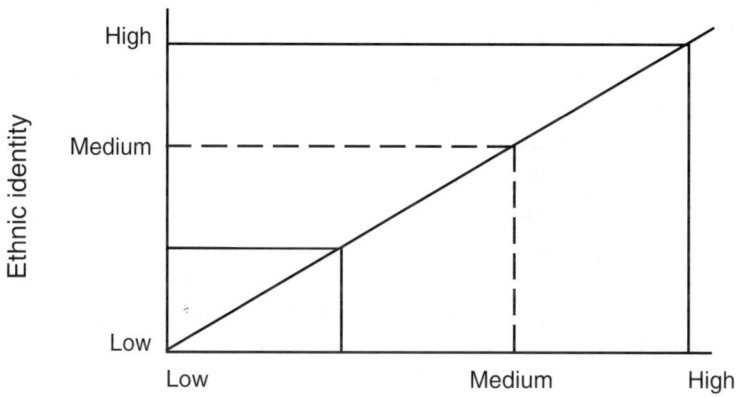

Americans, Japanese, Koreans, Malaysians, Brazilians and so forth, even though they may be members of ethnic minorities in their countries. My survey shows that the level of national identity was high among the Chinese (as well as among the Malays and Indians). For example, when forced to choose between being called Singaporean or Chinese, 82 per cent preferred to be known as Singaporean while only 18 per cent preferred to be called Chinese in 1969. When asked in 1969 if they were willing to fight and die for Singapore, 81 per cent were fairly (33%) or very (48%) willing to do so. The majority of them were also pro-integration of various kinds such as approving multiracial housing, multiracial friendship, multiracial schooling, acceptance of out-groups as neighbours, colleagues, bosses, and so on.

In 1989, a survey was conducted by me and Tan Ern Ser on ethnic and national identity and other issues (Chiew and Tan, 1990). When asked how they felt being a Singaporean, 81 per cent felt positive while 12.9 per cent were ambivalent and only 6.1 per cent expressed negative feelings. The majority of the Chinese Singaporeans were positive about Singapore: (1) 88 per cent believed there was a future for them in Singapore, (2) 86 per cent felt that Singapore was a good place to raise children, (3) 77 per cent thought that Singapore was a good place to make a living, (4) 75 per cent did not think that Singapore was a boring place to live in, and so forth. When asked whether they had ever considered emigrating, 85.7 per cent of the Chinese Singaporeans answered in the negative. The 1989 survey shows again high levels of identification with Singapore among the Chinese Singaporeans.

National and ethnic identity: Four phases of identity development

It is quite common or normal for people to have more than one identity. People may identify themselves as human, American, Afro-American or black, doctor or professional, artist, and so on. According to American psychologist Gordon Allport (1958), these identities form concentric circles of identity, where the inner entities or groups such as self, family, or school alumni are small intimate circles while the outer entities are large collectivities such as ethnic group, national group or humanity itself, which may span national boundaries. According to Allport, identification with groups within the same circle may lead to identity conflict. If one person is identified with Basketball Team A, he is unlikely to support equally strongly Basketball Team Z when these teams compete. He may support Basketball Team A and the NAACP (National Association for the Advancement of Colored People): there is no cognitive or social conflict in such dual identities located in different circles. Hence, many whites identify themselves quite comfortably as both American and white, and likewise some people identify themselves as both black and American, or woman, nurse, black and American.

In the case of Singapore, early and recent Chinese immigrants had or have strong ethnic Chinese identity (as a psychological state or process). Self-identity as a British subject or as a Singaporean took time or generations to develop. Such processes of identification may take longer for some but shorter time for others to form. Thus, not all second-generation local-born individuals identify themselves as Singaporeans as readily and as strongly. In general, national identity evolves gradually more or less 'step-wise'. The first-generation Chinese immigrants cannot be expected to cast away their cultural practices overnight while they slowly internalize some of the local norms in order to survive in a new environment, like learning to speak a few words of English or bazaar Malay or a different Chinese dialect. They have a strong ethnic Chinese identity because they view themselves as Chinese, practise Chinese culture habitually in their daily life and are labelled by others as Chinese. Slowly they internalize more local norms, beliefs (such as joining a Hakka church) and values, and thus become increasingly bicultural. If they live in a Chinese enclave such as Chinatown, these processes of acquiring elements of alien cultures may be slower for them than for those who live with members of other cultures in close proximity.

These processes of localization and multicultural acculturation carry on to the next and the next generation. Thus, over an individual's lifetime or over the generations, identities evolve or develop from the ethnic Chinese identity to an identity as Singaporean Chinese, that is, ethnic Chinese with varying amounts of Singaporean cultural elements or local way of life. As ethnic groups integrate more and more in schools, in the HDB or private housing neighbourhoods, at the various places of work, in community centres or clubs, and so forth, over generations, a common or Singapore way of life—local norms, beliefs, values and Singlish—evolves and enlarges in scope over time.

In this concept, Singaporean Chinese, "Chinese" is the noun and "Singaporean" is the adjective that qualifies the noun. "Chinese" is the dominant component while "Singaporean" is the subsidiary component. These Chinese are Singaporean Chinese as distinct from Hong Kong Chinese, Taiwan Chinese, mainland Chinese or American Chinese. They have certain cultural traits in common: hence, they are all Chinese. What they do not share differentiate them as Singaporean Chinese, Taiwan Chinese, American Chinese, and so on. These differences are often subtle.

It is hypothesized that over the generations or over an individual's lifetime, the Singaporean Chinese evolve into Chinese Singaporeans as they acquire more and more Singaporean traits. In this concept, Chinese Singaporean, "Singaporean" is the noun and the dominant identity while "Chinese" is the adjective that qualifies the noun. These Singaporeans are different from other Singaporeans such as Malay Singaporeans, Indian Singaporeans, Eurasian Singaporeans and British Singaporeans. These people have not yet become Singaporeans without ethnic Chinese, Malay, Indian, Eurasian or British characteristics. Singapore society has not yet evolved into a society of only Singaporeans. Psychologically, it is not impossible that some individuals view themselves as "purely" Singaporeans without ethnic characteristics or ethnic identity. The first Senior Minister, Mr Rajaratnam, publicly stated more than once that he was first, a Singaporean, second, a Singaporean, and third, a Singaporean. This is an example of the self-proclaimed "true blue" Singaporean from head to toe and from skin to the psyche or heart.

I hypothesize that there are, roughly, four phases of identity development among Singapore citizens of Chinese descent: (1) ethnic Chinese identity, (2) Singaporean Chinese identity, (3) Chinese Singaporean and (4) Singaporean (see Figure 2). I believe that a very small proportion belong to the first phase: these individuals are likely to be the elderly and poorly educated or the recent arrivals. A substantial proportion belong to the second phase and they either tend to be older and not so well educated or are Chinese-educated and middle-aged. I believe that the majority, particularly the young, belong to the third phase of Chinese Singaporeans, educated in EL1 and CL2. Those who belong to the last phase appear, at the moment, proportionately small.

Figure 2: Four phases of ethnic-national identities

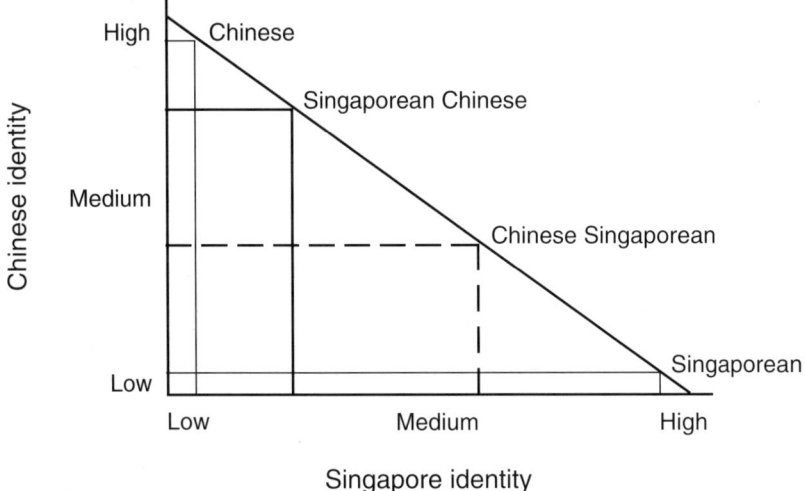

Limits to National Identity in Globalizing Singapore

Globalizing Singapore and global citizens

In an increasingly interconnected world where people, ideas, values, beliefs, norms, lifestyles, goods, business practices, capital and so on, cross national boundaries via the Internet, airlines, shipping, and so forth, national identity is in danger of losing its appeal or grip on citizens. Some Singapore citizens spend a good part of a year working abroad—perhaps three months in China, one month in Australia, one month in Indonesia, one month in Vietnam, two weeks in London, and two weeks in Cambodia. Their diversified interests, friends, business partners make them feel like global citizens.

Today, Singapore citizens who work abroad are not the clerks, maids or bus drivers. They are mainly members of the professional-managerial class—the professionals, managers and business owners.

As China opens up its economy and society more and more, more and more Chinese Singaporeans will be working in China in their attempt to corner a segment of the huge market of 1.22 billion consumers. If Yeo Hiap Seng can sell just one packet of its soft drinks per year to each Chinese, it has a potential market of 1.22 billion packets per year. Hence, these venturesome Chinese Singaporeans are brushing up on their spoken

Mandarin and Chinese dialects, and written Chinese. They also read up on Chinese history and culture (eg, Confucian and Daoist philosophies, and folklore or customs, etc). They project their situational ethnic and sub-ethnic identities in order to build *guanxi* (networking) for instrumental and other reasons.

Now mainland Chinese look up to Chinese Singaporeans for the latter's knowledge of the world outside China, particularly Western management practice, technology, products, and the Chinese Singaporeans' access to capital and bank credit. Eventually, given sustained and high economic growth, mainland China's corporations will grow in size and number, and their managers and professionals will become increasingly sophisticated and will match the ability and influence of Chinese Singaporeans. At that point, the "Singaporean" brand will begin to lose its "gloss": the Singaporean identity will carry less prestige. At that point, some big Chinese corporations may be hiring Chinese Singaporean managers and professionals to work for them as they will be able to pay Singaporean salaries.

It is projected that China's economy will surpass that of the United States, given its huge population and higher economic growth rates compared with those of America, in about three decades. A former World Bank economist and current CEO of a Washington consulting firm (*The Straits Times,* 25 May 2001, p 24) predicted that by 2025, China would become the world's largest economy, accounting for about 26 per cent of global output while the United States' global output would be about 22 per cent. China may take a longer time[1] to reach this level of economic development. Whether it takes three decades or four or five, as China's economy grows and grows over the next few decades, Chinese products, music, movies, magazines, people and capital will gradually spread around the world just like Coca-Cola, Microsoft Windows, Hollywood movies, American drugs, American cars, Palm PDAs, management praxes and so forth today.

Some may argue that American products are so dominant or popular because of successful branding. Can the Chinese produce brands as powerful as Coca-Cola, McDonald's, Amazon.com or Palm over the next few decades? Some of these American brand names are new, like "Amazon.com"

---

1   A Taiwanese reader of the *Lianhe Zaobao* report dated 2 July 2001 on my paper phoned me and asserted that it would take mainland China about 100 years to match the US in GNP and that Chinese culture would not be able to spread as much as the American culture because the Chinese do not have brands as powerful as General Motors, Coca-Cola or Hollywood. His constructive feedback helped me to elaborate on my theoretical arguments.

and "Palm". Others like "Coca-Cola" and "Ford" have been household names in the US for a long time but have become international brand names only in the last two or three decades. But times have changed from the telegraph and fax machines used just two decades ago to the current broadband instantaneous Internet communication which connects the world at low cost. The present younger generation of Chinese who have heard about the Cultural Revolution have different mindsets from that of the previous generation who experienced the trauma of the Revolution. The next generation may not even hear of the Cultural Revolution or life under the Command Economy of shared poverty and coerced consensus. These young Chinese would be born in an age of instant communication and interconnectivity through newer and newer, and faster and faster electronic communication devices. The world would be their classroom where learning curves would be shortened geometrically. I believe that under these circumstances, Chinese entrepreneurs would be able to produce their own Coca-Cola or Amazon.com brands at even faster speed and greater reach over the next few decades.

The future Chinese mass culture will not be like Third Sister Liu's anti-landlord songs but more like the hard rock music of Wu Bai or 500. Chinese glossy magazines, CDs, VCDs, movies, TV soap operas, novels and so forth will flood the world market like American and Japanese products today, as the Chinese are beginning to flood the Indian market today with Chinese goods.

Mainland China's culture will first affect Chinese Singaporeans working and living in China. Chinese culture will affect Singapore's professional-managerial class first. Chinese movies, music, TV programmes, magazines, fashion and so on will eventually 'filter' down to Singapore's clerks, hawkers, taxi drivers, students and home makers as they penetrate Singapore society gradually but steadily.

This cultural penetration, like the American mass culture before it, will spread like a virus and be likely to enhance ethnic Chinese identity and ethnic Chinese cultural identity (Chineseness) among Chinese Singaporeans from all walks of life to different extents. Our Westernized young will become both Westernized and resinicized and may become truly bilingual in English and Chinese and multicultural (Chinese, Singaporean and Western). They will remain Chinese Singaporeans but qualitatively different from the present Chinese Singaporeans according to their cultural mix.

The projected resinicization a few decades down the road is likely to check the further development of the Singaporean identity. China's growing influence is hypothesized to make it difficult for Chinese Singaporeans to evolve into Singaporeans. That is, identity development is likely to freeze at the third phase, the Chinese Singaporean, as unstoppable globalization takes its toll, making the making of "One People [Singaporeans], One Nation [Singapore]" very difficult to achieve. If the Singaporean identity is not 're-engineered' forcefully and persistently over the next few decades among the young and old, resinicization will come sooner and easier. The (Chinese) music (or culture) comes with the yuan (or trade). Soon Chinese and English will become the two dominant Internet languages of communication and persuasion.

Foreign talents and problems of repluralization

Singapore's economy has just started to restructure the second time in preparation for the coming of the "new knowledge-based economy" or KBE. With increasing globalization and the proliferation of the Internet and e-business, companies in Singapore face global competition. Just a decade ago, bookshops in Singapore competed among themselves locally. Now, with a click of the electronic mouse, books can be ordered from bookshops in America and elsewhere and at competitive prices. Bookshops in Singapore almost suddenly face competition from the largest bookshops around the world. Likewise, American stocks and shares and Dell computers can be bought at a click, bypassing local brokers and computer retailers.

To meet this fierce and ruthless competition, companies around the world compete for the best staff to enhance their competitiveness. Top managers and professionals work for any corporation which offers the best package. The world is borderless to them as they fly around the globe to wherever they are in demand. Singapore, too, is forced to join the rat race for "talents" or professionals and managers in areas where demand exceeds supply. For instance, Singapore's industries need 10,000 IT professionals but its training capacity can produce only a few thousand. In the face of shortage of skilled manpower, there are two options: (1) corporations recruit them from abroad or (2) corporations should not expand but maintain the *status quo*. The latter option will restrict economic growth and is not a viable option. The former option means bringing in more and more foreigners who bring with them their foreign cultures and lifestyles, some of which are likely to conflict with local ones. In 2000, there were 754,524 non-residents (who were neither citizens nor PRs) working or living in Singapore. They comprised 18.8 per cent of the total population of 4,017,733 persons. Thus, almost one in five in the population was a foreigner.

Though there is no ethnic breakdown of non-residents available now, I suspect that most of them were Indians from India and Chinese from Malaysia, China, Hong Kong and Taiwan because the percentage of Chinese in the resident population decreased by one percentage point (from 77.8 to 76.8 between 1990 and 2000) while that of the Indians increased by 0.8 percentage point (from 7.1 to 7.9). The cultures that they brought with them are not too different from those of the local-born citizens of Chinese and Indian origins. Among residents of Chinese descent, the census report shows that 81.7 per cent were born in Singapore and 9.4 per cent were born in Malaysia. Only 5.0 per cent were born in China, Hong Kong and Taiwan and 1.0 per cent were born in Indonesia. The remaining 2.9 per cent were born in India, Pakistan, Bangladesh, Sri Lanka and elsewhere.

It is relatively easier to attract people with the required skills or expertise from low-income and less liberal countries like China, India and Sri Lanka, than people from high-income and more liberal countries like those in North America and Western Europe and Japan. These latter countries also compete for "talents". While many Chinese from China, Hong Kong and Taiwan may wish to work in the United States, some find Singapore society with 77 per cent Chinese more socially and culturally comfortable.

Not all Westerners bring in "exotic" cultures. The Americans, British and Australians who come to work in Singapore do not add much to the existing British-American culture. The French, Germans, Italians and others, who are very few in number, do bring in cultures and languages that are very different from the local cultures. But their cultural impact is likely to be insignificant due to their small numbers.

Many of these expatriates may use Singapore as a stepping-stone. For instance, some Chinese from mainland China may work here for a few years and then move on to the United States, using their working experience in Singapore as a credential for their upward social mobility. But many stay and become, initially, PRs and then citizens. So long as Singapore's economy continues to grow and its political stability is sustained, its open door policy will continue to attract foreigners. Consequently, repluralization and the depluralization will become an ongoing process.

Summary and Conclusion

During the last three decades, Chinese Singaporeans made progress in education, occupation, housing, home ownership and income. They also experienced changes in terms of religion (more Buddhists, Christians, "freethinkers", and fewer Daoists), dominant language used at home (Chinese dialects losing ground to Mandarin and English), greater "basic" literacy in both Chinese and English, later marriage, fewer children born, and more remaining single. Some of these latter changes were correlated with social class progress. For instance, those who had higher educational qualifications and those who lived in bigger dwellings tended to speak Mandarin and English more than those with lower educational attainment and smaller housing units. Those who professed to have no religion tended to be younger and better educated. Thus, these paralleled developments in education, income, religion, literacy and so forth were interconnected. Consequently, as further progress is made in education, income and so on in future, further changes in religion, literacy and so forth will occur.

This article also hypothesizes the gradual evolution of identity in four phases: Chinese identity, Singaporean Chinese, Chinese Singaporean and Singaporean. The emergence of China as an economic superpower in the 21st century is hypothesized to arrest the progression from the third to the last phase. As China's economic power increases, its cultural influence will also spread, and will eventually affect Singaporeans from the professional-managerial class first and ultimately filter down to touch the life of almost every Singaporean to different extents. Future generations of Chinese Singaporeans are likely to become truly bilingual in Chinese and English, and multicultural (ie, resinicized, Singaporean and Westernized culturally). English and Chinese will become the two dominant Internet languages of communication and persuasion as the Asia-Pacific Age dawns.

References

Allport, Gordon W. *The Nature of Prejudice*. New York: Doubleday Anchor Books, 1958.
Chiew, Seen Kong. *Singaporean National Identity*. MSoc Sci thesis. Singapore: Department of Sociology, University of Singapore, 1971.
Chiew, Seen Kong, and Tan Ern Ser. *Singaporean: Ethnicity, National Identity and Citizenship*. Singapore: The Institute of Policy Studies, 1990.
Department of Statistics, Singapore. *Report on the Census of Population 1970 Singapore,* Vol II. Singapore: Department of Statistics, 1973.
———. *Singapore Census of Population 1990: Economic Characteristics*. Singapore: Department of Statistics, 1993.
———. *Singapore Census of Population 2000: Advance Data Release*. Singapore: Department of Statistics, May 2001.
———. *Singapore Census of Population 2000: Advance Data Release #1— Changing Educational Profile*. Singapore: Department of Statistics, nd.

———. *Singapore Census of Population 2000: Advance Data Release #2—Religion.* Singapore: Department of Statistics, nd.
———. *Singapore Census of Population 2000: Advance Data Release #3—Language and Literacy.* Singapore: Department of Statistics, nd.
———. *Singapore Census of Population 2000: Advance Data Release #4—Economic Characteristics of Singapore Resident Population.* Singapore: Department of Statistics, nd.
———. *Singapore Census of Population 2000: Advance Data Release #6—Households and Housing.* Singapore: Department of Statistics, nd.
———. *Singapore Census of Population 2000: Advance Data Release #7—Household Income Growth and Distribution.* Singapore: Department of Statistics, nd.
———. *Singapore Census of Population 2000: Advance Data Release #8—Marriage and Fertility.* Singapore: Department of Statistics, nd.
———. *Statistics on Marriages and Divorces, 1965–1999.* Singapore: Department of Statistics, nd.
Tay, Wan Joo Mary. *Trends in Language, Literacy and Education in Singapore.* Census Monograph No 2. Singapore: Department of Statistics, nd.
The Straits Times, 19 May 2001, S16.
The Straits Times, 25 May 2001, p 24.
Yeh, HK Stephen. *Households and Housing.* Singapore: Department of Statistics, nd.

Chapter 3

THE CHANGING DEMOGRAPHIC SITUATION OF MALAYSIAN CHINESE

Tey Nai Peng

Introduction

This article examines the changing demographic trends of the Chinese population in Malaysia between 1970 and 2000. During this period, the size of the Chinese population increased by 53 per cent from 3.72 million to 5.69 million. The changing demographic situation of the Malaysian Chinese will be studied in terms of the changes in size, rate of growth, age-sex structure, geographical distribution and their proportion to the total population, as well as the demographic processes that brought about such changes.

Despite the fact that most Malaysian Chinese are now second- or third-generation–born in this country, they still retain their cultural distinctiveness within the multi-ethnic society. To some extent, the distinctiveness in cultural practices and socioeconomic behaviour of the Malaysian Chinese may be attributed to the "affirmative" policies of the government in social restructuring. The classification of the Malaysian population according to ethnic affiliation is extended to a host of official statistics, such as those for education, employment, ownership of shares, assets and businesses, and so forth. In this article, the changing demographic situation of the Malaysian Chinese will be compared with that of the other ethnic groups, in particular, the Malay majority.

Population Size and Rate of Growth

Prior to World War II, the growth of the Chinese population in Malaysia was mainly the result of large-scale immigration from Guangdong and Fujian provinces in southern China. With the restrictive immigration policy after the War, natural increase became the major determinant of changes in the size and character of the Chinese Malaysian population. By the mid-1950s, the Chinese had become a fairly settled population (Saw, 1988).

According to the population census of 1911, there were 694,970 Chinese in Malaya. They constituted about 30 per cent of the total population of about 2.34 million. Their number increased steadily to about 1.5 million in 1957, when the country achieved independence, and this was 37 per cent of the total population in Malaya. In 1970, when the first pan-Malaysian population census was taken, the number of Chinese was estimated at 3.72 million, and this had increased to about 5.69 million by the turn of the century (see Table 1).

Table 1: Population size (in thousands) and the relative size of the Chinese population to the total population by region, 1970–2000

	1970	1980	1991 (Tot pop.)	1991 (M'sians)	2000 (Tot pop.)	2000 (M'sians)
Malaysia						
Total population	10,439.4	13,745.2	18,379.7	17,574.3	23,274.7	21,889.9
Chinese	3,719.1	4,414.6	4,945.0	4,945.0	5,691.9	5,691.9
% Chinese	35.6	32.1	26.9	28.1	24.5	26.0
Peninsular Malaysia						
Total population	8,826.7	11,426.0	14,797.6	14,475.4	17,714.4	16,991.8
Chinese	3,286.0	3,865.4	4,251.0	4,251.0	4,740.0	4,740.0
% Chinese	35.8	33.8	28.7	29.4	26.8	27.9
Sabah						
Total population	636.4	1,011.0	1,863.7	1,398.9	2,603.5	1,988.7
Chinese	139.2	164.0	218.2	218.2	262.1	262.1
% Chinese	21.3	16.2	11.7	15.6	10.1	13.2
Sarawak						
Total population	976.3	1,307.6	1,718.4	1,700.0	2,071.5	2,008.8
Chinese	293.9	385.2	475.8	475.8	537.2	537.2
% Chinese	30.1	29.5	27.7	28.0	25.9	26.8

Sources: Population censuses, 1970, 1980, 1991 and 2000.

The Chinese population in Peninsular Malaysia increased most rapidly in the 1920s, registering an average rate of growth of 4.1 per cent per annum for the 1911–21 period. Since then, their rate of growth hovered around 2.5 per cent per annum up until 1970. Although the number of Malaysian Chinese increased by more than 2 million between 1970 and 2000, their rate of growth decelerated to 1.7 per cent per annum during the 1970–80 period, and fell further to 1.0 per cent during the 1980–91 intercensal period, before reversing to a more rapid growth of about 1.6 per cent between 1991 and 2000. As will be shown later, the changing rate of growth was brought about by the interplay of various factors, such as changes in the marital structure, marital fertility and international migration.

Table 2 shows that the Chinese population was growing at different paces in the different regions and states between 1970 and 2000. In the 1970s, the Chinese population registered an average rate of growth of between 1 per cent (in Malacca and Perak) and 4 per cent in Selangor. Between 1980 and 1991, the deceleration in the rate of growth occurred in all the states, and there was actually a decrease in the number of Chinese in the states of Pahang, Perak and Perlis. Data from the 2000 Population and Housing Census show an increase in the rate of growth of the Chinese population in Selangor, Johor and Pahang. On the other hand, there was a decrease in the number of Chinese in Trengganu, Kelantan, Perak and Perlis. The Chinese population remained rather constant in Malacca and Negri Sembilan from 1980.

Table 2: Annual rate of population growth (Chinese and total population) by state, 1970–80, 1980–91, 1991–2000

	1970–80 Chinese	1970–80 All races	1980–91 Chinese	1980–91 All races	1991–2000 Chinese	1991–2000 All races
Malaysia	1.7	2.8	1.0	2.6	1.6	2.6
P. Malaysia	1.7	2.6	0.9	2.4	1.5	2.5
Johor	2.2	2.5	1.7	2.5	2.1	2.6
Kedah	1.2	1.6	0.7	1.8	0.8	2.1
Kelantan	2.1	2.7	1.2	2.7	-1.1	0.9
Malacca	1.0	1.4	0.0	1.2	0.1	2.0
N. Sembilan	1.3	1.8	0.1	2.1	0.0	1.9
Pahang	2.8	4.6	-0.4	2.8	1.0	1.9
Perak	1.0	1.5	-0.4	0.8	-1.0	0.4
Perlis	1.8	2.0	-0.2	2.3	-1.2	0.8
P. Pinang	1.8	2.1	0.5	1.4	0.7	1.8
Selangor	4.0	4.3	2.6	4.2	5.4	6.1
Trengganu	1.7	2.9	0.7	3.7	-2.0	1.2
W.P.K.L.	3.1	6.6	0.8	2.1	0.1	1.3
Sabah	1.6	4.4	2.6	5.5	2.5	4.0
Sarawak	2.4	3.9	1.9	2.5	1.3	2.1
Labuan	—	—	—	—	0.9	3.6

Sources: Population censuses, 1970, 1980, 1991 and 2000.

During the 1970–2000 period, the rate of growth of the Chinese population was considerably lower than that of the total population in all states, and this resulted in significant changes in the ethnic composition. Regional differentials in the rate of Chinese population growth brought about greater concentration in a few states—notably Selangor, Sabah and Johor.

The crude rate of natural increase of Malaysian Chinese declined in all the three regions, and at a faster rate than that of the Malays (see Table 3). Hence, even in the absence of out-migration, the Chinese proportion in the total population declined nevertheless.

Table 3: Crude rate of natural increase by ethnic group, 1970–98

| Year | Crude rate of natural increase of Malaysian Chinese | | | Pen. Malaysia | |
	Pen. Malaysia	Sabah	Sarawak	Malays	Indians
1970	23.9	25.2	32.9	28.6	22.0
1975	21.3	22.7	26.8	27.8	22.5
1980	19.7	23.3	25.8	28.3	22.8
1985	17.4	19.6	19.6	32.2	20.4
1990	14.5	19.3	20.1	27.1	17.4
1994	15.6	17.0	19.5	26.3	18.7
1998*	15.7	—	—	22.3**	17.4
1999*	15.3			20.8**	10.0
2000*	17.2			20.7**	16.6

*Refers to Malaysia.
**Refers to Bumiputra.
Source: Department of Statistics, *Vital Statistics, Peninsular Malaysia,* various years.

The crude rate of natural increase of the Malaysian Chinese was higher than the rate of population growth in the 1970s and 1980s. During the last intercensal period (1991–2000), the rate of population growth of the Malaysian Chinese followed closely their rate of natural increase. This indicates that the outflow registered in the previous two decades had come to a halt.

Components of Population Growth of Malaysian Chinese

Until World War II, international migration played an important role in determining the growth and structure of the Chinese population in Malaya. However, with the cessation of Chinese immigration into Malaya after the War, the natural increase has been the main determinant of the increase of Malaysian Chinese and their demographic characteristics. Table 4 shows that the number of foreign-born had decreased from about 900,000 in 1931 to around 284,000 by 1980. Consequently, the proportion of Malaysian Chinese who were foreign born fell rapidly from about 80 per cent in 1921 to 25 per cent in 1957, 7.3 per cent in 1980 and merely 3.1 per cent in 1991.

Table 4: Foreign-born Chinese in Peninsular Malaysia, 1921–80

Year	Chinese population	Foreign-born	Percentage foreign-born
1921	857,653	682,502	79.6
1931	1,285,173	900,486	70.1
1947	1,884,534	707,024	37.5
1957	2,333,756	595,326	25.5
1970	3,286,000	410,399	12.5
1980	3,865,400	283,516	7.3
1991*	4,945,000	153,000	3.1

*Refers to Malaysia.

Note: Information from the 2000 Population Census regarding place of birth by ethnicity was still unavailable at the time this report was written.

Sources: Saw Swee Hock, 1988; and Department of Statistics, 1995a.

Data show that for the period 1947–2000, population increase of Malaysian Chinese was the result of natural increase, which was partly offset by migration deficits. Given the comprehensiveness of vital registration, it is possible to estimate the number of out-migrants by comparing the natural increase with population growth enumerated in population censuses. Table 5 shows that the out-migration of Malaysian Chinese had significant impact on the growth of their population up until the 1980s. The out-migration rate of Malaysian Chinese was estimated at close to 10 per cent of their population for the 1947–91 period. The heaviest outflow was registered during the 1980–91 period when migration deficits were slightly more than half of the natural increase. Evidence from the

2000 Population Census shows that the outflow ceased during the last decade. The increase in the number of Chinese during the intercensal period 1991–2000 corresponded very closely to that of natural increase.

Table 5: Components of population growth in Peninsular Malaysia, 1947–91

Period		Population increase	Natural increase	Net migration	Migration rate (%)
1947–57*		449,200	642,500	-193,300	-10.3
1957–70*		797,600	1,044,400	-246,800	-10.6
1970–80*		519,900	775,100	-255,200	-8.2
1970–80**	All	591,597	786,857	-195,260	-6.0
	Male	282,929	387,858	-102,929	-6.2
	Female	306,668	398,999	-92331	-5.7
1980–91**	All	385,538	777,339	-391,801	-10.1
	Male	200,794	389,941	-189,147	-9.7
	Female	184,744	387,398	-202,654	-10.6
1991–2000@		746,900	750,000	–3100	-0.0

Sources: *Saw Swee Hock, 1988; **NPFDB (1983); ***Chan and Tey (2000).
@Based on vital statistics (1991–99) and 2000 Population and Housing Census.

Proportion of Chinese to the Total Population

Consequent upon the slower rate of growth of the Chinese relative to that of the other ethnic groups in the country, the Chinese proportion to the total population declined steadily from 35.6 per cent in 1970 to about 24.5 per cent in 2000 (or about 26.0% of Malaysian citizens), at an accelerated rate from the 1980s (see Table 1). The declining Chinese proportion can be attributed to the higher rate of natural increase among the Malays, and the increased inflows of migrant workers and their families from neighbouring countries. According to the 2000 Population Census, there are now about 1.38 million non-Malaysians out of a total population of 23.3 million. In Sabah, the Chinese proportion in the state decreased dramatically from 21.3 per cent in 1970 to 10.1 per cent in 2000 consequent upon large-scale immigration of Indonesians and Filipinos. However, the Chinese still made up about 13.2 per cent of Malaysians in Sabah.

While all the states had an increase in Chinese population in the 1990s, the rate of increase was much lower than that of the general population such that the proportionate share of the Chinese in each state continued to decline rather sharply over the years (see Table 6).

Table 6: Chinese population by state, 1970, 1980, 1991 and 2000

State	Chinese population				Chinese population as percentage of all Malaysians in each state			
	1970	1980	1991	2000	1970	1980	1991	2000
Johor	504.2	628.9	759.1	916.7	39.5	38.4	36.1	35.4
Kedah	184.7	208.4	225.9	241.4	19.3	18.6	16.6	14.9
Kelantan	38.7	47.9	54.4	49.1	5.6	5.4	4.6	3.8
Malacca	160.3	176.7	176.1	178.3	39.7	38.0	33.7	29.1
N. Sembilan	183.6	209.7	211.1	211.9	38.1	36.6	29.7	25.6
Pahang	158.3	209.6	199.7	218.3	31.4	26.2	19.0	17.7
Perak	666.4	737.2	706.5	643.1	42.4	40.8	36.0	32.0
Perlis	19.9	23.8	23.2	20.8	16.4	16.0	12.3	10.3
P. Pinang	436.7	521.5	551.1	588.7	56.3	54.6	50.1	46.5
Selangor	382.0	567.5	758.4	1230.3	38.9	37.4	32.4	30.7
Trengganu	22.6	26.7	28.9	24.3	5.6	4.9	3.7	2.8
W.P.K.L.	373.9	507.5	556.5	560.1	57.7	51.9	47.5	43.5
Sabah*	139.2	164.0	218.2	271.6	21.3	16.2	15.6	13.3
Sarawak	303.5	385.2	475.8	537.2	31.1	29.5	28.0	26.7

*Includes Labuan.

Sources: General Reports of the Population Censuses 1970, 1980, 1991 and 2000.

The decrease in the proportionate share of the Chinese population to the total population was most pronounced in the younger cohorts, consequent upon the more rapid decline in fertility as compared with the Bumiputra. Table 7 shows that in 2000 Malaysian Chinese below 15 years of age made up just about 20 per cent of the population in that age group, as compared with about 36 per cent among those in the older age groups. This implies that even in the absence of emigration, the Chinese proportion will become progressively smaller in the future.

Table 7: Population size (Chinese and all races) by age group, 2000

Age group	Malaysians	Chinese	Percentage Chinese
0–4	2,504,193	476,803	19.0
5–9	2,558,020	513,630	20.1
10–14	2,425,807	498,792	20.6
15–19	2,268,257	524,032	23.1
20–24	1,875,443	482,350	25.7
25–29	1,665,483	444,059	26.7
30–34	1,608,793	449,367	27.9
35–39	1,564,735	462,134	29.5
40–44	1,398,936	437,763	31.3
45–49	1,120,040	371,391	33.2
50–54	888,119	314,045	35.4
55–59	600,589	216,535	36.1
60–64	538,420	194,286	36.1
65+	873,081	306,721	35.1
All age groups	21,889,916	5,691,908	26.0

Source: Department of Statistics, 2001.

Population Distribution

Since 1970, about two-thirds of the Chinese population have been living in five of the states—Johor, Perak, Penang, Selangor and Kuala Lumpur. Socioeconomic development and structural transformation of the economy have brought about increased mobility, resulting in rapid urbanization and redistribution of the population. During the last three decades, there was significant redistribution of the Chinese population across the states. In 1970, Perak had the largest Chinese population, followed by Johor and Pulau Pinang. By 1991, the pole position had been taken over by Johor and Selangor. In 2000, the largest Chinese concentration was in Selangor (21.6%), followed by that in Johor (16.1%), Perak (11.3%), Pulau Pinang (10.3%) and Kuala Lumpur (9.8%). The corresponding figures for 1991 were 15.3, 15.4, 14.3, 11.1 and 11.3 respectively (see Table 8).

In 2000, only 5.2 per cent of the Chinese were living in the predominantly Malay East Coast states in Peninsular Malaysia—Kelantan, Trengganu and Pahang. The proportion of Malaysian Chinese living in Sabah and Sarawak increased somewhat over the last three decades, on account of net inflows and higher fertility in these two states.

Table 8: Population distribution of Malaysian Chinese by state, 1970–2000

State	1970	1980	1991	2000
Johor	14.1	14.2	15.4	16.1
Kedah	5.2	4.7	4.6	4.2
Kelantan	1.1	1.1	1.1	0.9
Malacca	4.5	4.0	3.6	3.1
N. Sembilan	5.1	4.8	4.3	3.7
Pahang	4.4	4.7	4.0	3.9
Perak	18.6	16.7	14.3	11.3
Perlis	0.6	0.5	0.5	0.4
P. Pinang	12.2	11.8	11.1	10.3
Selangor	10.7	12.9	15.3	21.6
Trengganu	0.6	0.6	0.6	0.4
W.P.K.L.	10.5	11.5	11.3	9.9
Sabah	3.9	3.7	4.4	4.8
Sarawak	8.5	8.7	9.6	9.4
Total	**100.0**	**100.0**	**100.0**	**100.0**

Sources: Population censuses, various years.

While the National Development Policy (previously, the New Economic Policy) was aimed at urbanizing the Malays, it has strengthened the urbanization process in the country in general and this accounts for the growth in urban living among the already more highly urbanized Chinese. This can be seen in the rise of the level of urbanization among Malaysian Chinese from 47 per cent in 1970 to 56 per cent in 1980, 76 per cent in 1991 and 88.6 per cent in 2000.

Reflecting the concentration of the Chinese in the urban areas, they made up some 59 per cent of the urban population in 1970. However, the demographic dominance of the Chinese in the urban areas declined steadily to 50.3 per cent in 1980, 40.8 per cent in 1991 and 33.9 per cent in 2000, while the proportionate share of the Bumiputra in the urban areas increased from 27.6 per cent to 37.9 per cent, 47.4 per cent and 50.0 per cent during the same period. The decline in the proportionate share of the Chinese population in the urban areas could be attributed to lower fertility relative to that of the Bumiputra, as well as the higher propensity of the Bumiputra to migrate to the urban areas in line with the objectives of the National Development Policy. In 2000, the Chinese made up only 9 per cent of the rural population, down from 26.1 per cent in 1970.

An index based on the ratio of the proportion of the Chinese in each state's population to the proportion of the Chinese in the national population was calculated to examine the Chinese concentration (Chan and Tey, 2000). In general, the Chinese population concentration index was higher in the more developed states, such as Selangor (with an index of 1.37 in 1991), Penang (1.92), Johor (1.32), Perak (1.36) and Malacca (1.27), while it was lowest in the less developed states—Kelantan (0.16), Trengganu (0.13), Perlis (0.45) and Sabah (0.47).

Age-Sex Structural Shifts in Population

The age-sex structure of the Malaysian Chinese has changed considerably since 1970. Their median age increased from about 19 years in 1970 to almost 26 years by 1991 and about 29 years by 2000. The proportion aged 15 and younger declined from 43 per cent in 1970 to 30.4 per cent in 1991 and 26.2 per cent in 2000. Those in the age group 30–59 registered the largest proportionate increase over the 1970–2000 period, resulting in the reduction in age dependency burden in the short and medium terms. However, in the longer run, continued fertility decline would result in the ageing of the population, as indicated by the rapid increase in the ageing index from 15.6 per cent in 1970 to 24 per cent in 1991 and 33.6 per cent in 2000. In the not too distant future, the old-age dependency burden will become more severe, as experienced in the more developed countries. There is therefore an urgent need for the government and the community to formulate strategies and programmes to grapple with the challenges of an ageing population.

As in the case of the total population, there are relatively more males than females among the Malaysian Chinese in most of the age groups. At the state and district levels, the observed age structure and sex ratio may be attributed to the selectivity of migration in terms of age and gender (Table 10). Generally, states which register a higher rate of population growth tend to have a younger age structure as compared with those that experience slow or negative growth.

Table 9: Age distribution of Malaysian Chinese, 1970–2000

Age group	Number				Percentage distribution			
	1970	1980	1991	2000	1970	1980	1991	2000
0–14	1338	1345.8	1504.3	1489.2	42.7	36.9	30.4	26.2
15–29	842	1036.9	1324.6	1450.4	26.9	28.4	26.8	25.5
30–44	466.9	670.7	1128.8	1349.3	14.9	18.4	22.8	23.7
45–59	275.4	336.8	620.1	902.0	8.8	9.2	12.5	15.8
60–74	174.6	202.8	272.0	403.8	5.6	5.6	5.5	7.1
75 and over	34.4	58.1	95.2	97.2	1.1	1.6	1.9	1.7
Total	3131.3	3651.2	4945	5691.9	100.0	100.0	100.0	100.0
Ageing index*	15.6%	19.4%	24.4%	33.6%	Median (19)	Median (22)	Median (26)	Median (28.8)

*Persons aged 60 and above divided by persons below 15 years times 100.

Source: Department of Statistics, 1983; 1995; and 2001.

Table 10: Age-sex structure of Malaysian Chinese by state, 2000

State/Territory	Population ('00)			Percentage			
	Both sexes	Males	Females	Sex-ratio	0–14	15–64	65 & over
Johor	916.7	473.3	443.4	107	28.4	67.1	4.6
Kedah	241.4	123.2	118.2	104	27.5	66.3	6.2
Kelantan	49.1	25.3	23.8	106	28.5	64.8	6.7
Malacca	178.3	89.5	88.8	101	26.1	67.3	6.6
Negri Sembilan	211.9	108.1	103.8	104	26.8	66.9	6.3
Pahang	218.3	113.9	104.5	109	26.9	67.7	5.4
Perak	643.1	325.7	317.4	103	25.8	66.1	8.1
Perlis	20.8	10.8	10.0	108	27.9	64.2	7.9
Pulau Pinang	588.7	295.5	293.2	101	22.8	70.6	6.6
Selangor	1230.3	633.5	596.8	106	26.5	69.7	3.8
Trengganu	24.3	12.7	11.6	109	26.7	67.3	6.0
FT Kuala Lumpur	560.2	285.0	275.2	104	20.6	74.5	4.9
Sabah	262.1	137.0	125.1	110	26.9	67.8	5.3
Sarawak	537.2	275.3	261.9	105	29.7	65.4	5.0
Malaysia	5691.9	2913.7	2778.2	105	26.2	68.4	5.4

Source: Department of Statistics, 2001.

Changes in the Level of Fertility

In 1947, the Chinese had the highest crude birth rate (CBR) at 44 per thousand population) among the three main ethnic groups in Peninsular Malaysia. However, they were much more responsive to socioeconomic development in their demographic behaviour (Leete and Tan, 1993; Lim, 1983). Consequently, by the 1950s the Malays and Indians were registering a higher CBR than the Chinese. Table 11 and Figure 1 show that over the last three decades, the CBR of Malaysian Chinese was considerably lower than that of the Malays and, to a lesser extent, the Indians as well. Given the low level of mortality among all the major ethnic groups in the country, the course of fertility transition will be the main determinant of future population growth and composition.

Table 11: Crude birth rate of Malaysian Chinese (by region), compared with that of Malays and Indians in Peninsular Malaysia

Year	Chinese			Peninsular Malaysia	
	Pen. Malaysia	Sabah	Sarawak	Malays	Indians
1970	30.5	30.8	38.3	36.1	29.6
1980	25.2	29.0	30.3	33.6	29.8
1990	19.5	24.4	23.8	31.7	23.4
1994	20.6	21.5	23.4	30.8	24.2
1998	20.5	—	—	29.1	22.5
1999	20.1			28.6	22.3
2000	22.0			28.2	21.9

The total fertility, which takes the age-sex structure into account, is a more refined measure of fertility than the CBR. While Chinese CBR in Peninsular Malaysia declined by some 35 per cent during the two decades between 1970 and 1990, their total fertility rate fell more steeply, by 51 per cent (Chan and Tey, 2000).

The age pattern of fertility among Malaysian Chinese has undergone significant changes. While the fertility level has declined for each age group, the fall has been more rapid for the younger and older women. Between 1970 and 1994, the age-specific fertility rate of the Chinese in Peninsular Malaysia declined as follows: 15–19 years, 60 per cent; 20–24 years, 55

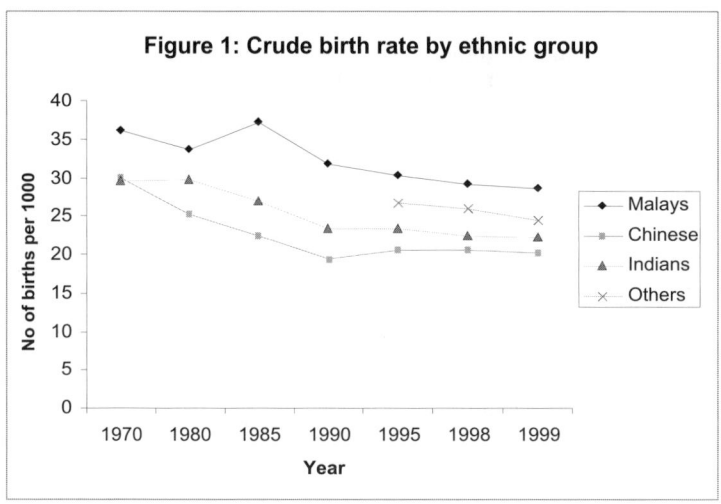

Figure 1: Crude birth rate by ethnic group

per cent; 25–29 years, 30 per cent; 30–34 years, 35 per cent; 35–39 years, 58 per cent; 40–44 years, 83 per cent; and 45–49 years, 91 per cent. Marriage and childbearing postponement have resulted in the rapid decline in fertility among young Malaysian Chinese women. Reduced fertility among older women is the result of earlier termination of childbearing.

Despite a temporary rise in the number of births among Malaysian Chinese between 1987 and 1988, the number of births again fell by 1989. Since 1990, however, there has been an increase in the level of fertility among women in the prime reproductive age group (see Table 12 and Figure 2). The reversal in the trend of the CBR is not merely the result of age-sex structural change, but rather a real increase in fertility among the Malaysian Chinese.

Table 12: Age-specific fertility and total fertility rate of Malaysian Chinese in Peninsular Malaysia (selected years)

Age group	1970	1980	1990	1991	1992	1993	1994	1995	1996	1997
15–19	25	25	9	11	10	10	10	10	10	10
20–24	190	161	75	90	91	93	85	80	77	70
25–29	280	243	164	183	188	196	195	193	194	191
30–34	222	163	135	135	138	146	149	149	158	160
35–39	136	69	58	57	58	61	57	59	59	61
40–44	59	22	10	10	10	10	10	10	10	10
45–49	11	4	1	1	1	1	1	1	1	1
TFR	4615	3435	2260	2435	2483	2582	2532	2510	2544	2511

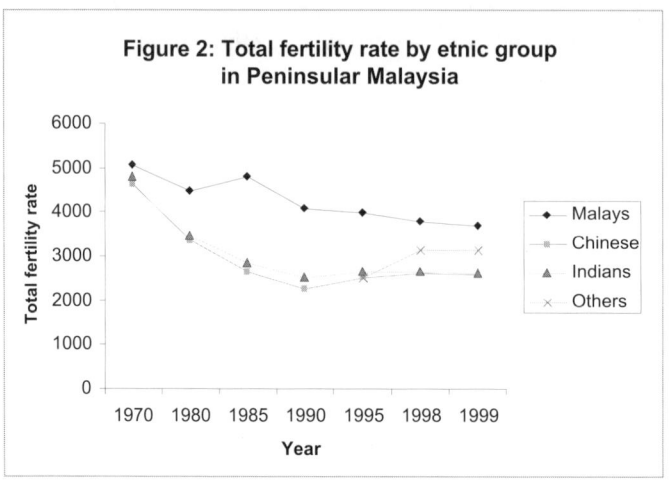

Figure 2: Total fertility rate by etnic group in Peninsular Malaysia

Proximate Determinants of Fertility

Rapid fertility decline among Malaysian Chinese has been brought about by the spectacular socioeconomic development in the country, mediated through postponement in age at marriage and contraceptive use. Since the launching of the National Population and Family Development Programme in 1966, several national fertility surveys have been conducted to provide the necessary data for in-depth study of the determinants of fertility and family planning practice.

Past studies have identified educational improvement, urbanization, women's work and attitudinal change as having a significant impact on fertility through their influence on the marital patterns and contraceptive use. Among Malaysian Chinese, the proportion of currently married women in the reproductive age group who had ever used contraception increased from 68 per cent in 1974 (Chander et al, 1977) to about 88 per cent since 1984 (Hamid et al, 1988). Contraceptive prevalence rate also increased to about 70 per cent in 1994 (unpublished data from the 1994 Malaysian Population and Family Survey). Studies by Hamid et al (undated) and Tey et al (1988) clearly demonstrate the significant impact of contraception in bringing about the sharp decline in the fertility level of the Malaysian Chinese.

Overall, age at marriage has been rising steadily over the years. More and more Chinese are remaining single, particularly among the younger ones, and this is true for both sexes in Peninsular Malaysia, Sabah and Sarawak. According to the 1991 Population Census, the singulate mean ages at first marriage for Malaysian Chinese males and females were 29.8

years and 26.3 years respectively. The corresponding figures for the total population were 28.3 and 24.7. The 1991 census data show that about 7 per cent of Malaysian Chinese women aged 40–49 were never married. The proportion of women who remain unmarried is probably higher now, as more and more women have attained higher education and are working. The changes in the marital structure are likely to contribute to reducing the crude birth rate, along with changes in marital fertility and age-sex composition. A decomposition of the decline in crude birth rate (National Population and Family Development Board, undated; Chan and Tey, 2000) shows that between 1970 and 1980, changes in the age-sex structure would have increased the CBR by 85 per cent, while changes in marital structure and marital fertility would have reduced CBR by 39 per cent and 76 per cent respectively. In the following decade, changes in these two factors would have reduced CBR by 61 and 67 per cent respectively, while changes in age-sex structure would have increased it by 28 per cent.

Changes in Mortality

Socioeconomic development and an efficient health programme have resulted in a sharp decline in the level of mortality (see Table 13 and Figures 3 and 4). The crude death rate among Malaysians of all races is now one of the lowest in the world. Infant mortality rate, too, has been declining for all the ethnic groups across the country. The improvement in mortality has resulted in longer life expectancy. Life expectancy for Malaysian Chinese males increased from 58 years in 1957 to 72 years in 1999, while that of the females increased from 67 years to 78 years (see Figure 3).

Table 13: Crude death rate of Malaysian Chinese (by region) as compared with that of the Malays and Indians in Peninsular Malaysia

Year	Chinese			Peninsular Malaysia	
	Pen. Malaysia	Sabah	Sarawak	Malays	Indians
1970	6.2	5.6	5.4	7.5	7.6
1980	5.4	5.7	4.5	5.3	7.0
1990	5.0	5.1	3.7	4.6	6.1
1994	5.0	4.5	3.9	4.5	5.5
1998	4.7	—	—	4.5	5.5
1999	4.9	—	—	4.6	5.7
2000	4.8	—	—	4.6	5.3

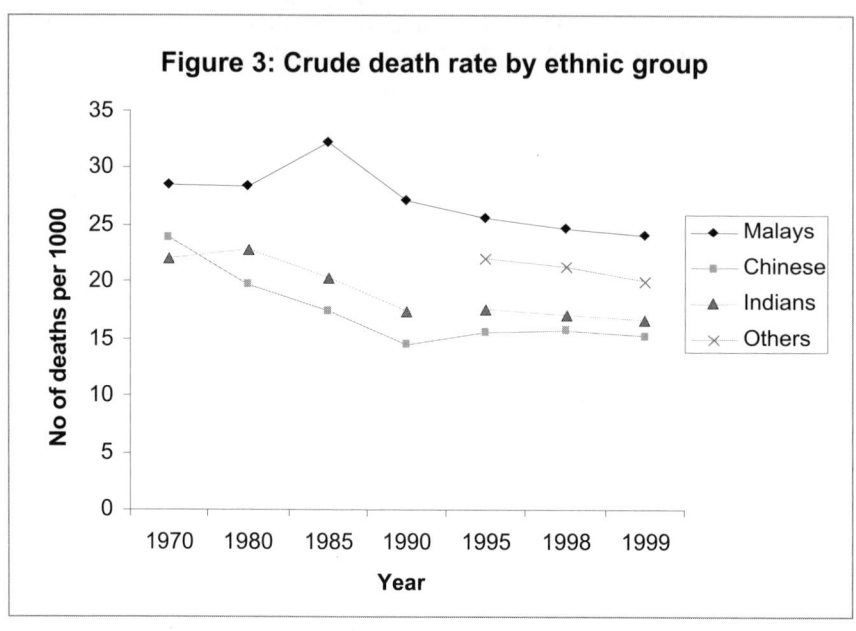

Figure 3: Crude death rate by ethnic group

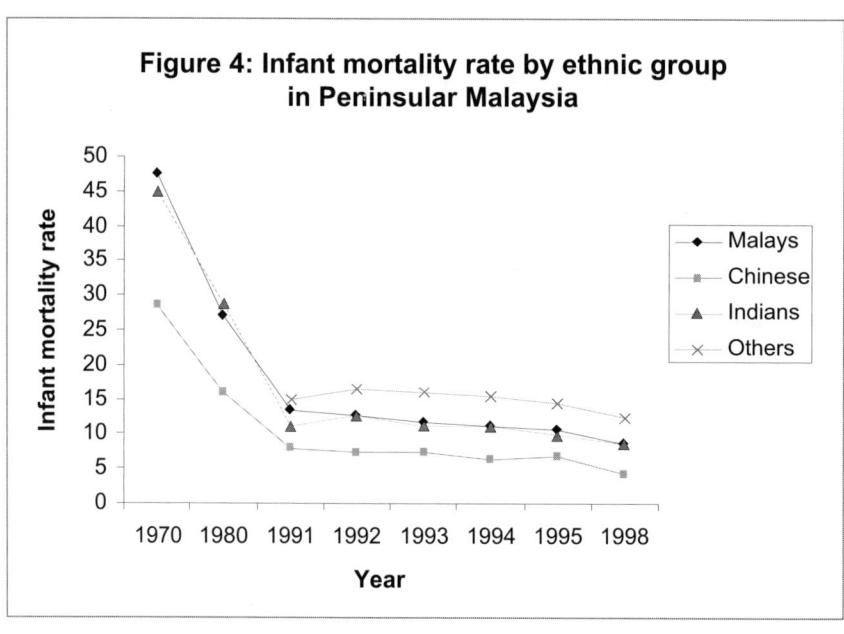

Figure 4: Infant mortality rate by ethnic group in Peninsular Malaysia

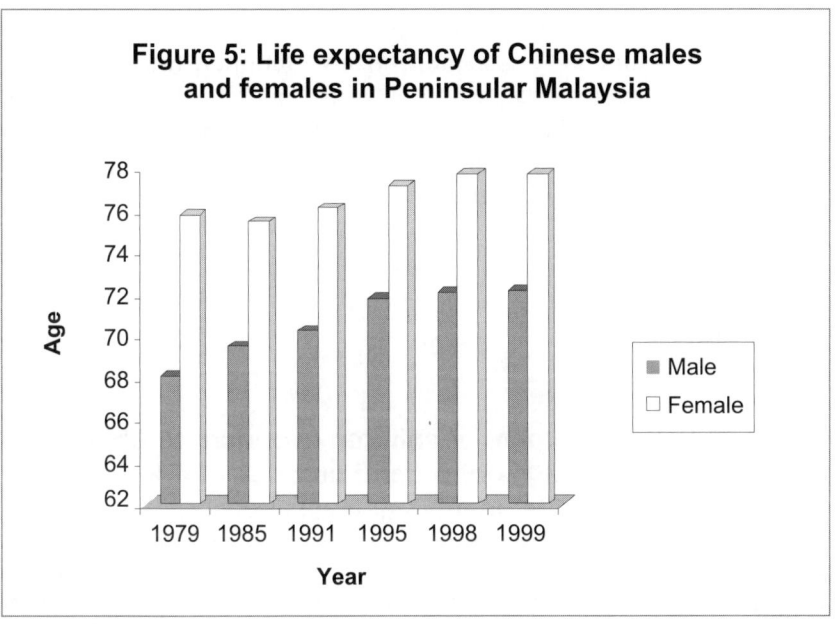

Figure 5: Life expectancy of Chinese males and females in Peninsular Malaysia

Summary and Conclusion

The Malaysian Chinese are one of the largest groups outside mainland China and Taiwan. They constitute the largest non-indigenous population in Malaysia. However, with rapid fertility transition, the Chinese proportion to the total population is dwindling and it has caused some concerns among community leaders. The Malaysian Chinese Association, one of the main component parties of the ruling National Front, has recently launched the Cupid Club to provide an avenue for matrimony among the unmarried persons. Incentives in the form of cash and kind have also been provided by some community groups and clan associations to encourage women to have babies.

Unlike many Chinese populations that have achieved replacement level or below replacement level fertility, the reversal in the declining fertility trends among Malaysian Chinese during the last decade means that their number will continue to increase for some time. Given the low level of mortality, and the unlikely scenario of a new wave of international migration, fertility will be the main determinant of population changes of the Malaysian Chinese in the future. What seems certain is that their fertility level will remain much lower than that of the Malays, and this will result in the further shrinking of the Chinese proportion.

Malaysian Chinese have always placed great emphasis on education and human resource development. For most families, the educational expenditure constitutes a large portion of the household budget. Many couples are restricting the number of children to ensure that they can be equipped with the necessary skills to participate in nation-building and to compete in an increasingly borderless world.

Appendices

Table A1: Mean number of children ever born to Chinese women by marriage cohort and duration of marriage, Peninsular Malaysia

Marriage cohort	Exact duration of marriage (years)								% childless after 5 years of marriage
	2	5	8	10	12	15	20	25	
1950–54	0.8	2.5	3.9	4.6	5.3	6.2	6.8	7.0	3
1955–59	0.9	2.5	3.8	4.4	4.9	5.5	6.0	6.3	2
1960–64	0.9	2.4	3.4	4.0	4.3	4.5	4.8		2
1965–69	1.0	2.3	3.3	3.7	3.9	4.2			1
1970–74	1.0	2.1	2.8	3.2					2
1975–79	1.0	2.0							2

Source: Hamid Arshat, Tan BA, Tey NP and M Subbiah, *Marriage and Family Formation in Peninsular Malaysia: Analytic Report on the 1984/85 Malaysian Population and Family Survey* (Kuala Lumpur: National Population and Family Development Board, 1988).

Table B: Distribution of births by birth order of Malaysian Chinese (1970, 1980 and 1990) and of the Malays and Indians (1990)

	Chinese			Malays	Indians
Birth order	1970	1980	1990	1990	1990
First	22.2	31.2	30.7	21.5	29.9
Second	18.5	26.2	28.0	19.1	25.4
Third	15.7	18.6	20.9	17.3	18.7
Fourth	12.0	11.3	11.9	13.5	11.5
Fifth	9.0	6.0	5.2	10.1	7.0
Sixth	6.9	3.0	2.0	6.8	3.7
Seventh	5.5	1.6	0.8	4.6	1.9
Eighth and above	10.2	2.1	0.5	7.1	1.9
Total	100.0	100.0	100.0	100.0	100.0

Source: Chan KE and Tey NP, "Demographic Processes and Change", in *The Chinese in Malaysia* (edited by Lee KH and Tan CB), Oxford University Press, 1999.

Table C: Peninsular Malaysia: Percentage of Malaysian Chinese ever married, by age and gender, and singulate mean age at marriage, 1970, 1980 and 1991

	Males			Females		
Age group	1970	1980	1991	1970	1980	1991
15–19	2	1	0.8	6	5	2.5
20–24	14	12	8.0	40	37	24.8
25–29	55	49	37.1	79	72	64.4
30–34	81	78	68.4	91	87	83.2
35–39	90	90	83.8	94	92	89.3
40–44	94	93	90.5	97	94	92.0
45 and over	93	95	93.8	97	97	94.2
SMAM	27.3	28.0	29.8	24.2	24.9	26.3

Source: Department of Statistics, 1983 (Volume I) and 1991 (Volume II). Figures for 1970 and 1980 refer to Peninsular Malaysia, and figures for 1991 refer to Malaysia.

Table D: Percentage distribution of all ever-married women in Malaysia according to status of first marriage by years since first marriage and ethnic group

Years since first marriage	First marriage intact	% widowed	% divorced	N
Malays				
<10 years	97.7	0.5	1.8	439
10–19 years	87.8	2.3	9.9	354
>19 years	70.6	7.1	22.3	184
Chinese				
<10 years	99.4	0.0	0.6	178
10–19 years	94.6	2.0	3.1	197
>19 years	87.3	8.9	3.8	79
Indians				
<10 years	97.6	1.2	1.2	161
10–19 years	93.2	3.4	3.4	116
>19 years	74.3	20.0	5.7	70

Source: Khalipah Mohd Tom, *1988 Malaysian Family Life Survey Report*.

Table E: Mean number of children ever born according to socioeconomic characteristics, controlling for ethnicity

	N	Ethnic groups				
		Malays	Chinese	Indians	Others	Total
Age at first marriage						
Less than 18	(891)	5.2	4.0	4.6	3.9	4.9
18–20	(1186)	4.1	3.6	3.2	2.7	3.8
21–23	(1116)	3.0	3.0	2.6	2.3	3.0
24+	(1241)	2.3	2.2	1.9	2.1*	2.2
Place of residence						
Urban	(2411)	3.3	2.7	2.8	2.3	3.0
Rural	(2033)	4.0	3.5	3.4	3.9	3.9
Wife's education						
No formal education	(357)	5.3	4.1	4.4	4.5	4.8
Primary	(1680)	4.8	3.5	3.8	3.1	4.2
Secondary	(2064)	2.9	2.3	2.0	1.8	2.6
Tertiary	(343)	2.4	1.7	1.8	2.3*	2.2
Husband's education						
No formal education	(103)	4.6	3.6	4.4	2.7*	4.3
Primary	(1561)	4.8	3.4	3.6	3.5	4.3
Secondary	(2107)	2.9	2.7	2.4	2.2	2.8
Tertiary	(479)	2.7	2.0	2.0	2.1*	2.4
Total	(4444)	3.7	2.9	3.0	3.2	3.4

Sources: Chan Kuan Thye—based on 1994 Malaysian Population and Family Survey, LPPKN.

References

Chan, KE, and Tey NP. "Democratic Processes and Changes". In *The Chinese in Malaysia*, edited by Lee KH and Tan CB. Singapore: Oxford University Press, 2000.

Chandra, R, VT Palan, Nor Laily Aziz and Tan BA. *Malaysian Fertility and Family Survey—1974, First Country Report*. Kuala Lumpur: Department of Statistics and National Population and Family Development, 1977.

Chan, Kuan Thye. "Socio-economic Determinants of Childbearing in Peninsular Malaysia". Project paper submitted to the Faculty of Economics and Administration, University of Malaya, in partial fulfilment for the degree of Master of Applied Statistics, 2002.

Department of Statistics, Malaysia. *Vital Statistics, Peninsular Malaysia*. Kuala Lumpur: Department of Statistics, Malaysia, various years.

_____. *1970 General Report of the Population Census*. Kuala Lumpur: Department of Statistics, Malaysia, 1972.

_____. 1983. *1980 General report of the population census*. Kuala Lumpur: Department of Statistics, Malaysia.

_____. *1991 General Report of the Population Census*. Kuala Lumpur: Department of Statistics, Malaysia, 1995.

_____. *2000 General Report of the Population Census*. Kuala Lumpur: Department of Statistics, Malaysia, 2001.

Hamid, Arshat, Tan BA, Tey NP and M Subbiah. *Marriage and Family Formation in Peninsular Malaysia*. Analytic report of the 1984/85 Malaysian Population and Family Survey. Kuala Lumpur: National Population and Family Development Board, 1988.

Hamid, Arshat, Y Takeshita, Tan DA and Tey NP. *Fertility Trends in Peninsular Malaysia 1957–70 and 1970–80: Application of a Decomposition Technique*. Kuala Lumpur: National Population and Family Development Board, nd.

Khalipah, MT. "Marriage Trends among Peninsular Malaysia Women". In *Report of the Malaysian Family Life Survey II*. Kuala Lumpur: National Population and Family Development Board and Rand Corporation, USA, 1992.

Leete, R, and Tan BA. "Contrasting Fertility Trends among Ethnic Groups in Malaysia". In *The Revolution of Asia Fertility-Determinants, Causes and Implication*, edited by R Leete and I Alam. Oxford: Clarendon Press, 1993.

Saw, Swee Hock. *The Population of Malaysia*. Singapore: Singapore University Press, National University of Singapore, 1988.

Tey, NP, Tan BA, Tan PC and Kwok KK. *Direct and Indirect Determinants of Fertility in Peninsular Malaysia*. Kuala Lumpur: National Population and Family Development Board, 1988.

Part II

Politics, Identity and Education

Chapter 4

PERANAKAN CHINESE IDENTITIES IN SINGAPORE AND MALAYSIA: A RE-EXAMINATION*

Leo Suryadinata

In recent years, there have been more studies on the ethnic Chinese, especially with regard to their identities. There are a few in-depth studies on the Peranakan Chinese in Malacca (by Tan Chee Beng), Penang (by Ho Eng Seng) and Singapore (by Jurgen Rudolph). These studies are significant and have thrown new light on these Chinese. Tan Chee Beng has also done a general study on the Peranakan Chinese beyond the Straits Settlements. Benefiting from the above fine studies, this short article focuses on the evolution of Peranakan Chinese identities. It re-examines these identities in Singapore and Malaysia, right from the colonial era to the present. Were various terms used to refer to the Peranakan very similar, if not identical? Was the Peranakan identity a sociocultural identity or a political identity or both? Was this a self-identity or others-given identity? Were the Peranakan Chinese confined to the British Straits Settlements? The article also deals with the life experience of the Peranakan Chinese after independence, what the Peranakan identities today are and what the future holds for them.

"Peranakan" and Other Related Terms

It is generally known that the ethnic Chinese in Singapore and Malaysia are heterogeneous. One of these groups, known as the Peranakan Chinese or *Cina Peranakan*, is also known as "Straits Chinese", "Straits-born Chinese", and "Baba" (male Peranakan Chinese) and "Nyonya" (female Peranakan Chinese). Nowadays, some writers and the Peranakan themselves use these terms interchangeably, but in fact they are not identical.

---

*Acknowledgement: I would like to thank Yeo Kim Wah for his comments and suggestions.

Peranakan

Peranakan, a Malay word, is now used as a generic term to refer to the local-born Chinese who speaks Malay or a local language at home. The present meaning of the term is the descendants of the union between indigenous people (*anak negeri*) and foreigners.[1] It is not known when the term first came into existence.[2] In the 19th century, *The Hikayat Abdullah*, which was written by the Munshi Abdullah, did not mention the term *peranakan* but mentioned two *baba* in British Malaya.[3] His son, Mohamed Ibrahim, wrote a book and mentioned the term *peranak awak* to refer to the people in Penang who were born locally of Siamese or Burmese fathers and Chinese mothers.[4] But the meaning is different from our ordinary usage. In fact, in the mid-19th century, the term *peranakan* was already quite popular. According to a dictionary published in 1856, the Malays called the "mixed race" of Chinese descendants "Peranakan China" (*Peranakan Cina*, according to the current spelling) during that time.[5] Later, the term *peranakan* was used as the abbreviation of *Peranakan Cina*, as if the Peranakan question was a solely Chinese phenomenon.

In fact, there were many types of Peranakan. The term was used to refer to the Indian Peranakan or "Jawi Peranakan", who were the descendants of Indian Muslims and Malay women. Nevertheless, because of the large number of Peranakan Chinese, the term *peranakan* has generally been associated with the Chinese community.

The Peranakan phenomenon was not confined to Singapore and Malaysia. It was quite common to the region as a whole, including Indonesia and the Philippines. While the term *peranakan* has been used in Indonesia, a different term—"mestizo"—has been used to refer to a similar group in the

---

1   *Kamus Dewan* (Kuala Lumpur: Dewan Bahasa, 1970), p 26.
2   *Sejarah Melayu* (the Malay Annals, written in the 16th century) did not record the term *peranakan*.
3   Abdullah, the contemporary of Sir Stamford Raffles, mentioned "Baba Cheng Lan" and "Baba Hok Guan". See Abdullah bin Abdul Kadir, *The Hikayat Abdullah* (an annotated translation by AH Hill), Kuala Lumpur: Oxford University Press, 1970, pp 75 and 266.
4   He explained that in the course of time, the progeny of such unions with Penang Chinese became more and more numerous. See *The Voyages of Mohamed Ibrahim Munshi* (translation with an Introduction and notes by Amin Sweeney and Nigel Phillips) (Kuala Lumpur: Oxford University Press, 1975), pp 90–91.
5   See John Crawfurd's *A Descriptive Dictionary of the Indian Island and Adjacent Country* (London, 1856), cited in Tan Chee Beng, *Chinese Peranakan Heritage in Malaysia and Singapore*, Kuala Lumpur: Fajar Bhakti, 1993, p 21.

Philippines. However, unlike the mestizos in the Philippines, who became Filipino rather than Chinese, the Peranakan Chinese in Singapore, Malaysia and Indonesia remained largely "Chinese" in terms of their identity. The reasons were complex and religion was definitely an important one.

The emergence of this Peranakan Chinese community is well known. This was due to the fact that earlier Chinese migrants were males who were either bachelors or married men who came to Southeast Asia without their spouses. They married local women,[6] especially those who were nominal Muslim or non-Muslim, and with their children, they formed a new kind of community, which had the characteristics of both the Chinese and the Malay in their sociocultural make-up. This hybrid culture was distinct from either Chinese culture or Malay culture. The major characteristic was the use of the Malay language. A large number of Peranakan children never developed a command of the Chinese language and could only converse in the Malay language, as was the case with the Peranakan in Batavia (Java), Malacca and Singapore. Recent studies also confirm that in the missionary schools where the Chinese language was taught, the medium of instruction was Malay.[7] The attire was also a mixture of Chinese and local dress. In fact, the female Peranakan wore Malay dress and had Malay hairstyles. The food was also distinct as it included Malay ingredients but pork—the preferred Chinese meat—was retained. These Peranakan Chinese were not only found in Java but also outside Java, and in peninsular Malaya and Singapore.

Nevertheless, it should be pointed out that during the colonial era, until the 19th century, the term *Cina Peranakan* in Indonesia was used to refer to Chinese Muslims.[8] In fact, it was also the case when the term was first used in British Malaya. It was used to refer to the mixed descendants of Indian Muslims (eg, Jawi Peranakan). Nevertheless, when it was applied

---

6   A number of studies on the Chinese in colonial Malaya and Singapore show that indeed many Chinese married non-Chinese (local women); see Chen Yusong (Tan Yock Seong), *Xinjiapo huawen beimingjilu*, Hong Kong: Chinese University of Hong Kong, 1972, p 13; also Zhuang Qingyong, *Maliujia, Xinjiapo huawen beiwen jilu*, Taipei, 1998, p 46. On the intermarriage between Chinese men and indigenous women in Indonesia (Java), see Li Minghuan, "Batavia's Chinese Society in Transition: Indications Based upon the Tandjoeng Cemetery Archives 1881–1896", *Asian Culture*, no 24 (June 2000), pp 90–107.
7   See a recent paper by Zhuang Qingyong (David Chng), *1819–1844 nian Xinjiapo de huawen xuetang*, Taipei, May 2001 (unpublished).
8   Many Dutch writings mentioned this fact, for instance, F de Haan, *Oud Batavia*, vol II (Bandoeng, 1935); See also Mona Lohanda, *The Kapitan Cina of Batavia, 1837–1942*. Jakarta: Penerbit Djambatan, 1996, p 6.

to the Chinese in 20th century Dutch Indonesia and British Malaya, it did not have the religious connotation any more. The term *peranakan* was used by both the foreign rulers and the Malay-speaking local population to refer to the partially "assimilated" local-born Chinese. Subsequently, the Chinese themselves also accepted this term for their "identity". The term is a cultural rather than a political category.

Straits Chinese/Straits-born Chinese

When the British colonized peninsular Malaya and Singapore, the Peranakan Chinese came to be known as the Straits Chinese. This was due to the fact that they were in the Straits Settlements, which were formed when, in 1826, Penang, Singapore and Malacca were placed under one administration and came to be known as the British Straits Settlements. Strictly speaking, the term refers to the birthplace rather than the culture of the Chinese. However, some used the term to mean the Peranakan Chinese. For those people who used the term for a cultural group, they often wrongly used "Straits-born Chinese" to refer to the Straits Chinese. This was due to the fact that in the Straits Settlements, some Chinese were newer migrants and culturally were not hybrid; hence, the preference for the use of the term "Straits-born Chinese" rather than "Straits Chinese".[9]

This was not entirely correct either. It is true that the Peranakan Chinese were local-born (Straits-born) but not all Straits-born Chinese were Peranakan. Among the Straits-born Chinese, some were still culturally non-Peranakan, or Sinkeh (*xinke*). For instance, the Malacca-born Chen Sheng Tang (Tan Seng Tong) was not only Chinese-speaking but also a well-known Chinese language writer.

Also, unlike the term *peranakan*, which was used by the Malay-speaking population as well as the foreign rulers, the term "Straits Chinese" was used by those who were English-educated, as there is no Malay equivalent of this term. The Malays themselves, when referring to these Chinese, used either *Peranakan Cina* or "Baba" (or "Babah"). The non-English-educated Peranakan Chinese also used the term "Baba" to refer to themselves. No one is certain about the origin of the term "Baba". It might have emerged before the coming of the Dutch or the British, and it was not confined to the Peranakan Chinese in the Straits Settlements. In both northern Sumatra (eg, Medan) and West Java (eg, Jakarta and Bogor), this

---

9   See Ye Zhongling (Yeap Chong Leng), *Chen Shengtang wenji* (Singapore: Singapore Society of Asian Studies, 1994).

term was known and used by the local 'Malay' population as well as the Peranakan Chinese themselves.[10]

Baba and Straits Chinese

However, JD Vaughan, who wrote a classic on the Straits Chinese (1879), stated:

> The Chinese born in the Straits are called Baba to distinguish them from those born in China. The term "Baba" is used by the natives of Bengal to designate the children of Europeans and it's probable that the word was applied by Indian convicts at Penang to Chinese children and so came into general use. The word "Baba" is given in Douglas's Hokkien Dictionary as meaning a half-caste Chinese from the Straits. In the Straits, however, the term is applied to all Chinese born there, half or not.

Tan Chee Beng maintains that the term was initially used in the Middle East.

The use of the term "Baba" to refer to Peranakan Chinese was not confined to the Straits Settlements. In northern Sumatra and West Java, for instance, the term "Baba" was also used during the colonial era. However, it was not used beyond West Java. This was perhaps due to the intensive interaction between the Chinese in West Java (including Jakarta) with those in Singapore, and between the Chinese in northern Sumatra (including Medan) and those in Penang.

The term "Straits Chinese" is still used today, although it is more appropriate for reference to a historical period when the Straits Settlements were in existence. After Malaya's independence, although there are still descendants of the Straits Chinese, few are in fact still using this term to refer to themselves for obvious reasons. The Straits Settlements are no longer in existence, and after the formation of Malaysia, which combined Malaya and Singapore, together with Sarawak and Sabah, in 1963, the Straits Chinese were no longer occupying higher positions in society. The Straits Chinese British Association (SCBA), for instance, was renamed the Singapore Chinese Peranakan Association in 1964.[11] The terms "Peranakan" and "Baba/Nyonya" have been popularized. It seems that only when the

---

10 A well-known Peranakan writer at the end of the 19th century and the beginning of the 20th century, Lie Kim Hok, was often called "Baba Kim Hok" by others. See Tio Ie Soei, *Lie Kim Hok (1853–1912)*, Bandung (1958).
11 Lee Kip Lee and Lee Liang Hui, "A Brief History of the Peranakan Associations", in *Sixth Baba Convention: 26–27 November 1993, Shangri-la Hotel, Singapore; Theme: Our Linguistic Heritage* (Singapore: The Peranakan Association of Singapore, 1993), p 30.

writers want to talk about these people in a historical context, or to discuss their cultural legacy, then the term "Straits Chinese" is used. This is the case in a book by Dr Khoo Joo Ee entitled *Straits Chinese: A Cultural History* (1996).

If the term "Straits Chinese" is historical with limited geographical connotations, the terms "Baba/Nyonya" and "Peranakan" appear to have a wider usage and longer history as these are not restricted to a historical place. Some recently published books such as *The Babas Revisited* by Felix Chia, *Memoirs of a Nonya* by Queeny Chang, and the Memoirs of Shirley Lim Giok-Lan, who calls herself a "Nyonya Feminist" show that these writers still consider themselves as members of this group.[12] In fact, in Singapore and Malaysia, the terms "Baba" and "Nyonya" have a longer life span than in Indonesia. I have not come across any Indonesian Peranakan descendants who wrote books and included the words "Baba" and "Nyonya" in the titles.

Actually, the terms "Baba" and "Nyonya" have been loosely used in the past as well as today. In Singapore and Malaysia, the Baba and Nyonya are not necessarily those who speak Malay or are culturally Malay. As pointed out by Png Poh Seng, so long as a female member of the family dresses herself in a sarong or has a *konde*, they are considered Baba. This kind of definition may be considered too loose but if we use self-identity as the basis of an identity, if the people concerned call themselves Baba/Nyonya, it is difficult to say that they are not, especially if the local Baba community considers these people its members.

There is no doubt that there are still Baba and Nyonya or Peranakan today. Even among the Chinese communities in Singapore and Malaysia, the Chinese-speaking Chinese continue to refer to the Malay-speaking or partially assimilated Chinese as Baba or *tusheng huaren*. In Indonesia, the Chinese-speaking Chinese used *qiaosheng* to refer to the *tusheng huaren*.[13] The original meaning of these two terms simply mean either "local-born foreigners" (*qiaosheng*) or "local-born Chinese" (*tusheng huaren*) without any cultural connotation.

---

12 Felix Chia, *The Babas Revisited* (Heinemann, 1994); Queeny Chang, *Memoirs of a Nonya* (Eastern University Press, 1981); and Shirley Lim, *Among the White Moonfaces: Memoirs of a Nyonya Feminist* (Times Books International, 1996).

13 The term *tusheng huaren* means "local-born Chinese"; when used to refer to the Baba, it, therefore, has a cultural connotation rather than just an indication of birthplace. However, one can argue that this Mandarin term can also be used to refer to the local-born Chinese-speaking Chinese who were locally oriented in politics, although this usage is not common among the Chinese-language writers.

Typical Peranakan or Baba?

The difficulty of establishing any standard markers of Peranakan or Baba is thus clear. It may be more realistic to consider Peranakan Chinese as a spectrum ranging from those who are most Malaynized ("localized", as Tan Chee Beng calls it) to least Malaynized. While the Penang Baba are least Malaynized, the Malacca Baba are most Malaynized. The Malaynization involves the use of language and the adoption of dress and cuisine.

It should be pointed out that within one area (eg, Malacca or Penang), there are also variations. Not all Penang Peranakan are Hokkien-speaking. Some might be similar to the Malacca Baba but it appears that the majority are Hokkien-speaking. In Malacca, the same can also be said. Some might be similar to those in Penang but the Malay-speaking Peranakan are dominant.

Another characteristic is the small number of Peranakan Chinese communities in the Straits Settlements. We don't have figures of the number of the Peranakan Chinese as such, but we do have the census figures of Straits-born (later, British Malaya–born) Chinese in the late 19th century and the first half of the 20th century. According to the 1881 census (see Table 1), the Straits-born Chinese numbered 25,268 and formed 14.5 per cent of the total Chinese population. By 1891, however, the number had increased to 34,757 and constituted 15 per cent of the total Chinese population in the Straits Settlements. Since the 19th century, mass Chinese immigration had not taken place; therefore we can assume that the majority of the Straits-born Chinese were Peranakan. We can safely argue that the Peranakan Chinese did not exceed 15 per cent of the total Chinese population. In other words, the non-Peranakan Chinese formed the absolute majority of the Chinese population in the Straits

Table 1: Number and percentage of local-born Chinese in the Straits Settlements (1881 and 1891)

Year	1881		1891	
Territory	Number	Percentage	Number	Percentage
Penang	10,477	15.5	16,981	19.3
Malacca	5,264	26.7	4,971	27.4
Singapore	9,527	11.0	12,805	10.5
Total	25,268	14.5	34,757	15.3

Source: Computed from *Report on the Census of the Straits Settlements, 1891* (Singapore, 1892), pp 36–37, 46–47, 94–95, 134–35.

Settlements. The proportion of the Peranakan would be even smaller if we were to consider the Federation of Malaya as a whole.

In the first half of the 20th century, the number of the local-born (ie, born in British Malaya and Singapore) in the Straits Settlements began to grow steadily (see Table 2). It should be noted that in the 20th century, the number of new Chinese immigrants increased tremendously, particularly in Singapore and Penang. These immigrants settled down and raised their families, which explains the significant increase of local-born Chinese. I would like to argue that the offspring of these newcomers were culturally different from the earlier settlers. They were still Sinkeh rather than Peranakan.

Table 2: Number and percentage of local-born Chinese in Penang, Malacca and Singapore

Year Territory	1901	1911	1921	1931	1947	1957
Penang	23,569 (24%)	35,529 (32%)	52,041 (38%)	76,854 (46%)	173,261 (70%)	266,723 (72%)
Malacca	4,955 (26%)	7,366 (21%)	13,130 (29%)	22,494 (35%)	63,028 (66%)	95,211 (79%)
Singapore	15,498 (10%)	43,833 (20%)	79,686 (24%)	150,033 (36%)	437,243 (58%)	741,605 (68%)
Total	44,022 (16%)	86,778 (23%)	144,857 (29%)	249,381 (38%)	673,532 (63%)	1,103,539 (72%)

Sources: *Report on the Census of the Straits Settlements, 1901* (Singapore, 1902), p 19; *The Census of British Malaya, 1921* (printed in London, 1922), p 95; *A Report on the 1947 Population Census* (Kuala Lumpur, 1949); *1957 Population Census of the Federation of Malaya*, Report No 14 (Kuala Lumpur, 1961), computed from Table 1 and Table 7B; and Saw Swee Hock, *The Population of Singapore* (Singapore: ISEAS, 1999), pp 33 and 47.

If we assume that 15 per cent of the Chinese in the Straits Settlements were Peranakan, the rest, that is, about 85 per cent of them, were non-Peranakan.

The presence of Peranakan and non-Peranakan communities in the Straits Settlements also explained the existence of different Chinese organizations. The organizations were divided along these sociocultural lines. The Baba had their own mutual help association (eg, *Qingde hui*)[14] and the Straits Chinese British Association (SCBA) and the State Chinese (Penang) Association, while the Sinkeh had their own clan associations, often known as *bangs* (based on dialect groups, such as Fujian *huiguan*, Keshu *gonghui*, etc)[15] and sociopolitical organizations such as the Kuomintang. The Chinese Chambers of Commerce, which were established under the instruction of the Chinese (Ching) government, were Sinkeh-dominated.[16]

It is also interesting to note that the economic activities of the Peranakan and Sinkeh tended to be quite different. While the Peranakan were mainly involved in shipping, banking and tin mining, the Sinkeh, on the other hand, were "farmers" and traders. The type of business was linked to the cultural and language background. As shipping and the banking business requires a knowledge of English, naturally the English-educated Baba were better equipped than their Sinkeh counterparts.

The patterns in political activities were also formed along sociocultural lines. The Peranakan elites, being British subjects, were politically oriented towards the colony and the United Kingdom, while the Sinkeh were China-oriented and considered themselves part of the larger Chinese nation. The orientation began to change at the end of World War II with the establishment of the major political Malayan parties. The SCBA, the Baba association which was politically pro-British, was a contrast to the Malayan branch of the Kuomintang, which was a Sinkeh party. The left-wing organization, the Malayan Communist Party (MCP), was politically "international" but still closely linked with China and dominated by the Sinkeh. The situation, of course, was different at the end of World War II. The Chinese in Malaya/Malaysia, both Peranakan and Sinkeh, began to readjust their positions to the new developments.

Baba and Peranakan

How significant are the terms "Baba", "Nyonya" and "Peranakan" in the context of culture and politics? In the past, Baba or Peranakan identity was significant, especially during the colonial era, when the British colonial power tended to use the Baba to serve their political interests. Are the Baba or Peranakan still relevant on the political scene today? In fact, both in Singapore and West Malaysia, it appears that the division is no longer

---

14 On *Qingde hui*, see Lin Xiaosheng (Lim How Seng), *Xinjiapo huashe yu huashang*, Singapore: Singapore Society of Asian Studies, 1995, p 100.
15 Ibid.
16 Yen Ching-hwang, "Ch'ing China and the Singapore Chinese Chamber of Commerce, 1906–1911", in *Southeast Asian Chinese and China: The Politico-Economic Dimension*, edited by Leo Suryadinata, Singapore: Times Academic Press, 1995, pp 133–60.

between Peranakan and Sinkeh, or between Baba and non-Baba, but between different kinds of education. Among the older-generation Chinese in Singapore, the division was between the Chinese-educated and the English-educated, but among the younger generation, such division is less obvious as they receive a similar type of education. However, in West Malaysia, the division is between the Malay-educated and the Chinese-educated. Nevertheless, the so-called Baba community, or more appropriately, the Peranakan community, still exists. The community, nonetheless, is declining and its political significance has also diminished.

Before proceeding further, one has to point out that the term "Baba", which has sometimes been used very rigidly—that is, to mean "Malay-speaking Chinese"—is misleading. In fact, there are at least two types of Baba: the Malacca Baba and the Penang Baba. (With regard to the Singapore Baba, they are an offshoot of the Malacca Baba and, hence, do not really present a new category.)[17] The former, who are the Malay-speaking Baba, have been used as the 'standard' for the Baba, as if all Baba were/are Malay-speaking. Many are not aware that the Penang Baba are Hokkien-speaking. Nevertheless, they are still called Baba because of the influence of the Malay culture over them. The Malacca Baba speak Malay (low Malay) with Hokkien vocabulary while the Penang Baba speak Hokkien with Malay vocabulary. One can argue that the Penang Baba are more Chinese than the Malacca Baba in linguistic terms but both communities consider themselves Baba or Nyonya.

Nevertheless, some writers are of the view that the Peranakan in Penang are not "Baba" precisely, and that their language is Hokkien with Malay words. This is due to the fact that "Baba" is defined in terms of the Peranakan in Malacca. In the 1950s, for instance, Diana Ooi did not use the term "Baba" to refer to the local-born and English-educated Chinese but the term "English-educated Chinese", as if all Baba in Penang were English-educated.[18] Others continued to feel that the correct way to refer to them was "Straits Chinese".[19] Yet others insisted that they were Baba and Nyonya.[20]

---

17 Felix Chia, *The Babas Revisited*, Singapore: Heinemann Asia, 1994, p 11. Chia states that "Excepting a few, all families of the Singapore Babas trace their roots to Malacca."

18 Diana Ooi, "The English-educated Chinese in Penang", Master's thesis, University of Malaya, 1957.

19 Khoo Joo Ee, *Straits Chinese: A Cultural History*, Kuala Lumpur: The Papin Press, 1996; "The Straits Chinese Today", *Suara Baba: The Voice of the Peranakan Associations in Malaysia and Singapore,* no 2 (November 1993), p 2.

20 Ho Eng Seng, "Problems of Identity among the Overseas Chinese: A Historical Examination of the Baba Chinese in Penang", Honours essay for the major in Social Sciences, Stanford University, Department of Anthropology, June 1986.

Khoo Joo Ee maintains that

> the term "Baba" has colonial connotations and "Straits-born Chinese" is anachronistic insofar as the Straits Settlements no longer exist in a political unit. "Peranakan" is preferably labelled. Yet such definition is irrelevant for the Baba who are absorbed in the larger Chinese community. However, for citizenship and present-day political entities, "Peranakan" becomes mandatory. In private and non-political affairs, "Peranakan" is less used. The "Baba-Nyonya" term is still prevalent among the Malays and [in] the Peninsular Community.[21]

This is perhaps true that for the older-generation Baba, the terms "Baba" and "Nyonya" are more popular than "Peranakan" among the Peranakan Chinese themselves. Even the books and memoirs by Queeny Chang and Shirley Lim use "Nyonya" or "Nonya" in the title rather than "Peranakan". Long after the change of names of Baba organizations to "Peranakan" organizations, the term "Baba" for the Peranakan congress is still used. For instance, the Peranakan Association of Singapore in 1993 held the Sixth Baba Convention rather than the "Peranakan Convention".[22] At the convention, apart from the Peranakan Association of Singapore, four Peranakan organizations were present: they were the Persatuan Peranakan Cina Pulau Pinang, Persatuan Peranakan Cina Melaka, Gunong Sayang Association (Singapore) and Persatuan Peranakan Cina Kelantan.[23] Nevertheless, all of these organizations used "Peranakan" in their formal/official names. Perhaps this was due to the fact that the term "Peranakan" is a Malay/Indonesian term while "Baba" is a non-Malay term.

The SCBA, Political Identity and Peranakan Identity

However, one has to point out that "Baba" and "Nyonya" do not have colonial connotation but "Straits Chinese" does. It is not surprising that the Straits Chinese British Association (SCBA), which was established in 1900, changed its name to "Singapore Chinese Peranakan Association" in November 1964, when Singapore was part of Malaysia, and eventually adopted the name "Peranakan Association" in February 1966. "Straits Chinese" implies pro-

---

21 Khoo Joo Ee, "The Straits Chinese Today".
22 See *Sixth Baba Convention, 26–27 November 1993*.
23 Ibid, contents page. The name of Persatuan Peranakan Cina Kelantan, however, is not listed. I was present at the convention and listened to the presentation of the spokesman of that organization on 26 November 1993.

British Peranakan Chinese and, hence, was considered anachronistic. The members used to consider themselves "King's Chinese" or "Queen's Chinese". Their political loyalty, before independence, was to the British.

It is also interesting to note that after the establishment of the SCBA, in Malacca, a similar organization was formed. However, in Penang, the Baba Chinese refused to establish such an organization as it was too exclusive—it tended to differentiate the Baba from the larger Chinese community.[24] Apparently, the Straits Chinese (in a cultural sense) were weak and other existing Chinese organizations such as the Chinese Chamber of Commerce and the Chinese Town Council, both dominated by the Sinkeh Chinese, were strong. Eventually, the Baba Chinese in Penang established the State Chinese (P) Association (SCA—note that the term "Straits Chinese" does not appear in the name). It is again interesting to note that after Malaya's independence, the association came to be known as the Persatuan Peranakan Cina Pulau Pinang. Perhaps this was in accordance with the Baba's fight for their indigenous status.

The Malaysian situation is different from that of Singapore as it is an indigenous state where the indigenous population, or Bumiputra, have more rights than the non-indigenous population. The ethnic Chinese, in general, are trying to gain the indigenous status; hence, some Peranakan Chinese seek to claim the status based on their "unique" status. In Khoo Joo Ee's words:

> The Straits Chinese [sic] combined Chinese, Western and Malay cultures in aspects such as language, dress, cuisine and occupation. This identity is a fragile one, with Straits Chinese striving to assert their identity as genuine indigenous people of Malaysia and Singapore. They drew on several ethnic traditions yet transcended them into a new identity. The syncretism achieved by the Baba went beyond the political coalition which exists between the different races in present-day Malaysia.[25]

Khoo Joo Ee is correct when she maintains that some of these Baba Chinese attempted to seek "indigenous" (Bumiputra) status because the Malaysian constitution differentiates indigenous people and non-indigenous people and accord them different rights. However, their attempt to be recognized as such has so far been unsuccessful. The ethnic Chinese—both Baba and non-Baba—continue to be regarded as an "immigrant race" rather than an "indigenous race" and, hence, have no claims to Bumiputra status.[26]

---

24 Ho Eng Seng, "Problems of Identity", pp 55–56.
25 Khoo Joo Ee, "The Straits Chinese Today".
26 In fact, Dr Mahathir stated clearly in his 1970 book that "the Malays are the original or indigenous people of Malaya and the only people who can claim Malaya as their one

In fact, in Malaysia, many descendants of the Straits Chinese or Baba have rapidly been resinicized. This is largely a result of the government policy which is based on "race" and "indigenism". However, the rise of China, the resurgence of ethnicity worldwide and the spread of democratic ideas are also responsible for the resinicization of the Chinese in Malaysia. Many send their children to Chinese primary schools—which are part of the national education system—to learn the Chinese language.[27] Only after completing six years of primary education in Chinese, do they enrol in the national secondary schools, which use Malay as the medium of instruction. Some continue to study in Independent Chinese-medium schools and are resinicized further.[28] One young scholar wrote in 1986 that the Baba Chinese in Penang no longer existed as they had already merged with the Penang Chinese in general. Those Baba Chinese that he could identify were in their seventies![29] Perhaps this was a slight exaggeration, but certainly the number of so-called Baba in Penang was extremely small.[30]

---

and only country. In accordance with practice all over the world, this confers on the Malays certain inalienable rights over the form and obligations of citizenship which can be imposed on citizens of non-indigenous origin" (Mahathir bin Mohammad, *The Malay Dilemma*, Singapore and Kuala Lumpur: Times Books International, 1996, p 133). In 1986, the Malaysian Chinese Association (MCA) attempted to challenge this concept. There was a convention resolution which declared that "the three major races are originated from other countries. Therefore, none of them should brand the others as immigrants and claim themselves natives". This resolution angered the Malays and heightened tension between the MCA and UMNO (reported in *Asiaweek*, cited in Harold Croach, *Government and Society in Malaysia*, NSW: Allen and Unwin, 1996, p 107). The MCA later quietly abandoned this stand.

27 See Tan Chee Beng, *The Baba of Melaka: Culture and Identity of a Chinese Community in Malaysia*, Petaling Jaya: Pelanduk Publications, 1988; Tan Chee Beng, *Chinese Peranakan Heritage in Malaysia and Singapore*, Kuala Lumpur: Fajar Bakti, 1996; John R Clammer, *Straits Chinese Society: Studies in Sociology of the Baba Communities of Malaysia and Singapore*, Singapore: Singapore University Press, 1980.

28 There are about 60 such schools in Malaysia, funded by the Chinese community. Tan Liok Ee has published many excellent studies on Chinese education in Malaysia. See, for instance, Tan Liok Ee, "Chinese Independent Schools in Malaysia: Varying Responses to Changing Demands", in *Changing Identities of the Southeast Asian Chinese since World War II*, edited by Jennifer Cushman and Wang Gungwu, Hong Kong: Hong Kong University Press, pp 61–74; *The Politics of Chinese Education in Malaya, 1945--1961*, Kuala Lumpur: Oxford University Press, 1997; "Chinese Schools in Malaysia: A Case of Cultural Resilience", in *The Chinese in Malaysia*, edited by Lee Kam Hing and Tan Chee Beng, Shah Alam, Malaysia: Oxford University Press, 2000, pp 228–54.

29 See Ho Eng Seng, "Problems of Identity", p 2.

30 In 2001, I met an ex-Penang woman in Singapore who was in her late forties and claimed to be a Nyonya.

However, after Singapore's separation from Malaysia in 1965, the Baba also faced new challenges. The bilingual policy, which defines mother tongue in terms of "racial language", has a tendency to resinicize the Baba Chinese. The descendants of the Baba begin to learn Chinese again. However, the emphasis on English permits the Baba to continue maintaining their English-educated Chinese identity rather than the old Baba identity.

English-educated and Chinese-educated?

Some observers maintain that after the two countries became independent, when we refer to the sociopolitical scene of the ethnic Chinese, it is more relevant to talk about the division between the Chinese-educated and English-educated.

In Malaysia, for instance, it is true that the MCA was first led and controlled by the Baba (eg, Tan Cheng Lock and Tan Siew Sin). But as time passed, the non-Baba Chinese began to lead the organization (eg, Lee San Choon and Tan Koon Suan). The current president, Ling Liong Sik, and his deputy, Lim Ah Lek, may be considered Baba, but more see them as English-educated. In fact, many top leaders in the MCA now are either Chinese-educated (eg, Chan Kong Choy) or bilingual (eg, Chua Jui Ming). The rank and file of MCA members are also Chinese-educated.

With regard to Chinese non-governmental organizations (NGOs), these are divided between the Chinese-educated and the English-educated, not between the Baba and the non-Baba. This is due to the small size of the Baba community and the popularity of Chinese education. Many Chinese, including the Baba, have sent their children for primary Chinese education. Some English-educated Chinese politicians have also picked up Chinese and are able to converse in Mandarin, although with a rather limited vocabulary. The division between the Chinese-educated and English-educated is often blurred, but it is still real as the Chinese schools are flourishing.

The situation in Singapore is quite similar. Prior to independence, many Peranakan were in politics; so were non-Peranakan. The first generation of top political leaders in Singapore belonged to the community of the so-called Straits Chinese. They were Peranakan but also English-educated. However, with the passing away of this first generation, there was an emergence of new leaders who were not necessarily Peranakan but were English-educated. Gradually, leaders have become bilingual, with English as their major language. However, unlike in Malaysia, where

Chinese-medium schools are still in operation, in Singapore the national education system tends to produce one type of leaders.

Post-Independence Peranakan Associations

Despite unfavourable conditions, some Baba wanted to perpetuate their heritage. They continued the old associations, giving these new names. We have mentioned the Peranakan Association of Singapore, which originated from the SCBA; the Persatuan Peranakan Cina Melaka, which was based on the SCBA Malacca branch; and the Persatuan Cina Pulau Pinang, which was based on the SCA. There is also a new Persatuan Peranakan Cina Kelantan, which is not well known. According to some reports, these associations have small memberships. It seems that it is difficult for them to develop further.

Conclusion

It shows that the official term "Peranakan" has now replaced other terms in reference to local-born and partially assimilated Chinese, but in Singapore and Malaysia, the terms "Baba" and "Nyonya" continue to be used. However, the identity of the Peranakan Chinese is far from clear. While it is clear that all Peranakan Chinese share the influence of Malay culture, especially language, there is, nevertheless, a wide spectrum of this influence, ranging from language to food and dress.

While the meaning of "Peranakan Chinese" has differed from period to period, it nevertheless continues to survive today. Other terms such as "Straits Chinese", "Straits-born Chinese" and "Baba" have had shorter life-spans as they are history- and geography-bound. In fact, "Straits Chinese" and "Straits-born Chinese" have become historical terms. With the exception of the old folk who can still be called "Straits Chinese" and "Straits-born Chinese" owing to their birth dates and birthplaces, it is anachronistic to use the terms to refer to the Chinese who were born and brought up in Singapore and Malaysia after independence.

The terms "Baba" and "Nyonya" have also been declining in usage, although in Singapore and Malaysia they are still used interchangeably with "Peranakan Chinese". Nevertheless, younger Peranakan Chinese no longer identify themselves as Baba and Nyonya. In West Java, where the terms were once widely used, they have gradually fallen into disuse. Few Chinese Indonesians understand the meanings of the terms today.

The self-identity and perception of others are equally important for the perpetuation of "ethnic identity". During the colonial era, the terms "Straits Chinese" and "Straits-born Chinese" were preferred, as the group of Chinese they identified in British Malaya (including Singapore) appeared to form the upper class of the Chinese community. However, with the end of colonialism, the terms were used less and less as more Chinese came to regard them as anachronistic. There has been a shift to "Baba" and "Nyonya" and "Peranakan Chinese", which represent merely cultural rather than sociopolitical identities.

The function of identity is also crucial. During the colonial period, to be Straits Chinese meant a socially higher and even "superior" status than that of other Chinese.[31] However, in Malaysia today, to be Straits Chinese is anachronistic, and, hence, the term is abandoned. Nevertheless, the status of Baba and Peranakan can still claim links with the Malays—who are the ruling elite. Therefore, it is still useful socially and politically to claim to be part of the indigenous scene. However, with racial and religious polarization, the Peranakan Chinese face new challenges. With globalization and the rise of Chinese culture, many Peranakan children are being exposed to non-Baba cultures, with some eventually becoming more "Chinese" and less "Malay".

The retention of the Baba identity in Singapore does not have social and political "values" since the multi-ethnic ruling elite is predominantly Chinese. Although the city-state is located in the so-called Malay seas, the rise of China as an economic giant and globalization continue to 'dilute' the Baba culture. Nevertheless, some Peranakan individuals still attempt to salvage this culture, as it is underdeveloped. The objective conditions are not favourable and the Peranakan identity is gradually fading from the scene.

---

31 Before World War II, in the Straits Settlements Legislative Council, all the 14 Chinese members in the period 1900–41 were Peranakan.

Chapter 5

THE MODERN TRANSFORMATION OF CHINESE POLITICAL LEADERSHIP IN COLONIAL SINGAPORE*

CF Yong

During the entire era of colonial rule, Singapore's evolving multiracial community generally and its Chinese community in particular were constantly subjected to international influences and internal dynamics for change. In the long march of history, the Chinese political leadership was likewise under the twin pressure with modernizing effects. This article will examine the traditional Chinese political leadership of the 19th century and analyse changing historical circumstances which brought about its modern transformation in the 20th century.

During the 19th century, the traditional Chinese political leadership came mainly from two sources. One, the Kapitan China system, which, although officially ended in 1826, was unofficially continued until the institution of the Chinese Protectorate in 1877. The other, the Chinese secret societies, which were transplanted from South China with social, political and economic objectives. Until 1890, these societies were tolerated, recognized and legitimized by the British. Their importance as a political force will be discussed later.

The Kapitan China system as adopted by the British first in 1786 in Penang and then in 1819 in Singapore had its origins dating back to the 16th century when the Portuguese ruled Malacca. This system of appointing Chinese headmen as Kapitan Chinas was continued by the Dutch in 1641 when they took over the colony. From 1641 to the transfer of Malacca to the British in 1824, the Dutch appointed no less than 13 Kapitan Chinas, some of whose careers have been reasonably well documented.[1]

---

*Acknowledgement: I would like to thank Mrs RB McKenna for assisting me in revising this article.

1   David KY Chng, *History of the Chinese in Singapore and Malacca: Some Notes*, Singapore: South Seas Society, 1990, pp 7–31.

David Chng's research confirms that the British appointed two Kapitan Chinas between 1819 and 1826, heretofore unregistered in most Singapore history writing.[2] The first Kapitan China was a Cantonese, named King An, a trader in opium and other merchandise who had commercial dealings with European businessmen. A second Kapitan China, Tan How Seng, was a Hokkien. He was a middleman and construction contractor. He also owned four land titles before he went bankrupt and died in 1823.[3]

These Kapitan Chinas had onerous tasks to perform, being empowered to deal with police, judicial and civil matters of the Chinese community. To help King An's performance, the British provided two Assistants and 12 Elders to assist him in carrying out his duties. However, the British only provided two Assistants to Tan How Seng. The British dismantled the Kapitan China system in 1826 when the Straits Settlements came under the control of one Presidency, with a Court of Judicature to cover all three settlements to deal with judicial matters.[4]

Despite the abolition of the system, the British found it difficult to rule Singapore's Chinese community on their own without resorting to the help of Chinese collaborators. The British did not have a single Chinese-speaking officer capable of communicating with the various dialect groups in Singapore until the 1870s. Besides, the English East India Company was short of funds for the maintenance of law and order. In any case, the Straits Settlements government lacked the political will to stamp out the burgeoning power of the Chinese secret societies. Thus, the British were compelled to look for new collaborators in ruling the Chinese in Singapore. Carl A Trocki has accurately provided a list of new collaborators, including the Straits Chinese, the secret society headmen, the revenue farmers and Baba merchants who had come to occupy semi-official positions.[5] In short, the British co-opted the Straits Chinese community leaders and secret society headmen as their new collaborators, confirming the former as the favoured political and economic elite. The Straits Chinese consisted of both Straits-born and naturalized British subjects who retained the essence of a Baba culture but increasingly identified themselves with the colonial rulers. Wong Lin Ken has made interesting observations on the Straits Chinese, praising

---

2   Ibid, pp 33–43.
3   Ibid, pp 40–41.
4   Chan Gaik Gnoh, "The Kapitan Cina System in the Straits Settlements", *Malaysia in History*, vol 25, 1982, p 79; and CS Wong, *A Gallery of Chinese Kapitans,* Singapore: Ministry of Culture, 1963, p 28.
5   Nicholas Tarling, ed, *The Cambridge History of Southeast Asia,* vol 2, The Nineteenth and Twentieth Centuries, Cambridge: Cambridge University Press, 1992, p 89.

them for playing an active role as middlemen in Singapore's entrepot trade. In his view, their economic success was owed largely to "a knowledge of English, and the habits and commercial procedures of the Western merchants, as well as the language, habits and needs of the multifarious Asian traders".[6] With great wealth accumulated, some of the Straits Chinese, like Cheang Hong Lim, were able to venture into the lucrative revenue farms. Having benefited from the economic development and political stability of the British rule, the Straits Chinese leaders were most responsive to assisting the British in maintaining law and order whenever secret society or communal disturbances erupted in Singapore.[7] In return, the British appointed them JPs, who could be called upon to serve as jurors in court cases. Some served as municipal commissioners while a few were nominated to serve on the Legislative Council, founded in 1867. Among a long list of important and influential Straits Chinese leaders were Tan Tock Seng (1798–1850), Tan Kim Seng (1805–64) and Tan Kim Ching (1829–92). These served as *de facto* Kapitan Chinas of the post-1826 era.[8]

Despite their Baba cultural background, the Straits Chinese leaders had gradually undergone Westernization and modernization processes. They had adopted Western business and trade practices and had acquired English language and communication skills. Like their 20th-century counterparts, they began to develop a passion for education generally. Being financially prosperous, they showed their charitable temperament towards their less fortunate countrymen by funding the building of temples and maintenance of funeral grounds, founding private hospitals and establishing schools and providing free education to children of Chinese immigrants. Thus, these modernizing and civilizing influences created an enlightened leadership pattern and tradition, based on wealth, influence, high social status and the values of social justice.

If Kapitan Chinas and the Straits Chinese leadership were the creation of European colonial powers, then the Chinese secret societies, known as the Triad, Tien Ti Hui, the Ghee Hin, the Ghee Hok, among others, were a product of an age-old Chinese political tradition of the imperial era, rooted in rural China. When transplanted early in the 19th century to Singapore, they were political in nature for their anti-Manchu sentiments. As their numbers and influence grew, they degenerated into social and economic

---

6 Wong Lin Ken, "Singapore: Its Growth as an Entrepot Port, 1819–1941", *Journal of Southeast Asian Studies,* vol 9, no 1, March 1978, p 59.
7 Song Ong Siang, *One Hundred Years' History of the Chinese in Singapore,* Singapore: University of Malaya Press, 1967, pp 88, 166, 174, 403.
8 Ibid, p 174.

power struggle, feuds, riots and communal disturbances, and crime. Their *raison d'etre* was that they fulfilled the needs of immigrants by "providing a range of networks, both for the essential material, social and spiritual underpinnings of day-to-day life, and—equally important—for maintaining social cohesion in the colony".[9] Besides, the Chinese secret societies had control over the supply of immigrant labour, a crucial factor in the development of the economy in British Malaya.[10] By the mid-19th century, they had become a political force in their own right when they became involved in the 1846 funeral riot, the 1850 anti-Chinese Catholic converts campaign, the 1854 riot and the 1857 communal disturbances.

By 1857, the Ghee Hin had come of age with the building of a central lodge at Lavender Street, Rochore, in charge of five other branches along the lines of dialect groups.[11] In 1879, there were at least ten Chinese secret societies in Singapore, with a total of 924 registered office-bearers and 23,858 registered members. Two years later, the registered membership rose to 33,103 out of a Chinese population of 72,571 in Singapore, or 45 per cent of the Chinese population.[12]

Despite some grey areas with regard to the Chinese secret societies, it is possible to characterize the 19th-century leadership. First, their leaders were never faceless and unmonitored since they were well known to the authorities by virtue of being leaders or by registration from 1869. Second, although some of their leaders were literate in the Chinese language and were conversant with their own specific dialects, few appear to have been able to speak English. Third, a majority of the leaders appear to have come from the working class; some, nevertheless, prospered under colonial rule to become owners of properties and other assets. Coincidentally, these leaders often emerged as leaders of their own dialect groups, founding dialect associations, such as the Ningyang and Chayang Associations, or managing their affairs as office-bearers.[13] Fourth, despite various attempts to suppress the secret societies, some colonial administrators had considerable goodwill

---

9   David KY Chng, *Heroic Images of Ming Loyalties: A History of the Ghee Hin Kongsi Leaders in Singapore*, Singapore: Singapore Society of Asian Studies, 1999, p 59.
10 Yen Ching-hwang, *A Social History of the Chinese in Singapore and Malaya, 1800–1911*, Singapore: Oxford University Press, 1986, pp 110–16; and Wong Lin Ken, *The Malayan Tin Industry to 1914*, Tucson: The University of Arizona Press, 1965, pp 236–39.
11 David KY Chng, *Heroic Images of Ming Loyalties,* pp 10–11.
12 Maurice Freedman, "Immigrants and Associations: Chinese in Nineteenth-century Singapore", *Comparative Studies in Society and History,* vol 3, no 1, October 1960, p 32.
13 David KY Chng, *Heroic Images of Ming Loyalties,* pp 55–57, 59.

towards their leaders. WA Pickering, the first Protector of the Chinese from 1877, believed that the secret society leaders were generally co-operating with the government,[14] while JD Vaughan, another administrator and later on a lawyer, even defended the leaders for doing "some good by adjusting petty quarrels and in supporting and maintaining the sick and poor".[15] By virtue of the fact that the secret society leaders were called upon to assist the government in quelling riots or communal disturbances, Maurice Freedman concludes that the colonial government made use of the secret societies as an instrument of government.[16] Fifth, in an expanding capitalist economy in Singapore, it would seem inevitable that the secret society leaders would come into close contacts with the Straits Chinese leaders in social and commercial fields, such as the supply of labour and the control and operation of the opium syndicate.[17] ML Wynne, an early expert on the Chinese secret societies, suspected that prominent Straits Chinese leaders, such as Tan Tock Seng, Tan Kim Seng, Lee Cheng Tee, Tan Beng Swee, Cheang Sam Teo and Cheang Hong Lim, had close relations with the Triad and the Tokong.[18] Sixth, an examination of the Rules of the Ghee Hok of mid-19th century Singapore sheds interesting light on headmen's enormous power over their members. Apart from being filial towards their parents, members must obey the orders of their headmen, who had the power of dismissal under certain circumstances. Stealing from fellow members and adultery involving the wife of another member, or introducing a lawbreaker or a government employee into the society, constituted grounds for sacking. Moreover, the Rules of the Ghee Hok set high moral standards for members, including prohibition against making or dealing in illicit *chandu* and spirits and assistance rendered to members in distress.[19] Although colonial authorities often perceived the Chinese secret societies as *imperium in imperio*, the Rules of the Ghee Hok suggest that members had to obey and respect colonial law and order.

The power enshrined in the Rules of the Ghee Hok aside, its leaders

---

14 Maurice Freedman, "Immigrants and Associations", p 32.
15 JD Vaughan, *The Manners and Customs of the Chinese,* Singapore: Oxford University Press, 1992, 4th printing, p 110.
16 Maurice Freedman, "Immigrants and Associations", p 34.
17 Carl A Trocki, *Opium and Empire: Chinese Society in Colonial Singapore,* Ithaca and London: Cornell University Press, 1990, pp 117–82.
18 ML Wynne, *Triad and Tabut: A Survey of the Origins and Diffusion of Chinese and Mohammedan Secret Societies in the Malay Peninsula, 1800–1935*, Singapore: Government Printing Office, 1941, p 351.
19 JD Vaughan, *The Manners and Customs of the Chinese,* pp 117–20.

enjoyed power in several other areas since it was the largest and the most powerful secret society in the 1870s. In 1879, for example, the Ghee Hok had 4,728 members with 304 office-bearers. The membership represented about 20 per cent of all members registered with the ten secret societies.[20] To organize, mobilize and lead a large institution like the Ghee Hok called for strong, dynamic and decisive leadership and leadership qualities. A brief profile of the top leader, Chua Moh Choon (1819–79), will illustrate the character and qualities of the man. Born in a Teochew prefecture, Guangdong province, Chua migrated to Singapore in 1838 and joined the Triad as a member. During the 1850s, Chua emerged as the leader of the Ghee Hok, which had become involved in the 1854 riot. In 1861, Chua led his armed members against the Tan clan members, resulting in his arrest and imprisonment. In 1864, he was granted naturalization as a British subject. From then on, he branched out into various businesses, including the running of brothels[21] and the operation of the coolie trade.[22] It may be surmised that Chua's good fortunes were largely due to the British need for his strong leadership to maintain law and order in a secret society–infested Chinese community in Singapore. W Blythe has this to say about his long career of intrigue:

> To the Chinese of Singapore, Chua Moh Choon was the embodiment of power. His word was law because he had the means to enforce it. Not only was he the unchallenged head of the largest and most unscrupulous Hoey in the town but he was also in the confidence of the principal officers of the Government, and was thus in a position to blacken the name of anyone who failed to do his bidding.[23]

However, change was afoot as colonial rule deepened with the introduction of new political and education policies and as China's cultural and political influences began to make impact on the Chinese community in Singapore from the 1870s.

To analyse this historical phenomenon, it is imperative to identify and trace the sequence of events and major players in Singapore history. In 1877, the Chinese Protectorate was instituted to deal with all affairs Chinese in the colony. For the first time, there was a Chinese expert in WA Pickering to take charge of Chinese immigration and emigration, labour, opium-

---

20 Maurice Freedman, "Immigrants and Associations", p 32.
21 *Lianhe Zaobao*, 5 July 1987.
22 Song Ong Siang, *One Hundred Years' History*, pp 175–76.
23 Wilfred Blythe, *The Impact of Chinese Secret Societies in Malaya: A Historical Study*, London: Oxford University Press, 1969, p 211.

smoking, gambling and prostitution and, more importantly, Chinese secret societies. The founding of the Chinese Protectorate signalled the beginning of an end to indirect rule. Pickering tightened control over the secret societies by re-registering their office-bearers and members. As the secret societies were still legal, these measures did little to eliminate the constant threat to peace and order by irresponsible members. However, the arrival of a new governor, Sir Cecil Clementi Smith, in 1887 saw the policy change from control to one of total suppression. A bill on the suppression of the Chinese secret societies was introduced in the Legislative Council in February 1889 and was passed after some strong opposition from the Unofficial members of the Council. Known as "Ordinance 1 of 1889, An Ordinance to amend the Law relating to Societies", it came into operation in January 1890, empowering the Governor in Council to dissolve any registered society by *Gazette* notification.

The proscription of Chinese secret societies had important historical significance for the Chinese community. The creation of a Chinese Advisory Board in 1889 with representation from various Chinese dialect groups helped patch up relationships between the government and the Chinese community. Through the Board, the Chinese community leaders were able to air their views on matters close to their hearts. The demise of the secret societies cleared the field for the rise and development of new and modern political leaderships. The emergence of China-oriented nationalists, be they reformists or revolutionaries, were to dominate the immigrant Chinese community for the next 50 years. During the interwar years, a more radical group of Chinese communists brought with them communism and Marxism, which were to dog the colonial authorities until the 1960s.

A second colonial policy which had profound impact on the emergence of modern political leadership by the turn of the century was also initiated by Sir Cecil Clementi Smith in 1884. This was the institution of the Queen's scholarships to enable the brightest students from English secondary schools to compete for two scholarships each year and to complete their university studies in Great Britain. Among a host of Queen's scholars who returned to contribute to public life were Lim Boon Keng (1869–1957) and Song Ong Siang (1871–1941). CM Turnbull has succinctly summarized their contribution as follows:

> they became leaders in the professions and took their place alongside the wealthy merchants as legislative councillors, municipal councillors, and Justices of the Peace. The English-educated professional Asian elite provided a new type of leadership and began a subtle Westernizing and modernizing of Singapore society, including a respect for Western education and

professional success, opening the way for the Asian community to assimilate and accept Western medicine, the British judicial system and European educational methods.[24]

A third government policy which institutionalized the political structure and determined future constitutional development of the Straits Settlements was the establishment of a two-chamber legislature in 1867. The Executive Council was empowered to present government bills for debate in the Legislative Council before executing them. The Legislative Council consisted of a majority of Officials and a minority of nominated Unofficials from Singapore's multiracial community. Although neither type of members were elected, nomination to the Legislative Council allowed representation of the various ethnic communities and practice in parliamentary procedures for English-speaking community leaders. Thus, the structure and operation of the Legislative Council provided an avenue for the emergence of a legitimized English-educated Straits Chinese leadership, serving as spokesmen for the Chinese population in Singapore in general.

If the above internal dynamics produced *modern* political leadership of the Straits Chinese community, then the China influences from the 1870s were to create diverse leadership patterns and strains of the immigrant Chinese community. The establishment of a Chinese Consulate in Singapore in 1877 set the scene for a protracted battle for the minds and hearts of the Chinese between the Chinese Consul and the Chinese Protector. Described by Song Ong Siang as "a man of enlightenment and liberal education",[25] Tso Ping Lung (1850–1924), a bilingual scholar and diplomat, played a decisive role in evoking the cultural and intellectual awakening of the Straits Chinese and immigrant Chinese in Singapore. In 1881, he encouraged the wealthy Chinese-educated leaders to launch a Confucian revival movement by promoting a series of lectures on the values of Confucianism. In 1882, Consul Tso founded a literary club, the Hui Hsien She (the Society for the Meeting of Literary Excellence), for the benefit of the immigrant community. He personally set topics for monthly essay and poetry competitions and graded them himself. Monetary awards for good compositions came from his own purse.[26] During his long tenure of ten years, there were at least 1,000 participants in essay and poetry contests.[27]

---

24 CM Turnbull, *A History of Singapore, 1819–1988*, Singapore: Oxford University Press, 1989, 2nd edition, pp 116–17.
25 Song Ong Siang, *One Hundred Years' History*, p 210.
26 Tan Yeok Seong, *Ya Yin Kuan Wen Chun*, Singapore: South Seas Society, 1983, vol 1, p 123.
27 *Lianhe Zaobao*, 17 January 1988.

Through these activities, he succeeded in stimulating their concerns for China's endemic crisis and arousing them to take an interest in cultural, social and moral issues of the Chinese in British Malaya. In short, he laid the cultural and intellectual groundwork for the blossoming of political nationalism among the Chinese in the 1890s.

Consul Tso also won the goodwill of the Straits Chinese community in Singapore by founding a debating club for them. In 1882, he presided at a fortnightly meeting in English of the Celestial Reasoning Society. Debate topics consisted of politics, social problems and cultural issues of the Straits Settlements or China. These debates sharpened the minds and debating skills of the Straits Chinese and prepared them for social, cultural and political stirrings as a distinctive community group.

Indeed, Consul Tso's many good works did not go unnoticed. When he left Singapore in 1891, even Governor Clementi Smith heaped praises on him by reporting that Consul Tso had performed his duties with excellent tact, discretion and ability and helped the government in many projects for relieving the poor and helpless Chinese in the colony.[28]

In the 1880s, the Ch'ing government sold honours, including brevet titles and ranks to wealthy Chinese community leaders, with a view to winning the latter over to the Ch'ing regime. From 1890, the Ch'ing launched numerous diplomatic drives by despatching diplomats, dignitaries, officials and envoys to British Malaya for fact-finding, fund-raising, trade and educational missions, which were all well received.[29] Given time and more favourable conditions, the pro-Ch'ing nationalism could well have taken root but for the defeat of China by the Japanese in the first Sino-Japanese War (1894–95) and subsequent political agitation which culminated in the Hundred Days of Reform during 1898.

The 1890s was a decade of national crises in China and political tensions of the Chinese overseas. The politicized Chinese in Singapore responded in two opposing ways. A reform movement led by Khoo Seok Wan (1874–1941) and Lim Boon Keng went on to found the first Chinese political party in Singapore in 1900. Known as Pao Huang Hui (the Emperor Protection Society), the reformers supported K'ang Yu-wei's reformist programmes for China, including the constitutional monarchy.[30] What was

---

28 Edwin Lee, *The British As Rulers: Governing Multiracial Singapore, 1867–1914*, Singapore: Singapore University Press, 1991, p 182.
29 Yen Ching-hwang, *Community and Politics: The Chinese in Colonial Singapore and Malaysia*, Singapore: Times Academic Press, 1995, p 215.
30 Ibid, p 215.

modern about the Pao Huang Hui was that it had persuasive and coherent ideology and had two print media, *Thien Nan Shin Pao* and *Jit Shin Pao*, to propagate it. It also utilized a front organization, the Hao Hsueh Hui, known in English as the Chinese Philomatic Society, to promote a monthly public lecture for 300 members. It had a considerable support base as the Cantonese community in Singapore backed K'ang's reformism.

The other strain of Chinese nationalism was politically and ideologically more radical, for it aimed at the overthrow of the Ch'ing dynasty by force and the creation of a Chinese Republic. From 1895 to 1900, as Chinese community leaders were not ready to accept radical solutions to China's problems, it was left to a small band of political refugees and agitators, such as Yu Lieh, to foment a revolutionary movement among workers and members of the Chinese secret societies. In 1901, Yu founded a political organization, the Chung Ho T'ang, to undertake the task. Yu liaised with a small group of local young Chinese revolutionaries of Straits Chinese background, such as Teo Eng Hock (1871–1957), Tan Chor Nam (1884–1971) and Lim Nee Soon (1879–1936), and, together, they co-founded the first revolutionary newspaper in Southeast Asia, *Thoe Lam Jit Poh*, in 1904. In 1906, Sun Yat-sen himself visited Singapore and presided at an inauguration meeting for the founding of the T'ung Meng Hui (the United League), a topic deserving more analysis in the context of the modern transformation of Chinese political leadership.

The Straits Chinese were just as politically restless and culturally awakened as their China-born counterparts during the 1890s. The Celestial Reasoning Society's activities of the 1880s, the return of Lim Boon Keng and Song Ong Siang in 1893 and the publication of the *Straits Chinese Magazine* in 1897, all contributed to the creation of a Straits Chinese identity as a potent but minority community. Finally, the spirit of reform and the euphoria emanated from the British military victory in the South African War in 1900 propelled the Straits Chinese to organize their own Straits Chinese British Association (SCBA) in August that year. A pledge of undivided loyalty to the Queen and Empire was of utmost importance as the first priority of the Queen's Chinese.[31]

Just how *modern* were the Pao Huang Hui, the Chung Ho T'ang, the T'ung Meng Hui and the SCBA?

The answers lie in the use of modern ideologies and modern print media for propaganda purposes, the input of modern intellectuals, the effective use of front organizations, the practice of a modern concept of democracy and a commitment to social, cultural and educational development.

---

31 Song Ong Siang, *One Hundred Years' History*, pp 319–20.

Briefly, all early 20th-century Chinese political leaderships had well-argued and developed ideologies, be they anti-Manchu nationalism, pro-Ch'ing reformism, Western imperialism, or Straits Chinese liberalism and social Darwinism, whereas these ideologies had been glaringly absent during the previous century. Modern intellectuals broke the monopoly of the Straits Chinese community leaders and the Chinese secret societies. The use of modern print media and front organizations, such as reading clubs and drama troupes for political purposes, was modern in technique and function.[32] The annual election of office-bearers of the SCBA and the T'ung Meng Hui was democracy at work. Finally, political leaders of the early 20th century were all committed to promoting cultural and educational wellbeing. One of the SCBA's objectives was "to encourage higher and technical education for the Chinese in some practical way".[33] Likewise, the leaders of the Pao Huang Hui and the T'ung Meng Hui were active promoters of modern Chinese education as panacea for the ills of China and the poor social status of the Chinese overseas.

Among the four political societies examined thus far, the Chung Ho T'ang fell by the wayside as it was absorbed by the T'ung Meng Hui in 1906. The Pao Huang Hui ceased to exist in 1901 when Khoo Seok Wan split with K'ang Yu-wei and dissociated himself from the reformist movement altogether. However, supporters of K'ang entrenched themselves in a newly founded Chinese Chamber of Commerce as their main power base.[34] The T'ung Meng Hui, transformed in 1912 as the Kuomintang (KMT), lasted until 1949, when it was banned a third time by colonial authorities. The SCBA still existed in 1965 as a declining and innocuous political force. It is important to note that during the interwar years, new international influences helped create in Singapore two modern political leaderships, the Malayan Communist Party (MCP) and Tan Kah Kee's non-partisan leadership. It is thus important that each of the leaderships be examined in some detail in the context of modern development within a politically and ideologically polarized community.

A brief analysis of the four major political leaderships from 1900 to 1941 will illustrate how each had travelled under rigid colonial control.

As a political pressure group, the SCBA had a comparatively smooth plain sailing with 800 members in 1900, but its membership declined to

---

32 Yen Ching-hwang, *Community and Politics*, pp 264–86.
33 Song Ong Siang, *One Hundred Years' History*, p 320.
34 CF Yong, *Chinese Leadership and Power in Colonial Singapore*, Singapore: Times Academic Press, 1992, pp 23–46.

386 in 1931, when Singapore was in economic recession. Having enjoyed the trust of the government, its leaders invariably became Legislative Councillors, Municipal Commissioners and Justices of the Peace. The SCBA projected various images to the public as social reformers, promoters of English language, education and culture, founders of modern capitalist enterprises, such as banks, shipping companies and insurance institutions, and defenders of law and order. Moreover, they played colonial politics hard and to the best of their ability. They performed creditably in the Legislative Council as seasoned speakers and debaters. When Singapore and the Empire were under duress, as was the case in World Wars I and II, they joined the local volunteer corps, donated relief funds and purchased aeroplanes towards British war efforts. As critics, they exercised their rights to chastise government policies deemed to be damaging their interests or those of the Chinese community at large. When Governor Clementi downgraded the importance of English education and language and introduced a controversial Aliens Bill to exert political control over Chinese immigration, labour and non-British subjects via registration, they unanimously opposed these moves without compunction.[35] However, it was in the battle for constitutional development that showed the political vision of early Singapore's nationalists. In 1922, SJ Chan, a barrister and an active SCBA member, voiced the need to elect Straits Chinese members to the Chamber rather than government nominations. In 1924, Song Ong Siang followed suit by agitating for direct representation for all British communities in the colony. He suggested that an Asian member be invited to serve on the Executive Council.[36] In 1926, Tan Cheng Lock spoke at length at a Council meeting of the need to expand the size of the Legislative Council. He contended that the government should create a majority of Unofficial members within the Council to serve as opposition. He aired his nationalistic sentiments thus:

> Our ultimate political goal should be a united self-governing British Malaya with a Federal Government and Parliament for the whole of it, functioning at a convenient centre, say, at Kuala Lumpur, and with as much autonomy in purely local affairs as possible for each of its constituent paths.[37]

---

35 CF Yong, "Sir Cecil Clementi and the Straits Chinese, 1930–1934", *Journal of South Seas Society,* vol 49, 1994, pp 34–56.
36 Andrew Docherty, "The Straits Chinese in Singapore, 1900–1941", MA thesis, History Department, Flinders University of South Australia, 2000, p 224.
37 *Proceedings of the Legislative Council, Straits Settlements,* 1 November 1926, B 161.

Although there was no self-governing Malaya in prewar years, the SCBA's persistent agitations over constitutional and political matters prompted the government to establish in the 1930s the Straits Settlements Legal, Medical and Civil Services to accommodate qualified Asians as junior members of the government services. However, the Malayan Civil Service (MCS) remained closed to Asians in the colony.

The Singapore KMT was an outgrowth of the T'ung Meng Hui. It had a chequered history as it incurred the wrath of the government on three occasions, 1925, 1930 and 1949. It waxed and waned, depending on the fluctuating fortunes of its China counterpart and on its ability to broaden its support base and to groom new local leaders for continuity. As fundamentally a China-oriented party, it had some highlights. After the fall of the Ch'ing dynasty, party members capitalized on the euphoria by holding the first election in 1913 for office-bearers. They elected a 123-member office-bearing committee from a membership of 2,000. Oddly, seven top leadership positions were held by Straits Chinese, including Tan Chay Yan, Teo Eng Hock, Lim Boon Keng, Tan Boo Liat, Lim Nee Soon, Tan Chor Nam and CS Yin. The social origins of these office-bearers were diverse, businessmen being the majority and a sprinkling of intellectuals and professionals. More importantly, the KMT created a new power base in a new chamber of commerce, the Chinese Merchants General Chamber of Commerce (CMGCC), founded in 1912. With branches and sub-branches and a number of reading clubs, the KMT presented itself as a potent and formidable political force within the Chinese community. Despite the fact that the KMT in British Malaya suffered two bans on political grounds, such as its association with Chinese Communism and its organization being an *imperium in imperio*, it survived into the postwar years. In 1948, it reached another high point with 23 branches and 5,000 members,[38] capable of challenging rival political forces.

The KMT movement left behind some durable legacies. It promoted Chinese education by funding, maintaining and staffing vernacular Chinese schools with modernizing effects. It founded a number of social and reading clubs in Singapore, thus enriching the social and cultural life of members. It published and controlled various Chinese newspapers, thereby improving the intellectual standards of their readers. Being China-oriented in its activities, it may be argued that the KMT impeded the progress towards the making of a Singapore identity.

---

38 CF Yong and RB McKenna, *The Kuomintang Movement in British Malaya, 1912–1949*, Singapore: Singapore University Press, 1990, p 209.

A third political force, the MCP was as important as it was international, with its historical links to the China CCP and the Comintern in Moscow. Before the founding of the party in April 1930, Chinese political refugees, Communist Party members and Hainanese Communist cadres contributed to organizing youths, women, labour unions and night schools. The Hainanese Communists dominated the party hierarchy for at least ten years from 1926.[39] Having survived the Depression years and Clementi's onslaught, they launched three massive waves of labour unrest in Singapore and Malaya from 1936. They capitalized on rising nationalist fervour arising from the Sino-Japanese War (1937–45) by organizing numerous Anti-Enemy Baching-up Societies (AEBUS) for popular support for their anti-war and anti-Japanese cause. As a working class leadership and movement, the MCP had come a long way within so short a time. It flexed its political and industrial muscles and became the most dreaded foe in the eyes of colonial authorities. In 1941, it was the strongest and best organized political party with a membership of 5,000 for British Malaya, 40,000 AEBUS members and 50,000 Malayan General Labour Union members.[40]

What characterized the MCP leadership?

It was firstly a working class-cum-intellectual movement, with union leaders and intellectuals constituting the top party hierarchy *vis-à-vis* the Malayan KMT movement, dominated largely by wealthy community leaders. Despite its China and Moscow connections, it was substantially a Malaya-oriented party with an increasing number of Malayan and Singapore-born Chinese being drawn into anti-colonial struggle. Its Malayan orientation is illustrated by its mobilization of the masses for social justice and for the creation of a 'Soviet Republic' in Malaya, which was to remain a dream. Part of its success in prewar years was the flexible use of the Marxist class line (labour unrest) and the Maoist mass line (united front tactic for mass mobilization). However, the MCP had failed to make itself a multiracial party and this was the party's Achilles' heel in the end. What made the MCP so different from all other Chinese political leaderships was not just its radicalism in ideology and action but also its strong anti-colonial posture.

A fourth contending political force that emerged during the interwar years was Tan Kah Kee's non-partisan leadership, based on traditional Chinese community institutions, such as clan and dialect associations, social,

---

39 CF Yong, *The Origins of Malayan Communism*, Singapore: South Seas Society, 1997, pp 141–44, 167, 273.
40 Ibid, pp 234, 274–75.

educational and cultural organizations, guilds, clubs and professional bodies and, to a lesser extent, secret societies.

Tan Kah Kee (1874–1961) came into the political limelight in 1912, when he successfully led a fund-raising campaign for the maintenance of law and order in his home province, Fujian, in the aftermath of the 1911 Revolution. His status as a community leader was enhanced in 1919 when he co-founded the Singapore Chinese High School. Two years later, he achieved international fame by single-handedly financing the Amoy University. A feather in his cap in 1923 was his successful assumption of the top leadership of a millionaires' club in Singapore, the Ee Hoe Hean Club. As club president, he could mobilize club members, many of whom were community leaders in their own right, for sociopolitical actions. From 1923 to 1928, Tan welded a hard core of talented club members who were to become his close friends, loyal supporters and brains trust. These included Hau Say Huan (1883–1944), Chew Hean Swee (1884–1961), Lee Chin Tian (1875–1965) and Sng Choon Yee, among others.[41] Sng Choon Yee's role in Tan Kah Kee's political legitimization by the British was crucial since the former was on the government payroll as the Chief Chinese Translator of the Chinese Affairs Department. In 1931, Sng was promoted as Chinese Secretary for the Secretary for Chinese Affairs, AB Jordan, becoming the latter's right-hand man. As a link man between Tan Kah Kee and the government, Sng's role was to smooth out any problems of Tan's with his Department and to relay any feedback the government might have on his leadership and actions. With Sng's support and government blessing, Tan moved on to lead numerous fund-raising campaigns for China relief funds. These included the Shantung Relief Fund (1928–29), the Malayan Singapore Committee for Premier Chiang's Birthday Aeroplane Fund (1936), the Singapore China Relief Fund (1937–41), the Southseas China Relief Fund Union (1938–49) and the Singapore Chinese Mobilization Council (1941–42). Naturally, each of these campaigns involved the use of untold community manpower and resources and created in its wake a quickened politicization process. Take the Singapore China Relief Fund, for example. It was sanctioned by the government in the first place. Tan Kah Kee's leadership was needed to forestall both the KMT and the MCP from capturing it. With Tan Kah Kee at the helm, the British could expect a "properly constituted" fund to carry out orderly campaigns without resorting to anti-Japanese boycott, which would damage Singapore's economy, or inciting racial riots, which would impair Anglo-Japanese

---

41 CF Yong, *Chinese Leadership and Power*, p 106.

relationships.[42] Under Tan Kah Kee's leadership, a massive fund-raising campaign was soon turned into a mass political movement. Apart from utilizing traditional community institutions for fund-raising, it was not difficult for the Fund to foster closer links with various sociopolitical elites within the Chinese community, such as the Straits Chinese and English-educated, the MCP's front organizations, and the KMT and its networks, for a common goal of China relief. Chinese nationalism was at its height during the remaining years of the prewar era. Herein lie the legend and legacy of Tan Kah Kee's leadership in modern Singapore politics—his non-partisanship as a successful strategy for the mobilization of community support towards China's salvation.

In summary, it may be observed that each of the four leaderships had its own constituents and niche. With the exception of the MCP, co-operation among leaders of these organizations was commonplace. Political and ideological rivalry was more covert and circumspect. While the SCBA, the KMT and the MCP were modern political parties with sophisticated ideologies, Tan Kah Kee's leadership was clearly more traditional as his support base was rooted in traditional Chinese community institutions. In terms of influence and popularity, Tan Kah Kee had an edge over the others.

A second modern transformation of the Chinese political leadership took place in the 1940s, a decade of major historical events of great importance. Such events as the Japanese Occupation (1942–45), the Malayan Union (1946–47), the Malayan Emergency (1948–60), the Cold War (1946–89) and the Chinese Civil War (1946–49) had ramifications on the fortunes of prewar leaderships and the emergence of new political parties for self-government and independence.

The Japanese Occupation and ramifications changed the political leadership map of postwar Singapore in more ways than one. For the returned colonial rulers, it was a culture shock with tarnished image of superiority and invincibility and with questionable moral right to reimpose colonial rule.[43] In response to the loss of British Malaya, the Colonial Office in London set up a Malayan Planning Unit in 1943 to map out a new constitution for post-Occupation Malaya. Known as the Malayan Scheme, it provided rather generous citizenship qualifications to non-Malays but at the same time greatly undermined the privileged position of the Malays

---

42   CF Yong, *Tan Kah-kee, the Making of an Overseas Chinese Legend*, Singapore: Oxford University Press, 1989, 2nd printing, pp 202–04.
43   Eunice Thio, "The Syonan Years, 1942–1945", in *A History of Singapore*, edited by Ernest CT Chew and Edwin Lee, Singapore: Oxford University Press, 1991, p 110.

and their rulers. The British hurriedly succumbed to Malay nationalist agitations and demands by framing a new Federation of Malaya constitution which came into force in 1948. On the implications of the Malayan Union Scheme, Wang Gungwu observes that "in one bold and abortive act, the British succeeded in releasing the energies of all three main communities and inducing them to consider their potential rights in a new Malaya".[44] In other words, communalism had a field day in the Malayan Union, with each community forming its political party, such as the United Malays National Organisation (UMNO), the Malayan Indian Congress (MIC) and the Malayan Chinese Association (MCA). However, in Singapore, with the exception of the Malay Nationalist Party (MNP), multiracial political parties sprang up with the rise of the Malayan Democratic Union (MDU) in 1946 and the Singapore Progressive Party (SPP) in 1947, ready to reap the benefit of constitutional change.

The MCP made considerable capital gains out of the Japanese Occupation as the only effective resistance movement. With British blessing and material support, the MCP developed into a sizeable military force of 5,000 strong, divided into eight regiments. Known as the Malayan People's Anti-Japanese Army (MPAJA), Chinese guerrillas were armed and trained for jungle warfare. These trained soldiers were to return to the jungle again in 1948 and to take up arms against the British colonial rule when the British reverted to their anti-Communist policy of the prewar years in a climate of growing Cold War conflicts between the Soviet bloc and the Free World.

If the Japanese Occupation created a potent MCP, it also gave rise to a Singapore nationalism which ultimately aimed at the attainment of independence, within or outside Malaya. The three and a half years of the Japanese interregnum were the most important of Lee Kuan Yew's life.[45] His unpalatable experience of Japanese rule made him a staunch anti-colonialist. When speaking in 1961, Lee confirmed that he and his generation who went through the Japanese Occupation emerged determined that no one—neither the Japanese nor the British—had the right to push them around.[46] If further proof is needed, then a 1955 Colonial Office file which contains a dossier on Lee will be sufficient:

---

44 Wang Gungwu, *Community and Nation: Essays on Southeast Asia and the Chinese*, Singapore: Heinemann Educational Books (Asia) Ltd, 1981, p 204.
45 Lee Kuan Yew, *The Singapore Story*, Singapore: Singapore Press Holdings, 1998, p 74.
46 Yeo Kim Wah and Albert Lau, "From Colonialism to Independence, 1945–1965", in *A History of Singapore*, edited by Ernest CT Chew and Edwin Lee, p 117.

Arriving back in Singapore in August 1950 he was interviewed by the Commissioner of Police where he contended that he was a Socialist, not a Communist, had no regard for Lim Hong Bee, whom he considered had tricked the Malayan students, but said that he regarded the present trouble in Malaya solely as a private war between the British Government and the M.C.P. Should the former win he would press for immediate self-government and rapid Malayanisation.[47]

For the sake of continuity, it is in order to examine the fate of the SCBA, the KMT, the MCP and the Tan Kah Kee leadership of the postwar era, in addition to a new Chinese-dominated political party, the People's Action Party (PAP), founded in 1954.

The SCBA, being one of the main targets of Japanese repression, dwindled in numbers and influence. Besides, many of the able Straits Chinese lost their lives while serving in the Singapore Volunteer Corps against the Japanese invasion of the island.[48] The SCBA was somewhat unpopular in a changed environment when anti-colonialist fervour was engulfing Singapore. It strove to preserve its British national status with attached privileges while at the same time opposing the proposal for a Singapore citizenship enfranchising the China-born, Chinese-educated and Chinese-speaking sector of the community. Moreover, it strongly supported the colonial policy of expanding English education and maintaining English language as the only official language in the legislature, at odds with the multilingual policy of the Singapore Chinese Chamber of Commerce.[49] In 1951, Lee Kuan Yew was elected Secretary of the SCBA but became impatient with the slow pace of the Straits Chinese politicians. He realized that the future of Singapore did not belong to the Queen's Chinese but to those who could command wider support.[50]

Still a key player in Malayan and Singapore politics, the MCP entered the postwar years with trepidation and uncertainty. They soon encountered some stormy weather in the industrial and political fields. Under the leadership of Lai Teck, the MCP adopted a united front strategy of working for a self-government by constitutional means. Under conditions of legality and in a seemingly level playing field, MCP cadres were frenetic in extending their power and influence in ex-soldiers' associations, women's

---

47 CO 1030/403, Briefs for Secretaries of State's visit to Federation of Malaya and Singapore, 1955, which contains biographical notes on Lee Kuan Yew, p 8.
48 Eunice Thio, "The Syonan Years, 1942–1945", p 111.
49 Yeo Kim Wah, *Political Developments in Singapore, 1945–1955*, Singapore: Singapore University Press, 1973, p 138.
50 CM Turnbull, *A History of Singapore, 1819–1988*, p 246.

bodies, youth and student organizations, trade unions, and social, cultural and educational societies. Amidst organizational and recruitment drives, the MCP in Singapore mobilized trade unions for strikes and stoppages in the name of social justice. In 1947, the governments of Singapore and the Malayan Union readily admitted that the MCP controlled 75 per cent of organized labour in the two territories.[51] In the political arena of Singapore, the MCP achieved a major breakthrough by establishing close liaisons with two non-Communist political bodies. One of them, the Malayan Democratic Union, was organized by middle-class English-educated intellectuals, such as John Eber and Philip Hoalim, for the creation of a self-governing Malaya within the Commonwealth. The other, the PMCJA (Pan-Malayan Council of Joint Action)–PUTERA (Pusat Tenaga Ra'ayat), was a loosely united front organization embodying anti-British and anti-UMNO forces in 1947 and 1948. By 1947, the MCP had increased its membership to 11,800, and then posed a threat to the colonial government.[52]

So alarmed was the Governor-General for Malaya, Malcolm MacDonald, that he convened an urgent meeting with 13 other high government officials on 26 June 1947 to discuss the threat of Communism in Malaya and Singapore. At this historic Special Conference, Malcolm MacDonald declared that "Communism was Enemy No. 1" in Malaya and Southeast Asia,[53] while canvassing countermeasures and strategies for combating it. Among urgent measures suggested were the setting up of government-controlled trade unions, the persuasion of political moderates in Singapore to form political parties for the election of six Unofficial members of the Legislative Council in 1948 and the strengthening of the Malayan Security Service for intelligence gathering of Communist activities. The issue of the legality of the MCP was raised and discussed but no decision was made. In January 1948, Malcolm MacDonald appointed a Special Committee to seriously consider the banning of the MCP.[54] However, the British had the decision made for them when the MCP launched an armed insurrection in June 1948.

The 1948 Malayan Emergency sealed the fate of the MCP in Singapore. It was driven underground between 1949 and 1953 and was totally crippled

---

51 MR Stenson, *Industrial Conflict in Malaya*, London: Oxford University Press, 1970, p 124.
52 JD Dalley, "Threat of Communism in Malaya and Singapore, 1947", containing Minutes of Special Conference held under the Chairmanship of HE the Governor-General, at 10 am on Thursday, 26 June 1947, in the Governor-General's Office, Singapore, p 9.
53 Ibid, pp 2, 7.
54 CO 537/2679/14355/6, Political Intelligence Journals, 1948, Sir F Gimson, Governor of Singapore, to Mr Bourdillon, dated 7 February 1948.

with the detention of 14 out of 16 top leaders of the Singapore City Committee.[55] It was not until 1954 that the MCP in Singapore was revived to direct an open united front struggle for self-government in Singapore.

Although both the KMT and the Tan Kah Kee leadership survived the ordeal of the Japanese Occupation, they soon became inextricably embroiled in China politics generally and in the politics of the Chinese civil war, raging in the country since 1946, in particular. By overtly siding with Mao Tse-tung against Chiang Kai-shek and China KMT, Tan Kah Kee forfeited his non-partisanship, and thus much of his prewar power base, with the exception of his fellow provincials and their organizations. The confrontation between these two factions took the form of political, ideological and polemical battles and, at times, polemical debates in opposing newspapers became overheated and acrimonious. On one occasion in September 1946, Tan Kah Kee, as Chairman of the Southseas China Relief Fund Union, cabled President Truman of the United States, slamming the KMT government and its ministers for being corrupt, incompetent, tiresome, bigoted, dictatorial and incapable of reforming China. On the other hand, the Fund Union praised the Yenan government for being popular and democratic. Further, it advised the US President to change his China policy by stopping aid to Chiang Kai-shek and by withdrawing US naval, air and land forces from China so as to bring the Chinese civil war to a speedy end.[56] This, then, was the so-called "Cable Crisis" which created prolonged animosity between the antagonists, resulting in deepened division within the Chinese community in Singapore particularly.

Oddly enough, the Malayan Emergency had unpredictable ramifications for both the MCP and the Tan Kah Kee leadership. In the eyes of the British, Tan Kah Kee was unashamedly pro-Mao, hence, leaning towards the left in China and Malayan politics. In order to neutralize the Tan Kah Kee forces and to prevent Tan Kah Kee from providing any moral support to the MCP, the British 'persuaded' Tan to issue a press statement on 22 July 1948, stressing the importance of law and order and disapproving the Malayan Communist insurgency.[57] A combination of British pressure and Mao's personal invitation for his return helped Tan Kah Kee take the course of action he did—to return to China in May 1950 for good. This, then, ended an era in which Chinese nationalism was an incurable passion and

---

55 Yeo Kim Wah and Albert Lau, "From Colonialism to Independence, 1945–1965", in *A History of Singapore*, edited by Ernest CT Chew and Edwin Lee, p 127.
56 CF Yong, *Tan Kah-kee, the Making of an Overseas Chinese Legend,* p 312.
57 Ibid, pp 325–26.

contagious disease for many of the politicized China-born and Chinese-educated in British Malaya.

For the Singapore KMT, a change of government policy was on the cards since the Malayan Emergency. It was finally proscribed in May 1949 on the grounds that the KMT was a foreign political party which "militates against the growth of Malayan civic consciousness" and a ban would encourage the Chinese to develop "a real sense of loyalty to Malaya as the country of their adoption".[58]

In the postwar years, the Singapore Chinese Chamber of Commerce was as much a political organization as it was commercial since it became heavily involved in Singapore politics over the issues of citizenship, language and education. The emergence of a nucleus of pragmatic, far-sighted and resilient leaders, such as Lee Kong Chian, Tan Chin Tuan, Tan Lark Sye, Lien Ying Chow, Ko Teck Kin, Tan Keong Choon and Soon Peng Yam, was mainly responsible for its proactive policy towards the issues mentioned. In response to the quickened tempo of decolonization from 1948, the Chamber fought and won Singapore citizenship for the China-born, multilingualism in both the Singapore City Council and the Legislative Assembly and the founding of the Democratic Party (DP) to contest the 1955 election on communal issues the Chamber championed.[59] Denounced by Lee Kuan Yew as "a stooge party of Formosa"[60] and by left-wing opposition as a "millionaires' party",[61] the DP won only two seats out of the 20 it contested. Although the Chamber's electoral experimentation was a failure, its prolonged campaign for the franchising of the China-born residents contributed to the passing of the Singapore Citizenship Ordinance of 1957. This liberal Ordinance practically added 220,000 China-born residents to the electoral rolls. By 1959, eligible voters had increased from a mere 72,000 in 1952 to over 500,000, returning the PAP to manage a self-governing Singapore.

This leads us to the PAP, a multiracial and multilingual political party dominated by a group of English-educated Chinese intellectuals and professionals, headed by Lee Kuan Yew.

From its formation in 1954, the PAP projected a radical left-wing image in the Singapore political scene—the ending of colonialism by constitutional

---

58 CO 537/4835/54463, Control of Foreign Political Parties, 1949, see letter from Sir F Gimson to the Secretary of State for the Colonies, CO, 17 February 1949.
59 CF Yong, *Chinese Leadership and Power*, pp 278–79; and Yeo Kim Wah, *Political Developments in Singapore*, pp 135–53.
60 Ibid, p 270, as quoted in *The Straits Times*, 18 March 1955.
61 Ibid, p 272.

means being its immediate task. In 1959, when it won power to rule a self-governing Singapore, it reaffirmed that its political platform was independence for Singapore through merger with a democratic, socialist and non-Communist Malaya.

The rising popularity and dominance of the PAP from 1955 were partly due to the reaction against the two previous ineffective governments, the first led by an erratic David Marshall, Singapore's first Chief Minister, and the second led by his successor, Lim Yew Hock, whose government was weak, corrupt, but staunchly anti-Communist. They could also be attributed to the successful operation of a united front strategy to win over not just the English-educated constituents but the raw, vibrant and anti-colonial Chinese-speaking and Chinese-educated world. To break into that world, the PAP, willingly or unwillingly, accepted and tolerated pro-Communist elements within its rank and file, since the latter had considerable muscle from trade union and student support.

As in 1947, the British in the 1950s still regarded Communism in Singapore as their main threat. In their view, the Communists "dr[e]w on the political enthusiasm of the young and gain[ed] assistance from the political passivity of the middle-aged and moderate Chinese and from emotional and cultural appeals to a strong and resurgent Modern China".[62] With the pro-Communist elements still entrenched within the PAP in 1959, the British were most concerned, likening the moderate PAP leaders as "riding a tiger".[63] From 1959 to 1965, one of the tasks of the PAP was a successful management of Communism in Singapore, including the so-called Operation Coldstore of February 1963 to detain Communists and their supporters. The PAP took on both colonialism and Communism but each time they returned safely from the dens where tigers crouched.

In conclusion, it would seem clear that the modern transformation of the Chinese political leadership took place in two crucial periods of Singapore history—the 1890s and the 1940s. Each of these historical periods produced somewhat diverse but, nevertheless, modern leaderships with new character and content. The first period of the 1890s created two major strains of leadership: one China-oriented, which included the Pao Huang Hui, the Chung Ho T'ang, the T'ung Meng Hui, the Malayan/Singapore KMT and the Tan Kah Kee leadership; and the other, the SCBA of the Queen's and

---

62   CO 1030/651, Internal Political Situation in Singapore, 1957–59, which contains United Kingdom/United States/French Discussions, Brief for United Kingdom Delegation on Singapore, item 6, no page number given.
63   Ibid, item 6, no page number given.

King's Chinese, who began to exert some influence and left behind legacies in Singapore society. With the exception of the MCP, none harboured any political ambition of overthrowing colonialism.

In contrast, the 1940s helped produce a new breed of leaders, locally born, from among the Chinese and English-educated constituents, who dared challenge colonialism and who aspired to reconstruct a modern Singapore society as master of its own house. This was unmistakably a victory for Singapore nationalism, which had been largely absent in the contending leaderships of the prewar years.

In the process of tracing the rise and demise of Chinese political leaderships in the colonial era, it becomes apparent that the British were unable or unsuccessful in preventing the emergence of Chinese political parties and ideologies. However, they proved to be the final arbiters as to which political party should be denied their *raison d'etre* and which political leaderships should be the successors of colonial rule. Is it any wonder then that one of the most enduring political legacies of the colonial rule was the continuation of an English-educated elite which is still dominating Singapore politics today?

Chapter 6

RECONCEPTUALIZING CHINESE IDENTITY: THE POLITICS OF CHINESENESS IN SINGAPORE

Eugene KB Tan

The geopolitical realities facing Singapore, an economically successful city-state with a population comprising almost 77 per cent ethnic Chinese, have dictated that it exercises great caution in positioning itself with regards to its multi-ethnic and multireligious society and region. The management of ethnic Chinese identity and culture as well as the relationship with Communist China is a delicate exercise in balancing the needs of nation-building, economic development and regime maintenance. This article examines the policy impulses and implications for the changes in reconceptualizing the Chinese-Singaporean identity, which can be attributed to the needs of regime maintenance, buttressed by Confucian ethos, as well as to the security and economic demands of state- and nation-building against the backdrop of a rising regional hegemon in China.

A Quick Overview of the Chinese in Singapore[1]

The statistical notes on the Chinese population in Singapore from the 2000 census would be of interest as demographic indicators of future issues (Department of Statistics, Singapore, 2001). In 2000, the ethnic Chinese comprised 76.8 per cent of the total resident population in Singapore with the median age of 35 years, which was the highest when compared with those of the other races (29 years for the Malays and 33 years for the Indians and Others). Over the last ten years, the median age of the Chinese population had 'aged' by five years from 30 to 35. This is not surprising given that the average number of children born to the Chinese had moved

---

1   A succinct sociohistorical overview of the Chinese community since the founding of Singapore by Raffles and the issues facing the community can be found in Kwok Kian Woon (1998).

from above replacement level to below replacement level in ten years—from 3.4 in 1980 to 2.8 in 1990, and to 2.5 in 2000. In the same period, the average Chinese household size had fallen from 4.8 persons in 1980 to 4.2 in 1990 and to 3.6 in 2000.

The majority of the ethnic Chinese were Buddhists (53.6%, up from 39.4% in 1990), followed by those claiming "no religion" (18.6%), Christians (16.5%), Taoists and those with "Chinese traditional beliefs" (10.8%) and practitioners of other religions (0.5%). Ethnic Chinese believers of Taoism and Chinese traditional beliefs had declined in number significantly—it was the most popular religion among the Chinese in 1980 (38.2%).

In terms of language literate in, ethnic Chinese literate in Chinese only constituted 32 per cent; in English, only 16.4 per cent; in Chinese and English, 48.3 per cent. In terms of language most frequently spoken at home, Mandarin was the most popular with 45.1 per cent (up from 30.1% in 1990). However, an observation has been made that while Chinese Singaporeans are speaking more Mandarin, they are not reading or writing sufficiently in Chinese.[2] Younger Chinese families are much more likely to be English-speaking than older ones. In 1988, only 20 per cent of the Primary 1 cohort came from English-speaking homes. By 1998, the figure had doubled to 40 per cent.[3] As a result of the Speak Mandarin campaign and the no-dialect policy in the media, Chinese dialects have declined significantly in popularity. They were the most popular languages in 1990 with 50.3 per cent speakers and by 2000, this group had declined to 30.7 per cent. English saw a slight increase with from 19.3 per cent speakers to 23.9 per cent. Economically, the ethnic Chinese's average monthly household income from work in 2000 was S$5,219, which was the highest among the races and was also above the national average of S$4,943.

Despite Singapore's Chinese-majority complexion, an Institute of Policy Studies survey in 2000 revealed that the Chinese-Singaporean sense of national pride, although high, did not rank as high as the Indian and the

---

2   See "Fewer here reading and writing Chinese", *The Straits Times*, 7 March 2001, H5. There is also the concern with declining readership of Chinese newspapers among the younger generation, see speech by Prime Minister Goh Chok Tong at the *Lianhe Zaobao* 75th Anniversary Gala Dinner, 6 September 1998, available at <http://app.internet.gov.sg/data/sprinter/pr/archives/1998090602.htm>.

3   Figures provided by BG Lee Hsien Loong, Ministerial Statement on Chinese Language in Schools in Parliament, 20 January 1999, available at <http://app.internet.gov.sg/data/sprinter/pr/archives/1999012002.html>. This is also the case with the Indian community: see "'More Indian pupils now speaking English at home", *The Straits Times*, 4 August 2001, H2.

Malay. Similarly, ethnic Chinese recorded the lowest index scores for citizen-nation psychological ties (Tan and Ooi, 2000).

Within the regional geopolitical setting, Singapore has been careful in nurturing an independent image and downplaying its Chinese majority polity, notwithstanding its Chinese-majority make-up and its strong economic and cultural ties with China and Taiwan. Indeed, Leifer refers to Singapore as "the centre of Overseas Chinese achievement in South-East Asia" (2001: 208). Thus, Singapore's sensitivity to the feelings of its neighbours saw it establishing formal diplomatic ties with China in 1990 only after Malaysia and Indonesia had normalized relations with the regional giant. As Leifer (2000: 18) observes,

> Within its regional environment, a corresponding admiration is mixed with envy and resentment in important part because of the prevailing ethnic-Chinese cultural identity of the island-state and the persistence of the regional middleman role of local Chinese entrenched during the colonial era. That identity has been reinforced from the late 1970s by the government's policy of encouraging the study and use of Mandarin by the vast majority of the population, albeit in conjunction with that of English. That attempt at reinforcing cultural identity has made managing relations with closest neighbours a matter of continuing difficulty and those with the People's Republic of China a matter of acute sensitivity.

There was also the ideological danger posed by China, which was a propagator and active supporter of Communism in Southeast Asia. This was of concern to the Special Branch, the colonial internal security apparatus, from as early as the 1920s (Ban, 2001).[4] The halcyon days of decolonization in Southeast Asia and the Communist-nationalist rivalry in mainland China engaged Malaya/Malaysia and Singapore intensely. Anti-colonialism had a heady mix with anti-revolutionary nationalism. In Singapore, the hold of Communist ideology on the Chinese-educated Chinese was pervasive in the late 1940s up to the mid-1960s, which led Lee Kuan Yew (1998: 280) to remark that,

> ... it was difficult to identify good Chinese-educated candidates who would remain loyal when the Communists opened fired on us [PAP] ... we were fishing on the same pond as the Communists, who exploited both Chinese nationalism and Marxist-Maoist ideas of egalitarianism ... Their mental terms of reference were Chinese history, Chinese parables and proverbs, the

---

4 For a detailed study of Chinese politics in pre-World War II Singapore, see Yong (1992) and Yen (1995).

legendary success of the Chinese communist revolution as against their own frustrating life in Singapore.

But the idea of a Communist united front in post-World War II Singapore is perhaps a misnomer arising from British "heightened official paranoia" (Harper, 2001: 13, 15; see further, Harper, 1999: chaps 2–3). On the cultural gulf between the Chinese-educated and the English-educated in Singapore, Lee (2000: 546–47) added:

> A people steeped in Chinese values had more discipline, were more courteous, and respectful to elders. The result was a more orderly society. When these values were diluted by an English education, the result was less vigour and discipline and more casual behaviour. Worse, the English-educated generally lacked self-confidence because they were not speaking their own native language. The dramatic confrontations between the communist-led Chinese middle school students and my own government brought home these substantial differences in culture and ideals, represented in two different value systems.

But this struggle had impacted significantly upon the "English-educated" PAP elites as well as the "'Chinese-educated' political elites" (Sai and Huang, 1999). The official historiography on the merger, Sai and Huang note, was portrayed as "a Herculean struggle between non-communists and communists" with Chinese education being heavily politicized and "woven into the master narrative as another 'sinister' communist attempt to feed on the dissatisfaction of the Chinese-educated so as to create agitation and tension for political mileage" (Sai and Huang, 1999: 144–45). "The biggest single theme that galvanized the Chinese-speaking was Chinese culture, and the need to preserve Chinese traditions through the Chinese schools. It was not a proletarian issue; it was plain, simple chauvinism" (Lee Kuan Yew, 1998: 185–86). Indeed, much of the merger and the immediate aftermath of separation from Malaysia in August 1965 centred on issues of Chinese education (which is a key dimension of Chinese culture and identity) and have been narrated as the PAP English-educated, multiracial non-Communists triumphing over the Chinese-educated Communists and chauvinists. A key element in the PAP's tactics was "making one notion of 'Chinese-ness', supposedly the communist one, criminal" (Sai and Huang, 1999: 146). Likewise, the British colonial authorities also linked Communism with Chinese ethnicity (Hack, 2001:

---

5   One must not forget that labour issues intertwined with race and ideology. For a discussion on the ethnic Chinese role and identity and the associated nationalist and

234–43).[5] It is this juxtaposition of ethnic and ideological identities that had been firmly imprinted in the national psyche of that period and formed the background to the differences between the "Chinese-educated" and "English-educated" Chinese.

The bruising experience of the PAP's pioneer leaders with the pro-Communist elements resulted in the ruling party and government consciously developing new parapolitical organizations such as the People's Association (PA), Citizens' Consultative Committees (CCCs) and the Community Centre Management Committees (CCMCs) as alternative structures and institutions for political mobilization. The concern then was with the Chinese Chamber of Industry and Commerce, clan associations and powerful and influential Chinese businessmen, who had considerable resources and support to exert influence on local politics "especially on issues regarding culture and language" (Chan and Ng, 2001: 41; Yong, 1992: 273–84). The government opted to alienate the powerful and influential Chinese business community through its "two-legged" policy in which multinational corporations and government-linked companies were co-opted to drive the economic modernization programme (Huff, 1994: 320, 355–57). This strategic economic bypass reduced the degree of government's dependence on the Chinese business community and reduced the latter's influence.

However, the increasing need for a more broad-based economic development, including nurturing small and medium enterprises, has resulted in Chinese capital being integrated back into the economic mainstream (Chan and Ng, 2001: 39).[6] The campaign to build an "Enterprise Ecosystem", with more emphasis being given to the hitherto neglected small and medium enterprises in the deliberate attempt to nurture technopreneurship as well as to compete in the burgeoning China market, will see ethnic Chinese gain increasing prominence in the economic sphere in the years ahead.[7] It is also likely that they will develop into a political constituency which the government will have to manage.

    Communist influence in the development of labour relations in pre-independent Singapore, see Trocki (2001).
6   Chan and Ng (2001) periodizes the history of Chinese business in Singapore into four periods (1819–1958, 1959–75, 1975–89, 1989–present), which roughly coincide with the changes to the management of ethnic relations in independent Singapore.
7   A discussion on the broadening of the industrial base in Singapore's economy in the light of the 2001 economic slowdown can be found in Deputy Prime Minister Tony Tan's speech entitled "The Singapore Economy—Challenges, Prospects and Policies" (available at <http://app.internet.gov.sg/data/sprinter/pr/weekly/2001081304.htm>).

Waxing and Waning of Chineseness in Singapore: The Context

Vasil (1995) divides the Singapore's government's policy on the management of its ethnic diversity into three phases. The first phase, from 1965 to 1979, was characterized by the drive to build a multiracial state. The impetus was the strategic need to avoid being seen as a "third China". More importantly, on the domestic front, there was the pressing need to build a new society from the ashes of the failed "Malaysian Malaysia" project.[8] To this end, the PAP government de-emphasized the Chineseness of what was, in the main, a Chinese-majority island-state.

The focus then was to develop a Singaporean Singapore identity, while recognizing the special position of the indigenous Malays. In terms of the government's approach to education, the focus was on English as the first language for purposes of international commerce, industry and science. The economic rationale alone was good enough to justify the importance placed on the English language. More significantly, the impact on Chinese education and schools was to gradually reduce their relative value in the eyes of Chinese parents and the employers. It should be noted that the fears of destroying Chinese culture, language and education though latent were not a severe problem. Yet the government was very cautious in managing what Lee Kuan Yew called, "a sacred heritage dear to the hearts of all Chinese, especially the poorly educated merchant millionaires and shopkeepers of Singapore" (1998: 170).

The issue of Chinese schools and education was handled very deftly by the PAP's Chinese vanguards such as Ong Pang Boon, Lee Khoon Choy and Jek Yeun Thong (see Sai and Huang, 1999). This was supported by Lee Kuan Yew's conscious efforts in ensuring that the Communists and the chauvinists could not denounce him as a "deculturalized Chinaman" who "preferred English to Chinese as the more important medium of instruction in the schools" (Lee Kuan Yew, 1998: 221–22). The government had its way with Nanyang University (fondly known as "Nantah"), widely perceived by the Chinese-educated as the jewel of Chinese education in Southeast Asia but a bastion of resistance to the government in the field of Chinese education. In 1975, Nanyang University adopted English as the language of instruction and, in 1980, it merged with the University of

---

8   Note that the concept of a multiracial nation for Malaya was probably first discussed and developed by the Straits-born Tan Cheng Lock as early as the 1920s. For a succinct discussion of his ideas on multiracialism, see Christie (2001: 118–22).

Singapore to form the present National University of Singapore. Yet, the non-existence of Nantah today rankles a segment of the Chinese population. Nantah was founded as a symbol of Chinese culture and received widespread legendary support from the local as well as regional Chinese community for its founding. Today, there are still calls to revive Nantah.[9]

Where Phase II (1979–90) was concerned, the Speak Mandarin campaign (launched in 1979) was the beginning of the "Asianization" of Singapore. This marked the emphasis on the return to one's cultural roots and heritage as a form of cultural and moral compass in the midst of modernization (some would read it as Westernization). Embedded in the drive was also the concern that the ethnic Chinese were running the risk of being deculturalized. At the same time, the opening of China under Deng Xiaoping heralded significant economic advantages for co-ethnics and Singapore. This was, however, predicated on the Chinese being able to communicate in the lingua franca of the mainland Chinese and an understanding of the Chinese psyche. Thus, the economic value of Mandarin had an undercurrent in the Speak Mandarin campaign. The Special Assistance Plan schools were also introduced in 1979 to preserve the best of the old Chinese schools and also encourage good academic performance in a rich Chinese environment. It was also in the 1980s that the drive towards Confucianism in Singapore's political governance was initiated. The highwater mark was when Confucian Studies was made an approved subject under the Religious Knowledge programme, when ostensibly one would not regard Confucianism as a form of religion (Kuo, 1996).

The concern with the loss of one's cultural heritage, especially among the younger generation, ensured that the Asianization of Singapore continued under Phase III (since 1990). In the early 1990s, the "East Asian Miracle" provided boisterous impetus for Singapore to be the self-declared spokesman on the so-called "Asian Values". And while Confucianization apparently took a back seat, the vehicle for its tacit promotion came under the rubric of Asian Values.

---

9   Probably the most well-known expression for the revival of Nantah was put forth by poet and calligrapher Pan Shou in 1998. He urged renaming the NTU as it would "quieten the hearts of many … If one waits till the next century, it will become an issue of another 100 years". See "Rename NTU, says Pan Shou", *The Straits Times*, 27 August 1998, p 1. Interestingly, NTU President Dr Cham Tao Soon said that he was confident that the name change from "NTU" to the old name "Nantah" would take place in the next ten years. See "NTU can become Nantah once more, says its president", *Today*, 9 July 2001, p 1. See, also, Sai and Huang (1999) and Kwok (1998).

The Creation of Chinese Cultural Elites[10]

The ascendancy of the Chinese language and culture required the foundation of Chinese cultural elites. By 1997, the government was concerned that while Mandarin was gaining popularity, the Chinese community lacked the foundation of a sufficient pool of cultural elites. These elites "have deep knowledge of Chinese language, culture, history, literature and traditions".[11] Where the government was concerned, bilingualism and the mother tongue policy were critical in maintaining social discipline and social values and facilitating economic utility. Deputy Prime Minister Lee Hsien Loong put it succinctly:

> The Government's long-standing policy on bilingualism and learning of mother tongues in schools remains unchanged. English is and will remain our common working language. It is the language of global business, commerce and technology. But the mother tongue gives us a crucial part of our values, roots and identity. It gives us direct access to our cultural heritage, and a world-view that complements the perspective of the English-speaking world. It provides us the ballast to face adversity and challenges with fortitude, and a sense of quiet confidence about our place in the world. Maintaining our distinctiveness and identity as an Asian society will help us to endure as a nation. This applies to all ethnic groups.

Language was seen as the key to unlock the wisdom, legacy and virtues of a 5,000-year-old civilization and supporters welcomed such efforts to promote the Chinese cultural heritage. Not surprisingly, the emphasis on bilingualism and the mother tongue in schools had its detractors. Detractors were concerned that the focus on the proficiency of mother tongue as an important criterion for doing well in the education system here unduly punished students who were weak in the mother tongue for some reason or other. It was also reported that the uncompromising policy on bilingualism and mother tongue for the ethnic Chinese students was one of the reasons cited for emigration of young Chinese families.

In an attempt to bridge the middle ground, the government made a

---

10 Quotes in this section, unless otherwise stated, are taken from Deputy Prime Minister BG Lee Hsien Loong's Ministerial Statement on "Chinese Language in Schools" in Parliament, 20 January 1999; available at <http://app.internet.gov.sg/data/sprinter/pr/archives/1999012002.html>.

11 Prime Minister Goh Chok Tong in his National Day Rally Speech in Mandarin, 24 August 1997; available at <http://app.internet.gov.sg/data/sprinter/pr/archives/199708240c.htm>.

comprehensive review and announced changes to the teaching of the Chinese language, which it regarded as "a vital issue". Announced in 1999, the changes had the twin aims of "(1) reproducing a core group of Singaporeans who are steeped in the Chinese cultural heritage, history, literature and the arts—we need them to be Chinese language teachers, writers, journalists, community leaders, MPs and Ministers; and (2) to set realistic standards in CL [Chinese Language] for all pupils, including those from English-speaking homes".

On the production of a Chinese cultural elite, BG Lee Hsien Loong elaborated that:

> The Chinese cultural elite are an important source of strength for our multiracial, multireligious society. Their group instincts, political and social values, and social cohesion complement the different spirit and outlook of English-educated Singaporeans. Chinese High School and Raffles Institution are both outstanding schools, but the pupils they produce are sharply of different moulds. Singapore society would be poorer, and weaker, if it had only one of the two.

He was also quick to caution:

> But we cannot aim to preserve our Chinese elite exactly in the form of the 1950s or 1960s. That was a product of the particular phase of our history: postwar colonial Singapore, in an anti-colonial struggle for independence. The Chinese elite played a major role, both on the Communist and non-Communist sides. Their support was again important later, in an anti-communal struggle after Singapore entered Malaysia. That period has passed. Even in China, Hong Kong and Taiwan, the values and culture have not remained static. They have evolved differently, in response to different political and social pressures. So the Chinese elite in Singapore must develop, and help Chinese culture to play its rightful role in shaping our cosmopolitan society and knowledge economy of the 21st century.[12]

As for setting realistic standards for the mother tongue policy, which also saw the creation of the Chinese Language B syllabus, BG Lee remarked:

> We must accept the human limits of our pupils. Very few can be equally proficient in two languages ... I myself did not find Chinese easy in secondary school and pre-U, despite being in a Chinese school throughout and speaking Chinese at home with my father ... We must set our Chinese requirements at

---

12 See "Alumni group to groom Chinese elite", *The Sunday Times*, 18 February 2001, p 32.

a realistic level, particularly for CL, which the main bulk of the students take. The standard cannot just depend on what we like to see, but also on what empirical experience tells us that students can reach and cope with.

Yet, a term like "Chinese elite" is bound to cause relative unease; never mind if the offer is open for the other races to have their own cultural elites.[13]

The Electoral Politics of Chineseness

The distinction between the Chinese-educated and English-educated is now overlaid by the distinction between cosmopolitan and heartlander, which arguably is also a metaphor for the English-speaking and Chinese-speaking (see discussion below). This overlays the earlier divide between the English-educated and the Chinese-educated. Notwithstanding this development, the government has paid close attention to the issues of Chinese language, culture and education. It should be noted that the Chinese-educated Chinese continue to see themselves as being marginalized (Kwok, 1998: 215). Although this group is declining in numbers, there are political repercussions, especially during the elections.

The PAP has felt the need to be sensitive to the Chinese-educated given their numbers. In this regard, there is the constant fear of being outflanked or for others to be seen to be more Chinese than the PAP leadership. This was amply demonstrated in the 1997 general election where Workers' Party candidate Tang Liang Hong was accused by the PAP of being a "Chinese chauvinist", anti-English-educated and anti-Christian. Senior Minister Lee Kuan Yew drew a distinction between Singapore being a "China base" and "an ethnic Chinese base", with the former being dangerous (see also George, 2000: 108–13; and Kwok, 1998: 215). The electoral battle in 1997 drew attention to the uneasy relationship between the Chinese-educated and English-educated Chinese even after 30 years of nation-building. It highlighted the fact that despite prominence given to Chinese culture and language as a bulwark against Western decadence and individualism, new fissures were developing. More accurately, one could see the configurations of the putative distinction on the basis of values, talent and economic mobility.

---

13 Warren Fernandez, "S'pore still walks language tightrope" and Chua Lee Hoong, "These days, one language can highlight three divides", in *The Straits Times*, 23 January 1999, p 59.

Beyond refining policies that emphasize Chinese language and culture, the PAP places the onus on itself to field a sufficient number of candidates who are deemed acceptable to the Chinese-educated or who have the necessary Mandarin and/or Chinese dialect proficiency. Given that Mandarin is increasingly popular, the need to woo the Chinese-educated and lower-income electorate ("heartlanders" in PM Goh's terminology) will remain part of the dynamics at play on the electoral landscape. Indeed, the government has formed a Chinese community liaison group which comprises mainly Chinese-educated MPs. This group is tasked with helping the government to be "attuned to sentiments in the politically important Chinese-speaking community ... [and] to make sure this community does not feel marginalized in increasingly English-speaking Singapore".[14] One feedback that has been highlighted is that the government should make "a special effort to retain our [Chinese] culture and traditions".[15] The ruling party cannot allow another political party to be more Chinese than itself; otherwise, the PAP could potentially lose a critical and influential vote-bank.

The challenge is to maintain an even keel in seeking to capture the ethnic Chinese vote—electoral expediency can quietly undermine the multiracial policy by unwittingly encouraging ethnic outflanking. In Singapore's case, intra-Chinese outflanking can have negative knock-on effects on how the other racial groups might canvas for their own cultural and political space.

Attributes of Chineseness and Confucianism in Singapore's Political Discourse

> *This value-transformation [to individualism] was regarded with concern by the government because it was seen to influence national competitiveness, prosperity, and even survival as a nation.* (Hill, 2000: 187)

I would like to examine two issues—the dominant Confucian ethos in Singapore political governance and the heartlander-cosmopolitan

---

14　Leong Weng Kam, "MPs begin new round of visits to Chinese groups", *The Straits Times*, 16 February 2001, H8.
15　This was revealed by Prime Minister Goh's speech in Chinese in the 2001 National Day Rally; the English translation of this speech can be found at <http://app.internet.gov.sg/data/sprinter/pr/archives/2001081901.htm>.

distinction—which, although appearing to be tangential to the issues of Chinese culture and identity, demonstrate the creeping Chineseness in Singapore's political discourse as well as the boundaries of a new distinction within the Chinese community.

The starting premise for the political leadership here is that language and culture can act as a cultural ballast and provide the necessary inoculation against deculturalization. The landmark Goh Keng Swee 1978 Education Report and the Ong Teng Cheong 1979 Moral Education Report set the scene for the promotion of Mandarin (and the other mother tongues) and laid the groundwork for the propagation of Asian Values. The Asian Values discourse gives a civilizational-cum-philosophical dimension and justification to the particularistic style of governance in Singapore. Yet it is this conflation of the needs of state-building with nation-building that has pushed aspects of Chineseness to the forefront of political discourse in Singapore and has created some unease among the minorities about Singapore's national identity.

At the core, the issue is whether a Singaporean Singapore identity is too Chinese-dominant such that the national identity and value system become problematic for the minority races to internalize. What is clear is that with the particularistic political culture in Singapore, which is heavily influenced by neo-Confucianist thinking, the Singapore political leadership subscribes to the Confucian precept that leaders have a moral duty to act in the collective interest. It is from this that they derive their moral authority to govern.[16] This system of government is presumed to be virtuous and to be trustworthy. As such, it should not be subjected to the pervasive scrutiny that political leaders in liberal democracies are subjected. To do so would undermine the integrity of the political system and governance would be more difficult and its focus diffused, imperilling the common good. Indeed,

---

16 Lee Kuan Yew argues that good government is what people want and that cultural values *a la* "Asian Values" play a determinant role in deciding the political norms of a society:
> What Asians value may not necessarily be what Americans or Europeans value. Westerners value the freedoms and liberties of the individual. As an Asian of Chinese cultural background, my values are for a government which is honest, effective and efficient in protecting its people, and allowing opportunities for all to advance themselves in a stable and orderly society, where they can live a good life and raise their children to do better than themselves ... Very few democratically elected governments in the Third World uphold these values. But it is what their people want ... It is Asian values that have enabled Singapore to contain its drug problem ... (quoted in Han et al, 1998: 376–83 at 380).

the government's imprimatur has been given Confucian notion of good government by good men. The White Paper on Singapore's Shared Values affirmed:

> The concept of government by honourable men (*junzi*) who have a duty to do right for the people, and who have the trust and respect of the population, fits us better than the Western idea that a government should be given as limited powers as possible, and should always be treated with suspicion unless proven otherwise.[17]

In January 1999, at the Davos World Economic Forum, Lee Kuan Yew stated that he had in his speeches all along referred to "Confucianist values" rather than "Asian Values". He added that, "When the West, especially Western journalists, use the term 'Asian values', they mean it as an antithesis to Western values. But there are actually many kinds of Asian values".[18] It is questionable whether given the multi-ethnic make-up of Singapore, Confucianist values in whatever packaging would find resonance in the non-ethnic Chinese population let alone the Chinese community. It would be hard to deny the Confucian core of Singapore's Shared Values although rigorous efforts were made, prior to the adoption, to highlight the Shared Values' commonality with all the cultural traditions and value systems of the major racial groups. While once subtle, the Confucianist dimension can now be arguably perceived to be more evident in the Singapore conception of good government. Confucianism, even if modified to suit local needs, is still regarded as being Chinese and this questions its universal appeal to non-ethnic Chinese Singaporeans even if its modified variant is incorporated as the cornerstone of Singapore's political philosophy.

Translated into practice, the Asian Values school sanctions, on the principle of cultural specificity, a less universalistic stance in areas where adherence to international norms is less critical in the functioning of a modern economy and where sociocultural values and principles of political governance are at stake. This inevitably results in cultural relativism justifying why the Singapore way is unique and superior to Western liberal democracy. The emphasis on duties, rather than rights, and the priority of society's interests can be distilled on closer observation. This idea and belief of collective security and wellbeing, manifested in the community's interests

---

17 For an elaboration of the Confucian *junzi*, see Wm Theodore de Bary (1991: 24–45).
18 See "'Asian values'? I didn't use this term, says SM", *The Straits Times*, 30 January 1999, p 6; "Looking to the Future", *Asiaweek*, 21 May 1999, p 34. Note that this begs the question of the supposed cultural universality of Asian values.

gaining precedence over the individual is commonly characterized as "communitarianism". However, this tends to result in the blurring of distinctions among state, community and individual interests. Nevertheless, the community-first philosophy and aspects of Asian values are now enshrined in Singapore's Shared Values, which the government introduced in January 1993.[19]

Ironically, Singapore-style communitarianism, while stressing cultural particularity, might well in time result in a potentially fragmented society. In emphasizing a civilizational discourse in ensuring that there is a cultural ballast to maintain the desired value system amid economic imperatives of globalization and liberalization, resort has been made to the separate ethnic, cultural and religious values and identities. A neo-Confucianist approach might cohere with the majority Chinese but would certainly smack of ethnic domination where the minorities are concerned. If an overarching identity cannot be forged, centrifugal forces would be set in motion undermining the nation-building efforts.

The Intra-ethnic Divisions: the Heartlander-Cosmopolitan Divide

At the National Day Rally in 1999, Prime Minister Goh Chok Tong spoke of the heartlander-cosmopolitan divide in Singapore society. The coinage of the description of these two groups of Singaporeans was in the context of his discussing whether Singapore would endure. For the purposes of the discussion, I have tabulated the Prime Minister Goh's delineation of the differences between cosmopolitans and heartlanders on the following page.

---

19 The Shared Values, which are akin to a national ideology, enshrine the political ethos deemed vital to Singapore's survival. They are also said to reflect the sociocultural mores of Singapore society and mobilized as an axiom of faith by which Singaporeans of all races and religious beliefs could subscribe to and live by as part of the nation-building process. The Shared Values are: (1) Nation before community and society above self; (2) Family as the basic unit of society; (3) Community support and respect for the individual; (4) Consensus, not conflict; and (5) Racial and religious harmony. The element of the community, beginning with the family as the smallest unit and the state as the largest, is patently evident. The Shared Values are also expected to be a safeguard against undesirable values permeating from more developed countries that are detrimental to Singapore's social fabric (White Paper on Shared Values, 1991). See also Meyer (2000) for a discussion on the centrality of the family in Confucian thought.

	Heartlanders	**Cosmopolitans**
Attributes	"... make their living within the country. Their orientation and interests are local rather than international. Their skills are not marketable beyond Singapore. They speak Singlish. They include taxi-drivers, stallholders, provision shop owners, production workers and contractors. Phua Chu Kang is a typical heartlander. Another one is Tan Ah Teck. If they emigrate to America, they will probably settle in a Chinatown, open a Chinese restaurant and call it an "eating house".	"... their outlook is international. They speak English but are bilingual. They have skills that command good incomes— in banking, IT, engineering, science and technology. They produce goods and services for the global market. Many cosmopolitans use Singapore as a base to operate in the region. They can work and be comfortable anywhere in the world."
Utility to Singapore ("Both heartlanders and cosmopolitans are important to Singapore's wellbeing.")	"Heartlanders play a major role in maintaining our core values and our social stability. They are the core of our society. Without them, there will be no safe and stable Singapore, no Singapore system, no Singapore brand name."	"Cosmopolitans, on the other hand, are indispensable in generating wealth for Singapore. They extend our economic reach. The world is their market. Without them, Singapore cannot run as an efficient, high performance society."
Challenge for Singapore	"... to get the heartlanders to understand what the cosmopolitans contribute to Singapore's and their own wellbeing ..."	"... to get the cosmopolitans to feel an obligation and sense of duty to the heartlanders."

The terminology is unfortunate because in stereotyping, it is by no means clear who a heartlander is and who, a cosmopolitan. Given Singapore's racial and socioeconomic make-up, it can be argued that the typical cosmopolitan is akin to your "English-educated"/English-speaking Chinese while the heartlander is a "Chinese-educated"/Chinese-speaking Chinese. It refreshes the characterization of the Chinese-educated and English-educated Chinese in a new form although the substance of the differences is undiluted in any significant way.

Yet the cosmopolitan-heartlander divide is not about dollars and cents *per se*; the divide is about values and talents. The heartlanders are characterized as the culture carriers as "they play a major role in maintaining our core values and our social stability. They are the core of our society". In short, the heartlander provides the cultural ballast for a disciplined society that would help ensure continued survival and prosperity. On the other hand, the cosmopolitan is a global citizen whose loyalty is probably fluid. The cosmopolitan is valued for his economic contributions—he is the economic dynamo who is modernized (read "Westernized") and, in PM Goh's words, "indispensable in generating wealth for Singapore".

What can be discerned is that one segment of Singapore's population provides the cultural and moral anchor; the other segment is an economic dynamo but whose loyalties are more fluid, dictated by economic considerations and enjoying, in Ong Aihwa's description, "flexible citizenship". Hence, the Prime Minister's caution that "If cosmopolitans and heartlanders cease to identify with each other, our society will fall apart". In short, the social and political obligations are demarcated. There cannot be room for envy by the heartlander of the cosmopolitan. At the same time, the cosmopolitan must exercise his moral duty towards the heartlander although it is unclear what this obligation and sense of duty should be. The attributes ascribed to the two groups mirror those of the Chinese-educated and English-educated and their relative adaptability to globalization. Ultimately, the heartlander-cosmopolitan distinction does not assist in bridging the differences in a globalized world. Instead, it hardens the supposed differences and preserves the cultural-economic divide within the Chinese-Singaporean community in stark terms.

Origins of Nation-Building in Singapore: the Sun Yat-sen connection?

The modern nation-state, as Benedict Anderson suggests, tends to project its history back to a geographic and cultural entity with a long past so as to derive some dimension of heritage, legitimacy and standing born of the *longue duree* (Anderson, 1991). The dialogue between tradition and modernity in the reconceptualizing of Chinese identity has its resonance in Singapore. At the same time, the resonance has its unevenness and its contradictions. Indeed, Singapore's restless search for a national past that is inspiring has led to Chinese national history, or the Chinese civilizational discourse, being intertwined with Singapore's historiography. One area is in defining the national past, which requires the "invention of tradition", national myths, national heroes that can be internalized by the citizenry (Hobsbawm and Ranger, 1983).

In attempting to hitch the Singapore independence story onto the larger canvas of international history and relations, as well as the Chinese civilizational discourse, Singapore's nationalism has been identified as having its inspirations from Dr Sun Yat-sen's 1911 revolution. Singapore and the ethnic Chinese living there then are now portrayed as having shaped and contributed to the diasporic nationalism. The villa, which Sun used as his temporary headquarters in Southeast Asia for his revolutionary cause between 1900 and 1911 and at which he stayed when he visited Singapore, was gazetted as a national monument in 1994. Now renamed the "Sun Yat Sen Nanyang Memorial Hall", it was opened by Senior Minister Lee Kuan Yew on 12 November 2001, which was Sun's birthday. The event also marked the 90th anniversary of the Chinese revolution.[20]

The revival of interest in Sun—as manifested in the Sun Yat Sen Nanyang Memorial Hall—is also a celebration of the cultural idea of being Chinese as well as the transformation of the Chinese mind catalysed by Sun. Trade and Industry Minister BG George Yeo has recently expressed that:

> The 1911 revolution contributed to Singapore's anti-colonial movement and, later, independence. And the Chinese nationalism awakened by Dr Sun provided a lot of energy for Singapore's nationalism. The villa [the Sun Yat-sen villa] is a testament to the historical contributions our forefathers made to that important revolution, not only with money but also with their blood and their lives. Singapore Chinese should take great pride in this.[21]

In this historiography, Singapore's nationalism is traced to the 1911 revolution, which, of course, has its roots in late 19th century China. This claim to lineage with Chinese civilizational nationalism is a quantum leap whose resonance is uncertain and likely to be contested. The potential to marginalize the non-Chinese racial groups is significant if indigenous Singaporean nationalism is ignored or not given due credit along side Sun's. Thus far, the Chinese revolution has not been officially narrated as part of

---

20 Leong Weng Kam, "Sun Yat Sen Villa to recount his life", *The Straits Times*, 29 August 2001, H8. See Huang (2001) for a discussion of the villa's shifting status in Singapore's history.
21 Quoted by Kao Chen in "Historical villa's very slow face-lift", *The Sunday Times*, 26 March 2000, p 36; and Kao Chen, "Sun shone at this old villa", *The Sunday Times*, 2 April 2000, pp 52–53. McKeown reminds us of the nature of Chinese identity at the turn of the 20th century: "To be Chinese, anywhere in the world, was to be a representative of the motherland, to have a stake in the future of China, and to recognize the claims of China and Chinese culture over one's loyalty" (2001: 94).

Singapore's official past but it portends a potential approach to the nation-building in Singapore that seeks to consign Singapore's birth as part of a longer and revolutionary movement in terms of time, ideas and race. This desire for lineage with the *noblesse oblige* of Chinese nationalism can be argued as stemming from an insecurity of Singapore's thrust into independence.

However, this invented tradition of the origins of Singapore's nationalism is a historical rupture and a leap of historical logic considering that Sun and the Chinese revolution were never given credence in the official historiography of the origins of Singapore nationalism. The 'elevation' of Sun and his ideas stands in stark contrast to the two prominent World War II figures who physically fought on Singapore soil against Singapore's aggressors and would therefore have closer affinity to Singapore nationalism than Sun's diasporic nationalism. Major-General Lim Bo Seng and Lieutenant Adnan Saidi, two local heroes during the Japanese Occupation, have recently been deemed unsuitable for elevation as national heroes as they were "defending Singapore for the British, not independent Singapore".[22] But Lim Bo Seng and Adnan Saidi are certainly more in keeping with popular memory and will remain as "military heroes".[23] Sun Yat-sen's supposed heritage for Singapore's nation-building can be categorized as "non-consensual memory" that is hard-pressed for recognition even within the ethnic Chinese community, much less the other races.[24] As Gillis reminds us (1994: 5): "Identities and memories are not things we think about, but things we think *with*."

Although overseas Chinese (Chinese migrants) have been regarded

---

22 PM Goh Chok Tong at the Prime Minister's Forum, Nanyang Technological University, 11 May 1999. The Royal Malaysian Armed Forces have 'adopted' Lt Adnan in recognition of his loyalty and bravery and have made a movie based on him to improve the image and morale of the Malaysian armed forces: "Reel boost for image of armed forces", *The Straits Times*, 11 December 1999, p 54. On the reinsertion of World War II memory into the national narrative of survival and the Singapore national identity project, see Wong (2001).

23 A portrait of Lim Bo Seng hangs prominently in Singapore's SAFTI Military Institute Library. Lim is also commemorated in an exhibition on Force 136 in Fort Siloso on Sentosa. There is a growing Chinese language literature on Force 136, the unit Lim is associated with. Adnan's and the Malay Regiment's heroism are commemorated at the Kent Ridge battlefield site. I am grateful to Mr Kwa Chong Guan for our discussion on this topic.

24 A recent Singapore theatre production on Sun Yat-sen focused on Sun's mistress, Chen Cuifen, although the intent of drawing the political and historical significance of Sun was also evident. See "Women in Waiting", *The Straits Times*, 11 June 2001, L6–L7.

as "the hearth of the Chinese nationalism", this reputation "was earned more by default than intention" (McKeown, 2001: 90; see also chapters 1–3 and 8 on diasporic nationalism). This short illustration of contrasting acceptance and rejection of putative candidates for Singapore's national heritage makes one wonder if the selective adoption of aspects of Chinese national history can be truly accepted if the framework for their incorporation as part of Singapore's national past is contested, if not lacking in resonance among the racial minorities. Yet, it is an unusual application of race to a national discourse that patently needs to be more multiracial and cross-cutting in its appeal and resonance. Singapore's independence had and continues to have broad-based multiracial support. To segment the origins of this collective memory and elevate the role of a sojourner in Singapore, and whose appeal to the Chinese then living here was as Chinese "nationals", is arguably constructing new memories and identities that are unlikely to add value to the nation-building efforts. Instead, it may unwittingly over-emphasize the role of the ethnic Chinese over the other races in Singapore's independence story.

Reassertion of Chineseness

Perhaps the most evident reassertion of Chineseness in Singapore, outside the realm of education, would be in the economic arena. Here one can discern the Singapore strength of straddling East and West as well as the affinity to China by virtue of Singapore's majority race being co-ethnics with Asia's rising power.

One instance would be Singapore's positioning itself as a hub for "knowledge arbitrage" in the field of Chinese business networks. Singapore has aimed to leverage on knowledge arbitrage, which refers to the knowledge and ability to take advantage of market differences in labour costs and product markets within the so-called Chinese commonwealth to maximum advantage (Kao, 1993). This facilitates companies in sourcing for the best production sites based on the determinants of cost of manufacture of products, access to markets and distribution channels. In this age of mobile capital and the expected ascendancy of China as a political and economic power, Singapore has ingeniously transformed its role from mere traders or middlemen to that of the international arbitraguer. This command of cross-cultural accommodation makes Singapore enterprises valuable joint venture partners for foreign multinationals seeking a local partner in Southeast Asia and in China.

In the realm of economics, China is simultaneously seen as a challenge, an opportunity and a threat to Singapore's and Southeast Asia's wellbeing. Sino-Singapore economic relations have been expanding rapidly and China's accession as a member of the World Trade Organization and its hosting of the Olympic Games in 2008 offer further scope for economic ties to develop further. In a bold way, Singapore is attempting to rebrand itself and enhance its competitiveness *vis-à-vis* China by embracing China as its economic hinterland. Singapore seeks to strategically position itself as a gateway for foreign investors intending to break into the China market.[25] Between 1990 and 1999, bilateral trade between Singapore and China increased steadily at an average annual rate of 12 per cent, tripling from 23 billion renminbi (S$5.2 billion) in 1990 to 73 billion renminbi (S$16.3 billion) in 1999. In 2000, Sino-Singapore total trade expanded by 32.4 per cent to 97 billion renminbi (S$21.6 billion). This growth rate outstripped Singapore's growth in total world trade of 23 per cent. Sino-Singapore trade continued to register double-digit growth in the first five months of 2001, reaching 41 billion renminbi (S$9 billion). Today, China is Singapore's sixth largest trading partner and an impressive 40 per cent of Singapore's bilateral trade is accounted for by Guangdong province alone.[26] Not content with the coastal regions, Singapore is seeking to tap the first offerings of China's strategic look West policy. The initial focus has been on business opportunities in the relatively uncharted inner provinces of Xinjiang and Shaanxi.[27] Other initiatives include having government scholars spend a year in China and working with their counterparts to acquire intimate knowledge of China.[28]

All these efforts are part and parcel of the imperative to boost Singapore's share in the China market; the realization is that the cultural affinity and ties as well as good political relations provide an advantage which should be more rigorously tapped. At the same time, Singapore is also alive to the need to cope with the "Chinese juggernaut" which has resulted in lower foreign direct investments in Southeast Asia. Another area that could potentially affect Singapore's economy is closer cross-straits economic relations, which are expected to see the China and Taiwan

---

25 On the growing influence of Michael Porter's cluster theory and need to integrate a city-region with other economic units as a driver of prosperity, see Porter (2000; 2001).
26 Statistics are obtained from speech by Mr Yeo Cheow Tong, Singapore's Minister for Communications and Information Technology, at the official opening ceremony of the joint venture between PSA Corporation Ltd and Guangzhou Harbour Bureau in Guangzhou, China, on 17 July 2001.
27 "BG Yeo in Xinjiang next week", *The Straits Times*, 18 August 2001, p 4.
28 "Govt to find ways to enter China market", *The Straits Times*, 26 July 2001, p 3.

economies integrating fully (Ministry of Trade and Industry 2001). It is clear that the Singapore government approach to China in the economic sphere is to co-opt the opportunities and ameliorate the threats.[29]

Furthermore, Singapore has initiated the following endeavours as a contribution to research and public education on the Chinese overseas: (1) the establishment of the Chinese Heritage Centre in 1995, under the auspices of the Singapore Federation of Chinese Clan Associations, which "can help Singapore develop into an important centre of Sinic studies in the Pacific Rim"; and (2) the establishment of the National Chinese Internet Programme (NCIP) to implement the national initiative to develop Singapore into a cyber-hub for the Chinese Internet. The National Library Board is working jointly with local and foreign organizations and experts in the development of Huayinet, a virtual resource centre on overseas ethnic Chinese communities.[30]

Several other initiatives have been attempted as part of the overall effort of carving for Singapore "a role in the development of Chinese culture and its evolving civilization".[31] In 1991, the Singapore Chinese Chamber of Commerce and Industry initiated the inaugural biennial World Chinese Entrepreneurs Convention in Singapore. Located in Singapore, the Convention Secretariat also manages the online World Chinese Business Network. The government has also been encouraging the various clan associations to reconceptualize their role in the cultural and economic life of the 21st century in order to attract younger members and to reap potential economic benefits from ties based on cultural affinities (see also Liu, 1998). This is also part and parcel of the Asian Values discourse, which still exerts a dominant hold with the Singapore political elite.

Furthermore, Singapore-China ties have grown from strength to strength, with Singapore's development experience being seen as a point of reference and possible blueprint for China.[32] The Singapore model of soft authoritarianism appeals to China (Foot, 2000: 153–57; Bolt, 2000:

---

29 The flurry of ministerial speeches in July and August 2001 on China is evidence of the concern of China's economic growth.
30 The URL for Huayinet is <http://www.huayinet.org>. See Andersson (2001) for a discussion of the intellectual capital among ethnic Chinese academics.
31 Speech by BG George Yeo, Minister for Trade and Industry, at the launch of Huayinet, 11 February 2000; available at <http://app.internet.gov.sg/data/sprinter/pr/archives/2000021101.htm>.
32 It is outside the scope of this article to discuss the intricacies of Sino-Singapore relations; excellent overviews and analysis can be found in Leifer (2000, especially pp 108–12), and Khong (1999). See also Cheung and Tang (2001) for an analysis of the Chinese provinces foreign economic relations, especially with Chinese overseas communities.

143–49).³³ To quote the Senior Minister, "After Deng Xiaoping's southern tour in 1992, delegations from various parts of China visited Singapore to understand how we promoted rapid economic development while maintaining social discipline. We were happy to share our experience with our Chinese friends."³⁴ Industrial parks overseas—in particular, the Suzhou Industrial Park project—are portrayed as instances of Singapore exporting its development model (Gidlund, 2001; Lee, 2001). China has also sought to learn how Singapore's manages the political and social control of infocommunications technology (Lynch, 1999: 211). Over the past decade, increasing economic, political and military contacts have complemented cultural affinity. As Lee proclaimed,

> Successful Chinese communities overseas are a spur to action in China. China's leaders have been studying them ... just by being ourselves, making progress in our lives, Chinese abroad become a powerful pull factor in China's evolution forward. We are living examples of Chinese people, imbued with Chinese culture, doing immensely better because we work under a different system. [quoted in Bolt (2000: 93)]

In the military sphere, Singapore subscribes to the criticality of the triangular equilibrium between China, Japan and the United States of America. Singapore's defence ties with China have recently been described as "progressing on a step-by-step basis" as part of the emerging dynamic geopolitical situation (Karniol, 2001: 32). All things considered, where foreign relations are concerned, given the multifaceted dimension of China-Singapore relations, this cosy state of affairs can be potentially troubling if China seeks to assert quasi-hegemonic dominance of the region and this, in turn, triggers a fresh wave of Sinophobia in Southeast Asia.³⁵

---

33   Castells (2000: 306) observes: "It [Singapore] may also prefigure a successful model for the twenty-first century: a model that is being sought, consciously, by the Chinese communist state, pursuing the developmental goals of a nationalist project." See also Long Hua, "China favours Singapore as political model", *The Straits Times*, 6 July 2001, p 21 (first published in *Hong Kong Economic Journal*).
34   Speech by Senior Minister Lee Kuan Yew at the ceremony to mark the achievements of China-Singapore Suzhou Industrial Park (SIP) 7 Years of Development, 8 June 2001, Suzhou. Not all of Lee's political views are acceptable to the China leadership and this has led the Chinese censors to delete and rewrite parts of Lee's memoirs: see "Chinese censors cut parts of Lee Kuan Yew memoirs", *International Herald Tribune*, 7 August 2001, p 4.
35   As Henry Kissinger reminds us, "China will insist on a political role commensurate with its growing economic power" (2001: 114). On the myths, which can be accentuated to threats, surrounding relations between China and Southeast Asia and China and the Chinese overseas, see Wang (1999; 2000), Goodman (1997/98) and Zha (2000).

The Speak Mandarin campaign has been successful in phasing out Chinese dialects. The new objective of the campaign is to promote "Mandarin as the social language of the Chinese. The educated elite should use more Mandarin socially".[36] The recent debate over the adoption of Western names in preference over or to the exclusion of dialect/*hanyu pinyu* names is one reflection of the saliency of Chinese identity issues.[37] Similarly, the themes that constantly surface include the concerns of Nantah alumni, including their grievance that their contributions have not been adequately recognized; the welfare of Chinese language teachers in schools; the standard of Chinese Language in schools; the revitalizing of Chinese grass-roots organizations such as clan associations; and the loss of Chinese culture among the younger generation.[38]

Conclusion

What is evident in examining Vasil's three-phase typology of ethnic management in Singapore is the confident assertion and promotion of the Chinese identity in tandem with the growing international political and economic stature of China. However, there are implications for nation-building in Singapore. This dialogue between tradition and modernity in the realm of Chinese identity and culture continues in Singapore. While the distinction is no longer the Chinese-educated versus the English-educated *per se*, the differences between the two subgroups within the Chinese community persist. I have suggested that the heartlander-cosmopolitan divide is a new metaphor. This state of affairs mirrors the

---

36 For PM Goh's remarks, see the English text of his National Day Rally speech in Mandarin, 27 August 1994; available at <http://app.internet.gov.sg/data/sprinter/pr/archives/199708240c.htm>. On the evolution of the Speak Mandarin Campaign, see Promote Mandarin Council (2000). The Speak Mandarin Campaign website can be found at <http://mandarin.org.sg>.
37 See, for instance, "Chinese, but they prefer English names", *The Straits Times*, 20 June 2001: H2; and "Ease of use no excuse for dropping Chinese names", *The Straits Times*, 27 June 2001, H1.
38 It is interesting that the successful takeover bid of the Overseas Union Bank by the United Overseas Bank was born out of the desire to keep the entrepreneurial spirit of the Chinese businessmen-founders of both banks alive. This resulted in the government-linked bank, DBS Bank, being unsuccessful in its takeover bid. See "UOB's takeover bid: not just a matter of dollars and cents", *The Straits Times*, 30 June 2001, S15. For an examination of the early Chinese entrepreneurs' contribution to the Singapore economy, see Huff (1994: 208–35).

earlier division in Singapore between the English-educated Chinese and the Chinese-educated. The English-educated Chinese are regarded as being the elites at the centre of power and influence, with the Chinese-educated being at the periphery.

Beyond the goal of nation-building, one cannot ignore the subtle forces and influences of the "ideology of pragmatism" in the management of Chinese identity in Singapore. The hues of Confucian political governance, economic imperatives linked with the burgeoning market and influence as well as the potential threat of China and the ever-present need to ensure electoral support have led to policies and directives that have edged towards a reconceptualization of Chinese identity, which inclines towards a reassertion of the Chinese language, culture and identity. This conflation of nation-building with state-building has led to aspects of Chinese identity, culture and language taking a disproportionate presence over the last 20 years. Such a move has, of course, caused unease among Singapore's minority races and Singapore's immediate geopolitical locale. It would also gradually weaken the multiracial ethos here as it touches a raw nerve among the minorities who have the latent fear of being overwhelmed by the assertion of Chinese identity and culture.[39] This is not to suggest that discrimination on racial grounds has increased in the last two decades. Rather, the concern is that "they will be left out of an increasingly Chinese Singapore" (George, 2000: 162). Prime Minister Goh Chok Tong's reminder is timely:

> ... the outlook of the Chinese community in Singapore has been attuned to its geopolitical environment. The Singaporean Chinese recognize and accept that Chinese culture and Mandarin must be advanced within the multiracial context of Singapore and the political and social milieu of Southeast Asia. They know that the destiny of Singapore is in Southeast Asia. They preserve their heritage but subsume its display under the broader complexion of Singapore nationalism. They leave Singaporeans of all races in no doubt that their political standpoint is solidly based on the national interest of an independent Singapore in Southeast Asia.[40]

---

39 Cf William KM Lee (2001), who controversially argues that the leaders' narrow interpretation of Singapore's success "as result of Chinese cultural influence" and that the privatization of social security policy there has led to in-group posturing, which "promotes a notion that the Chinese are a different species and culturally superior to other ethnic groups".

40 Speech by Prime Minister Goh Chok Tong at the launch of *The Encyclopedia of the Chinese Overseas* at the Chinese Heritage Centre, Nanyang Technological University, 26 October 1998; available at <http://app.internet.gov.sg/data/sprinter/pr/archives/1998102602.htm>.

Singapore's policy of multiracialism is likened to "four overlapping circles" in which the different communities maintain their cultural identity and heritage. The overlapping area must continue to enlarge. Ultimately, the Chinese-Singaporean community, as the dominant majority, needs to be more sensitive to the feelings of the racial minorities at a time when the ethnic Chinese in the region are relatively more confident in asserting their cultural heritage and identity. In the midst of creeping Chineseness in Singapore's society, the challenge is to ensure that the Chinese Singaporean does not become blind to the multiracial composition of Singapore or that Chinese identity becomes conterminous with the Singapore national identity. Such racial hegemony must never be allowed to take root for it will surely tear at Singapore's delicate and maturing social fabric.

References

Anderson, Benedict R O'G. *Imagined Communities: Reflections on the Origin and Spread of Nationalism*. Rev ed. London: Verso, 1991.

Andersson, David E. "Emerging Knowledge Networks in Eastern Asia". In *Asia Pacific Transitions*, edited by David E Andersson and Jessie PH Poon. New York: Palgrave, 2001.

Ban, Kah Choon. *Absent History: The Untold Story of Special Branch Operations in Singapore, 1915–1942*. Singapore: Raffles, 2001.

De Bary, Wm Theodore. *The Trouble with Confucianism*. Cambridge, MA: Harvard University Press, 1991.

Bolt, Paul J. *China and Southeast Asia's Ethnic Chinese: State and Diaspora in Contemporary Asia*. Westport, CN: Praeger, 2000.

Castells, Manuel. *End of Millennium*. 2nd ed. Malden, MA: Blackwell Publishers, 2000.

Chan, Kwok Bun, and Ng Beoy Kui. "Singapore". In *Chinese Business in Southeast Asia: Contesting Cultural Explanations, Researching Entrepreneurship*, edited by Edmund Terence Gomez and Hsin-Huang Michael Hsiao. Surrey: Curzon Press, 2001.

Cheung, Peter TY, and James TH Tang. "The External Relations of China's Provinces". In *The Making of Chinese Foreign and Security Policy in the Era of Reform, 1978–2000*, edited by David M Lampton. Stanford, CA: Stanford University Press, 2001.

Christie, Clive. *Ideology and Revolution in Southeast Asia, 1900–1980: Political Ideas of the Anti-Colonial Era*. Surrey: Curzon Press, 2001.

Department of Statistics, Singapore. May 2001. *Singapore Population*. Available online at <www.singstat.gov.sg>.

Duara, Prasenjit. "Nationalists among Transnationals: Overseas Chinese and the

Idea of China, 1900–1911". In *Ungrounded Empires: The Cultural Politics of Modern Chinese Transnationalism*, edited by Aihwa Ong and Donald Nonini. London and New York: Routledge, 1997.

Foot, Rosemary. *Rights beyond Borders: The Global Community and the Struggle over Human Rights in China*. New York: Oxford University Press, 2000.

George, Cherian. *Singapore: The Air-conditioned Nation, Essays of the Politics of Comfort and Control, 1990–2000*. Singapore: Landmark Books, 2000.

Gidlund, Janerik. "Illiberal and Successful? In Search of Sustainable Regional Growth in Authoritarian States". In *Asia Pacific Transitions*, edited by David E Andersson and Jessie PH Poon. New York: Palgrave, 2001.

Gillis, John R. "Memory and Identity: The History of a Relationship". In *Commemorations: The Politics of National Identity*, edited by John R Gillis. Princeton, NJ: Princeton University Press, 1994.

Goh, Keng Swee, and the Education Study Team. *Report on the Ministry of Education 1978*. Singapore: Singapore National Printers, 1979.

Goodman, David SG. "Are Asia's 'Ethnic Chinese' a Regional Security Threat?" *Survival* 39, no 4 (1997/98): 140–55.

Hack, Karl. *Defence and Decolonisation in Southeast Asia: Britain, Malaya and Singapore, 1941–1968*. Surrey, Richmond: Curzon Press, 2001.

Han, Fook Kwang, Warren Fernandez and Sumiko Tan. *Lee Kuan Yew: The Man and His Ideas*. Singapore: Singapore Press Holdings and Times Editions, 1998.

Harper, TN. "Lim Chin Siong and the 'Singapore Story'". In *Comet in Our Sky: Lim Chin Siong in History*, edited by Tan Jing Quee and KS Jomo. Kuala Lumpur: INSAN, 2001.

―――. *The End of the Empire and the Making of Malaya*. Cambridge: Cambridge University Press, 1999.

Hill, Michael. "'Asian Values' as Reverse Orientalism: Singapore". *Asia Pacific Viewpoint*, vol 41, no 2: 177–90.

Hobsbawm, Eric, and Terence Ranger, eds. *The Invention of Tradition*. Cambridge: Cambridge University Press, 1983.

Huang, Jianli. "Dissonant Narratives of the Past: Positioning the Sun Yat Sen Villa in Singapore". Paper presented at the international conference on the "Ethnic Chinese in Singapore and Malaysia: A Dialogue between Tradition and Modernity", Singapore, 2001.

Huff, WG. *The Economic Growth of Singapore: Trade and Development in the Twentieth Century*. Cambridge: Cambridge University Press, 1994.

Kao, John. "The World Wide Web of Chinese Business". *Harvard Business Review* 71, no 2 (1993): 24–36.

Karniol, Robert. "Interview with Dr Tony Tan Keng Yam, Deputy Prime Minister and Minister for Defence of Singapore". *Jane's Defence Weekly* 35, no 26 (27 June 2001): 32.

Khong, Yuen Foong. "Singapore: A Time for Economic and Political Engagement". In *Engaging China: The Management of an Emerging Power*, edited by Alastair Iain Johnston and Robert S Ross. London: Routledge, 1999.

Kissinger, Henry. *Does America Need a Foreign Policy? Toward a Diplomacy for the 21st Century*. New York: Simon and Schuster, 2001.

Kuo, Eddie CY. "Confucianism as Political Discourse in Singapore: The Case of an Incomplete Revitalization Movement". In *Confucian Traditions in East Asian Modernity: Moral Education and Economic Culture in Japan and the Four Mini-Dragons*, edited by Tu Wei-ming. Cambridge, MA: Harvard University Press, 1996.

Kwok, Kian Woon. "Singapore". In *The Encyclopedia of the Chinese Overseas*, edited by Lynn Pan. Singapore: Archipelago Press and Landmark Books, 1998.

Lee, Kuan Yew. *From Third World to First: The Singapore Story 1965–2000, Memoirs of Lee Kuan Yew*. Singapore: Singapore Press Holdings and Times Editions, 2000.

———. *The Singapore Story: Memoirs of Lee Kuan Yew*. Singapore: Singapore Press Holdings and Times Editions, 1998.

Lee, William KM. "Ethnicity and Ageing in Singapore". *Asian Ethnicity* 2, no 2: 163–76.

Lee, Lai To. "The Lion and the Dragon: A View on Singapore-China Relations". *Journal of Contemporary China* 10, no 28: 415–25.

Leifer, Michael. *Singapore's Foreign Policy: Coping with Vulnerability*. London: Routledge, 2000.

———. *Dictionary of the Modern Politics of South-East Asia*. 3rd ed. London and New York: Routledge, 2001.

Liu, Hong. "Old Linkages, New Networks: The Globalization of Overseas Chinese Voluntary Associations and Its Implications". *The China Quarterly* 155: 582–609.

Lynch, Daniel C. *After the Propaganda State: Media, Politics, and 'Thought Work' in Reformed China*. Stanford, CA: Stanford University Press, 1999.

McKeown, Adam. *Chinese Migrant Networks and Cultural Change: Peru, Chicago and Hawaii, 1900–1936*. Chicago, IL: The University of Chicago Press, 2001.

Meyer, Jeffrey F. "Concord and Conflict from a Confucian Perspective: The Paradigm of the Family". In *Ideas of Concord and Discord in Selected World Religions*, edited by Joseph B Gittler. Stamford, CN: JAI Press, 2000.

Ministry of Trade and Industry. *Convergence of Cross-Straits Economic Interests and Implications for Singapore*. Singapore: Ministry of Trade and Industry, August 2001 (accessed on 15 August 2001 @ www.mti.gov.sg).

Ong, Aihwa. *Flexible Citizenship: The Cultural Logics of Transnationality*. Durham, NC: Duke University Press, 2000.

Ong, Teng Cheong, and [the] Moral Education Committee. *Report on Moral Education 1979*. Singapore: Singapore National Printers, 1979.

Porter, Michael E. "Locations, Clusters, and Company Strategy". In *The Oxford Handbook of Economic Geography*, edited by Gordon L Clark, Maryann P Feldman and Meric S Gertler (with the assistance of Kate Williams). Oxford: Oxford University Press, 2000.

———. "Regions and the New Economics of Competition". In *Global City-Regions: Trends, Theory, Policy*, edited by Allen J Scott. Oxford: Oxford University Press, 2001.

Promote Mandarin Council. *Mandarin: The Chinese Connection*. Singapore: Ministry of Information and the Arts, Singapore, 2000.

Sai, Siew Min, and Huang Jianli. "The 'Chinese-educated' Political Vanguards: Ong Pang Boon, Lee Khoon Choy and Jek Yeun Thong". In *Lee's Lieutenants: Singapore's Old Guard*, edited by Lam Peng Er and Kevin YL Tan. St Leonards, NSW: Allen and Unwin, 1999.

Tan, Ern Ser, and Ooi Giok Ling. *Citizens and the Nation—IPS Survey of National Pride and Psychological Ties to the Nation*. Singapore: Institute of Policy Studies, 2000.

Trocki, Carl A. "Development of Labour Organisation in Singapore, 1800–1960". *Australian Journal of Politics and History* 47, no 1 (2001): 115–29.

Vasil, Raj K. *Asianising Singapore: The PAP's Management of Ethnicity*. Singapore: Heinemann Asia, 1995.

Wang, Gungwu. *China and Southeast Asia: Myths, Threats and Culture*. Singapore: World Scientific and Singapore University Press, 1999.

———. *The Chinese Overseas: From Earthbound China to the Quest for Autonomy*. Cambridge, MA: Harvard University Press, 2000.

Wong, Diana. "Memory Suppression and Memory Production: The Japanese Occupation of Singapore". In *Perilous Memories: The Asia-Pacific War(s)*, edited by T Fujitani, Geoffrey M White and Lisa Yoneyama. Durham, NC: Duke University Press, 2001.

Yen, Ching-hwang. *Studies in Modern Overseas Chinese History*. Singapore: Times Academic Press, 1995.

Yong, Ching Fatt. *Chinese Leadership and Power in Colonial Singapore*. Singapore: Times Academic Press, 1992.

Zha, Daojiong. "China and the May 1998 Riots of Indonesia: Exploring the Issues". *The Pacific Review* 13, no 4 (2000): 557–75.

Chapter 7

BUREAUCRATIC PARTICIPATION AND POLITICAL MOBILIZATION: COMPARING PRE- AND POST-1970 MALAYSIAN CHINESE POLITICAL PARTICIPATION

Ho Khai Leong

> People vote their resentment, not their appreciation. The average man does not vote for anything, but against something.
>
> — *William Bennett Munro*

Introduction

One major hallmark of meaningful citizenship is individual or organized participation in the political process. Participation ranges from passive observation from the sidelines to active involvement such as standing for elected office. Citizens' political participation, however, does not necessarily lead to influence or power in governance. There exists a gap between participatory politics and policy output. The incongruence between these two entities sometimes can be daunting. Power at the base in the form of electorate mobilization may not necessarily be translated into power at the apex of the political hierarchy. As Robert J Pranger remarks: "Power means the relatively greater ability some persons have to control (or dominate) a hierarchically structured group's resources."[1] Representation in the government, while duly acknowledged, has diminished in significance. Indeed, the same author argues, "representation is now fading into more oligarchic forms of power."[2]

In political science literature, discussions on political participation tend to concentrate on two major issues: the value of political participation

---

1 Robert J Pranger, *The Ellipse of Citizenship*, New York: Holt, Rinehart and Winston, 1968, p 13.
2 Ibid, p 13.

to individuals and the political system, and the causes of participation and non-participation. In this article, I am more interested in the patterns of political participation, specifically ethnic Chinese political participation, and their implications on the Malaysian political development.

With this theoretical premise, this article argues that the political participation of ethnic Chinese in Peninsular Malaysia can be conceptualized as a two-facet phenomenon, that is, political mobilization and bureaucratic participation. Malaysian Chinese electorates mobilized at the grass-roots level generally are sympathetic to the political oppositions while the Chinese political elites share power with the Malay political class in the form of bureaucratic involvement. The Chinese-based political parties (ie, MCA, Gerakan and DAP) do fulfil the different functions of a political party, namely representation, elite recruitment, socialization, mobilization and organization of government—each in its own unique way. This article does not quarrel with the arguments that the Malaysian Chinese are politically marginalized—indeed, they have been relatively deprived of power in the major decision-making processes in the UMNO-dominated government, despite the fact that they are "represented" in the government by Chinese-based political parties, or that they have been "encapsulated" in the Malaysian political process.[3] This article suggests, in addition to these arguments of political marginalization and encapsulation, there is a counter-current that is equally intense and forceful, occurring at the mass level, that has made ethnic Chinese political participation a complex and multifaceted phenomenon.

In general, this article discusses the transformation of Chinese political participation in Peninsular Malaysia before and after 1970, which witnessed the implementation of the New Economic Policy (NEP) after the racial riots of 1969. It will first examine the characteristics of the Malaysian political system *vis-à-vis* the impact on Chinese political participation. The period *circa* 1970–71 is chosen as the major turning-point in the transformation of regime pattern, which bears significant ramifications for both inter- and intra-ethnic relations. Next, the patterns of Chinese political participation in these two periods are analysed. The major arguments are: (1) the NEP has transformed the Malaysian political system into a more Bumiputera-centric polity, which has important implications for balance of power; (2) that the

---

3   For these arguments, see Heng Pek Koon, *Chinese Politics in Malaysia—A History of the Malaysian Chinese Association*, Kuala Lumpur: Oxford University Press, 1988; and Judith Strauch, *Chinese Village Politics in the Malaysia State*, Cambridge, Mass: Harvard University Press, 1981.

Malaysian Chinese, who are part of the decision-making process in the government, have been further marginalized in the Malay-dominated state; and (3) in post-1970, political participation of the Malaysian Chinese has taken the form of bureaucratic involvement at the elite level and mobilization at the mass level.

There is one caveat, though. Since the period under discussion is extremely long, recent developments in the 1990s will only be mentioned in passing. It is the author's view that the political changes in Malaysia affecting ethnic Chinese participation in the 1990s deserve a more thorough examination than the limitation of this short article.

The Malaysian Political System: Pre- and Post-1970

The essential feature of the pre- and post-Malaysian state is that of Malay dominance. Malay interests and ethos have prevailed in almost all decisions, and domestic policies are predominantly defined in those terms. From this perspective, Malay ethnic interests cannot be challenged, and Malay official thinking perceives any challenge from non-Malays as ultimately an unstable force which would bring chaos to the system. This understanding has been quite explicitly stated by Malay political elites as well, though challenged by an increasing number of non-Malay politicians and intellectuals.[4]

Malay dominance, of course, has its historical roots. It was first embedded in the special rights provision in the Malayan Constitution. In the Constitution that came into operation in 1957, Malay special rights received constitutional sanction and protection. Article 153 of the Constitution authorized a system "to safeguard the special position of the Malays through a system of quotas applied to the public service, to scholarships, to training privileges and to licences for any trade or business" while the Yang di Pertuan Agong was entrusted with the responsibility of reserving for the Malays "such proportion as he may deem reasonable of positions in the public service".[5]

In multiracial Malaysia, politicians have generally found that appeals to racial loyalties have been the most effective means of mobilizing political and economic support among the masses. As such, the political expediency of the ethnic quota system increases the likelihood that it will continue to

---

4   Abdullah Ahmad, *Issues in Malaysian Politics*, Singapore: Singapore Institute of International Affairs, 1988.
5   *Federal Constitution*, Kuala Lumpur: Government of Malaysia, p 145.

be a feature in Malaysian politics. This view, of course, has been challenged by the non-Malay community. For the non-Malays, the referent unit of politics as Malay community interests is dubious at best. Some commentators have argued that the so-called *merdeka* "bargain"—that the Malays get political power and the Chinese economic power—did not have the tacit agreement of the majority of the non-Malay community. Even if there were a consensus, it would have lost its legitimacy and validity three decades after independence.[6]

One important turning-point in Malaysian politics was the racial riots in 1969, and the implementation of the New Economic Policy (NEP) that followed. It has been argued that the NEP has been able to transform the Malaysian state from a quasi-consociational system to a more Bumiputera-centric system.[7] Indeed, the origin of the NEP took advantage of the change that the 1969 racial riots had made in the perception of Malaysian ethnic relations. The National Operations Council (NOC) attributed the major causes of the riots to three factors: the lack of progress in the implementation of Bahasa Malaysia (Malay) as the national language, non-Malays' challenge of the privileged positions of the Malays, and the unemployment situation of both Malay and non-Malay youths. Solutions to all these problems, it was thought, were to be found in the NEP, which had the overriding objective of achieving "national unity" by (1) eradicating poverty irrespective of race, and (2) restructuring the Malaysian society by closing the economic gap between the ethnic groups.[8]

The NEP has been the major cause of a shift in political resources to the Malays. Hence, the bulk of issues dealing with ethnic configurations are resolved through a process of Malay domination. Bargaining, to the extent that it is meaningful, occurs around the edges of the issues involved. It is quite clear that the UMNO-led coalition government has not responded to the basic demands coming from the non-Malay electorate, if only through the respective ethnic-based parties in the coalition.

There are two observations to be made in regard to the post-1970 Malaysian regime. First, it reveals a Malaysian polity best understood as a hegemonic, not a consociational, system.[9] At best, it is a quasi-consociational.

---

6   Tan, Chee Beng, "Ethnic Aspects of the Constitution", in *Reflections on the Malaysian Constitution*, Penang: ALIRAN, 1987, pp 251–52.
7   Ho, Khai Leong, "Political Indigenization of the State in Peninsular Malaysia", in *ASEAN in the Global System*, edited by HM Dahlan, J Hamzah, JH Ong and AY Hing, Kuala Lumpur: Penerbit UKM, 1997, pp 210–24.
8   *Second Malaysia Plan*, Kuala Lumpur: Government of Malaysia, 1971.
9   Ho, Khai Leong, "Political Indigenization of the State in Peninsular Malaysia", pp 210–24.

Second, one of the most important factors effecting such a change has been the rise to political prominence of the two-headed Malay elite. Strategies of Malay class domination have now replaced the strategies of consensus formation.

The general conclusion, therefore, is this: the emphasis on Malayness in the NEP has provided one particular ethnic group with a larger claim to the rightful and legitimate prerogative of control over the state and the society. The effects of the NEP in having created a two-headed Malay elite have added a class dimension to the ethnic tensions. While the provision for Malay special rights was a product of Malay "political" nationalism in the 40s and 50s, Malay "economic" nationalism in the form of the NEP in the 70s constituted a comparable conviction in the economic arena. Taken as a whole, these economic and political processes have resulted in the emergence and consolidation of a political ethos defined as Malayism.

Malaysian Chinese Politics, pre-1970: "Horizontal Solidarity" and "Vertical Division"

The transformation of the state described above had important implications for Malaysian Chinese political participation in the period under discussion.

The most important clue of the quasi-consociational state in pre-1970 Malaysia was the coalition of the three ethnic communities in the Alliance. Much of this coalition existed only at the elite level. Within the political organization of the UMNO, MCA and MIC, the top elites had, albeit disagreements and conflicts of interests, attempted to cement a "horizontal solidarity" among them. They were mostly Western-educated, conservative, strongly nationalistic, and deeply committed to communal interests. They shared an experience that was unique in Malaysian political history. Decisions were made with the participation of these leaders, although their role in policy-making might not be equally significant. By all accounts, the Alliance during the initial period of its association was more broadly based in terms of ethnic participatory decisions.

The coalition of ethnic elites functioned at two levels of the bargaining process: internal and external. First was the internal bargaining among the ethnic elites themselves. This happened, for example, in the negotiations of the Constitution in 1957. Second was as a united group with an external entity. This was illustrated in 1957 when the UMNO-MCA-MIC Alliance claimed independence from the British.

Vertically, the various ethnic groups were segregated in a plural society.

Political interactions and communications were extremely limited at individual, group and organizational levels. While ethnic groups accommodated each other in their daily lives, there was very little exchange of political views.

While there were inter-ethnic divisions, there were also internal divisions among the ethnic Malaysian Chinese. Indeed, the Malaysian Chinese elites were not homogeneous. They were divided by circumstances and traditions, cultural heterogeneity, and class.[10] Intra-Chinese divisions were also accelerated by pro-Malay policies. These divisions were found even within the one organization that united the Chinese: the MCA. In the first years of its formation, the MCA significantly united the Chinese. Before its formation, the Chinese were political divided between three main groups: the Kuomintang (KMT), the Malayan Communist Party (MCP) and the Straits Chinese British Association (SCBA). The KMT represented conservative and right-wing Chinese political activists while the MCP consisted of radical and left-wing groups. Unlike both the KMT and the MCP, which were linked to similar conflicting movements in China, the SCBA was Malayan-based in its political affiliation. Among these groups, it was the KMT which generally

---

10 For a general treatment of the subject, see Wang Gungwu, "Chinese Politics in Malaya", *The China Quarterly*, no 42, July/September 1970; Tjoa Hock Guan, "Chinese Malaysians and Malaysian Politics", *Southeast Asian Affairs*, 1975; and Lee Kam Hing, "Three Approaches in Peninsular Malaysian Chinese Politics: The MCA, the DAP and the GERAKAN", in Zakaria Haji Ahmad, *Government and Politics of Malaysia*, Singapore: Oxford University Press, 1987. See also Judith Strauch, "Tactical Success and Failure in Grassroots Politics: MCA and DAP in Rural Malaysia, 1972", *Asian Survey*, 19 (12) 1978: 1280–94.

For studies on the MCA, see Margaret Roff, "Malayan Chinese Association, 1948–1965", *Journal of Southeast Asian History*, vol 6, no 2 (Sept 1965): 40–53; Chan Heng Chee, "The Malayan Chinese Association", MA thesis, University of Singapore, 1965; Lim San Kok, "Some Aspects of the Malayan Chinese Association 1949–69", *Journal of the South Seas Society*, vol 26, no 2, 1971: 31–48; Heng Pek Koon, *Chinese Politics in Malaysia—A History of the Malaysian Chinese Association*, Kuala Lumpur: Oxford University Press, 1988; and Roy H Haas, "The Malayan Chinese Association, 1958–1959: An Analysis of the Differing Conceptions of the Malayan Chinese Role in Independent Malaya", MA thesis, Dekalb, Northern Illinois University, 1967.

For a study of the DAP, see Michael Ong, "The Democratic Action Party and the 1978 General Election", in *Malaysian Politics and the 1978 Election*, edited by Harold Crouch, Lee Kam Hing and Michael Ong, Kuala Lumpur: Oxford University Press, 1980; and Chew Huat Hock, "Democratic Action Party in Post-1969 Malaysian Politics: The Strategy of a Determined Opposition", MA thesis, Australian National University, 1980.

There is, however, no single treatment on the GERAKAN. For an unpublished source, see Jeffrey Quah, "A Multi-Racial Approach to Malaysian Politics: A Case Study of Parti Gerakan Rakyat Malaysia", BA thesis, Franklin and Marshall College, Lancaster, Pennsylvania, USA, 1989.

had the support of the powerful Chinese Chambers of Commerce (CCC) and the voluntary organizations, *huay kuans*, which were organized along dialect, trade or clan lines.

The UMNO's dominance within the Alliance made the MCA less capable of delivering rewards to their ethnic-group client. While bargaining existed, the decisions were usually in favour of the UMNO. Hence, the MCA consistently failed to satisfy the demands of its Chinese electorate. It, therefore, became alienated from the Chinese grass roots, who began to withdraw their support. Indeed, the MCA's inability to deliver cultural, political and economic goods led to elite-mass political divisions within the Chinese community.

Meanwhile, Chinese-based opposition parties emerged. They were the Democratic Action Party (DAP) and the Gerakan Rakyat Malaysia (Gerakan).[11] The DAP was formed in 1965 after its parent organization, the Singapore-based People's Action Party, left Malaysia. It was a consistent critic of the MCA. The Gerakan was inaugurated in 1968 and it brought together key leaders from two other non-Malay opposition parties, the United Democratic Party and the Labour Party. These two political parties were highly vocal in criticizing the Malay-dominated state and its policies, and championed non-Malay rights in terms of education, language and culture. With these alternatives, the Chinese electorate was able to have a choice in terms of selecting its own representatives. Political divisions within the Chinese community, in particular among the electorate, were intensified.

The Barisan Sosialis also attracted many Chinese voters during this period. The political elites in this camp were able to advocate many of the cultural, education and political issues close to the ethnic Chinese electorate. However, when the two Chinese-based opposition parties emerged on the Malaysian political scene, they took over some of the major issues of the Barisan Sosialis, and eventually the socialists lost their appeal.

The most distinguishing feature in the Malaysian political system as far as ethnic Chinese political participation was concerned was the representation they enjoyed at the elite level. Important cabinet positions, such as the portfolio of the finance ministry, were held by MCA politicians traditionally. Many important issues were decided in the UMNO's favour, however. The appearance of political representation remained as an important selling point for the MCA to its supporters and sympathizers.

---

11 Lee, Kam Hing, "Three Approaches in Peninsular Malaysian Chinese Politics: The MCA, the DAP, and the GERAKAN", in Zakaria Haji Ahmad, *Government and Politics of Malaysia*, Singapore: Oxford University Press, 1987.

Malaysian Chinese Political Participation, post-1970: "Political Mobilization" and "Bureaucratic Participation"

As indicated earlier, the 1969 general election and the racial riots that followed impacted significantly on both Malay and Chinese politics. The percentage of votes received by the Alliance for the first time went below 50 per cent. The significant shift of the Chinese votes to the opposition in many ways continued in the next two decades with only one or two exceptions.

At this point, let me take a step backwards to examine the two sets of variables which significantly affected Malaysian Chinese political participation. These two sets of evidence are: voter turnout rates and the percentages of votes the Barisan Nasional (BN) and the Chinese-based parties received in the general elections.

Table 1 shows voter turnout rates in Malaysia's parliamentary and state elections from 1959 to 1990.

Table 1: Voter turnouts in Malaysia's parliamentary and state elections, 1959–90

Year	Voter turnout in parliamentary election	Voter turnout in state election
1959	73.30	74.30
1964	78.90	78.90
1969	73.60	73.90
1974	75.10	75.40
1978	75.30	76.90
1982	74.39	74.47
1986	69.90	71.68
1990	72.00	73.20

With the exception of the 1986 general elections, voter turnout rate in the Malaysian parliamentary elections was over 70 per cent. This is considered high among developing nations. The figure is higher for state elections, showing a consistency in the voting pattern of Malaysian voters. Table 2 shows the results of Malaysia's parliamentary elections from 1959 to 1990.

Malaysian official statistics do not show voter turnout or voting according to ethnic groups. There is no way of telling how a Malay, Chinese or Indian voted in the elections and what parties he/she voted for. But the general indications at the grass roots and available evidence suggest that most urban ethnic Chinese votes went to the opposition (especially the

Table 2: Percentages of votes in Malaysia's parliamentary elections, 1959–90

Year / Vote percentage	Alliance/BN	DAP	PAS	Independents	Others
1959	51.8	—	21.30	4.80	22.1
1964	58.5	—	14.60	0.70	26.2
1969	44.9	11.9	20.90	1.80	20.5
1974	60.7	18.3	—	6.00	15.0
1978	57.2	19.1	15.50	4.60	3.4
1982	60.5	19.6	14.50	3.80	1.7
1986	57.6	21.1	15.30	3.20	3.0
1990	52.0	16.5	6.57	3.08	14.4*

*Semangat 46

DAP). Even the MCA leaders have periodically made the comment that their party candidates received only approximately 30 per cent of the Chinese votes, and the DAP leaders have claimed that theirs had 80 per cent of the Chinese votes. From these two tables and the rhetoric of Chinese political leaders, one can make two general observations:

1. Malaysia's voter turnout rate has been relatively high compared with that of other developing nations; that voter turnout in urban areas was higher than voter turnout in rural areas; and that Chinese voter turnout was higher than that of other ethnic groups.
2. approximately 20 to 30 per cent of Chinese votes went to BN candidates; the rest to the opposition's.

A case in point is the 1986 general elections.[12] While the UMNO achieved one of its best victories, MCA emerged from this election with one of its worst results. It contested 32 parliamentary seats and won only 17. Of the 69 state seats the party contested, it won 43. The 17 parliamentary seats that the MCA won accounted for only 9.6 per cent of the total 177 seats in the parliament, the lowest percentage the party had won in any election (see Table 3).

One way to look at the response of the ethnic Chinese voters to the MCA and to examine its implications for the political process is to look at the support of the ethnic groups in the constituencies. The results indicated

---

12 The analysis is based on Ho Khai Leong, "The 1986 Malaysian General Elections: An Analysis of the Campaign and Results", *Asian Profile*, vol 16, no 3 (1988): 239–56.

Table 3: MCA's performance in parliamentary elections, 1955–86

Year	Parliamentary seats won	Total number of parliamentary seats	Percentage of representation
1955	15	52	28.85
1959	19	104	18.27
1964	27	104	25.96
1969	13	104	12.50
1974	19	114	16.67
1978	17	154	11.40
1982	24	154	15.58
1986	17	177	9.60

Sources: *Election Commissions Reports*, 1955 to 1982, and *The New Straits Times*, August 1986.

that of the 17 seats that the MCA won, 15 of them were in constituencies where Malay voters constituted more than 34 per cent (see Table 4). The margin of votes enjoyed by the MCA candidates showed that the seats were won on the strength of Malay votes. Only two candidates were elected in Chinese "majority" constituencies, where ethnic Chinese voters constituted more than 50 per cent of the voting population. In the constituencies where the MCA won, however, the margin of victory was considerably smaller than had been anticipated.

Further analysis of the data shows that the 15 parliamentary seats that the MCA lost were all won by DAP candidates. It is worth stressing that the voter composition of these constituencies consisted of more than 49 per cent ethnic Chinese voters.

In sum, it is reasonable to suggest that the MCA candidates were elected on the basis of Malay votes. This pattern was repeated in the past few general elections and appears likely to be so. The MCA candidates in Chinese-majority constituencies were defeated. MCA representation in the parliament and government remained quite consistent in the last 20 years.

These three aspects of the MCA performance point to one conclusion: the Chinese voters seemed to have forsaken the MCA. As the results indicated, a protest movement in the Chinese community against the establishment was taking effect. It could be argued that this protest existed on two levels: against the BN and against the MCA itself. As stated earlier, the performance of the BN government cast a shadow of apprehension and doubt on the voting populace. Not surprisingly, therefore, the ethnic Chinese community was less than happy with the administration. The MCA is a

Table 4: MCA candidates and their constituencies by ethnic group, Malaysia's general elections of 1986

	Name	Constituency	Malay voters	Chinese voters	Indian voters	Result
1	Lim Ann Koon	Ampang Jaya	68.5%	25.9%	4.6%	won
2	Chew Kam Hoy	Padang Serai	55.2%	20.6%	3.7%	won
3	Oo Gin Sun	Alor Star	54.8%	38.8%	5.5%	won
4	Kok Wee Kiat	Selandar	52.2%	36.3%	11.3%	won
5	Law Lai Heng	Pontian	52.2%	46.8%	1.0%	won
6	Wong Choon Wing	Lipis	51.6%	26.2%	12.5%	won
7	Lee Kim Sai	Hulu Langat	48.1%	41.6%	9.6%	won
8	Teng Gaik Kwan	Raub	47.9%	43.6%	7.2%	won
9	Loke Yuen Yow	Tanjung Malim	44.2%	36.1%	17.8%	won
10	Chua Jui Meng	Bakri)	43.8%	54.3%	1.8%	won
11	Woon See Chin	Senai	41.1%	52.8%	6.1%	won
12	Ng Cheng Kuai	Lumut	40.9%	46.5%	12.3%	won
13	Ling Liong Sik	Labis	38.3%	46.7%	14.9%	won
14	Tan Koon Swan	Gopeng	38.3%	45.9%	13.1%	won
15	Chan Siang Sun	Bentong	34.5%	55.6%	8.8%	won
16	Kee Yong Wee	Sungai Besi	31.4%	59.0%	8.7%	lost to DAP
17	Yim Koh Kheong	Seremban	31.0%	56.7%	11.5%	lost to DAP
18	Liu Thai Heng	Puchong	27.3%	56.5%	15.0%	lost to DAP
19	Lee Phon Yong	Petaling Jaya	27.0%	61.0%	10.6%	lost to DAP
20	Wong Seng Chow	Rasah	26.9%	49.3%	22.8%	lost to DAP
21	Lee Jong Ki	Bayan Baru	24.7%	66.2%	8.8%	lost to DAP
22	Tan Chong Keng	Bukit Mertajam	24.3%	66.6%	9.1%	lost to DAP
23	Ng Cheng Kiat	Kelang	23.8%	58.6%	16.5%	won
24	Soo Chin Ann	Kota Melaka	22.1%	72.0%	3.5%	lost to DAP
25	Chaw Chek Sam	Bagan	22.0%	62.5%	15.1%	lost to DAP
26	Chin Fook Yen	Kampar	16.4%	74.9%	8.5%	lost to DAP
27	Ling Chooi Seng	Kluang)	14.1%	72.2%	na	won
28	Ooi Foh Seng	Batu Gajah	14.1%	75.8%	10.1%	lost to DAP
29	Wong Chin Chye	Ipoh	12.3%	66.4%	19.6%	lost to DAP
30	Ng Khek Kiung	Pasir Pinji	8.6%	86.4%	4.2%	lost to DAP
31	Yap Fook Hing	Bukit Bintang	8.3%	83.5%	7.9%	lost to DAP
32	Chua Kok Tee	Seputeh	7.6%	83.1%	8.6%	lost to DAP

Source: Data obtained from *The New Straits Times*, 5 August 1986.

member in the BN coalition, and votes of protest by Chinese voters against the government inevitably were cast against the MCA because of a perception of the community at large of growing Chinese helplessness and political impotence to influence policy within the administration.

Despite the lack of grass-roots Chinese support, the MCA appeared to have done well in terms of representation in the coalition government at the cabinet level. Table 5 shows the MCA representatives in government from 1955 to 2001. The number of ministers appeared to be consistent (4), except in 1980–81 and 1986–87 (5 and 6 respectively). The number of deputy ministers increased over the years, and this is the portfolio which the UMNO seemed to be more willing to allocate to the MCA. The bureaucratic involvement of the MCA in the government increased marginally over time as compared with its popular electorate support which at best remained constant.

Table 5: MCA representatives in government, 1955–2001

Year	Minister	Deputy Minister	Parliamentary Secretary
1955–58	4	1	0
1958–63	4	1	0
1964	4	2	2
1964–66	4	2	2
1967–68	4	3	1
1968–73	4	1	0
1973–74	4	1	0
1974–76	4	3	1
1976–78	4	3	2
1979	4	6	0
1980–81	5	5	1
1982	4	6	1
1983–85	4	6	1
1986–87	6	6	1
1988	4	6	1
1989–90	4	6	1
1991–94	4	6	2
1995–99	4	6	2
2000	4	6	2

How did the Gerakan perform in the 1980s? As a regionally based party in Penang, it lacked national appeal. Chinese support for the party was not very consistent. In 1969, participating in an election for the first time, it did well, winning 8 out of the 14 seats it contested. In the 1974 elections, however, after it had been co-opted into the Barisan Nasional, the number of parliamentary seats of the Gerakan was reduced to 5. In 1978, it won 4 seats. In the 1982 elections, the number of seats went up by one to 5, and it retained the same number of seats in both the 1986 and

1990 elections. In 1990, its founder member, Lim Chong Eu, was defeated by Lim Kit Siang, the secretary-general of the DAP, and for a while, the party suffered very low morale. It received votes from both the Chinese and non-Chinese, as witnessed in the state voting in Penang, although its image was essentially a Chinese-based party. Its influence in government remained limited, as its political leaders were given less important ministerial portfolios.

The DAP, however, was not very different from the MCA and Gerakan in terms of parliamentary and state elections. In the 1969 elections, the DAP claimed victory, winning 13 seats, the same as the MCA, and replaced the Pan Malayan Islamic Party as the country's strongest opposition party. In 1974, it only won 9 seats. During the 1978 general elections, there was a swing of support back to the DAP, which won a total of 15 seats, a majority of which were from the state of Penang. This electorate support, however, was withdrawn in the 1982 elections when it lost 10 of the seats it had captured in 1978 and won only 6 seats. In 1986, it won 24 seats, one more than the MCA and the Gerakan combined. In the 1990 elections, the number of its seats decreased slightly to 20 (see Table 6).

Table 6: Performance of the DAP in general elections, 1969–90

Year	Parliamentary seats	Percentage of votes cast	State seats	Percentage of votes cast
1969	13	11.9	31	NA
1974	9	18.3	23	NA
1978	16	19.1	2	NA
1982	9	19.6	12	NA
1986	24	21.1	37	NA
1990	20	17.2	44	NA

This is only half the story, however. Looking at the percentages of votes received, the numbers were quite consistent. The DAP remained a favourite of many urban Chinese. This was its strength as well as its weakness. By and large, the DAP still is an urban- and Chinese-based party. It has been unable to make a breakthrough in rural areas, and it is not likely to attract rural and Malay voters. In the 1990 general elections, it relied heavily on Semangat 46 to deliver Malay votes, but was disappointed by Semangat 46 performance. It will continue to be a champion of urban and Chinese rights, and is unlikely to shed its image of a Chinese-based party. Its limitations were apparent in the 1990 elections: despite the unprecedented challenge to the BN, the DAP was not able to make a breakthrough in the Chinese-majority state of Penang. Lim Kit Siang, its secretary-general, said the election was the biggest letdown in his political life.

What does all this leave for the roles of the Chinese interest groups in the political process? The Chinese Guilds and Associations (CGA) is a loose, informal clustering of associations. It is a coalition group which includes several major types of voluntary association: (1) the dialect/territorial associations formed at the provincial, prefecture, county and village level; (2) the clan/surname associations; (3) the trade guilds and the Chamber of Commerce; (4) the cultural, dramatic and/or musical societies; and (5) the social/recreational societies. Many of these organizations had their origin in the secret societies and clans in the early years of Chinese immigration into Malaya, and acted to reaffirm Chinese self-sufficiency.[13] The group became increasingly politicized in the past decade,[14] but has remained divided as to which political party to support. It has been limited by its communication and organizational capacity. The organizations that appear to lead the CGA are the United Chinese School Committees' Association (UCSCA), the United Chinese School Teachers' Association (UCSTA)—better known as *Dongjiaozong*—and the Federation of Chinese Associations, Malaysia, based in Kuala Lumpur.

The methods of participation of the CGA vary from the crass and venal to an anti-governmental concern. In recent decades, there has been not only an expansion in the CGA activities but also a transformation of their character. Two of the principal changes in the larger political environment—the marginalization of the MCA and the ascendancy of Bumiputerism—may well be giving rise not simply to more activity but entirely new kinds of activity or at least to enhance salience of some forms of activity at the expense of others. The change is designed to maximize its popular appeal.

---

13   Some examples of the relevant literature are: Wolfgang Moese, Gottfried Reinknecht and Eva Schmitz-Seiber, *Chinese Regionalism in West-Malaysia and Singapore*, Hamburg, 1979—see especially chapter 12, "The Clan Associations in West-Malaysia and Singapore" (by Eva Schmitz-Seiber), chapter 15, "Chinese Schools and Education (by Wolfgang Moese), and chapter 16, "Professional Associations in West-Malaysia and Singapore" (by Eva Schmitz-Seiber); Maurice Freeman, "Immigrants and Associations: Chinese in 19th Century Singapore", *Comparative Studies in Science and Society*, vol 3, 1960, pp 25–48; and Charles Gamba, "Chinese Associations in Singapore", *Journal of Malayan (Malaysian) Branch of the Royal Asiatic Society*, vol 39, no 2, 1966, pp 123–68.

14   Ho Khai Leong, "The Malaysian Chinese Guilds and Associations as Organized Interests in Malaysian Politics", Department of Political Science, Occasional Papers No 4, 1992, 36 pages.

It seems appropriate to predict that the approaches taken by the CGA will be altered by the strengthening of the government's hand in dealing with political opposition. There is also a cluster of phenomena, evident in the last three general elections, that demonstrate that in recent years, the attention of the CGA has been drawn towards electoral politics. But electoral politics has its limitations. The results of the elections suggest that even if the CGA were able to "deliver the vote", its influence over public policy-making would be circumscribed. Moreover, many leaders want to avoid over identification with one political party or the sponsoring of candidates in elections for fear of division within the organization as well as alienation of the wider public support that they seek.

At this point, it would be appropriate to look at the roles and functions of the various Chinese-based political parties. A number of general functions of political parties can be identified. The main functions are as follows:

1   Representation
2   Elite formation and recruitment
3   Goal formulation
4   Interest articulation and aggregation
5   Socialization and mobilization
6   Organization of government.

Both the MCA and the Gerakan fulfil to a certain extent the functions of representation and organization of government. "Representation" refers to the capacity of parties to respond to and articulate the views of both their members and the voters. Such representation in the government brings about stability and continuity in the system. For elite formation and recruitment, the two parties have done so with a certain degree of success, but they have not established themselves as an agent of socialization and mobilization of the Chinese electorate in the political process. That role has been played by the DAP and, to a certain extent, the CGA. The mobilizing forces for and against the regime are both present, and evidence suggests that there is growing disenchantment with the pro-system forces.

All in all, while the Malaysian Chinese do have representation in the government, popular pressure also exists from below in the form of electoral politics mobilized by opposition parties and interest group demands. The party and group that reflect political mobilization from below seem to be stronger in resources as well as strength, judging from the percentages of votes they received in the general elections and the popular support for issues they have raised. This situation does not offer comfort to those ethnic Chinese who want to have a stronger and more assertive representation in the government, since the UMNO's disregard of the MCA and Gerakan is unlikely to change. At the same time, however, the Chinese can find comfort in the fact that things will not get worse, if they can get their act together behind the DAP.

There is one issue remaining to be solved: political efficacy. If the ethnic Chinese perceive themselves to be ineffective in affecting public policies, why do they continue to participate? To answer this question, one has to think about efficacy in terms of how it affects political behaviour. Table 7 attempts to do this by deriving hypothesis from plotting efficacy feelings against the feeling of trust in the political system.

Table 7: Political efficacy and trust in the political system

	High level of trust in the system	Low level of trust in the system
High political efficacy	Participation that is supportive of the regime (A)	Participation that is designed to reform (or protest against) the regime (B)
Low political efficacy	Voting and "patriotic" support for the regime only (C)	Alienation and withdrawal from politics (D)

While there are no scientific data on the number of Malaysian Chinese in each of these categories, it is my postulation, based on the above analysis, that a majority of the Malaysian Chinese fall under category B—they participate in the belief that they will be able to make a difference or possibly change things. This trend of politicization of the Chinese community seems to have increased in the past ten years. Mobilization at this level is most intense during the general election periods and when specific controversial events occur.

Conclusion

Malaysian Chinese political participation in the period from 1970 to 1990 signalled both continuity and change. While the voting pattern of Chinese electorate seems to show a swing to the opposition candidates, the parties in the Barisan Nasional government continued to enjoy the confidence of the Malay communities as well as the elites. They were able to occupy bureaucratic positions in the government and, hence, could claim representation and legitimacy. The data also reveal that the urban-based Chinese had a greater voter turnout rate than the rural Malays, and almost 70 to 80 per cent of their votes went to the opposition.

Two sets of changes influenced the course of Malaysian Chinese political participation in the last decade. One set involved increased authoritarianism of the system. The issue was not so much Bumiputera-centric policies, but pro-Malay capitalist policies. The growing power of the executive during Mahathir's administration amounted to a deconsociationalization of Malaysian politics to a point that it became increasingly difficult to move some multi-ethnic policies through the process.

The third set of changes involved the inclination of the Chinese voters: the widely discussed shift to the opposition in the Chinese community. This shift was neither so sharp nor so unambiguous as has been indicated, but it was real. The results of the 1990 general elections seemed to be a logical consequence of the increased dissatisfaction of the Chinese public with Malaysian political development. The tantalizing question that remained, however, was whether the two trends—autocratism and increased opposition of Chinese voters—were somehow connected.

The 1990s witnessed a twist in these two trends. Mahathir's legitimacy was increasingly challenged both within UMNO and by PAS. Barisan Nasional candidates had to rely more heavily on Chinese voters in order to win given such a challenge. This tendency was reflected in the 1999 general elections. The challenge of PAS prompted the Islamicization programme of the Mahathir Administration, which had ironic consequences for ethnic Chinese support.[15] The Chinese electorate, as indicated, swung to the Barisan Nasional in the 1999 general elections, responding to some of the "sweet carrots" of the Mahathir government, which showed instantaneous support for Chinese educational and cultural projects.

The Anwar affair and the subsequent "Reformasi" movement, however, brought out one significant feature of ethnic Chinese political participation. There was a conspicuous absence of ethnic Chinese demonstrators on the streets, with the major exception of Tian Chua, the vice-president of the Justice Party who is presently in custody under the ISA. There are a few possible explanations. One, the ethnic Chinese viewed the Anwar affair as a Malay internal affair rather than a "national" affair. Second, there has

---

15 Patricia Martinez, "Mahathir, Islam, and the New Malay Dilemma", in *Mahathir's Administration: Performance and Crisis of Governance*, edited by Ho Khai Leong and James Chin, Singapore: Times Books International, 2001.

been no tradition of street demonstration in recent memory by the ethnic Chinese electorate. Only in the 1950s when the Barisan Sosialis was at its height of influence did Malaysia witness ethnic Chinese anomic protests on the streets. These explanations may suggest an important dilemma that Chinese citizens have: their orientations and awareness of issues are confined to their own parochial interests. While they are also concerned about administrative accountability, electorate gerrymandering, illegal immigrants and so forth, their major attention is on education, culture and political interests. The recent widespread protest of the Chinese community to the MCA's takeover of the two Chinese newspapers (*Nanyang Press* and *China Press*) is a case in point. The intensity of activities in this instance is much more than that generated against the Reformasi movement in the past two years. If the Chinese response to the Reformasi movement can be termed "spectatorial" and "transitional", then it is reasonable to suggest that its protest activities against the MCA's takeover could be classified as "gladiatorial".

Political participation of Malaysian Chinese will continue to exhibit the characteristics of bureaucratic involvement at the top governmental hierarchy and mobilized opposition at the grass roots in the foreseeable future. The more interesting factor for political observers to watch would be the constellation of Chinese voters in general elections. While organized groups in the Chinese community can be quite vocal and display opposition tendencies, such inclinations may not be strong enough to influence the general Chinese populace. The notion of a "critical minority" may not be an exaggeration to describe the significance of Chinese votes in general elections (winning seats for MCA, Gerakan and UMNO candidates), but to say that they would determine the future development of Malaysian politics (political succession, meta-policies or administrative restructuring) is probably too far-fetched.

Chapter 8

BAGGAGE FROM THE PAST, EYES ON THE FUTURE: CHINESE EDUCATION IN MALAYSIA TODAY

Tan Liok Ee

Chinese education in Malaysia,[1] in comparison with that in other Southeast Asian countries, has an exceptionally long, continuous and resilient history. From the early 19th century, there were small *sishu*[2] in Penang and Singapore, following long established traditional patterns of education in China. The earliest of these *sishu* are impossible to date accurately but among the most well known of the "old style" schools that can be documented are the *Wufu Shuyuan* in Penang and the *Chongwen Ge* and *Cuiying Shuyuan* in Singapore. Conventionally, the beginning of "modern", or "new style", Chinese schools in Malaysia dates back to the setting up of Chung Hwa Confucian School in Penang in 1904.[3] Chung Hwa Confucian School, together with many others set up at the beginning of the 20th century, exists to this day. There are today 1,284 national-type primary schools (NTPSs), 60 independent Chinese secondary schools (ICSSs) and three institutions of higher learning using Mandarin as their main medium of instruction.[4] In addition, many of the former Chinese secondary schools that, as part of the national school system, now teach mainly in Malay, are still considered to be "Chinese schools".

---

1 Malaysia, comprising the 11 states of the Federation of Malaya, Singapore, Sabah and Sarawak, was formed in 1963. Singapore separated from Malaysia to become an independent state in 1965. "Malaysia" is used here in a general geographic sense to cover the territories that after 1963 became a single political entity. "Malaya" will be used for the pre-1963 period.
2 *Sishu*, literally "private schools", were small teaching units of 20 to 30 pupils, taught by a single teacher, which might be set up by a family, a clan or a village committee, or by the teacher himself.
3 The *Wufu Shuyuan* is thought to have been established in 1819, the *Chongwen Ge* in 1849 and the *Cuiying Shuyuan* in 1854. On the early history of Chinese schools, see Tan Liok Ee, 1997, Ch 1; and Zheng Liangshu, 1998, pp 1–37.
4 These are Southern College in Johor, New Era College in Selangor, and Han Jiang College in Penang.

In a paper written several years ago, I attributed the exceptional resilience of Chinese education in Malaysia to "a unique mix of inter-related demographic, socio-cultural, economic and political factors [which] enabled the Chinese schools to negotiate the terms for their survival through different phases of their history".[5] That paper did not, however, bring out how the strategies of survival in the past have left several unresolved anomalies and recurrent problems, which could intensify or deteriorate. In addition, as circumstances changed, some sources of strength in the past have become areas of vulnerability today. This article is an attempt to review the sources of resilience in the past of Chinese education in Malaysia in the light of the vulnerabilities and problems in the present and the challenges likely to arise in the future—all part of a continuing dialogue between past and present, tradition and modernity, in the lives of Malaysians of Chinese descent.

The Past

Chinese schools grew in the first half of the 20th century in tandem with the changing character of the Chinese population. In the 1920s and 1930s, two decades which saw the transformation of pockets of transient and predominantly male immigrants into settled and permanent communities, the number of Chinese schools in the Malay Peninsula increased from 252 in 1921 to 1,015 in 1938. Another important period of demographic change was the postwar decade with its baby boom and the emergence of a 'normal' demographic profile for the Chinese population. During this period, the number of Chinese primary schools increased less dramatically—from 1,004 in 1946 to 1,333 in 1957—but the total enrolment in these schools more than doubled from 158,037 to 342,194. By 1957, in addition to the primary schools, there were 60 Chinese secondary schools with almost 50,000 students. Further, Chinese school students could by then continue their education in the Chinese language at the tertiary level in the Nanyang University, established in Singapore in 1956 through the efforts of community leaders in Malaya and Singapore.[6]

The vast majority of the Chinese schools were *minban xuexiao*—schools initiated and funded by local Chinese communities. Chinese schools could be found not only in towns but also in small villages, indeed, wherever there was a group of children needing a school and some local leaders prepared to take the initiative to organize one. Thus the schools had deep

---

5   Tan Liok Ee, 2000, p 229.
6   Tan Liok Ee, 1997, Ch 1.

roots within their respective local communities, depending on them for funding and leadership. The cost of land, buildings and equipment was met from donations, which were also collected sporadically to bridge the gap between fees and running costs. Local leaders had a social and moral obligation to keep the schools going and, together with the Chinese schoolteachers, enjoyed both status and respect for their role in fulfilling a social and cultural need. The Chinese schools equipped the younger generation with the basic literacy and numeracy skills, provided some essential general knowledge, inculcated traditional moral values, and sustained political and cultural links with the ancestral homeland.

The colonial state played a minimal role in meeting the educational needs of the children of immigrants, both Chinese and Indian. State power was used mainly in a "policing" role to prevent students and teachers from being recruited into militant or radical political movements. Financial assistance to Chinese schools was far below that provided to English and Malay schools except in the early 1950s, when the colonial government was compelled to take an interest in ensuring that Chinese schools existed in the 480 New Villages. Entire Chinese communities living on jungle fringes had been forcibly resettled in these New Villages as part of the strategy of cutting off support for the Communist Party of Malaya during the Emergency. A special scheme of aid for Chinese schools in the New Villages was instituted to help old schools relocate and to set up new ones where necessary because schooling for the children of families who had been uprooted from their homes was an important part of the colonial state's attempts to "win hearts and minds" in the war against the Communists.[7]

In the postwar context, the colonial government reviewed its *laissez-faire* education policy as it began to plan its strategy for decolonization. The existence of several school systems, teaching in different languages, was considered inimical to an education policy that must be directed at fostering national unity and moulding a national identity. In response, Chinese schoolteachers and management boards organized themselves into two organizations, popularly known as *Dongjiaozong*, to defend the principle of education in the mother tongue and the right of the Chinese schools to be part of the national education system.[8] In the few critical years before Merdeka, during which the constitutional and political framework of the country was

---

7 Ibid, p 55.
8 *Jiaozong* refers to the United Chinese School Teachers' Association formed in 1951, while *Dongzong* refers to the United Chinese School Committees' Association formed in 1953. On the role of the two organizations, usually referred to in Chinese as *Dongjiaozong*, see Tan Liok Ee, 1992.

determined, Malay and Chinese leaders were able to arrive at some important compromises on citizenship rights, language and education.[9]

As part of these compromises, the Chinese primary schools were accepted as national-type primary schools (NTPSs) *within* the national system in 1957, together with schools teaching in Malay, English and Tamil. Irrespective of their medium of instruction, all schools adopted a common curriculum to inculcate a shared national perspective. As NTPSs, the administrative and running costs of the schools were covered by government aid and their teachers became civil servants employed by the state. Since 1961, these NTPSs, together with other primary schools, have provided free primary education in Chinese. Chinese secondary schools, however, had to change their medium of instruction to English in order to be accepted within the national education system in 1961. Sixteen of the 70 Chinese secondary schools rejected these terms and became the first ICSSs, foregoing all funding from the state to preserve their autonomy.

These terms of survival for Chinese schools, both primary and secondary, that were negotiated during the immediate pre- and post-Merdeka years, have remained essentially unchanged. They have provided the rubric for free primary education in the Chinese language to continue to be available to children whose parents choose to send them to Chinese primary schools. But, consistent with the stated "ultimate objective" of national policy—which was to have *all* schools in the national system teach *mainly* in the national language—the 1961 Education Act gave the Minister for Education the discretionary power to change the medium of instruction to Malay.[10] This power was used to convert all English medium primary schools to schools teaching in the Malay medium in 1971, leading to a progressive change in the main medium of instruction within the entire national system. All national secondary schools, including the former Chinese secondary schools that joined the system in 1961, began teaching in Malay from the late 1970s and public universities changed their medium of instruction from English to Malay in the 1980s. This power of conversion, the subject of constant and vehement protests from Chinese organizations, was never invoked against the Chinese primary schools, which continue

---

9 Tan Liok Ee, 1997, Ch 4.
10 Paragraph 12 of the Razak Report states that "the ultimate objective of educational policy in this country must be to bring together the children of all races under a national education system in which the national language is the main medium of instruction". See Tan Liok Ee, 1997, Chs 5 and 6 for detailed discussions of the Razak Report, its implementation through the 1957 Education Ordinance and subsequent developments up to the 1961 Education Act.

until today to teach in Chinese. One important effect of the conversion of all English schools into Malay schools was that more Chinese parents sent their children to the NTPSs, stimulating a rise in enrolments that had been dipping drastically in the NTPSs in the late 1960s. Today, an estimated 90 per cent of Chinese children are enrolled in NTPSs.

The Present

The 1961 Education Act remained in force for 34 years, until the promulgation of the 1995 Education Ordinance. The new Ordinance does not carry the clause giving the Minister for Education discretionary powers to change the medium of instruction in primary schools. From one point of view, this means the position of the Chinese primary schools is now more secure. But the new Act still states that the national language should be the main medium of instruction in the national education system,[11] reaffirming an official position that has, in essence, remained unchanged since the debate on education policy started in the 1950s. This suggests that Chinese and Tamil schools have been, and will be, allowed to continue to exist but more as part of the baggage inherited from the past than as a commitment to the principle of educating young children in their home language. These schools are in a sense marginal within the national mainstream and, it is often alleged, marginalized in terms of attention from and treatment by the government. Allegations of discriminatory treatment are usually focused on three points: no provision for new or additional NTPSs, less generous grants, and insufficient attention on training more teachers. There is no doubt that the main focus of state funds is on Malay-medium national schools and there has been an unstated policy that the government will not set up any new or additional Chinese or Tamil schools.

The education system of Malaysia has expanded to meet the needs of a growing population. But, while the government has built more schools in new residential areas, they have invariably been national schools teaching in Malay; rarely are the new schools Chinese or Tamil schools. Between 1987 and 1998, the number of national primary schools increased from 4,856 to 5,283 whereas the number of Chinese primary schools dropped from 1,295 to 1,283.[12] The vast majority of the Chinese schools in existence today were established during the two main periods of demographic growth

---

11 See Malaysia 1995, sections 16–19.
12 UCSTA, 1999, p 66.

mentioned earlier, that is, between the 1920s and 1930s and in the first postwar decade. A survey of 911 Chinese primary schools in 1985 found that out of the 847 that provided information on their date of establishment, 779 (92%) were established before 1957, 65 between 1958 and 1969, and only 3 were established in the 1970s.[13] Malay politicians have responded negatively to calls from leaders of *Dongjiaozong* and other Chinese organizations that the government should set up Chinese schools in new housing areas where they are desperately needed. The UMNO Youth assembly in June 2001 explicitly opposed the building of any new Chinese and Tamil schools on the grounds that separate schools for different ethnic groups impeded national unity.[14]

The need for Chinese schools in new residential areas has arisen as a result of major demographic changes since the 1960s. Then, a significant majority of the Chinese lived in what were classified as rural areas, but between 1970 and 1980, the proportion of Chinese living in urban areas increased from 47.0 per cent to 56.1, rising further to 75.8 by 1991.[15] As a result, Chinese schools in urban areas are overcrowded while those in the rural areas have faced declining enrolment for several years. The effect on Chinese school enrolments could already be seen in 1978 when there were 40 schools with less than 45 students and 105 schools with less than 150 students.[16] In year 2000, 500 NTPSs had enrolments below 150 and 200 had less than 50 students.[17] In 2001, 18 NTPSs, 8 of which were located in Perak, had fewer than 10 students, while in Negri Sembilan, one Chinese school located in a plantation had a total enrolment of only 3 students![18]

The likelihood of more Chinese schools facing closure because their enrolments have dropped below sustainable levels has attracted a fair amount of attention. The Chinese population is increasingly concentrated in the major cities, with younger families living in new suburban areas where there are no Chinese schools. This outflow of the Chinese population to new suburban areas has also left old schools in inner-city areas with the problem of decreasing enrolment, a problem that is particularly acute in Penang, Kuala Lumpur and Selangor, where high urban densities have been dispersed to new suburbs. One possible solution to this problem is to relocate those schools with extremely low enrolments to areas of high population

---

13 UCSTA, 1985, pp 5–11.
14 *Sin Chew Jit Poh*, 21 June 2001.
15 Chan and Tey, 2000, pp 76–78.
16 UCSTA, 1987, p 9.
17 *Nanyang Siang Pao*, 30 November 2000.
18 *Sunday Star*, 10 June 2001.

density where there are no Chinese schools. However, government pledges, usually made before or during general elections, to provide land and funds for new premises to relocate affected schools have rarely materialized. A few attempts at relocation, mainly through the efforts of local-level Chinese leaders and politicians have been successful, for example, Shih Chung Branch School in Penang. But others have provoked controversy—a well-known case is the relocation of Damansara NTPS in Kuala Lumpur, which became the subject of contentious quarrels between one camp supporting and another opposed to its relocation.[19] Apart from issues specific to this particular controversy, there is a general divide of two opposing views on the issue of relocation. One side insists that it is the state's responsibility to establish new or additional Chinese primary schools wherever there is an obvious need for them as enrolment trends indicate they are the choice of 90 per cent of Chinese parents. The other takes a more pragmatic approach that does not confront head on the government's reluctance to establish more Chinese schools but seeks instead to engage federal and state education officials in ad hoc co-operative efforts with local Chinese leaders. Their objective is to find suitable land on which to relocate specific Chinese schools with extremely low enrolments to new housing areas with none.

During the colonial period, Chinese schools sprang up, grew, or shrank in response to local needs. Subject to being registered, new Chinese schools could be set up wherever they were needed. Neglect by the colonial authority and a tradition of *minban xuexiao* were the factors that led to the mushrooming of Chinese schools. Since independence, the state has played a dominant role in education, seeking greater control over all schools as the education system is viewed as an important channel for the nation-building process. The pattern of growth of small Chinese schools slowly growing to meet local needs is no longer possible today. The system of governance of the schools has changed. As *minban xuexiao*, the Chinese schools were set up and run by local communities whose leaders exercised

---

19 Damansara NTPS, originally a New Village school, found itself within the Federal Territory of Kuala Lumpur as the capital city and its satellites expanded. The decision to relocate the school became controversial when the school was moved in January 2001 to share premises with another Chinese primary school before the buildings on its new proposed site were up. This roused suspicions regarding the relocation and objections to the temporary move led to disagreement within the school's Board of Directors. The controversy became increasingly heated after Chinese politicians, from parties within the governing coalition as well as opposition parties, pitched in and a number of parents refused to move their children from the old site. See special series on the controversy in *Nanyang Siang Pao,* 9–11 February 2001.

almost complete control over decisions affecting the school. The school and, in particular, the staff, could be subject to the whims of powerful *dongshi* (directors) who had made the largest financial contributions to the school. This has changed with the schools' absorption into the national system as their administration and staff, and important decisions affecting the school, come under the Ministry of Education rather than the *dongshi*. The staff, including the principal, of the school are now employees of the state, subject to all regulations prevailing over civil servants. They no longer come directly under the control of the *dongshi*.

However, the *dongshi* remain important to many Chinese schools for two reasons. First, many of the Chinese primary and secondary schools which entered the national or publicly funded school system in 1957 and 1961 remain, in effect, semi-government schools as the school buildings and land belong not to the state but to the school board of management, or to organizations or individuals who act as trustees. In the 1985 survey of Chinese primary schools, out of the 889 schools which provided information about land and school buildings, 441 schools submitted that their land and buildings were owned by the *dongshi*, 127 had theirs owned by individuals or organizations, and 321 by the government. The last were most likely among the 480 New Village schools which were built on state land by the government in the 1950s. There is, in addition, an important distinction between whether the land is owned by the Federal government or by the local state government. The government policy was, and is, that a school can be fully assisted only if school buildings stand on Federal government land. Where the Federal government does not own the school buildings or the land on which the buildings stand, it does not contribute development funds to the school.

This is the situation for most Chinese schools, including many New Village schools, because the land on which they are sited belongs to the local state, rather than the Federal government. They receive much smaller grants than national schools, whose development and physical facilities are paid for fully by the state. Hence, Chinese schools have continued to rely on community efforts, almost always under the leadership of their *dongshi*, for development funds and even for maintenance and repair. The facilities of many Chinese schools in Penang, for example, are constantly upgraded through the efforts of their *dongshi*. Thus the *dongshi* remain an important social link between the schools and the communities where the schools are located, sustaining to some extent the *minban* tradition of the past. And where the *dongshi* have continued to make positive contributions, they continue to command the respect and co-operation of principals and their staffs, even though they have no power over their pay or promotion. This does not happen in all schools, of course.

In fact, the *dongshi* of the NTPS are in a nebulous position. Whereas in the past they were elected from the benefactors of the school according to a school constitution and existed formally as a body, today the Chinese schools technically have "instruments of government" which come under regulations set by the Minister for Education in accordance with the Education Act. In most cases, where the buildings and land of a school are not owned by the state, the Board of Governors is constituted from representatives from the Parent-Teacher Association, ex-pupils' association and nominees of benefactors and trustees of the school. The *dongshi* own the land and buildings, continuing to work for the school as a matter of history and convention. But it is the Federal government, through the state-level education departments, that controls all academic aspects of the school, including assigning students and staff to the school.

One area over which the *dongshi* have lost control is the appointment of principals and teachers. The principals and staffs of all Chinese schools, as civil servants, are appointed and posted to their respective schools by the Ministry of Education according to qualifications, years of service and standing on a multilevel salary scale. To a large extent, history and convention, as well as political pressure, have managed to sustain the practice of posting principals who are literate in Chinese to the Chinese primary schools. But this is a persistent area of concern where it is thought that the Chinese schools are most vulnerable to "being stripped of their definitive characteristics". A principal or senior assistant who cannot speak Chinese would not be able to conduct school assembly in Chinese, may not be sympathetic to or uphold "the traditions of a Chinese school", and would probably not work closely with the school's *dongshi*. In former Chinese secondary schools, which are now part of the national system, the teaching staff are trained to teach in Malay and some may not speak or understand Mandarin. Many staff members are not of Chinese descent. As staff and students become more multi-ethnic, these schools become indistinguishable from other government schools, despite their origin as Chinese schools. The persistent fear in the minds of many Chinese leaders is that the Chinese primary schools too will slowly "lose their identity" in a similar progressive slide into total conformity with the "ultimate objective" of national education policy. In 1987, the appointment of senior administrators in the NTPSs who were not educated in Chinese and therefore not literate in Mandarin created a furore, which led to intense bickering between Malay and Chinese politicians.

In a political context in which Chinese education has consistently been a sensitive 'nerve' in Chinese and Malaysian politics, it is interesting to note that the number of non-Chinese students in NTPSs has increased significantly in the past decade. In 2000, about 60,000 non-Chinese were NTPS students, representing 10 per cent of the total enrolment.[20] A study of Chinese schools in Sabah found that this trend had started in the 1960s and by the 1990s, as the Chinese moved to the towns, there were several rural NTPSs with no Chinese students at all! In 1997, non-Chinese pupils, mainly Kadazans, made up a third of the total enrolment of NTPSs in Sabah. More interesting still is the fact that non-Chinese sit on the Board of Governors of these schools and a Kadazan is the principal of an NTPS. This trend has attracted some debate, but, due to a different tradition of inter-ethnic relations and ethnic politics in Sabah, it has neither evoked controversy nor a sense of crisis.[21] In other states in Malaysia, some non-Chinese study in NTPSs because they happen to live near these schools. More often, the reasons cited by non-Chinese parents who enrol their children in Chinese schools are that these schools are well run, students are subject to strict discipline and achieve good results. In short, the NTPSs are considered to be good schools where children receive a good education and learn an additional language. Whether this trend will continue or even increase remains to be seen.

At the secondary level, enrolments in the ICSSs sagged dramatically in the 1960s but began to revive in the 1970s. *Dongjiaozong* leaders successfully campaigned to revive interest in the ICSSs, making them the base for a revival of the *Dongjiaozong* itself as the centre of a counter-hegemonic cultural and political movement.[22] The ICSSs provide the continuity of having a secondary education conducted mainly in Chinese for NTPS students who do not wish to proceed to national secondary schools where the medium of instruction is Malay. Since the 1970s, the *Dongzong* has conducted examinations for ICSS students to make these schools a viable alternative to national schools. These examinations are not recognized by the Malaysian government, which means that ICSS students cannot gain admission to teachers' training colleges or other institutions of higher learning run by the government, unless they also sit for the state-run public examinations. But the ICSS examinations have been accepted as the basis

---

20 *Nanyang Siang Pao*, 30 November 2000.
21 Seah Soo Lin, 2001, pp 10 and 199.
22 See Tan Liok Ee, 1988, on the revival of the ICSSs in the 1970s; and Tan Liok Ee, 1992, on the *Dongjiaozong* movement.

for admission into private colleges in Malaysia as well as universities in Singapore, Taiwan, Australia, the United Kingdom and the United States. Nevertheless, total enrolment in the 60 ICSSs has remained level, at between 54,000 and 59,000 over the past ten years, indicating that a plateau has possibly been reached in the expansion of ICSS enrolment. Another limiting factor on the expansion of the ICSSs is the problem faced by Chinese schools in the past—of meeting a constant gap between income from fees and the expenditures needed to keep the schools going. Funds for development of buildings and facilities aside, the amount needed just to bridge the gap between fees and the cost of running the schools for the 60 ICSSs in the country has been estimated to be 20 million Malaysian ringgit per year.[23] Apart from the state of Sabah, where some ICSSs have received regular grants from the state government, ICSSs in other states do not receive any funding from the government. They continue to be *minban xuexiao*, relying completely on the support of local Chinese communities to keep going.

The *Dongjiaozong* has continued to uphold the principle of mother-tongue education in opposition to the state's commitment to a unitary system of schools teaching mainly in the national language. Defending multi-lingualism and a diverse system of schools in Malaysia's plural society, it has advocated a "complete" system of education in Chinese from primary to tertiary level, pushing for the establishment of the Merdeka University throughout the 1970s until a Federal court decision in 1982 ruled that the Constitutional provisions for freedom to use the Chinese language did not extend to the establishment of a Chinese-language university in Malaysia. More than a decade later, however, three tertiary institutions teaching mainly in Chinese have been set up.

Official permission for these three institutions to be set up came after the government had adopted a more liberal policy towards private tertiary education in the mid-1980s as one way to meet the tremendous demand for higher education among non-Malays who found it difficult to obtain a place in public universities where an ethnic quota was maintained as part of the positive discrimination measures to increase the number of Bumiputera graduates in all areas of study.[24] Ethnic quotas on university admissions, and employment in the public sector, started in the early 1970s as part of

---

23 *Sin Chew Jit Poh,* 26 December 2000.
24 The number of private institutions of higher learning more than doubled from 156 in 1992 to 354 in 1996. By 1998, there were 574 such institutions. In addition, there were 11 public universities, including the International Islamic University, 31 teacher training colleges and 12 polytechnics run by the government. See Molly NN Lee, 1999.

the New Economic Policy's objective of restructuring society by redressing ethnic imbalances. Each year, the number of Chinese students who, despite excellent results, failed to obtain places in public universities in the course of their choice has attracted attention. The problem appeared to be particularly severe in the 2001 intake, provoking much discussion and debate on the quota system of admission. Issues of access to higher education, in relation to social mobility and justice, have consistently attracted as much concern as those related to the preservation of the Chinese language, Chinese schools and Chinese culture. At the tertiary level, private institutions teaching mainly in English, provide the most important and popular alternatives to state-run institutions as indicated in the 1997–98 academic year. Out of a total enrolment of 153,990 in state-run tertiary-level institutions, 43,379 (28%) were non-Bumiputera students. By comparison, 232,069 non-Bumiputera students were enrolled in 666 private universities, colleges or branches of foreign universities.[25]

The Future

The unresolved problems and issues of the past five decades are likely to persist into the future, which will no doubt also bring new and different challenges. With between 85 and 90 per cent of Chinese children enrolled in NTPSs in the past two decades, there will certainly be a much larger pool of ethnic Chinese with basic literacy in Chinese than ever before. This, however, has not, and may not, necessarily in the future translate into a larger proportion of Chinese choosing to study in ICSSs at the secondary level. The vast majority of the Chinese are, and probably will continue to be, educated within the national system, in Malay, at the secondary level. Out of this group, relatively few continue to study Chinese Language and Literature as a secondary school subject. The problem for the NTPSs is that teachers must be recruited from this small pool of students who have studied the subject beyond six years of primary education. Each year, the number who qualify for, and are interested in, training to be teachers for the NTPSs is far below the number needed. The problem of insufficient teachers, due partially also to government neglect, will make it increasingly difficult for the NTPSs to survive in the long run.

The choice of NTPSs for a significant proportion of Chinese parents has as much to do with their evaluation of the NTPSs as good schools that

---

25 *Sin Chew Jit Poh*, 5 September 2001, Education Supplement.

offer their children an edge in a highly competitive world as with a commitment to education in the mother tongue *per se*. Thus, NTPSs with a reputation for good results are crowded while less reputable ones within the same city suffer from lack of students. Today, many parents would like their children to know Chinese as they are aware of its growing importance, which may well increase congruent with China's growing economic strength and international standing. But many parents also want their children to acquire fluency in English, important as an international language and for education at the tertiary level. Indeed, experiments with bilingual schools offering Chinese children the opportunity to study both languages began as early as 1886 at Gan Eng Seng School in Singapore. The same sense of pragmatism led Chinese secondary schools to switch to using English as the medium of instruction in the 1950s.[26] Since political independence in 1957, functional literacy in Malay, the national language, is also essential. One challenge that the Chinese in Malaysia face, and which the NTPSs and ICSSs must provide the lead in exploring, is to work out the best balance and find the most effective teaching methods, for children to learn three languages simultaneously.

In recent years, as the government seeks to propel Malaysia with increasing momentum towards globalization and "fully developed" status, several ideas for change in the education system have been mooted, all of which will bring new challenges for the Chinese schools and the future of Chinese education. Let us consider a few particularly challenging scenarios. How will Chinese parents react if the government decides that for Malaysia to become more competitive globally, national schools must devote more hours to teaching English and use English to teach Mathematics and Science? What if the government, after a few years of planning and building, launches into single session schools which are able to keep their students in school for longer hours, co-ordinating better with parents' work hours, and offering time within the school curriculum to also teach Chinese as a second language? Another possibility is that the government may decide to build a few model Vision schools, providing within them new primary schools that are fully funded by the government and use Chinese as the medium of instruction for all academic subjects but with their students joining other schools within the Vision school complex for school assembly, music, physical and sports activities all conducted in Malay.[27]

---

26 Tan Liok Ee, 1997, Ch 6.
27 The idea of integrating students from different language streams through common facilities and activities was first proposed in 1985 and resuscitated in 1995 and again

All of the above have indeed been proposed in recent years though none have as yet been fully implemented. But if they were to be, the relative attractiveness of national primary schools in comparison with the NTPSs would change, challenging reassessment by parents and requiring changes in the NTPSs and the thinking of leaders of opinion in Chinese society. On the other hand, if national schools are taken in a more Malay and more Islamic direction, there will be further polarization with more Chinese selecting to go to Chinese schools. It should be noted here that in the 1961 Education Act, the orientation of education policy was towards the objective of nation-building and national unity. By comparison, the preamble in the 1995 Education Act, outlining the basic orientations for education policy, focuses more on the importance of knowledge, especially in the areas of science, technology and information, in a global world and the role of education in achieving the objective of full economic development.

Even if the above scenarios do not materialize, they present the Chinese schools in Malaysia with issues and challenges about their future that require careful consideration. The rhetoric of many supporters of Chinese education, reflecting a deep distrust of official intentions, perceived as historically determined to achieve the "ultimate objective" of a single system of schools teaching in Malay, has been defensive, backward-looking and resistant to change. Chinese schools are frequently called upon to uphold their "historical mission" of "defending and upholding mother-tongue education" and "never to lose their special characteristics/essence" (*yungbu bianzhi*). But what this "essence" is and what are the "special characteristics" or the "unique traditions" of the Chinese schools that must be preserved at all costs, are not always clear. That the medium of instruction should be Chinese is obvious, but must it be the sole medium or can it be the main medium with latitude for other languages to be used for a few subjects?

The high value placed on academic success and a tradition of enforcing "strict discipline" is yet another feature frequently mentioned as a *tezhi*, or special characteristic, of the Chinese schools. But remaining tied to old traditions of enforcing discipline and/or methods of teaching may be both a strength as well as a weakness. The Chinese schools are known for

---

in 2000 as Vision Schools. This proposal has been consistently opposed by leaders of the *Dongjiaozong* who see it as an attempt to erode the distinctive identity of the Chinese schools by progressively increasing the usage of Malay from extracurricular to academic activities. For reports of the controversy over the Vision School concept in 2000, see *Sin Chew Jit Poh,* October–November 2000, and the background article in *Star*, 5 November 2000.

enforcing a rigorous work ethic, giving lots of homework to their students, and adopting an authoritarian classroom approach. However, many educational psychologists today advocate radical changes in the traditional classroom relationship to encourage child-centred learning, de-emphasize rote memory work and stimulate creativity. The need for changes in pedagogical methods and classroom culture is something Chinese education organizations need to explore.

A distinctive feature of the Chinese schools, especially in the Malaysian context, is their historical origin as *minban xuexiao*. This was their strength in the past. In the present, where the NTPSs, though a legitimate part of the national system, are not fully funded by the government because their buildings and land are still held in private hands, this is both strength and weakness. Understandably, few schools have chosen to hand over their school buildings and land to the government, and are unlikely to do so, as this would mean severing links with the school's past and losing altogether the local community's claim to some say, however limited, in decisions affecting the school. Though this has meant the disadvantage of being denied development funds, it has sustained the strong symbiotic links between school and local community, usually to the benefit of the school. Where the *dongshi* involvement is motivated by traditional values of philanthropy, the school benefits from community support. But, where the *dongshi* are divided by different political affiliations, the school can become a site for political disputes, disruptive and damaging to the school.

Perhaps two other important points to keep in mind are that there is a wide diversity of opinions on many questions about education among the Chinese living in Malaysia and that there is also a diversity of local conditions in NTSSs, ICSSs and former Chinese secondary schools that are part of the national system. The situation in Sabah in which non-Chinese are accepted as *dongshi* and principals of Chinese schools is rather unusual. Similarly, that students and staff may be predominantly non-Chinese though the school continues to teach predominantly in Chinese is an interesting local variant. So is the fact that increasing numbers of non-Chinese students in Chinese schools affirm their status positively as schools of parental choice, though this may require these schools to make some changes in school culture and governance to accommodate a multi-ethnic student body. Another aspect of the Sabah situation is a stronger historical link of the Chinese schools with Christian organizations and more usage of English in the Chinese secondary schools. Unlike in other states, local conditions have made it possible for the government of Sabah to be supportive of ICSSs. While Sabah may in all these ways be unique, the importance of local factors and differences must be borne in mind in understanding the relative strengths and weaknesses of Chinese schools, and the appeal of Chinese education, in different locations within Malaysia.

In an ethnically diverse society with a wide range of differences in specific local conditions, the state should be more accepting and tolerant of diverse languages, different cultural traditions, and a wide range of different educational institutions, public and private. Equally, opinion leaders in Chinese society should manifest the same latitude towards diversity for Chinese schools in the country, allowing them to experiment with different ways of meeting local needs. Above all, in the discourse between tradition and modernity, rather than being tied to the past, the Chinese schools may well find that by taking the initiative to explore change, they may find new sources of strength to continue their resilient history into the 21st century and beyond.

References

Lee, Kam Hing, and Tan Chee Beng, eds. *The Chinese in Malaysia*. Shah Alam, Malaysia: Oxford University Press, 2000.

Malaysia 1995. *Education Bill*.

Lee, Molly NN. *Private Higher Education in Malaysia*. Penang: School of Educational Studies, Universiti Sains Malaysia, Monograph Series No 2/1999.

Seah, Soo Lin. "Perkembangan Sekolah-sekolah Cina di Borneo Utara/Sarah 1888–1970: Suatu Tinjauan Dari Segi Sejarah" (The Development of Chinese Schools in North Borneo/Sarah 1888–1970: A Historical Survey). MA thesis, Universiti Sains Malaysia, Penang, 2001.

Tan, Liok Ee. "Chinese Independent Schools in Malaysia: Varying Responses to Changing Demands". In *Changing Identities of the Southeast Asian Chinese since World War II*, edited by Jennifer Cushman and Wang Gungwu. Hongkong: Hongkong University Press, 1988, pp 61–74.

———. "*Dongjiaozong* and the Challenge to Cultural Hegemony 1951–1987". In *Fragmented Vision: Culture and Politics in Contemporary Malaysia*, edited by Joel S Kahn and Francis Loh Kok Wah. Sydney: Asian Studies Association of Australia in Association with Allen and Unwin, 1992, pp 181–201.

———. *The Politics of Chinese Education in Malaya, 1945–1961*. Kuala Lumpur: Oxford University Press, 1997.

———. "Chinese Schools in Malaysia: A Case of Cultural Resilience". In *The Chinese in Malaysia*, edited by Lee Kam Hing and Tan Chee Beng. Shah Alam, Malaysia: Oxford University Press, 2000, pp 228–54.

UCSTA. *1985 nian Quanguo Huawen Xiaoxue diaocha baogao* (Report of Nationwide survey of Chinese primary schools, 1985). Kuala Lumpur: UCSTA, 1985.

———. 1987. *Huaxiao Wenti Yantaohui teji* (Special issue on the Seminar on Problems of Chinese Primary Schools). Kuala Lumpur: UCSTA.

———. *Dongjiaozong Quanguo Fazhan Huaxiao Gongweihui 1999 nian gongzuo baogaoshu* (1999 Report of *Dongjiaozong* National Working Committee for the Development of Chinese Primary Schools). Kuala Lumpur: UCSTA, 1999.

Zheng, Liangshu. *Malaixiya Huawen jiaoyu fazhanshi*. Kuala Lumpur: Malaixiya Huaxiao Jiaosihui Zonghui, 1998, vols 1 and 2.

Part III

Culture and Entrepreneurship

Chapter 9

CHINESE ENTREPRENEURS IN MALAYSIA: TRADITIONAL AND MODERN

Jamie Mackie

How can we meaningfully apply words like "traditional" and "modern" to Malaysian-Chinese businessmen of the 19th and the 20th century? Most of them were no doubt predominantly traditional in outlook and business methods until as recently as 50 or 60 years ago, with a few notable exceptions; yet by the 1990s many were becoming increasingly modern in some senses of the word, but also retaining many traditional traits. So there have clearly been processes of change and interaction occurring constantly, both in the society generally and also in the behaviour patterns of individuals. But what are the criteria by which we can distinguish between the more traditional of them and the modern in either colonial Malaya or in post-independence Malaysia? Can such words even be defined with any precision at all, or do we simply have to think about them in terms of a spectrum, with two quasi-Weberian ideal-types at each end, along which we can see various individuals ranged towards one pole or the other (roughly, and all too subjectively), or hovering tantalizingly in the middle?

In his opening address to the conference on "Ethnic Chinese in Singapore and Malaysia: A Dialogue between Tradition and Modernity", Mr Wong Kan Seng spoke of the "constant dialogue between the traditional and the modern" throughout the history of the Southeast Asian Chinese, and of how the two outlooks have at times clashed but also "have constantly merged". That is very much the point I will be illustrating here. But instead of starting with a hair-splitting examination of definitions, I want to look first at some brief vignettes of individuals, in the hope that they will help us to form an impression of what the traditional-modern spectrum can tell us about all this. It turns out to be surprisingly hard to decide where or how to draw a firm line between the two types of Malaysian-Chinese entrepreneurs, even though some of them seem definitely to be located closer to one end of the spectrum than the other in various respects. Yet when we try to specify particular features that distinguish the two types, or align particular individuals across the spectrum, it is not easy to be precise about it. They may even shift across it over the course of a lifetime.

Can we safely say, for example, that among the tin-mining magnates of the late 19th century the most eminent of them, Loke Yew, was a more "traditional" or "modern" *towkay* than his near-contemporaries, Chung Keng Kwee or Foo Choo Choon? I am not sure how one would go about deciding that. Or that in recent times Robert Kuok has been more "modern" than, say, the less well-known William Cheng Heng Jem, of the Amalgamated Steel Corporation (Amsteel) and Lion group, just because Kuok has been so much more cosmopolitan, highly successful and internationally well known than Cheng—or than other wealthy towkays like Loh Boon Siew (Oriental Holdings, the Honda assembler) or Lim Goh Tong (of Genting fame)? Most people would have little hesitation in agreeing that Kuok has been one of the most thoroughly modern and cosmopolitan tycoons of the last half-century, or that Lee Kong Chian was hardly less outstanding in that respect in his time and was almost certainly the most modern in outlook of the mid-century group. In the early 20th century, the famous entrepreneur, Tan Kah Kee (who was not a Malayan Chinese but a resident of Singapore, although his rubber and pineapple interests were located mainly in Malaya), was strikingly modern in his business activities, although very traditional in other respects. But all of them were modern in diverse ways, while remaining quite traditional in other respects. Much the same could be said about the more traditional *towkays* of both the past and the present, I suspect. And it is the differences which are often most interesting and revealing, for the world is not a neat and tidy place in this respect; hence sharply defined categories can be altogether too arbitrary.

Aw Boon Haw (1882–1954) and Others

A good starting-point here might be some comments made about Aw Boon Haw, the famous "Tiger Balm king" of the early 20th century, who was one of the more traditional Chinese entrepreneurs of his time (although not strictly speaking a resident of Malaya but of Singapore, after his move from Burma in 1926), taken from a very useful survey of Singaporean entrepreneurs by Chan Kwok Bun and Claire Chiang.[1] Aw made a large fortune from Chinese medicines nearly a century ago, before becoming involved heavily in the modern world of newspapers, banking and assorted pharmaceuticals in the 1920-30s. He is described as very hierarchical, strict, paternalistic and, at the same time, benevolent and philanthropic (Chan and Chiang, 1994: 317):

---

[1] Much of the material in Chan and Chiang's book is based on interviews conducted by the Oral History Department of the Ministry of Information and the Arts. Useful additional sources on Aw Boon Haw are Chan (1998) and Yeoh and Teo (1996).

> The family business organization was hierarchical and nepotistic, with close family members heading the various business activities and children of trusted employees filling up various positions of their business firms ... [Aw was a patriarch and an autocrat] head of all his various businesses. He ran his business according to the traditional Chinese custom. His sons, daughters and nephews, though they were made managers of his various companies ... must refer to him for major decisions and they must make regular reports to him. He made all the decisions. No one dared suggest anything to him except perhaps through a close friend of Aw's. He felt that as head of the family he was to be obeyed at all times ... He was very strict and thrifty. He ran his household in the traditional Chinese way—with him as head of the family, to be respected and obeyed, never to be questioned, neither by his wives nor his children ... He did not want his children to learn the Western ways and to become too independent of their parents. Questioning their parents was something he would not tolerate in his children.

Two comments on a much younger man, Tan Lark Sye, convey much the same picture. Comparing him with his contemporary, Lee Kong Chian, the other great rubber king of the mid-century decades, who, like Tan, had also started his career under the legendary Tan Kah Kee in the post-1918 boom years of the rubber industry, one informant remarked that Tan was quite the opposite of Lee, who was generally considered very able in employing workers and making full use of talented people in his employ. Tan, on the other hand,

> did everything himself. He would not let others do it ... He declined with age. He had no successors to carry on the business.

His nephew, Tan Eng Joo, remarked that Tan was

> a strong-willed man and of course a self-made man. He managed the business the way he saw fit ... Aik Hoe prospered under him. But he never gave any importance to proper management. ... He was too concerned about the continuity of Aik Hoe, especially in its position as the leading firm in the rubber trade ... Being strong-willed and running the business as a one-man show, Tan insisted on continuing the way it was. ... In contrast, Lee Kong Chian reorganized Lee Rubber Company into a modern corporation with proper management. And as it came to pass, Aik Hoe faded with the passing away of Tan Lark Sye, while Lee Rubber continued to expand and prosper.

There we have one key aspect of the contrast between the old-fashioned and the modern very neatly encapsulated. We will look into other aspects later. It would not be difficult to find many other Straits Chinese of that time with similar traits to those of Aw Boon Haw and Tan Lark Sye—and no doubt many others even today, a couple of generations later, although probably fewer. So these cases serve to provide us with an ostensive definition of the traditional type to which many others approximate.

But they were not all like that, we should remember. Another facet of traditional values and business behaviour, revealing a different side of the "traditional" *towkay*, can be seen in the account of Tay Kia Hong's "compassion towards his workers, business partners, his wife and children", deeply rooted in his childhood sufferings at the hands of a cruel uncle and aunt in Muar in his teens (Chan and Chiang, 1994: 285). He had been sensitized by those experiences to an awareness of the needs of others and to a feeling that he should try to repay any consideration he had received; so in later life he gave a lot of money to charitable organizations (including a scholarship fund for the poor in Muar, where he had grown up) and he dealt generously with his workers when they were afflicted by hardships.

> Notions of propriety, reciprocity, decency and mutual respect for favours given and received were some of the many components of this business creed ... defined not only as "the proper way" of doing business but also as the "righteous", "honourable" and "moral" way of doing good (Chan and Chiang, 1994: 287).

Lim Goh Tong (1919–)

In contrast to these admirably succinct and illuminating glimpses into the personalities of two traditional Chinese *towkays*, I can best depict the qualities of one of today's more modern ones through the career of Lim Goh Tong (b 1919, Fujian) of the Genting (casino) group. He may not necessarily be the most modern in outlook or education of contemporary Malaysian-Chinese capitalists by any means, for his schooling was in fact very limited; but he has certainly been outstandingly successful in the modern world of corporate enterprise and high finance despite that. His was initially a typical "rags to riches" story of the old-style *towkay*, marked by unusual shrewdness and adaptability to changing commercial and political circumstances, not unlike those of many of his more traditional precursors (Searle, 1999: 228–29). He had nothing like the educational advantages that Lee Kong Chian or Robert Kuok enjoyed, or most of the new wave of post-1970s "paper millionaires".

Arriving in Kuala Lumpur as a penniless immigrant from China in 1937 at the age of 18, Lim started out as a carpenter and hawker working for his uncle. He soon established his own construction company, which boomed in the mid-1950s to become one of Malaysia's largest. At the same time, he diversified his investments into tin mining, iron ore and then into rubber and palm oil in the prosperous later years of the decade, in much the same manner as most of the big Chinese tycoons of that time. In 1965 he made his biggest leap towards mega-wealth when he had an extraordinary stroke of good luck in establishing the Genting Highlands tourist resort and obtaining government approval from Tunku Abdul Rahman for a casino licence to go with it. That was due in part to his having earlier built up friendly relations with Tan Sri Noah Omar, a member of the Johor executive council and father-in-law of Tun Razak and Tun Husein Onn. Up to that point his career had not been notably different from that of many other older-generation Chinese in Malaya whose stories had been broadly similar; nor was it notably more "modern" in character than theirs. But in the next phase of his career he showed that he had learnt how to operate very successfully in the modern world, as well as any of his predecessors or contemporaries.

> Lim shrewdly combined the advantage of a casino licence, state support and the opportunities afforded by the growth of Malaysia's stock exchange to adapt his business operations to the changing economic and political environment of the 1970s. In the process he vastly increased his already considerable wealth ... Genting soon became one of Malaysia's most profitable companies, a "blue chip" counter on the KLSE ... [and Lim] extensively diversified first in Malaysia and then abroad [as a hedge against any Muslim backlash against its gambling activities] (Searle, 1999: 228).

By 1980, Asiatic Development, one of his subsidiary companies, had such extensive holdings in rubber, palm oil and cocoa that it was ranked as one of Malaysia's five largest plantation companies, and among its most promising (Searle, 1999: 230–31; Gomez, 1999: 49–58). It diversified downstream into processing, refining and manufacturing. Lim also developed interests in paper manufacturing and property development, as well as overseas gambling operations of various kinds. Meanwhile he had "built up a core of trustworthy managers to help him run his multimillion dollar multinational group", with two of his daughters and three sons closely integrated into that group. He forged new alliances in keeping with Malaysia's shifting political tides, observes Searle (1999: 229), by assisting towards the achievement of state objectives and creating close personal relations with a wide range of UMNO leaders, although not in the manner of the "New Wealth" cronies of the 1980s so much as along the lines of Kuok 20 years earlier. I will return to that later in a comparison of Lim, Kuok and several others as examples of late 20th century modern businessmen, noting their similarities and differences.

Conceptual and Definitional Issues

Before we go any further, I want to consider whether we can get any closer to pinning down more precise definitions of what we mean by the words "traditional" and "modern" in this context. In doing so, I will not plunge into the conceptual thickets of deconstruction of such notions as tradition or traditional culture, or of "modernity" in its application to overseas Chinese business enterprises in the 20th century, even though a lot of further investigation needs to be done into the meanings that have been attributed to these notions at different times and places. But a few issues should be mentioned which will at least point us in that direction.

It is easier to say roughly what we mean by tradition than modernity since there are relatively fixed points of reference for the traditional Chinese outlook on life or ways of doing business, as the comment on Aw Boon Haw indicates well, whereas our ideas of what is modern are constantly changing. Seventy years ago Tan Kah Kee would have been generally regarded as one of the most modern of all Chinese capitalists in the Straits Settlements or the Nanyang generally, for he was quick to adopt new lines of business (pineapple canning initially, then rubber planting and remilling; later shipping, briefly, and in the 1920s the manufacture of tyres, shoes and numerous other forms of rubber goods), for all of which he had to utilize new technologies. His Singapore factory was described by Ormsby-Gore, a senior British parliamentarian, in 1928 as "one of the most remarkable enterprises in Asia ... a vast and varied factory that he has entirely built up and extended himself with Chinese management" (Yong, 1987: 66). His passion to develop new educational institutions in Xiamen was also a strikingly modern trait. Yet after his collapse in 1934, attention was drawn to some of his more old-fashioned or traditionally Chinese characteristics as well as his modern ones, especially his autocratic control of his business enterprises and reluctance to surrender ultimate authority over them. In contrast, his son-in-law, Lee Kong Chian, showed himself in the years following to be a significantly more modern entrepreneur, soon developing a deep and broad knowledge of the rubber trade in its broad global context, as well as of modern banking business after he became chairman of the Oversea-Chinese Banking Corporation, OCBC, and of how to create effective management structures. But Lee was a cautious rather than a daring entrepreneur ("Solid as a Rock" was an appropriate title for OCBC's first official history) of a very different stamp from the more modern members of the next generation of buccaneering Malaysian-Chinese entrepreneurs of the 1980s, or even the very cosmopolitan and well-educated Robert Kuok.

What, then, do we mean by "modern" in this context? Perhaps the simplest answer is just to stress the ability to see and learn how to use the advantages of new technology or modern science and the diverse methodologies behind it, which have so dramatically transformed the world since the 19th century, with all the changes they have led to. Or, more broadly, the ability to operate confidently in the modern world of business and changing industrial processes, without being handicapped by the limitations of traditional

Chinese methods of doing business (ie, the strongly familistic, personalistic and paternalistic features thereof; the reliance on *guanxi* and *xinyong,* but suspicion of Western notions of transparency or disclosure of accounts). Yet there's no one criterion of modernity, for there are so many ways of being modern, in business as well as in life. And while many Southeast Asian Chinese of the last century might have been affected by some aspects of modernity, most retained also some vestiges of their traditional Chinese culture, values and upbringing, in varying degrees. Much the same could be said of Westerners, of course (and, very clearly, of most Japanese); but the erosion of traditional values has been proceeding far longer in most Western countries and the tensions between the pulls of tradition and modernity have been less severe there than in China or among the overseas Chinese since the Opium War.

Even the notion of what is "traditionally Chinese" turns out to be more problematic than it seems at first sight, however, although it is often spelt out in terms of traditional Chinese cultural traits. But neither a political nor a cultural definition of the term is very satisfactory. In a 1991 symposium on "The Changing Meaning of Being Chinese Today", Myron Cohen argued that the sense of being Chinese did not have much to do with cultural traditions at all, either in mainland China or among the widely dispersed diaspora Chinese.[2] In fact, "iconoclastic nationalists" of the Fourth of May Movement had regarded Chinese tradition as a source of national weakness and wanted to embrace modernity as an alternative to it. Unlike Japan and some Western countries, which have "fed their nationalism by embracing their tradition so as to construct or even invent a far more glorious version of it", the Chinese attitude for much of the last century was to regard traditional culture as "feudalism" and totally unacceptable. Chinese nationalism has been "amazingly devoid of elaborated cultural content", as exemplified by the fact that modern national holidays have little cultural meaning, although the traditional lunar New Year and other festivals certainly do. The new definition of being Chinese "is firmly rooted in nationalism, in a concept of China as a nation-state ... Modern Chinese nationalism ... is not at all defined in the first instance within a larger cultural framework". For much of the population of the PRC, "nationalism

---

2   The article by the American anthropologist Myron Cohen, "The Living Tree", is one in a special issue of *Daedalus* devoted to the question: "What does it mean to be Chinese?" Most of the contributors deal with overseas Chinese views on that issue, but Cohen discusses mainland Chinese answers to it and the relevance of traditional Chinese culture there in the face of the challenges of modernity.

coexists with a sense of being Chinese still conditioned to varying degrees by traditional orientations ... [but] the cultural content of their nationalism is sparse indeed"—and presumably even more complex and problematic for Chinese residing outside China, where there is "an on-going crisis of identification ... as much a quest as it is a condition". Many Southeast Asian Chinese wanted over the last century to bring the benefits of modernity to China, particularly after seeing how greatly they had strengthened Japan, yet they were rarely eager to abandon their Chineseness in the process. In Yong Chin Fatt's fine account, Tan Kah Kee's determination to introduce modern education to Fujian through the schools and university he founded there—and also a vocational training school in navigation—was striking testimony to that; yet he also wanted the students there to retain their cultural roots in Chinese learning too (Yong, 1987). I suspect that few modern overseas Chinese would differ from him much in that regard, any more than any modern Japanese would.

How the transition from traditional to modern attitudes to doing business has occurred among 20th-century Chinese entrepreneurs in Singapore and Malaysia is a matter on which some interesting ideas have been put forward by Chan and Chiang (1994: 372–77) in their useful study of entrepreneurship in Singapore (and to some extent also Malaysia):

> While an entrepreneur would "modernize" by introducing new technology, learning new skills, and rationalizing and reorganizing his administrative and wage structures, it was not completely evident that he would, or wanted to, "modernize" his social relations. In fact, what he seems to have done continually was to "family-ize" social relations to reaffirm the "old-fashioned" traditional values of reciprocity and *ganqing*, or feelings for each other.

Management styles varied from authoritarian paternalism to benevolent paternalism, the latter directed more towards distant kin and non-kin (as a means to bind the workers' allegiance) and the former towards family or kin members. As enterprises grew larger, however, it became harder to sustain personalized and family-like paternalism and benevolence towards their workers, or to maintain the old autocratic forms of paternalism towards family members that had so often characterized the older generations of *towkays* in Southeast Asia. They had to meet "the continual challenge of having to modernize and rationalize an enterprise according to more universal criteria ... thus nepotism was relegated to a small role". But the question arises:

> How did they handle the norms and values such as reciprocity, benevolence and protection ... as well as the need for personal trust, loyalty and trustworthiness which they might now have to redefine?

They had to strike a balance there, "responding to the challenge in various ways ... rationalizing the organizational structure and adopting new managerial strategies and wage policies to find a middle path between old and new"— yet always maintaining a "tenacious adherence to family-type organization" and ultimate family control of the ownership of the enterprise.

Most of the entrepreneurs interviewed by Chan and Chiang were proud of having "modernized" their management structures, usually with a combination of Chinese and modern Western methods. The "family-ization" process began in various ways—monetary incentives, promotions, and non-tangible ways of winning their workers' gratitude and loyalty. But there was generally a recognition of the superiority of modern management methods in terms of employment practices and well-defined authority positions. The potential for conflict was recognized, however, between that and traditional management based mainly on trust, loyalty and mutual reciprocity. The entrepreneurs did not just choose between one or the other approach but tried to maximize the advantages of combining modern structural organization with a traditional mode of interpersonal communications.

What this account shows us, I think, is that the line of distinction between traditional and modern management styles is inevitably blurred and cross-cutting, or "constantly merging", as Mr Wong put it, although differing in details from case to case. But the basic features emerge clearly enough.

Two Eminent Tycoons: Traditional and Modern

Let us now look in more detail at two of the most famous Malaysian-Chinese *towkays*, Loke Yew and Lee Kong Chian, who reveal something of what we mean by traditional and modern businessmen, yet also show some features from both sides of the line of distinction between them.[3]

Loke Yew (1846–1917)

Although not necessarily the most "traditional" of the early Chinese *towkays* in Malaya, Loke Yew belongs well down towards that end of the spectrum

---

3   I was initially undecided on whether to cite Lee Kong Chian as the best example of the modern type or Robert Kuok, since they had some similar features. But Lee was born almost a generation earlier than Kuok and stood out among his contemporaries far more sharply for his adoption of modern methods of business. He was a pioneer in the rubber and banking industries to a greater degree and no less successful in the long run in creating two remarkable modern enterprises.

if judged simply by his career path and pattern of business activities. Like so many of his contemporaries, he spread his business interests across a wide and diverse range (a common risk-spreading strategy), far more than most, it seems. He had only a rudimentary education, yet he was shrewd in assessing where the opportunities for making rich profits were unfolding in the fast-changing British colony around the turn of the century.

Born to a poor peasant family in Guangzhou, he left for Singapore at the age of 13 and, like so many other rags-to-riches entrepreneurs of that time, he struggled through various menial jobs until he had saved up a modest sum with which to start his own shop in the late 1860s, which became the basis of his Hong Loong enterprise in Singapore.[4] He then set off to Larut to become involved in the tin-mining operations which were then starting to expand rapidly there, and he soon acquired his own tin mine at Kamunting. This venture was disrupted by the Larut civil war, however, in which his mines were laid waste and his workers scattered. But he soon recovered after obtaining a supply contract to the British troops engaged in the 1875 war against Maharaja Lela. The profits from that enabled him to return to tin mining, but when the price collapsed at the end of the 1870s he nearly became bankrupt. He turned instead to revenue farming in the 1880s and was involved over the next 20 years in a wide range of farms—general revenue farming, gambling, spirits, toddy, *candu*, attap and timber—in various districts of central Malaya, some of them in collaboration with Chiew Yoke, the Ghee Hin secret society leader with whom he had been closely involved in several property ventures after the great Kuala Lumpur fire of 1885. Meanwhile he had continued with his tin-mining ventures after the price recovered and made a considerable fortune from them, becoming one of the foremost of Malaya's tin magnates by the end of the century.

The diversity of his activities and business interests in that formative phase of his career is one of its most striking features, and it is one that persisted until the end of his life. But although tin became a more central part of his vast empire in his later years, it was never the whole of it. His property holdings in Kuala Lumpur alone are said by Butcher to have been, in fact, the main source of his great wealth (pers. comm.). A list of his business interests refers, in addition to tin mining and rubber estates which he acquired after 1905, two coconut plantations, oil mills, a cement factory,

---

4 This account of Loke Yew's life is based largely on Lee Kam Hing and Chow Mun Seong (1997: 123–25) and information kindly supplied by Dr John Butcher.

shares in Kwong Yik Bank, Straits Steamship Co, Straits Trading Co (the colony's first mechanized tin-refining operation), Malayan Collieries, Raub gold mine, an engineering company and Pahang Motorcar Service Co; in addition he had investments in a coastal steamer, a Banjarmasin coal mine and a Burmese rice mill (Lee and Chow, 1997:124). Yet when we compare this vast but almost ramshackle diversity of investments with the far more focused set of investments built up a few years later by Tan Kah Kee or Lee Kong Chian, the difference between traditional and modern approaches to business strategies becomes strikingly apparent.

That does not mean he was so old-fashioned that he made no use of modern technology when its advantages became apparent to him. He established Serendak Hydraulic Co as one of the early hydraulic mines, and introduced electric power at his Rawang mines in 1894, after creating Rawang Electric Supply Co in conjunction with an Indian entrepreneur. He was one of the first Chinese tin miners to make use of the ore refinery set up by Straits Trading and after buying shares in it he became a director over the last ten years of his life. In fact, his business activities over the last 20 or so years of his life appear to have differed greatly from the very traditional strategies of his earlier decades, when he relied heavily on his control of large numbers of immigrant labourers and on various tax-farming contracts. He appears to have become increasingly close to British officials and some planters in that later phase, both socially and in business partnerships. (He was also an enthusiastic patron of the Turf Club.) But he played only a modest part in the early boom years of the rubber industry and he was more famous for his tin-mining ventures than for rubber plantations.

Lee Kong Chian (1894–1967)

Lee Kong Chian must be ranked as one of the most remarkable Chinese businessmen of the 20th century in all Southeast Asia, for he was even more successful in some respects than his famous father-in-law, Tan Kah Kee, being primarily responsible for the establishment of two great commercial enterprises, the Lee Rubber Corporation and OCBC, which are both still flourishing more than 30 years after his death. He was an unusually successful institution-builder and an indisputably modern man, even though he clung to some traditionally Chinese features and values. Despite residing mainly in Singapore, he and his firms played such a prominent part in the growth of the Malayan rubber industry throughout the 20th century that he can appropriately be included here as one of the great Malaysian *towkays*.

Significantly, he had a very good start in life with a solid education in both Chinese and British schools and a sound grasp of English. He did not become actively involved in the business world until he was about 20— and then at the highest levels, not at all in the manner of the legendary rags-to-riches penniless immigrants.[5] In his first few years in Singapore he found work as a teacher in Chinese schools and as a translator for the newspaper *Lat Poh*; he also began training to be a surveyor, and enrolled for a correspondence course in civil engineering at a US college. After buying some shares in the National Product Company in 1914, he attracted the attention of its founder, who offered him employment as an assistant manager of the company. In 1916 he was recruited by Tan Kah Kee to become manager of his rubber department, reportedly because of his fluency in English—just at the time when the Malayan rubber industry and Tan's initial investments in it were beginning to expand rapidly. Tan was so impressed by him that he gave him the hand of his eldest daughter in marriage, after which his career took off dramatically. He headed the finance department of Tan's entire business corporation from 1921 until 1927 (at a time when Tan was spending a lot of time back in Xiamen building his schools and a university there, and was therefore very dependent on his managers in Singapore), but was by then becoming alarmed by the large debts Tan was incurring for his schools and decided to branch out on his own. His Lee Smoke House was founded at Muar in 1927 and soon grew into the Lee Rubber Corporation which became the flagship of the Lee Group.

Lee's business ventures flourished remarkably in the years after he set out on his own, despite the huge problems created for his companies by the 1930s Depression (which hit the rubber industry especially hard) and the Japanese occupation of Malaya and Singapore between 1942 and 1945. Lee Rubber, which became a limited liability company in 1931, grew to be one of the foremost companies in the industry, involved not just in plantations but also in remilling and processing plants, packing and exporting, with offshore companies in Sumatra and Thailand and later even in New York. Lee was chairman of the Rubber Traders Association at the end of the 1930s and became a dominating figure in the industry after the war. Other Lee enterprises included pineapple cultivation and canning (he

---

5   Lee Kong Chian was born in Fujian and came to Singapore at the age of nine to join his father after several years of elementary education in China; he then attended the Anglo-Chinese School, followed by several years at Yeung Shia School before returning to China at the age of 14 for his further education. He was studying civil engineering at the College of Mining and Communication in Tang Shan when the Republic was established by Sun Yat-sen. Lee returned to Singapore soon after, aged 18.

was known as "the pineapple king" as well as "the rubber king"), oil milling, sawmills, biscuit manufacturing and printing, while the Lee Group also had investments in nearly a dozen of the colony's major financial, insurance and trading companies. His most significant venture in the 1930s was the major part he played in bringing about the creation of OCBC in 1932 through a merger of three smaller Chinese banks which had been badly crippled by the Depression. Lee was a founding director and became chairman from 1937 to 1964, when it grew to be one of the largest and most solidly based banks in Southeast Asia, surviving the Japanese Occupation and the difficult years of the Emergency due to its cautious and prudent management and financial policies (Wilson, 1972). It built up branches throughout Southeast Asia, becoming the first truly multinational overseas Chinese bank, although the war and its aftermath shattered its hopes of maintaining that role after 1941. Lee happened to be in America at the time of the attack on Pearl Harbour, attending an international rubber conference on behalf of Malayan rubber interests, so he found himself stranded there throughout the war. That proved both beneficial and problematic for him, since it must have extended his knowledge of the modern world of finance and commerce considerably, although he was isolated from the other OCBC executives.[6] When he returned to Singapore in 1946, he was appointed by the British to the Advisory Council. But he resigned two years later to concentrate on his business interests and those of the rubber industry more generally at a time of exceptional difficulties and challenges from synthetic rubber.

By the 1960s the Lee Group had 18,500 acres of rubber under cultivation as well as 15 factories and 20 branch offices throughout the world. Since Lee Kong Chian's death in 1967 it has maintained its pre-eminence as the strongest rubber trading corporation in all Southeast Asia and has been a pioneer in the development of the new technologies which have transformed the natural rubber industry since 1945. The Lee Group, based mainly on Lee Rubber and OCBC, but also embracing a diversity of other interests, has made the generational transition to the second and third generations of the family with greater success, it seems, than any other large overseas Chinese business group in Southeast Asia.

---

6 During his years of involuntary residence in USA, Lee "lectured at the University of Columbia to US military and civil officers undergoing special training ... [and] also served in the US Red Cross and organized successful campaigns to raise funds for war victims in China" (Lee and Chow, 1997: 89). Meanwhile, senior OCBC officers were maintaining the bank's financial interests outside Singapore-Malaya in India, Australia and elsewhere (Wilson, 1972). In 1945–46 OCBC quickly resumed operations in the colony again in close co-operation with the returning British authorities.

The key to Lee's success in building up such a solid and adaptable conglomerate lay, to a large degree, in his ability to adopt modern management techniques (as mentioned earlier by Tan Eng Joo, to create "a modern corporation with modern management") and to keep abreast of the latest technologies, but also in his retention of various Chinese traits that won the loyalty of his workers. As Ng Kong Beng put it:

> Lam Aik Company [one of Lee Rubber's subsidiaries] functions according to Chinese business ways, but its management and organization are similar to those of the foreign companies. That is why it has become a very big company today and has been in existence for a long time ... In those days there were no fixed working hours, especially in the branches which dealt with the buying and selling of rubber ... If there were transactions, employees stayed back to complete the deals. If there was no work the staff could idle in the office. This was the Chinese way of doing business. It was entirely different from the way of the foreigners.
>
> I always felt there was something special about Mr Lee Kong Chian ... Something different. If the employees invited him to a sumptuous meal, they would be severely reprimanded ... He was a thrifty man ... yet he was generous in other ways ... His generosity and charitability was well known.

Lee Kong Chian's role as a community leader and philanthropist was not as outstanding as Tan Kah Kee's had been, but was nonetheless very substantial; the Lee Foundation, in particular, introduced a far more modern approach to philanthropic activities, even though the impulse towards them derived from a very traditional source.

Some Later Variants of the Modern Tycoon

An interesting comparison by Gomez (1999: 64–66) of three leading contemporary Malaysian-Chinese tycoons, Robert Kuok, Lim Goh Tong and Loh Boon Siew (Oriental Holdings), has direct relevance to the issues we are looking at here. He notes that Lim and Loh were both "penniless immigrants" with little formal education who built up large business empires by first establishing a strong corporate base and then diversifying successfully. Lim did so initially through his strong position in the construction industry, later through his Genting and other casino interests which provided him with a lucrative cash flow. Loh did likewise from a very different base as a retailer and assembler of Honda motorcycles and later cars, then as a manufacturer of automobile parts.[7] Neither had the kind of personal background that would have inclined them towards a strikingly new and modern type of business career, as Kuok had (and also

Lee Kong Chian, half a century earlier), yet they had both apparently learnt the skills required to operate with outstanding success in the modern world of corporate enterprise and high finance. Loh created a more narrowly focused business empire than Lim Goh Tong, vertically integrated around the automotive industry, and he floated his company's shares on the KLSE as early as 1963, long before most other Chinese firms did so; but he did not follow in the footsteps of the later "paper millionaires" who became rich by wheeling and dealing on the share market with borrowed money. In fact, he pursued essentially cautious financial policies, funding the expansion of his enterprises from his own capacity to generate capital, never even using rights issues to raise funds (Searle, 1999: 237–38). Loh also differed from both Lim and Kuok in that he made little use of political connections (or even of business links with other Chinese tycoons), whereas they benefited greatly from their political ties.

Kuok has been an utterly different, almost singular figure, for he had a head start as a modern entrepreneur, as Gomez notes, in his class background and elite connections, his good education and his early business training in a well-established family commodity trading firm—as well as an involuntary stint in London in the early 1950s where he became well acquainted with the London commodities exchange.[8] He was educated at Raffles College, where he got to know many of the later political leaders of Malaya and Singapore; then took over the family business after his father's death and went on to build up a wide-ranging sugar trading empire. By his early 30s he was already known as the "sugar king" of Southeast Asia (long before he became involved in modest sugar plantations in Perlis). His success has been attributed to his deal-making skills and "reputation

---

7   Loh Boon Siew (1916–95, b Fujian) came to Malaysia with his father at the age of 12. He had little formal education and worked initially as a mechanic, setting up his own workshop in 1934 and soon building up enough capital to buy some buses and establish the Penang Yellow Bus Co. He then ventured into selling used cars, auto parts and tyres. In 1958 he obtained the Malayan franchise for Honda motorcycles and by the mid-1970s he controlled about 70% of the national market for cycles. Oriental Holdings, which had been established in 1963 and listed publicly soon after, also became involved in auto assembling and then component parts. Although it engaged in some product diversification, it was focused mainly on manufacturing and was vertically integrated to a high degree. By 1992, Loh was reportedly the second wealthiest businessman in Malaysia (Gomez, 1999: 58–63).

8   For good accounts of Kuok and his business activities, see Gomez (1999: 40–49) and Heng (1997). The Kuok family felt obliged to move away from Malaya to London for several years after 1952, when Robert's youngest brother fled and joined the Communist guerrillas in the jungle, where he was killed by security forces.

for reliability, honesty and skill" as well as his "superlative cross-cultural networking skills ... equally at home in the hermetic world of Chinese *sinkehs* ... as he is in the cosmopolitan boardrooms of New York, London and Paris" (Heng, 1997: 33). Among the other factors that have been held to account for his success, two are distinctly modern—his use of competent and loyal professional executives alongside his sons and nephews, and his prudent financial management, manifested in his practice of making each unit of his empire a separate profit centre (Verchere, 1977: 12; Hiscock, 1997: 207–09; Friedland, 1991: 46–47). But his "unrivalled network of *guanx*i connections with leading businessmen and the political authorities in the Asian countries where he has business interests" testifies also to residues of traditional traits.

An even more interesting variant of the "modern" tycoon in Malaysia is William Cheng (b 1943, Singapore), who has some similarities with Loh Boon Siew for his technical expertise. He was educated only to secondary level and began work in his father's iron foundry in Singapore at the age of 16. He inherited the family's Malaysian operations on his father's death and got his first big break with a licence to establish Amsteel in the mid-1970s. His later flagship, Lion Corporation, so-named in 1981, grew out of a collection of his father's metal enterprises. It was listed on the KLSE soon after and subsequently diversified into more than 100 companies, embracing a wide range of metal products as well as chocolate and confectionery, retailing, property, finance, insurance and plantations. But steel products remained its primary focus. Amsteel got the Suzuki franchise to assemble and sell Suzuki motorcycles and later to manufacture their parts, including engines. So it was clearly a competent and technically sophisticated operation, with considerable vertical integration as well as the almost traditional horizontal diversification. Cheng has not been closely associated with any particular UMNO leaders, according to Gomez (1999: 100), although several are said to have bought into it, including Mirzan Mahthir. Through his holding companies he has retained a direct 35 per cent stake in Lion Corporation, which Gomez takes to mean that control of the group equity is still held by him. He has made good use of professional managers while apparently retaining ultimate control over key decisions. Only a man with a distinctly modern outlook and skills would be capable of creating such a diverse yet technically complex conglomerate.

Conclusion

I do not want to end on the rather negative note I started with, as if we could hardly categorize any of these Malaysian-Chinese tycoons as clearly "traditional" or "modern" (eg, with Aw Boon Haw and Loke Yew in the former camp, and Lee Kong Chian and Robert Kuok in the latter, but probably others too), since so many of them reveal a mixture of traditional and modern characteristics and it is the variations in the mix that are often worth exploring more fully. Quibbling over the use of one or the other of these terms seems to me not very fruitful. It is more useful to ask what other questions should be raised about them that are of relevance to these issues, or what further information about their management styles and strategies would be most useful to learn more about. On this I will simply make two suggestions, both very tentative.

The first is that different industries seem to call for—or perhaps generate—different kinds of skills or attitudes towards innovation in the realm of business activities and a different mix of traditional or modern traits. I have long been intrigued by a similar, partially related fact, that tin mining seemed to attract (or generate) much more entrepreneurial types of *towkay* in the late 19th century, most of them more traditional than modern in outlook, than rubber planting did later, for reasons which seem derived from both technological and sociocultural factors. That may have been because the returns on capital outlays in tin mines came faster and often very lucratively, whereas rubber planting required long gestation periods and, at the large plantation level, careful, patient management over many years. The great tin-mining tycoons like Loke Yew, Chung Keng Kee, Foo Choo Chin, Eu Tong Seng and others were able to build up large enterprises largely through their ability to mobilize and maintain a big labour force appropriate to the traditional, fairly rudimentary mining methods of the Chinese in the 19th century. They rarely ventured far down the path towards more modern and capital-intensive methods, apart from hydraulic sluicing (a fairly elementary step), and hardly ever engaged in the use of mechanical dredges until long after they were first introduced, since they required large capital outlays and efficient technological skills if steady profits were to be maintained in the face of high fixed costs. Curiously, Europeans had played a relatively small part in tin mining prior to the introduction of dredges (around 1910), being unable to compete with Chinese firms in such a labour-intensive industry, but they soon became increasingly dominant after that, until about the 1970s. If we ask why so few Chinese mining magnates made the transition to this more highly capitalized technology, the answer is surely not that they were incapable of mobilizing the capital needed to buy a dredge or of hiring the experts needed to work it, but that they had little incentive to invest in them so long as they could get a higher short-term rate of return on their capital from other activities, especially property development or trading. Later, most of them were no longer attracted as strongly towards tin mining as previously, at least until after World War II, when its profitability increased sharply. Tin mining would therefore not have drawn them far down the path towards technological or managerial modernization until well after 1950.

Rubber, on the other hand, seems to have been a very different story. Not many notably modern or entrepreneurial Chinese were involved in large-scale planting until the second half of the 20th century, apart from the great pioneer rubber planter, Tan Chay Yan, who was unusually forward-looking, and, later, Lee Kong Chian. That was perhaps not surprising during a period marked by gross overplanting and overproduction for much of the time between 1910 and 1941. Many Malaysian Chinese became involved in rubber cultivation as smallholders—or in small remilling operations—in those years; but relatively few had much opportunity or incentive to try to grow into big plantation owners by adopting modern methods of cultivation. That all changed after World War II, however, after the demand for rubber and its price increased sharply. Lee Loy Seng is the best example of a large-scale planter in the postwar period who acquired the skills needed to conduct rubber cultivation in accordance with the most advanced technical and managerial methods of that time. But there were quite a few others, too, of lesser note.

Second, I want to suggest that it may be useful to ask such questions as: what traits did the more traditional Chinese businessmen shed as they made their transitions towards modernity—and what new traits did they acquire? We have noted above some ideas posed by Chan and Chiang on this matter, but I would like to end by suggesting a few others. What did they shed? As we have seen, old-style wage structures and administrative systems were among the first things to go, while new technologies sometimes displaced older ones. Management structures tended to become less hierarchical as firms modernized, and less patriarchal. But old business strategies seem to have been retained more tenaciously—for example, the reliance on labour-intensive methods and quick short-term turnover of funds rather than long-term capital outlays in the earlier decades of adaptation to modernity (as in the tin industry) and, later, on diversification of investments into many different fields rather than vertical integration and specialization. Employment of non-family professionals as managers and financial or technical specialists had been spreading spasmodically throughout the 20th century and was now fairly widespread in most large corporations; it tended to be accompanied by a shift towards the abandonment of nepotistical reliance on family members alone. But it was rarely carried to the point where family ownership and control of the core enterprise were imperilled. Firms might go public in order to raise capital on a more flexible basis, but almost always in such a way that family control was ensured. Traditional values and reliance on *guanxi* and *xinyong* seem to have been among the last of the traditional traits to be abandoned, or subordinated to more modern values.

What did they usually acquire in the process of modernizing? New technologies and new ways of making or doing things in the first instance. The kind of mental flexibility which enabled them in the earlier days to see beyond the limitations of the traditional Chinese world-view. New language skills and the fluency needed to carry on business in English or other Western languages in many cases. (That was what enabled Lee Kong Chian to get his first big breaks. On the other hand, Tan Kah Kee had little or no knowledge of English.) Some familiarity with the kinds of business and financial principles that are taught these days in MBA programmes, whether at a rudimentary or more advanced level. In recent years, the skills needed to master or at least understand IT technologies—potentially the most profoundly transforming experience of all, we may find. In some cases (but not yet many?) some understanding of the basic methodological underpinnings of modern science and its broader epistemological impacts in other fields of modern thought. More widely, but not always very significantly, the conventionally recognized benefits of tertiary education in fields like science, economics and other technologies, at home or abroad.

As for deeper or more creative insights into the workings of the modern world and its global economy, I suspect that very few in Malaysia have made much progress in that direction yet, except, perhaps, Kuok. But in other developing countries some people have begun to do so, and we can expect that Malaysian-Chinese businessmen will in due course be found proceeding down that path also, even while retaining some elements of their "traditional" values, culture and outlook on life in other respects, like many other overseas Chinese in all parts of the world.

References

Chan, John SN. "An Exploratory Study of Aw Boon Haw's Thought". *Journal of the South Seas Society*, vol 52 (1998): 22–56.

Chan, Kwok Bun, and Claire Chiang See Ngoh. *Stepping Out: The Making of Chinese Entrepreneurs*. Singapore: Prentice Hall, 1994.

Cohen, Myron L. "Being Chinese: The Peripheralization of Traditional Identity". *Daedalus*, Spring 1991, vol 120: 113–35, of Proceedings of the American Academy of Arts and Sciences.

Friedland, Jonathan. "Kuok the Kingpin". *Far Eastern Economic Review* 7 (Feb 1991), pp 46–50.

Gomez, Terence Edmund. *Chinese Business in Malaysia: Accumulation, Accommodation and Ascendance*. Richmond, Surrey: Curzon Press, 1999.

Heng, Pek Koon. "Robert Kuok and the Chinese Business Network in Eastern Asia: A Study in Sino-Capitalism". In *Culture and Economy in Eastern Asia*, edited by Timothy Brook. Michigan: University of Michigan Press, 1997.

Hiscock, Geoff. *Asia's Wealth Club*. Sydney: Allen and Unwin, 1997.

Lee, Kam Hing, and Chow Mun Seong. *Biographical Dictionary of the Chinese in Malaysia*. Petaling Jaya: Institute of Advanced Studies, University of Malaya and Pelanduk Publications, 1997.

Lynn Pan, ed. *The Encyclopedia of the Chinese Overseas*. Singapore: The Chinese Heritage Centre, 1998.

Searle, Peter. *The Riddle of Malaysian Capitalism. Rent-seekers or Real Capitalists?* Sydney: Allen and Unwin, 1999.

Verchere, Ian. "The Changing World of Robert Kuok". *Insight*, August 1978.

Wilson, Dick, et al. *Solid as a Rock: The First Forty Years of Oversea-Chinese Banking Corporation*. Singapore: OCBC, 1972.

Yeoh, Brenda, and Peggy Teo. "From Tiger Balm Gardens to Dragon World: Philanthropy and Profit in the Making of Singapore's First Cultural Theme Park". Stockholm: *Geografiska Annaler*, Band 78, Heft Nr 1 (1996), Seite 27 42.

Yong, CF. *Tan Kah-kee: The Making of an Overseas Chinese Legend*. Singapore: Oxford University Press, 1987.

Chapter 10

TRADITIONAL ETHNIC CHINESE BUSINESS ORGANIZATIONS IN SINGAPORE AND MALAYSIA

Yen Ching-hwang

Introduction

In search of explanation for the rise of ethnic Chinese business in East and Southeast Asia in recent decades, scholars have offered a range of different theories. Historical, cultural, social, structural and strategic explanations are certainly important for the understanding of this phenomenon,[1] but there is still room for other explanations. A new angle to examine the dynamics of ethnic Chinese business is the institutional perspective. The question whether the traditional ethnic Chinese business organizations had any role to play in this process is the main focus of this study. There is also a popular but not fully answered question of what contributed to the dominance of the ethnic Chinese in business in Southeast Asia. Further, there is the question of the relationship between occupational monopolization and *Bang* (dialect and geographical entity) in the ethnic Chinese communities in Southeast Asia.[2] This study hopes to shed light on all these questions.

This study is concerned mainly with the traditional ethnic Chinese craft guilds and business guilds which constituted the mainstream of the traditional business organizations. In addition, it will deal with informal business organizations such as mutual-aid societies and businessmen's clubs.

---

1. For historical interpretation, see Wang Gungwu, "Merchants without Empires: The Hokkien Sojourning Communities" and "Little Dragons on the Confucian Periphery", in Wang Gungwu, *China and the Chinese Overseas* (Singapore: Times Academic Press, 1991), pp 79–101, 258–721; Robert Cribb, "Political Structures and Chinese Business Connections in the Malay World: A Historical Perspective", in Chan Kwok Bun (ed), *Chinese Business Networks: State, Economy and Culture* (Singapore: Prentice Hall, 2000), pp 176–92; Chin Kong, "Merchants and Other Sojourners: The Hokkiens Overseas, 1570–1760" (an unpublished PhD thesis, History Department, the University of Hong Kong, 1998). For cultural interpretation, see SG Redding, *The Spirit of Chinese Capitalism* (Berlin and New York: Walter de Gruyter, 1990); Yen Ching-hwang,

These subsidiary organizations, though operating on the periphery, lent support to ethnic Chinese businessmen and facilitate their activities.

Ethnic Chinese guilds originated in China. They were not the outgrowth of China's guilds, but rather they derived ideas and experience from China. The term "guild" has its origins in European history. In the Germanic languages, the "gild" (guild) originally meant "fraternity of young warriors practising the cult of heroes", and then any group bound together by ties of rite and friendship with mutual support among its members.[3] From the fifth to the tenth century, the guilds were predominantly social organizations not dependent on blood ties. They did not assume commercial character until around 1100 AD when craft guilds appeared in Italy.[4]

The earliest Chinese guilds can be traced back to the Song Dynasty (960–1279 AD). Robust domestic and foreign trade resulted in the rise of large cities during the Song, especially the Southern Song, Dynasty. To facilitate imperial control over the urban population, people of same trade were grouped together in a section of the city with recognized headmen, and they were given a designated term *hang* (literally meaning "line"), and their leader as *hangtou* ("head of a line") or *hanglao* ("elder of a line"). This Chinese term *hang* has been translated as "guild".[5] During the 16th

---

"Modern Overseas Chinese Business Enterprise: A Preliminary Study", in Yen Ching-hwang, *Studies in Modern Overseas Chinese History* (Singapore: Times Academic Press, 1995), pp 237–54; Yen Ching-hwang, "Tan Kah Kee and the Overseas Chinese Entrepreneurship", *Asian Culture*, vol 22 (Singapore: Singapore Society of Asian Studies, June 1998), pp 1–13. For social interpretation, see John T Omohundro, *The Chinese in Iloilo: Kin and Commerce in a Central Philippine City* (Athens, Ohio: Ohio University Press, 1981). For structural interpretation, see various articles contributed by Wong Siu-lun, Kao Cheng-shu, Ichiro Numazaki, Tu I-ching, Eddie CY Kuo and Tong Chee Kiong, in Gary Hamilton (ed), *Business Networks and Economic Development in East and Southeast Asia* (Hong Kong: Centre of Asian Studies, University of Hong Kong, 1991); and various articles contributed by Chan Kwok Bun, David Schak, Qiu Liben, Edmund Terence Gomez and Peter S Li, in Chan Kwok Mun (ed), *Chinese Business Networks* (Singapore: Prentice Hall, 2000). For strategic interpretation, see Victor S Limlingan, *The Overseas Chinese in ASEAN: Business Strategies and Management Practices* (Manila: De La Salle University Press, 1994).

2   See Mak Lau Fong, "Occupation and Chinese Dialect Group in British Malaya", in Leo Suryadinata (ed), *Chinese Adaptation and Diversity: Essays on Society and Literature in Indonesia, Malaysia and Singapore* (Singapore: Singapore University Press, 1993), pp 8–27; Yen Ching-hwang, *A Social History of the Chinese in Singapore and Malaya, 1800–1911* (Singapore: Oxford University Press, 1986), pp 116–23.

3   See Anthony Black, *Guilds and Civil Society in European Political Thought from the Twelfth Century to the Present* (London: Methuen, 1984), p 3.

4   Ibid, pp 4–6.

and 17th centuries (late Ming and early Qing period), the guilds took over the functions of the officially licensed brokers in some trades. The officially sanctioned brokerage that existed in Ming and early Qing times prevailed in every city and rural market. The brokers were licensed and were responsible to the government for the behaviour of roving merchants and for taxes to be collected on the goods.[6] In the 18th century (mid-Qing), Chinese guilds were predominantly merchant (business) guilds. They were identified as *huiguan*, literally meaning "clubhouse", and were formed by merchants who were away from their native places. This gave them a strong regional character. They enjoyed cordial relations with the government, protecting their members by setting prices for their merchandise, and worshipping special deities. In the early 19th century, a new kind of guild, craft or service guild, became important in the cities. Both business and craft guilds grew rapidly after China was forced to open its doors in the wake of the Opium War (1839–42).[7] It was in this historical context that the traditional ethnic Chinese business organizations were born and grew in an overseas environment.

Traditional Ethnic Chinese Craft Guilds

Traditional ethnic Chinese business organizations carried the hallmark of their counterparts in China—strong regional and kinship affiliations—with the nomenclature of *hang, gongsuo, gonghui, huiguan, ju* and *tang*.[8] Whatever name they assumed, they were better known as "guilds". They existed in the major ports and cities in East and Southeast Asia. There is no evidence to suggest a direct link between these early ethnic Chinese guilds and their counterparts in China. They were not the overseas branches of, nor had they strong links with, China's guilds. The circumstances of the overseas environment appeared to be of paramount importance in their birth. The ethnic Chinese were mainly responding to both the religious and economic needs in the new land they sojourned. Two types of early ethnic Chinese

---

5   See Kwang-ching Liu, "Chinese Merchant Guilds: A Historical Inquiry", in R Ampalavanar Brown (ed), *Chinese Business Enterprise*, vol 2 (London: Routledge, 1996), pp 210–11.
6   Ibid, pp 212–13.
7   Ibid, pp 213–18.
8   See Wu Hua, "List of Chinese Guilds in Singapore", in Wu Hua, *Xinjiapo huazu huiguan zhi* (Records of the Singapore Chinese Associations), vol 3 (Singapore: South Seas Society, 1977), front page; Sei'ichi Imahori, translated by Liu Guoyin, *Malaiya huaqiao shehui* (Overseas Chinese Society in Malaya) (Penang: Jiaying Association of Penang, 1972 ?), p 3; Kwang-ching Liu, op cit, p 213.

guilds can be discerned: craft guild and business guild. The former was the business organization of craftsmen: carpenters, tailors, blacksmiths, goldsmiths, building tradesmen and so forth. The latter was the business organization for a variety of business: import-export trade; grocery, tea and cloth trade; restaurant business and so on.

The existence of several craft guilds in early Penang and Singapore is beyond doubt. In Penang, the Hujing Goldsmith Guild (*Hujing tajin hang*) came into being in 1832.[9] It was followed by the North City Guild (*Beicheng hang*) for carpenters in 1856, the Nu City Guild (*Nucheng hang*) for concrete and brick layers in 1858, and the North Nu Guild (*Nubei hang*) for employee carpenters in 1886.[10] In Singapore, the carpenters' guild, the North City Guild (*Beicheng hang*), led the way in 1868. It was followed by the tailors' guild, the Hean Yuen Guild (*Xian Yan guan*) in 1880, and the employee carpenters' guild, the North Nu Guild (*Nubei hang*) in 1890.[11] Among the craftsmen, the carpenters were the most active in founding their guilds in protection of common interests. They set up four of the earliest Chinese craft guilds in Singapore and Malaya as listed above. The North City Guild of Penang, which came into being in 1856,[12] deserves special attention. "North City" (*Beicheng*) was the posthumous name of Nu Ban, the legendary craftsman in Chinese history who was worshipped as the patron deity of carpenters.[13] It was the worship of this patron deity that brought the ethnic Chinese carpenters together to found this guild. Scanty records do not allow us to reconstruct actual circumstances under which the guild was established. Nevertheless, the worship of the legendary craftsman, Nu Ban, appears to have been the motivating force behind this move.[14] What can be established from other evidence is that the majority of the carpenters in early Penang were Chinese from Taishan (or Toishan) district, Guangdong.[15] Writing about the Chinese in Penang in 1854, JD Vaughan,

---

9 Sei'ichi Imahori, ibid, pp 119–20.
10 Ibid, pp 99, 107 and 116.
11 See Wu Hua, op cit, pp 1, 8 and 12.
12 Sei'ichi Imahori, op cit, p 99.
13 Nu Ban, his surname was Gongshu while his name was Ban, was born in the Nu state (in modern Shandong province, East China) during the Spring and Autumn period of Chinese history. He was an expert craftsman, setting standards for the construction and building of boats and carts. He was deified after his death, and was worshipped as the patron deity of all carpenters. Because he was born in the state of Nu, he came to be popularly known as Nu Ban rather than Gongshu Ban. During the Ming Dynasty, he was posthumously conferred the title of *Beicheng hou* (Lord of North City) by an imperial decree.
14 Sei'ichi Imahori, op cit, p 99.
15 Ibid.

a British observer, noted that all the carpenters, blacksmiths, shoemakers and others engaged in laborious work were "natives of Quang-tung" (Guangdong). Here, the so-called "natives of Quang-tung" were most likely the Cantonese-speaking or sub-Cantonese-speaking group,[16] and the term could refer to the people of Taishan, one of the four famous districts in southern Guangdong from which many emigrated to North America and Australia. Although the Taishanese had already established their dialect association, the Ning Yang Association, in Penang in 1833,[17] the special religious needs of the Taishan carpenters led to the founding of the guild in 1856. Like their counterparts in China, religion played a significant role in the lives of members of the ethnic Chinese craft guilds.[18] The North City Guild served as the rallying-point for its members, who were required to participate in the ceremonies in honour of their patron deity, Nu Ban, on the 13th day of the sixth moon every year.[19] Perceived to possess enormous power, the patron deity was there not only to protect the guild members against any imminent dangers and provide job security, he also served as a symbol of unity and solidarity among members, thus checking any potential conflicts. As the followers of the legendary craft master, Nu Ban, the members regarded one another as brothers, and took the guild as an extended family. With the blessing of the patron deity and the protection of the guild, the members were able to co-operate and unite for a common goal—protection of jobs and business, and to defuse any conflicts that might arise from the practice of the same trade.

The membership of the North City Guild of Penang was not confined to carpenters; it also included other construction workers such as brick and concrete layers. The rules and regulations of the North City Guild of the 1880s stipulated that carpenters, brick and concrete layers were eligible for membership.[20] The applicant had to be recommended by a member and

---

16   See JD Vaughan, "Notes on Chinese of Pinang", *Journal of Indian Archipelago and Eastern Asia*, vol 8 (1854), p 3.
17   See "Taishan Ning Yang huiguan shiji" (A Short History of the Taishan Ning Yang Association of Penang), *Xing Bin ribao* (*The Xing Bin Daily*), 2 October 1951.
18   See Peter J Golas, "Early Ch'ing Guilds", in G William Skinner (ed), *The City in Late Imperial China* (Stanford: Stanford University Press, 1977; reprint, Taipei: Rainbow Bridge Book Co Ltd, 1983), p 577.
19   See "Pi-neng Nu Ban hang zhangcheng" (The Rules and Regulations of the Penang Nu Ban Guild [the successor of the North City Guild of Penang], revised and reprinted in November 1966). I have had this document in my possession since 1971. See also Sei'ichi Imahori, op cit, p 105.
20   Item 4 of the Rules and Regulations stipulated that those involved in *shui ni* (water and soil work) and *mu* (carpentry work) could apply for membership. I translate those involved in "water and soil work" as "brick and concrete layers". See Sei'ichi Imahori, ibid.

supported by another. The application had to be approved by all members who congregated on the birthday of the patron deity (13th day of the sixth moon in the Chinese calendar) for celebration. The membership of the guild in 1886 was estimated at 120.[21] The inclusion of the brick and concrete workers in the North City Guild revealed its desire to broaden its trade base. Perhaps the number of carpenters was still small though it was growing. Or perhaps it was due to the consideration that most of large construction works in Penang at that time were obtained by tender. The grouping of carpenters, brick and concrete layers would improve the chances of getting works.

Like any other guilds throughout the world, the economic role was the most significant for the ethnic Chinese craft guilds. To preserve a monopoly and to prevent competition in the trade were two obvious economic functions. To preserve the monopoly of a trade was not just to prevent the participation of outsiders in the business; more importantly, it was to exclude them from the guild. Since the majority of the carpenters were from the district of Taishan, Guangdong province, their distinctive sub-Cantonese dialect naturally barred carpenters speaking other dialects from joining the North City Guild. It was natural for early Chinese craftsmen speaking the same dialect to congregate for social activities and mutual aid. Thus, the dialect functioned as an excluding agent that barred other people from that particular organization. But the dialect barrier did not ensure that the Taishan carpenters would maintain the monopoly of their trade in the future when circumstances should change. There was a need to exclude carpenters or concrete workers of other dialect groups from joining the guild. In the "Rules and Regulations of the Penang Nu Ban Guild (the successor of the North City Guild)", revised in 1966, item 4 stipulated that applicants for membership must be persons from the province of Guangdong.[22] The phrase "persons from the province of Guangdong" should be interpreted more precisely as persons who spoke Cantonese or sub-Cantonese dialect. Although the Teochews and Hakkas, who spoke distinctively different dialects from Cantonese, were also from the province of Guangdong, they appear to have been excluded from joining the ranks of the guild.

To prevent competition among members for jobs or business was certainly a useful function of the ethnic Chinese guilds. The prevention did not take the form of prohibition, but in the promotion of co-operation and help. Neither the 1880s' version nor the 1966 revision of the Rules and

---

21 Ibid.
22 See "Pi-neng Nu Ban hang zhangcheng", item 4 "The Qualifications of the Membership".

Regulations of the North City Guild prohibited the poaching of jobs, business or apprentices. Instead, positive acts of promoting co-operation and mutual assistance were stipulated in the rules and regulations. Members were required to donate money for funerals and weddings, and they were also required to help each other in finding jobs.[23]

From a broader historical perspective, ethnic Chinese guilds served as an institution which helped perpetuate the monopolization of occupation by different dialect groups. I have argued elsewhere that the domination of certain branches of occupation and business by different dialect groups in the ethnic Chinese communities was mainly the result of the operations of dialect and clan organizations, and of the dialect-based secret societies being used as an effective control mechanism.[24] Like the secret societies, guilds were instrumental in the control of certain lines of jobs and business.[25] In this sense, the guild and the secret society were two sides of a coin that served the interests of ethnic Chinese dialect groups in the monopolization of occupation and business. The difference was that the former was an open and legal institution, while the latter was an informal and illegal one.

Underpinning these monopolistic craft guilds was the restrictive labour recruitment system—the apprentice system. Like their counterparts in Qing and early Republican China, they adopted an arbitrary three-year period.[26] This arbitrary period was not so much that the training required for a particular trade, but as Peter J Golas has pointed out, it was primarily a custom-sanctioned initiation before one could enter a trade.[27] In the case of carpenters' training, the apprentice was required to reside in the shop learning the skills as well as manning the shop, cleaning and running errands. He received no salary, but was provided with food, clothing and pocket money.[28] Given the fact that many of the Chinese craftsmen had been trained in China before coming overseas, they invariably transmitted their

---

23 See Sei'ichi Imahori, op cit, pp 105–06; and "Pi-neng Nu Ban hang zhangcheng", item 15.
24 See Yen Ching-hwang, *A Social History of the Chinese in Singapore and Malaya, 1800–1911* (Singapore: Oxford University Press, 1986), pp 116–23.
25 For the role of secret societies in the monopolization of occupations in early Singapore and Malaysia, see Mak Lau Fong, *The Sociology of Secret Societies: A Study of Chinese Secret Societies in Singapore and Peninsular Malaysia* (Kuala Lumpur: Oxford University Press, 1981), pp 45–46.
26 See Peter J Golas, "Early Ch'ing Guilds", op cit, p 566; and Sei'ichi Imahori, *Overseas Chinese Society in Malaya*, p 102.
27 Peter J Golas, ibid.
28 See Lin Yuqi, "Malaiya jianzhu ye de poushi" (The Analysis of the Construction Business in Malaya), in *Malaiya huaqiao jianzao hang lianhe zonghui kaimu tekan*

experience to the overseas guilds. They expected the apprentices to go through a training process similar to the one they had gone through. The relationship between master and apprentice was a complex and contradictory one. On the one hand, the master was expected to treat the apprentice as his son and teach him the required skills. In return, the apprentice was required to submit totally to the master and respect him like his father, and this master-apprentice relationship, like the father-son relationship, was to be harmonious. The old records of the North City Guild of Penang during the Xianfeng reign (1851–61) emphasized the so-called "law of nature" of human society that required the father to be benevolent and the son to be filial. This law was to be applied to the teacher-student (master-apprentice) relationship, which required the apprentice to be grateful and obedient.[29] This fictitious family relationship obliged the apprentice to respect his master as a son towards his father. On the other hand, the master was mindful that his apprentice could be his future competitor for jobs and business. He could decide to keep some secrets of the trade from him, and exploit him for his own benefits. However, since the majority of the Chinese carpenters in early Penang were from Taishan of Guangdong,[30] geographical and dialect affinities strengthened the master-apprentice relationship, and prevented any unpalatable exploitation of the apprentice.

Traditional Ethnic Chinese Business Guilds

Like the craft guilds, ethnic Chinese business guilds operated on the principles of monopoly and self-protection. The nature of urban life and the predominantly small business in the ethnic Chinese communities meant that a wide variety of business existed in the port cities in East and Southeast Asia. Trading was the focus of ethnic Chinese business life, and business guilds were born out of the need for trade and the special overseas environment. Those who were involved in the grocery trade, cloth trade, restaurant business and Chinese medicine were most active in organizing their guilds for the promotion of common interests. In Singapore, the Restaurateurs' Guild of Singapore (Xingzhou Gushu shenjing tang, founded in 1876), the Singapore Piece Goods Traders' Guild (Buhang shangwu ji,

---

(souvenir magazine of the Federation of the Malayan Chinese Building Guilds), cited in Sei'ichi Imahori, *Overseas Chinese Society in Malaya*, p 102.
29 See the North City Guild of Penang's old records, cited in Sei'ichi Imahori, ibid, p 114, note 18.
30 Ibid, p 101.

founded in 1908) and the Grocers' Guild of Singapore (Xingzhou zahuo hang) were among the earliest business guilds on the island.[31] In Kuala Lumpur, the Restaurateurs' Guild of Selangor (Xue Shenzhong tang, founded in 1892), the Builders' Guild of Selangor (Xuelane Jianzhao hang, or known as Selangor Kin Cho Hong, founded in 1917), the Selangor Wine and Spirit Dealers' Association (Xuelane Jiushang gonghui, founded in 1917) and the Selangor Grocers' Guild (Xuelane Zahuo hang, founded in 1924) were among the earliest Chinese business guilds in Malaysia.[32] Like the early craft guilds, the early business guilds were characterized by strong dialect affiliation: they were mostly founded by businessmen of the same dialect origins, and their membership was dominated by a single dialect group. For instance, the Singapore Piece Goods Traders' Guild was founded on 25 February 1908 by a small group of Teochew cloth businessmen headed by Chen Delun (Tan Teck Lun) and Wang Bangjie (Heng Pang Kiat), two known leaders of the Teochew community in Singapore.[33] The guild, located at 75B, Circular Road in the early 1970s, had 23 founding members, all of whom were Teochews who dealt in cloth and piece goods primarily from Europe and America.[34] This trend appears to have continued in the postwar

---

31 See Wu Hua, *Xinjiapo huazhu huiguan zhi* (The Chinese Associations in Singapore), vol 3, pp 6, 18–19; Yuan Xikang, "Xinjiapo Gushu shenjing tang yian zeyao" (Outlines of the Minutes of the Restaurateurs' Guild of Singapore), in Huang Guoquan et al (eds), *Xing Ma Gushu lianhe zonghui tekan* (Souvenir Magazine of the Federation of the Restaurateurs' Guilds of Singapore and Malaya (Singapore: The Federation of the Restaurateurs' Guilds of Singapore and Malaya, 1958), p 27; Liu Zhanliang, "Ben hang shilue" (A Short History of the Grocers' Guild of Singapore, in *Xingzhou zahuo hang wushi zhounian jinxi jinian tekan* (Souvenir Magazine of the Golden Jubilee Celebration of the Grocers' Guild of Singapore) (Singapore: Xingzhou zahuo hang, 1957), p 8.

32 See Li Jingpo, "Xue Shenzhong tang shilue" (A Short History of the Restaurateurs' Guild of Selangor), in Huang Guoquan et al (eds), *Xing Ma Gushu lianhe zonghui tekan*, p 162; Zhu Wen-shui, "Xuelane Jianzhao hang jianshi" (A Short History of the Builders' Guild of Selangor) and Zhou Jisun, "Xuelane Zahuo hang shilue" (A Short History of the Selangor Grocers' Guild), in *Xuelane hangtuan zonghui tekan* (Souvenir Magazine of the Federation of Chinese Guilds of Selangor) (Kuala Lumpur: Xuehua hangtuan zonghui, 1962), no page number; *Xuelane Jiushang gonghui jinxi jinian tekan* (Golden Jubilee Publication of the Selangor Wine and Spirit Dealers' Association) (Kuala Lumpur: Xuelane Jiushang gonghui, 1967), p 33.

33 See Wu Hua, *Xinjiapo huazhu huiguan zhi*, vol 3, p 18; Pan Xingnong, *Malaiya Chaoqiao tongjian* (The Teochews in Malaya) (Singapore: Nandao chubanshe, 1950), pp 72 and 137.

34 See "Xinjiapo Huaren bupiye" (The Chinese Piece Goods Trade in Singapore)—the report of a survey on the Singapore Chinese piece goods business conducted by the students of the History Department of Nanyang University, Singapore, 1971, p 5.

period. In 1950, the membership of the Singapore Grocers' Guild consisted of 106 shop members and 242 individual members. Only 10 shop members (mostly represented by the sole owner or the main partner) were non-Cantonese-speaking (6 Hokkien, 3 Hakka and 1 Teochew), while the remaining 96 represented Cantonese- or sub-Cantonese-speakers from Xinhui, Nanhai and Shunde. Among the individual members, only 6 out of 242 members were Hokkien (4) and Hakka and Teochew (1 each), and the rest or 236 were Cantonese and sub-Cantonese from Xinhui, Heshan, Shunde and Taishan.[35] This statistical evidence confirms beyond doubt that there was a strong link between business guilds and dialect groups. This fits nicely into the picture that the dialect monopolization of occupation and business was real and alive in the postwar and later periods.

Like the craft guilds, the business guilds also served as a mechanism through which dialect groups (*Bang*) could exercise their control over certain branches of occupation or business which they perceived to be within their rights and privileges to dominate. A *Bang's* monopoly could be undermined by changing political and economic circumstances and its inability to cope with the changes. The Teochew control over the planting of cash crops in Singapore and Johore (such as pepper and gambier) in the second half of the 19th century was well known.[36] But the rise of a new cash crop, rubber, at the beginning of the 20th century and the Hokkien control over it saw the decline of the monopolistic position of the Teochews in the plantation and its associated industries in Singapore and Malaya.[37] However, the change of political and economic circumstances could also add new sources

---

35 See "Hanghao tongxinlu" (Addresses of the Shop Membership of the Guild) and "Hangyuan tongxinlu" (Addresses of the Individual Membership of the Guild), in *Xinjiapo Zahuo hang sishisan zhounian jinian tekan* (Souvenir Magazine of the Celebration of the 43rd Anniversary of the Singapore Grocers' Guild) (Singapore: Xinjiapo Zahuo hang, 1950), pp 105–21.
36 See Siah U Chin, "General Sketch of the Numbers, Tribes, and Avocations of the Chinese in Singapore", *Journal of the Indian Archipelago and Eastern Asia*, vol 2 (1848), p 290; James C Jackson, *Planters and Speculators: Chinese European Agricultural Enterprise in Malaya, 1786–1921* (Kuala Lumpur: University of Malaya Press, 1968), pp 7–30; Carl A Trocki, *Prince of Pirates: Temenggongs and the Development of Johor and Singapore, 1784–1885* (Singapore: Singapore University Press, 1979), pp 88–91, 145–52.
37 For the rise of rubber and Hokkien participation in this new cash crop, see Wu Tiren, *Redai jingji zuowu—xiangjiao shu* (Rubber—the Tropical Cash Crop) (Singapore: Guanghua, 1951), pp 6–8; James C Jackson, ibid, pp 211–18; JH Drabble, *Rubber in Malaya, 1876–1922: The Genesis of the Industry* (Kuala Lumpur: Oxford University Press, 1973), pp 14–19; Tan Kah Kee (Chen Jiageng), *Nanqiao huiyi lu* (Autobiography) (Singapore: Chen Jiageng guoji xuehui, 1993), vol 2, pp 489, 492.

for the same trade, and this provided the opportunity for other dialect groups to participate, and the newcomers would form their own guilds to protect self-interests. Postwar Singapore saw the participation of Hokkiens and Hakkas in the piece goods business, which had hitherto been monopolized by Teochews. The rise of Japan as a new provider of textile goods gave the Hokkiens and Hakkas the opportunity to participate in this business. The Hokkien piece goods traders formed the Singapore Textile Dealers' Friendly Association, while the membership of the Singapore-Malaya Chinese Textile Merchants' Association was predominantly Hakka.[38] The sharing of the same business by different dialect groups would not necessarily lead to constant rivalry and conflict. The expanding market as a result of growing population could absorb more competitors who received supplies from different sources—Europe, North America, Japan and China, and enabled them to compete and coexist in the same trade.

The promotion of economic interests and the encouragement of mutual aid were the principal functions of the ethnic Chinese business guilds. They were usually stated in the aims or rules of the guilds. The desire to minimize competition and maximize profit served as the common ground for those far-sighted founders of the guilds, and then this desire was incorporated into the rules and regulations. In 1908, the desire to reduce keen competition among Teochew piece goods traders in Singapore brought into being the Singapore Piece Goods Traders' Guild. These traders had hitherto been hostile to each other because of business rivalry, and had even forbidden their apprentices to contact other apprentices for fear of their leaking out any business secrets.[39] This desire was commonly couched in a general statement found among the rules and regulations of the guilds. The statement "to cultivate good relationship among people of the same trade, and to advance common interests" (*lianlo tongye ganqing, gongmou tongye fuli*), commonly found among the rules and regulations of the guilds,[40] reveals the desire for co-operation for the common good. But the co-operation and interest in the common good were predicated on the ability of the guild to enforce the rules. Unlike their counterparts in China, which enjoyed

---

38 See "Xinjiapo Huaren bupiye", op cit, p 17.
39 Ibid, p 5.
40 See "Bincheng Lianshang gonghui zhangcheng" (The Rules and Regulations of the Penang General Merchants' Association), in *Bincheng Lianshang gonghui kaimu jinian ji zhounian huiqing hebian tekan* (Penang Lean Seong Kong Hoay [General Merchants' Association] Inaugural Ceremony and First Anniversary Combined Souvenir) (Penang: 1960), p 103.

considerable judicial authority,[41] the ethnic Chinese business guilds did not wield any legal power nor have any government support; they had to negotiate with members for the implementation of the rules. Sometimes, a deterrent clause was incorporated into the rules and regulations as part of members' obligation to obey the rules and decisions made by the guild.[42]

The lack of judicial power undermined the authority of the guilds and reduced their ability to enforce rules. Sometimes, this could result in the disfunctioning of the guilds. The example of the Guild of Chinese Medicines of Singapore (Xinjiapo Zhong Yao gonghui) is a case in point. The guild was founded in 1930 with the objective of protecting the common interests of the Chinese medicinal merchants.[43] With this long-term objective in mind, the guild introduced the so-called "genuine medicine and fair price" (*zheng yao zheng jia*) measure which obliged members to sell genuine goods at fair prices. To ensure the quality, the medicine sold by members had to be authenticated with a stamp from the guild, and the price set for the medicine had to be approved by the guild with a special code.[44] The authentication would weed out substandard and fake medicine, while regulation of prices would prevent unhealthy competition and overcharging. This measure was designed to lift the image of Chinese medicine and give the public more confidence. On a long-term basis, this would have ensured the continuous business for Chinese medicinal businessmen *vis-à-vis* the competition with Western medicine in the ethnic Chinese communities. The "genuine medicine and fair price" measure was approved by the executive committee of the guild in January 1946, and was rigorously enforced. Members were required to sign a commitment letter kept by the guild, and Singapore was divided into six districts with two elected leaders to oversee the operation of the new scheme. Any disputes arising from the new measure would be resolved by the district leaders with the support of their members. A wooden plate inscribed with the words "genuine medicine and fair price" was to be hung on the front of the members' shops, and

---

41 See Joseph Fewsmith, "From Guild to Interest Group: The Transformation of Public and Private in Late Qing China", in R Ampalavanar Brown (ed), *Chinese Business Enterprise*, vol 2 (London: Routledge, 1996), p 231.
42 See Rule Number 11 of the "Rules and Regulations of the Penang General Merchants' Association", op cit, p 103.
43 See "Xinjiapo huaren zhongyao hangye shi" (A History of the Singapore Chinese Medicinal Trade)—the report of a survey on the Singapore Chinese Medicinal Trade conducted by the students of the History Department of Nanyang University, Singapore, 1971, p 55.
44 Ibid, p 56.

investigators would be employed to check out the implementation of the measure.⁴⁵ The new scheme was put into practice in March 1947, but it failed to achieve the desired results after one and a half years' trial. Business competition, especially from non-members, the lack of judicial power of the guild, and the indifference of the colonial government in Singapore, were the main factors contributing to the failure of the new scheme.⁴⁶

Whatever rivalry and competition they might have, business guild members could not deny the fact that they shared some common needs such as mutual aid (including welfare). This was particularly felt in a foreign environment like Southeast Asia, with Western colonial or indigenous rulers speaking different languages. However, the linguistic barrier was not the only problem; there were problems of government legislation and external competition (foreign and indigenous) which would have direct bearing on everyone in the business. With the spirit of providing mutual aid, the guild was able to mobilize talents within the trading community and deal with the common problems. The collective power of the guild could change the legislation or external environment in favour of the trade. In 1954, when the colonial government of the Federation of Malaya imposed a 25 per cent tax on all imported Chinese medicines, the Selangor Chinese Medicinal Merchants' Guild (Xuelane Huaqiao yaoye gonghui), which was founded before the World War I, took the lead in organizing a petition against the new import duty. The petition gained strong support from other Chinese medicinal merchants' guilds in other states in Malaya and Singapore. The result of this concerted effort was the lifting of the tax on imported unprocessed Chinese medicine.⁴⁷

The ethnic Chinese business guilds also settled internal disputes among members, established contacts with foreign import-exporters,⁴⁸ assisted and promoted business, and strengthened relations between employers and employees.⁴⁹ Sometimes, large business guilds were also involved in running Chinese schools and other community charity functions in an attempt to improve

---

45 Ibid, pp 56–57.
46 Ibid, p 58.
47 See Lo Bojin, "Xuelane Huaqiao yaoye gonghui shilue" (A Short History of the Selangor Chinese Medicinal Merchants' Guild), in *Xuelane hangtuan zonghui tekan* (Souvenir Magazine of the Federation of Chinese Guilds of Selangor), no page number.
48 See Hong Majin, "Luetan benhui zhuzhi zhi dongji" (The Motives for the Founding of the Penang General Merchants' Association), in *Bincheng lianshang gonghui kaimu jinian ji zhounian huiqing hebian tekan* (Penang Lean Seong Kong Hoay [General Merchants' Association] Inaugural Ceremony and First Anniversary Combined Souvenir), p 93.
49 See Liu Zhanliang, "Ben Hang shilue" (A Short History of the Singapore Grocers' Guild), in *Xingzhou zahuo hang wushi zhounian jinxi jinian tekan* (Souvenir Magazine of the Jubilee Celebration of the Singapore Grocers' Guild), p 10.

the image of the guilds in the wider Chinese community. The Federation of the Selangor Chinese Guilds (Xuelane Hangtuan zonghui), formed in 1955 in Kuala Lumpur with 41 guilds in the state of Selangor, ran a Chinese primary school (the Huaqiao School), acted as a pressure group to press the government for the use of Chinese language in public places, and was involved in educational matters such as education policy and the support given to the founding of Nanyang University (a Chinese language university) in Singapore.[50]

The foundation of the business guild was the apprentice system, without which the particular line of business would have declined and disappeared. Like the crafts industry, the business line recruited its labour force through kinship, marriage and dialect connections.[51] These kin and dialect ties became especially important in immigrant societies because recruitment of labour started more frequently in China rather than overseas. Many successful Chinese entrepreneurs in Southeast Asia started with apprenticeship in a relative's or kinsman's business, in which they learnt the business fundamentals. The life stories of Zhang Bishi (Chang Pi-shih or otherwise known as Thio Thiau Siat), a prominent businessman in Southeast Asia in the late 19th and early 20th centuries; Yap Ah Loy (Ye Yalai or Ye Delai), the founder of Kuala Lumpur and a prominent tin miner; Wang Bangjie (Heng Pang Kiat), a prominent Teochew merchant in Singapore; and Foo Chee Choon (Hu Zichun), an eminent tin-mining tycoon in Perak, testify to this process.[52] The relationship between apprentice and employer (shop owner or business partner, or owner-manager) was similar to that of apprentice and master craftsman—paternalistic and sometimes oppressive.

---

50 See selection of newspaper reports on the activities of the Federation of Selangor Chinese Guilds, in *Xuelane Hangtuan zonghui tekan*, op cit, no page number.
51 See "Xinjiapo Huaren zhongyao hangye shi", p 24; "Xinjiapo Huaren bupiye", p 7.
52 Zhang Bishi arrived in Batavia from China at the age of 18, and he first worked as an apprentice in a rice shop. Yap Ah Loy worked as an apprentice in the shop of a kinsman, Yap Ng (Ye Wu) in Kesang, Malacca. Wang Bangjie worked as an apprentice in a cloth shop in Singapore after he arrived from China. Foo Chee Choon worked as an apprentice in a shop before he learnt the mining business from his uncle. See Kuang Guoxiang, "Zhang Bishi qiren" (The Story of Zhang Bishi), and "Xikuang dawang Hu Zichun" (Tin-mining King—Foo Chee Choon), in Kuang Guoxiang, *Bincheng sanji* (Anecdotal History of Penang) (Singapore: Shijie shuju, 1958), pp 99, 114; Wang Zhiyuan, *Ye Delai zhuan* (A Biography of Yap Ah Loy) (Kuala Lumpur: Yihua Publishing Company, 1958), pp 19–20; SM Middlebrook, "Yap Ah Loy" (an independent issue), *Journal of the Malayan Branch of Royal Asiatic Society* (Singapore: Malaya Publishing House Ltd, 1951), p 13; "Wang Bangjie xiansheng" (Mr Heng Pang Kiat), in Pan Xingnong (ed), *Malaiya Chaoqiao tongjian* (The Teochews in Malaya), p 72.

The apprentice was to be obedient, respectful and faithful towards the employer, while the employer was paternalistic and supposed to be caring. This relationship was perceived to be like the father-son relationship.[53] The apprentice was to start learning from cleaning, moving and packaging goods, cooking and running errands—the so-called mundane work—either in a Chinese medicinal shop, a grocery or a trading company.[54] He usually worked long hours with little or a token salary. There was no fixed period of apprenticeship, as it varied from business to business. Unlike the craft apprentice who had to learn specific skills in order to qualify as a craftsman, the business apprentice could pick up the essential knowledge of doing business by observation, but his promotion to a proper paid job (a formal employee status) in the shop depended very much on his relationship with the employer—such as how close his relationship with the employer was in terms of kinship or dialect ties—and his performance. The former seemed to play a bigger role in determining his promotion.[55] After he had acquired the knowledge of running the business and had accumulated some savings, he could leave and form a partnership with others to start in a similar line of business. When his business expanded and needed more helping hands, he would do as his former employer or relative had done—take on apprentices from among the children of relatives, kinsmen and friends either locally or from China, and this process would repeat itself continuously.

Whether this low-paying, long-hour and paternalistic apprentice system should be regarded as a hidden means of employer exploitation of cheap labour, or as a necessary training process to shape the prospective businessman's character is a matter for debate. In the absence of modern trade schools or business colleges, the apprentice system was the only means for training a future businessman. Long hours and low pay for doing petty and mundane tasks of apprenticeship are sometimes claimed to be the Chinese way of character-building—to become hard-working, thrifty and able to endure hardship. The acquisition of these qualities perhaps contributed to the success of a businessman. Of course, the system also worked to the advantage of the employer, who benefited from the low labour costs and indirectly increased his profit margin. This kind of mutual obligations and mutual benefits between apprentice and employer was very

---

53 See "Xinjiapo Huaren bupiye", p 6.
54 Ibid; "Xinjiapo Huaren zhongyao hangye shi", p 28; Tan Jingsheng, "Zahuo shengyai ershi nian" (Twenty Years of My Life in a Grocery Shop), in *Xingzhou Zahuo hang wushi zhounian jingxi jinian tekan* (Souvenir Magazine of the Jubilee Celebration of the Singapore Grocers' Guild) (Singapore: Singapore Grocers' Guild, 1957), p 15.
55 See "Xinjiapo Huaren zhongyao hangye shi", p 29.

much in keeping with the Confucian concept of mutual responsibility. Despite the rigours of the system, an apprenticeship was still coveted by many ethnic Chinese immigrants and local-born Chinese. From a broader perspective, the Chinese apprentice system has contributed to the growth in number of Chinese businessmen, and helped perpetuate the dominant position of ethnic Chinese in business in Southeast Asia.

It would be a mistake to assume that traditional ethnic Chinese business organizations are incapable of changing with time, and that they would disappear into oblivion or be replaced by new organizations. The traditional ethnic Chinese business organizations, like their counterparts in China, are capable of coping with change, and make themselves relevant in the modern world. Of course, the ability to cope with change varies with individual organizations, some being more capable than others. On the whole, the traditional ethnic Chinese business system contains seeds of change. The idea of change was partly derived from traditional Chinese culture. The core concept of change in *The Book of Change* (*Yi Jing*, or Romanized as *I Ching*), one of the five Confucian classics, is familiar to most Chinese. The idea of change has led to the ideas of progress, adaptation and reform. Kang Yuwei, the renowned Late Qing Confucianist reformer, exalted Confucius as a great reformer who had lived ahead of his time, and considered the idea of change and progress as inherent in Confucian teachings.[56] This idea of change and progress has filtered into the minds of ordinary Chinese, including the ethnic Chinese in East and Southeast Asia. The dictums of *qiong ze bian, bian ze tong* (difficulty leads to change, and change leads to adaptation) and *riri xin* (to renew every day), popularly held by the Chinese-educated in Singapore and Malaysia, indicate how much ethnic Chinese businessmen have been influenced by this long-valued concept.[57] This idea of change was reaffirmed for the earlier ethnic Chinese communities owing to their geographical position. Since most of the ethnic Chinese were urban folk residing in major ports in East and Southeast Asia, they were exposed more readily to outside influences, both Western and Chinese, through the media or business contacts. Many of the ethnic Chinese businessmen who had contacts with foreign businessmen were at the forefront of change, because they were more aware of what was going on outside the ethnic

---

56 See Kung-chuan Hsiao, "K'ang Yu-wei and Confucianism", *Momumenta Serica*, vol 18 (Nagoya, 1959), p 165; Jung-pang Lo, *K'ang Yu-wei: A Biography and a Symposium* (Tucson, The University of Arizona Press, 1967), p 6.

57 The author recalls that some Chinese shops had the phrases *ri xin* or *riri xin* incorporated in their names, in the small town of Mentakab, in the state of Pahang, Malaysia, in 1960s and 1970s.

Chinese communities. There were also businessmen who were influenced by newspaper reports of sociopolitical changes taking place in China. These outside influences would have impacted on their thinking and their attitude towards reform of the business organizations. The idea of change also grew out of the internal problems of the ethnic Chinese communities. Dialect and kinship differences led to competition and rivalry in business, and to attempts at monopolizing certain branches of business.

The awareness of change and progress was reflected in the public speeches of guild leaders and in guild publications. For instance, the souvenir magazine for the celebration of the anniversary of the Singapore Grocers' Guild, published in October 1950, contained many articles with progressive themes. They ranged from topics on "Chinese business to survive in the international business competition", "backwardness of ethnic Chinese business and industry", "the future of ethnic Chinese business", "economic status of the ethnic Chinese in Southeast Asia", to "employer-employee co-operation" and "unity and solidarity".[58] Although some of the contributors were not members of the Singapore Grocers' Guild, they were prominent ethnic Chinese businessmen affiliated with the guild,[59] and their progressive ideas and insights would have had impact on the members of the guild. In Penang, the awareness of the relative backwardness of ethnic Chinese and their traditional practices in early 1960 prompted some of the members of the Penang General Merchants' Association to suggest that "Ethnic Chinese business and industry have to catch up with time" and that they had "to reform obsolete practices".[60] Among the obsolete practices proposed for reform were "protracted bargaining" (*taojia huanjia*)

---

58 See Liang Bin, "Lun zhengqu qiaohui zhi guoji shichang" (On the Chinese Remittance and International Market); Huang Shufen, "Huaqiao shangye hougu yu qianzhan" (Retrospect and Prospect of the Ethnic Chinese Business); Feng Fuqi, "Lueshu laozi hezuo yu wo huaqiao shangye zhi guanxi" (On the Employer-Employee Co-operation and the Ethnic Chinese Business); Qiu Zhanghe, "Huaqiao shangye de tuanjie jingzhen he baozhang" (The Spirit of Unity and Its Guarantee of the Ethnic Chinese Business); Liang Junan, "Jiaqiang tongye de tuanjie" (Strengthen the Cooperation among the Grocers); Feng Jiaju, "Huaqiao shangye yu qiantu" (Ethnic Chinese Business and Its Future); Ke Tian, "Nanyang huaqiao yuanyu de jiangji diqei" (The Economic Status of the Ethnic Chinese in Southeast Asia), in *Xinjiapo Zahuo hang sishisan zhounian jinian tekan* (Souvenir Magazine of the Celebration of 43rd Anniversary of the Singapore Grocers' Guild) (Singapore: Xingzhou Zahuo hang, 1950), pp 21–25, 64–73.
59 Liang Bin was a leader of the Hong Kong Guang Yi Shanghui (Hong Kong Grocers' Guild), while Huang Shufen was a prominent Cantonese businessman and a leader of Singapore and Johore Cantonese communities.
60 See Chen Xiting, "Gongshangye ying yingtou ganshang shidai" (Ethnic Chinese Business and Industry Must Catch Up with Time); and Qian Chenxiang, "Xiang benhui

and "long opening hours". The "protracted bargaining" practice was considered to be a waste of time and as adding burden to the management, while the shortening of trading hours would help conserve energy.[61]

Informal Ethnic Chinese Business Organizations

Informal ethnic Chinese business organizations consisted mainly of two types: the mutual-aid society and the businessmen's club. They invariably played a supporting role for ethnic Chinese businessmen in their business activities.

Mutual-aid societies

The mutual-aid societies in the ethnic Chinese communities grew out of a desire for mutual assistance in times of crisis. The uncertainty of business and the nature of early Chinese immigrant society provided no guarantee for the perpetuation of wealth. The fluctuation of fortunes in the business world evoked fear of misery after the collapse of business. Wealth was not everlasting and dependable; it could dissipate overnight, leaving the families devastated. The formation of these mutual-aid societies was to meet this need. They began to appear in the major cities in Malaya and in Singapore. In Singapore, Kheng Teck Society (Kheng Teck Whay) came into existence in 1831,[62] while in Malacca, Kheng Leong Society (Kheng Leong Huay) was founded in 1891,[63] and it was followed by Ghee Kiat Society (Ghee Kiat Huay) in later years.[64] The members of these societies in the early stages were mostly businessmen. But as time passed, the societies opened up and broadened

---

tongye jin yiyan" (A Proposal to the Members of Penang General Merchants' Association), in *Bincheng Lianshang gonghui kaimu jinian ji zhounian huiqing hebian tekan, 1959–1960* (Penang Lean Seong Kong Hoay [General Merchants' Association] Inaugural Ceremony and First Anniversary Combined Souvenir, 1959–1960), pp 91–92, 94.

61 Qian Chenxiang, ibid, p 94.
62 See David KY Chng and Lim How Seng, "Xinjiapo Qing De Hui yanjiu" (The 153-Year-Old Kheng Teck Association of Singapore), *Asian Culture*, no 5 (Singapore: Singapore Society of Asian Studies, April 1984), p 54.
63 The Society claimed it was registered on 19 August 1891. See *Rules, Bye-laws and General Objects of Kheng Leong Huay and Kheng Leong Huay Mutual Aid Section, Malacca*, cover page revised in September 1957. I have this document in my possession.
64 The Rules of Ghee Kiat Huay, Malacca, do not indicate when the Society was founded. When I acquired the pamphlet in the 1970s, I was informed the Rules were probably amended in 1939. I suspect the Society could have been founded before the World War I.

their social base to include most adult Chinese.⁶⁵ The Kheng Teck Society was the earliest and the most important of them. Singaporean scholars Lim How Seng and David KY Chng have made a careful study of this organization, and have thrown light on its origin, structure and operation. They initially identified the 36 founders of the Society and examined its internal structure.⁶⁶ Lim How Seng further investigated its ideology, functions, social and historical significance.⁶⁷ What have been established by the studies of Lim and Chng are: the Society was established by 36 ethnic Chinese merchants in 1831 in Singapore; all founders of the Society were merchants of southern Fujianese origin, and some of them were leaders of the Hokkien *Bang* in Singapore and had strong connections with their counterparts in Malacca; the Society was primarily mutual-aid in objective and a welfare organization for ethnic Chinese merchants; and members of the Society, though English-educated, were imbued with strong Confucian values and loyalty to the Qing government.⁶⁸

What is relevant to our study is the main function of this Society and its implications. With the foresight of the founders, who contributed $100 (Spanish dollars) each, the Society had a flying start with its main objective of mutual aid.⁶⁹ The impressive $3,600 fund was invested in property which returned a stable and steady income. By 1914, the Society had seven shops the rental of which accounted for most of the income of $33,136.⁷⁰ The strong financial position of the Society enabled it to fulfil its main objective of helping members and their families in times of crisis. Members or non-

---

65 In the revised rules of Kheng Leong Huay, membership is open to persons of Chinese race of either sex; but the revised rules of Ghee Kiat Huay confine membership to all Chinese of the male sex over 20 years of age. See documents mentioned above.
66 See David KY Chng and Lim How Seng, op cit, pp 60–65.
67 See Lim How Seng, "Qing De Hui: Xinjiapo huashang huzhuhui de zuzhi yu yunzuo" (The Kheng Teck Association: The Dynamics of a Chinese Merchants' Mutual-Aid Organization in Singapore), *Asian Culture*, no 17 (Singapore: Singapore Society of Asian Studies, June 1993), pp 154–67.
68 See Lim How Seng, ibid, pp 158–65; David KY Chng and Lim How Seng, op cit, pp 58–65.
69 The $100 contribution was a large sum of money at the time. In the middle of the 19th century, an average agricultural worker in Singapore earned $3 to $4 a month, and his annual income did not exceed $50. This contribution represented two years' income of an average worker. See Yen Ching-hwang, *A Social History of the Chinese in Malaysia and Singapore*, p 144.
70 See Lim How Seng, "Qing De Hui: Huashang huzhuhui de zuzhi yu yunzuo", op cit, pp 160–62; see also the same article in Lim How Seng, *Xinjiapo huashe yu huashang* (Ethnic Chinese Society and Ethnic Chinese Businessmen in Singapore) (Singapore: Singapore Society of Asian Studies, 1995), pp 114–17.

members (presumably members' relatives or friends) could obtain loans from the Society by mortgaging land titles or jewellery when they were in financial difficulties. When a member's livelihood was threatened by sickness, the Society would render support with a sickness allowance. More importantly, the Society would take care of the member's family if he died in poverty; his widow and children would receive a monthly allowance until they could stand on their own feet; and the children of deceased members could apply for scholarships or loans.[71] In the period between 1907 and 1928, the Society spent, on average, over 30 per cent of its annual income on welfare, the bulk of it going towards members' benefit.[72] Two important implications are to be noted in relation to ethnic Chinese business activities. Firstly, this informal business organization acted as a modern insurance company in providing unemployment and sickness benefits as well as widow pension. This insurance policy would free ethnic Chinese businessmen from the fear of destitution in times of crisis, and reduce their level of worry and stress. This would improve their focus on doing business, and encourage their spirit of risk-taking, which was necessary if their business were to succeed. Secondly, this informal organization provided its members with a useful contact point where they could meet to exchange business ideas, market information, labour recruitment and so on.

Businessmen's clubs

Traditional ethnic Chinese businessmen's clubs assumed the form of a social club in providing a meeting-place and facilities for businessmen to meet after office hours. But they had important business significance. Traditional ethnic Chinese businessmen gained a reputation of doing business in an informal way: no formal negotiation sessions, valuing verbal promises and no formal contract signed. This informal approach presents a sharp contrast with the way business is done in the West, and sometimes, it has been dubbed "the Chinese way of doing business". This informality was a product of the Chinese perception of business relationship. In their view, business relationship was an integral part of a total relationship. They would not do business with adversaries but with friends, relatives, and people of same district or province whom they could trust. A successful business relationship was a long-term or lasting one. This traditional attitude of doing business made these clubs important in the building of business relationship. These

---

71   Ibid, pp 161, 116–17.
72   Ibid, pp 161–62, 117–18.

clubs assumed names such as *ting* (pavilion), *yuan* (garden) and *xuan* (porch or side room), or the more modern term *jilobu* (club). Song Ong Siang's *One Hundred Years' History of the Chinese in Singapore* lists at least four of such clubs in 19th-century Singapore, namely Ban Chye Ho Club, Cheng Kee Hean Club, Choon Guan Hock Club, and Kim Ban Choon Club.[73] Available Chinese sources add another four businessmen's clubs in that period. They were Chui Huai Lim Club, Shulin Yuan Club, Xiao Tao Yuan (Hsiao T'ao Yuan) Club and Ee Hoe Hean Club.[74] These clubs appear to have been founded by wealthy businessmen with strong dialect and regional affiliations.[75] For instance, Chui Huai Lim Club, probably the earliest ethnic Chinese businessmen's club, is said to have been founded in 1849 by Tan Seng Poh (Chen Chengpao), a Teochew opium farmer well known in Singapore and Johore, and it became a club popular with Teochew businessmen.[76]

Perhaps a better known and more established businessmen's club was Ee Hoe Hean Club, founded in Singapore in 1895. The founders of the club were mostly rich Hokkien merchants such as Lim Ho Puah (Lin Heban, father of famous entrepreneur Lim Peng Siang), Tan Cheng Siong (Chen Jenxiang, father of famous banker Tan Chin Tuan), Lee Cheng Yan, Tank Jiak Kim and Gan Eng Seng.[77] It was aimed at bringing both Chinese- and English-educated Hokkien businessmen together for recreational and social

---

73   See Song Ong Siang, *One Hundred Years' History of the Chinese in Singapore* (Singapore: University of Malaya Press, 1967), pp 98, 259, 291, 476, 552.
74   Song Ong Siang in his book lists a Chinese club in Kampong Java without a name, which I have now identified to be the Shulin Yuan Club whose members hosted a dinner in honour of Qing visiting dignitary Admiral Ting Juchang, who led a Chinese fleet to Singapore in April 1890. See *Lat Pau*, 15 April 1890, p 5; for Chui Huai Lim Club, see "Juihua lin jilobu" (The Chui Huai Lim Club), in Pan Xingnong (ed), *Malaya Chaoqiao tongjian* (The Teochews in Malaya), pp 343–44. For the existence of Xiao Tao Yuan Club, see Yen Ching-hwang, *The Overseas Chinese in the 1911 Revolution: With Special Reference to Singapore and Malaya* (Kuala Lumpur: Oxford University Press, 1976), p 55; for Ee Hoe Hean Club, see CF Yong (Yong Ching Fatt), *Zhanqian Xinghua shehui jiegou yu lingdou chen chutan* (Chinese Community Structure and Leadership in Pre-War Singapore) (Singapore: South Seas Society, 1977), p 31.
75   See Pan Xingnong, ibid, p 343.
76   Ibid; for identifying Tan Seng Poh as a big opium farmer in the region, see Song Ong Siang, *One Hundred Years' History of the Chinese in Singapore*, pp 131–32; Carl A Trocki, *Prince of Pirates: The Temenggongs and the Development of Johor and Singapore, 1784–1885* (Singapore: Singapore University Press, 1979), pp 143–44; Carl A Trocki, "Tan Seng Poh", in John Butcher and Howard Dick (eds), *The Rise and Fall of Revenue Farming* (New York: St Martin's Press, Inc, 1993), pp 249–54.
77   See CF Yong, op cit, p 31.

purposes.[78] It is clear that in its early stage, from 1895 to 1922, membership of the club was confined to Hokkien businessmen. It was not until 1923, when Tan Kah Kee (Chen Jiageng), the renowned ethnic Chinese entrepreneur and community leader, became the *zongli* (chairman or director) of the club that it was open to Chinese businessmen of other dialect groups.[79] Under the leadership of Tan Kah Kee (1923–47), the club was reformed and imbued with a new community spirit. It banned opium-smoking on the premises, encouraged punctuality and hygiene at social gatherings, and set up a small library.[80] When Tan Kah Kee was actively involved in China politics in the 1920s and 1930s, Ee Hoe Hean Club was turned into the headquarters for the mobilization of the ethnic Chinese in Southeast Asia to resist the Japanese invasion of China in both the Jinan Incident (1928) and the Overseas Chinese National Salvation Movement (1937–41).[81] The high political profile of Ee Hoe Hean Club after 1923 did not, however, overshadow its original function of providing recreational and social facilities for businessmen. These activities included opium-smoking (before 1923), playing mahjong,[82] drinking and feasting and so forth. More importantly, the club, like many other ethnic Chinese businessmen's clubs, provided a relaxed environment for businessmen, both Chinese- and English-educated, to mix. They chatted and exchanged useful business information, and negotiated business deals informally. A great deal of business was done through these informal meetings.

Conclusion

Several conclusions can be drawn from the above study. First, traditional Ethnic Chinese organizations were important institutional support for ethnic

---

78   Ibid, pp 31–32; Lim How Seng, "Yi He Xuan Jilobu shilue" (A Short History of the Ee Hoe Hean Club), in Huang Yihua et al (eds), *Yi He Xuan jiushi zhounian jinian tekan* (Souvenir Magazine of the Celebration of 90th Anniversary of the Ee Hoe Hean Club, Singapore) (Singapore: Ee Hoe Hean Club, 1985), p 37.
79   CF Yong, op cit, p 33; Lim How Seng, ibid, p 38.
80   Lim How Seng, ibid.
81   CF Yong, op cit, pp 34–36; Lim How Seng, ibid, pp 38–40; Yen Ching-hwang, "The Response of the Chinese in Singapore and Malaya to the Tsinan (Jinan) Incident, 1928", *Journal of the South Seas Society*, vol 43 (Singapore: South Seas Society, 1988), pp 1–22; CF Yong, *Tan Kah-Kee: The Making of an Overseas Chinese Legend* (Singapore: Oxford University Press, 1987), pp 160–67.
82   A very popular Chinese game, and it is still popular nowadays. I saw it being played when I visited the Club in 1990s.

Chinese business through their monopolization of certain lines of trade and as training ground for prospective entrepreneurs. Second, traditional ethnic Chinese business organizations were a mechanism through which *Bang* (dialect and geographical entity) perpetuated its control over business lines. The *Bang* monopoly, to a certain extent, disadvantaged the consumers, but guaranteed profit margins and generated competition in business activity. Third, traditional business organizations were a significant factor in the dynamics of ethnic Chinese business and were partly responsible for the dominance of the ethnic Chinese in business, especially in Southeast Asia. Fourth, traditional ethnic Chinese business organizations contained seeds of progress which enabled them to cope with changing circumstances. These progressive elements have helped transform the organizations and made them relevant in the modern world by changing or adding to their traditional functions. Just like many other ethnic Chinese kin and dialect organizations, they are capable of modernizing ethnic Chinese business. Fifth, the formal and informal business organizations (guilds, mutual-aid societies and businessmen's clubs) complemented each other, and helped to mould the special character of ethnic Chinese business.

Chapter 11

THE EMERGENCE OF MODERN CHINESE BUSINESS IN MALAYA: THE CASE OF THE STRAITS CHINESE AND THE OVERSEA-CHINESE BANKING CORPORATION

Lee Kam Hing

This article traces the rise of a group of Chinese entrepreneurs who, beginning in 1895, built the Oversea-Chinese Banking Corporation (OCBC) into one of the largest financial conglomerates in the Singapore-Malaysia region. These Chinese were led largely by Straits Chinese from Malacca and Singapore whose families had already been in the region for several generations. They went into economic sectors that were relatively new to them and where few local companies had succeeded. Even in China, where the forefathers of these Malacca and Singapore Chinese had come from, modern banking and insurance developed only towards the end of the 19th century. In that sense, these were new and modern institutions for the Chinese, whether in China or in Southeast Asia.[1] The first Chinese bank in China, the Commercial Bank of China, was established in Shanghai in 1897. The first Chinese insurance company, the Shanghai Yihe Gongsi Baoxian Hang, was established in 1865 in Shanghai.[2] The Straits Chinese succeeded in these two sectors of business because they adopted organizational forms and operational methods in business that were largely Western while retaining the traditional Chinese linkages.

The Chinese entered banking and insurance in Malaya and Singapore at a time when there was already a strong Western presence in those two fields. It was British companies that introduced banking and insurance into Malaya and Singapore in the early 19th century. British bankers and insurers, through agencies and, later, branch offices they established, dominated the

---

1   Wellington KK Chan, *Merchants, Mandarins, and Modern Enterprise in Late Ch'ing China,* Cambridge, Mass: Harvard East Asian Research Center, 1977, pp 39–63.
2   Pui Tak Lee, "Understanding and Practice of 'New Business' in Nineteenth-century China", in *Chinese Enterprise in Asia,* edited by Rajeswari Ampalavanar Brown, New York: Routledge, 1995.

two industries right up to the post-independence period in Malaysia and Singapore. Indeed, at the time the Chinese were venturing into banking and insurance they were already losing out to British capital in industries they had pioneered, such as tin mining. It was Chinese capital and labour that opened up large-scale mining during the mid-19th century. Likewise in the rubber industry, it was the Straits Chinese who undertook the first plantation. But by 1906, European mining companies using heavily-capitalized dredges were producing more tin than the Chinese ones using traditional methods. In rubber, European acreage grew rapidly from 168,000 in 1907 to 1,050,000 in 1918. In that year, Asian acreage was only 836,000. British dominance in tin and rubber has been attributed to their accessibility to larger capital, superior technology, and the support of the colonial state. It was these factors that were also to ensure their strong position in banking and finance.

The OCBC is currently among the top four banks in Singapore in terms of assets. With a capitalization of S$1.3 billion in the year 2000, it is currently the third largest company there. It is the second largest foreign bank in Malaysia, with over 25 branches and net assets worth RM20 billion. The OCBC is also the oldest and, probably, most diversified of all companies. The group has controlling stakes in Great Eastern Life Assurance (GE), which, with total assets of S$9,807 million in 1999, is the largest life insurance company in Singapore and the second in Malaysia. GE ranks 13th among the 100 largest Singapore companies. The OCBC also has controlling stakes in Overseas Assurance Corporation, one of the biggest general insurance companies in Singapore, and in Wing On Insurance. Recently, the OCBC acquired Sze Hai Tong Bank, the oldest surviving bank in Singapore. Over the years, the OCBC has been involved in various other sectors of the economy with stakes in banking, insurance, tin mining and smelting, rubber plantation, trading, hotels, properties, manufacturing, and investment. It once had significant holdings in Sime Darby, which is among the largest plantation companies in Malaysia. This group has been referred to as the OCBC–Sime Darby clique by Lim Mah Hui in an earlier study.[3] At one stage, the OCBC was the largest shareholder of Sime Darby with ten per cent of the equity. Through Sime Darby, the OCBC held interests in several other large companies which owned extensive rubber estates. The OCBC–Sime Darby combination therefore became the largest and most powerful of the conglomerates. Among its shareholders were some of the

---

3   Lim Mah Hui, *Ownership and Control of the One Hundred Largest Corporations in Malaysia*, Kuala Lumpur: Oxford University Press, 1981, pp 87–98.

most influential public figures. They included Tan Cheng Lock, the founder of the Malayan Chinese Association (MCA), and his son, Tun Tan Siew Sin, who also became president of the MCA and Malaysia's Finance Minister, as well as prominent British and Malay business figures.

How the Straits Chinese succeeded in establishing themselves in the modern financial sector is the focus of this study. In the process these Chinese helped create a broader class of Chinese in banking and insurance. Other Chinese groups had tried similarly to break into these modern industries. The most important was the Koe Guan group, led by the Khaw family. The Koe Guan group in Penang set up Khean Guan Insurance. Just as the Straits Chinese did, Koe Guan went into shipping, insurance and tin smelting. In banking, an attempt was made by a group of Cantonese in Singapore. They set up Kwong Yik Bank but it collapsed not long afterwards. Likewise, the Koe Guan group, which started out almost at the same time as the Straits Chinese group, had declined by the first decade of the 20th century and soon afterwards disappeared. The Straits Chinese were therefore only one of the groups of new Chinese entrepreneurs that emerged in the late 19th century. What is significant is that they were the first to progress successfully towards banking and insurance. Their enterprises proved durable.

There were several significant features in the emergence of the Straits Chinese OCBC Group. First, the key individuals in the creation of the OCBC came from a new generation of largely Western-educated Straits Chinese. They were admirers of Western science and technology. Innovative in business, they sought diversification into new ventures. Second, these Straits Chinese, in seeking modernization in business, also advocated reforms within the Chinese community. They held leadership positions in many Chinese organizations.

Third, these Western-educated Chinese were acceptable to the state authorities. British merchants and officials interacted more with this group than with the newer Chinese immigrants. Most of the latter had little education. In political outlook, the Straits Chinese were already seeing their future in Malaya and Singapore while the new immigrants were still China-oriented. These Straits Chinese represented the Chinese community in the Municipal Commission and the Legislative Council.

The Straits Chinese played economic and political mediating roles between the larger Chinese community and Western capital. In that sense they may be considered as brokers in a particular period between the new Chinese immigrants and British capital, and between the Chinese and the state. In this mediating role, a Hokkien commercial network was used by the Straits Chinese who themselves originated from the Fujian region of southern China. Through this Hokkien network, the Straits Chinese developed trading links with those of the same dialect group throughout Southeast Asia and southern China. This trade link was based on a commercial connection built by traders from Amoy in Fujian with indigenous producers and traders throughout the Southeast Asian region, including the Malay Archipelago, that dated back several hundred years. Later, Chinese traders from Singapore expanded this trade so that a predominant volume of regional trade in the pre-World War II period was conducted mainly by the Hokkiens. Necessities such as rice and sugar circulated in this regional trade. But it also included the shipping of export commodities such as rubber, copra and tin from the region to the major ports. Above all, the strength of the Straits Chinese was their willingness and ability, after consolidating their Hokkien network, to link up with those of the Cantonese and the Teochews.

These commercial networks of the Straits Chinese were important to British capital, which was then seeking investment opportunities and markets. A pattern of commercial collaboration developed. Increasingly, British merchants worked with Straits Chinese. They also recruited English-educated Chinese. In shipping, for instance, the coastal trade in the region dominated by the Chinese fed into the larger international trade centred in Singapore. Chinese coastal shippers linked up with the ocean-going British shipping lines.

For the Straits Chinese, business ventures with Western merchants in new industries went beyond profits and market share. These joint ventures gained for the Straits Chinese expertise and management skills in Western-type industries which they were relatively unfamiliar with. This was particularly the case with modern shipping, banking and insurance in which Western companies were more established and dominant.

The OCBC group provides a story of the emergence of a Chinese entrepreneurial class in Malaysia. Within it are encapsulated the major phases of Chinese business development as the merchants progressed from early planting operations and trade through to tin mining, revenue farming, shipping, rubber plantation and processing, and eventually to insurance and banking. But it was shipping, banking and insurance that perhaps presented a distinct phase as they created a new class of Chinese businessmen. Entry into the financial services sector achieved for these Chinese further social status, both within the Chinese community and the broader society.

Early Banking and Insurance

Banking and insurance were introduced into Malaya and Singapore in the early 19th century. They became increasingly important as the economy developed. Banks provided essential capital to start or to expand business. Insurance was important in the late 18th century when Western enterprises were venturing into business and to regions they were largely unfamiliar with. Insurance was necessary because it offered protection against risks in early trade and shipping. Then, too, the insurance industry was a form of capital accumulation. Premiums collected could be gainfully invested.

By the time banking and insurance arrived in Southeast Asia, they had acquired tested methods and organization. Long experience in tariff calculation and access to records of claims helped identify bad risks. Actuarial science was in regular use to calculate premiums. British insurers had, by 1860, combined to form Fire Offices Committees to share market information and to agree on tariff rates for the different classes of risks. Furthermore, British companies shared risks by reinsuring with one another. These developments helped British companies to lead in world insurance.

In the early development of banking and insurance in Malaya, the role of the British agency houses was important. Indeed, British agency houses were the pivot of Western capital in Malaya and Singapore as they came to hold commanding stakes in the tin, rubber, banking, insurance, and trading sectors. Agency houses included those that specialized in imports or exports, managed enterprises belonging to foreign investors, or those that combined all these activities. The agency houses looked after diverse Western investment activities such as the floating of tin and rubber companies in London, opening of estates, and acting as agents for insurers and trading companies. Some half a dozen agency houses dominated the modern sectors of the economy and these included Boustead and Company, Sime Darby, Harrison and Crosfield, and Borneo Company. Some agency houses became directly involved in banking or insurance. Borneo Company, one of Malaya's largest agency houses, was among the founders of the Hong Kong and Shanghai Bank. The company also helped start the Straits Insurance Company, the first locally incorporated insurance company in Singapore. The Chartered Bank itself was linked to some agency houses. A study of the lists of directors of various banks, insurance companies and agency houses will reveal that many of these organizations had shared interests.

The important role of agency houses was due to the fact that they were familiar with local conditions and had established a network of commercial connections. It was these which the insurance business tapped into. In addition, expenses, such as rental of premises or staff salaries, were borne by the trading houses. In turn, the agency arrangement proved convenient and beneficial to the trading houses. The agencies retained 15 per cent of the premium, and in many cases, were paid a share of the profits calculated over a period of three years. In any case, these agency houses needed insurance coverage for most of their other business. Buildings as well as goods, machinery and equipment had to be insured. Marine insurance was bought for goods shipped out and life insurance policies taken out for their expatriate staff. Retaining the 15 per cent commission on the premium reduced the cost of insurance for these trading houses.

The Chinese, during this period, largely relied on traditional organizations such as those based on dialect and district ties for sources of capital or to cover risks. Resources were pooled together for new ventures so that no single individual risked total loss. The traditional associations also offered some welfare support. For financing, there were the pawnshops where loans were secured against assets. But such loans were usually for consumption rather than investment purposes. Merchants or small businessmen usually turned to the *hui* or the rotating credit associations. These were associations of mutual assistance where resources were pooled. Then there were the Chinese moneylenders and the Indian *chettiars*. But the amount that could be borrowed was small, interest rate high and the loan period usually short. Remittance houses which mobilized and despatched savings of the Chinese in Southeast Asia were another source of funding. These houses handled remittance flows from Southeast Asia to China, and the accounts were used by Chinese merchants for their own trading and investment needs. Finally, a few Chinese businessmen turned to the Western banks through introduction from a comprador who stood also as guarantor of the loan. But as economic functions expanded, these traditional forms of insurance and financing proved inadequate.

During the late 18th and the early 19th century, a source of funding in Malaya and Singapore that became important came from the revenue farms. The revenue farm was a system of monopoly leased by the government, usually to wealthy Chinese merchants, to operate gambling or to sell opium and spirits. In the early years of British rule, when the administration of tax was not regularized, the rents from these farms were the main source of revenue to the government. Through the huge profits that could be made by Chinese leaseholders, the revenue farms created possibilities for capital accumulation. Large syndicates made up of wealthy merchants were formed to bid for the farm leases. Syndicates were formed to avoid competitive bidding among members and to pool their financial resources. Syndicates also became useful to revenue farmers as the population had become more diverse, and combinations of merchants from different dialect groups were needed to handle the more complex communities. An elaborate organization was needed to handle the distribution and sale of opium and to oversee gambling joints. The farm leaseholders generally turned to the secret societies or *kongsis* for such organizational support.

At the beginning of the 20th century, the changing political and economic environment necessitated, as well as facilitated, the Chinese moving into the modern financial sectors. The most important of these changes was the decision by the colonial authorities to phase out the revenue farm system. The lease of the last opium revenue farm ended in 1913 and with that, went the opportunity for the Chinese to accumulate capital by this means.

The revenue farm system had been phased out earlier in the Netherlands East Indies, and several Chinese revenue farmers from there had shifted to Malaya. Chinese merchants had, by then, begun diversifying into other economic activities. Of the new business, insurance and banking were regarded as profitable possibilities. Insurance was attractive because the industry did not require an initial outlay of funds as large as the rents required in the revenue farm system. Furthermore, premiums collected provided ready capital for investment. Not only was it an alternative source of capital accumulation, the insurance business also provided risk coverage for other investments.

The opening up of the Peninsula and the establishment of British rule in the Malay states created demands for new financial services. It was in the commercial centres of Penang and Singapore, where there were settled and growing communities, that the first local insurance and banking institutions were set up. But it was the European enterprises that Western insurers served. Western insurance companies were, for most of the period, wary about offering insurance to the Chinese. They knew very little about the community and less about its business forms. They considered dealing with the local merchants a hazard that far outweighed whatever profits that could be made. Even the early banks in Malaya and Singapore, which were largely British, catered mainly for European interests. The Mercantile Bank, the Hong Kong and Shanghai Bank, and the Chartered Bank provided financing to Western mines, plantations and trading houses.

It was a group of local British merchants who, in 1882, established the first insurance company in Singapore. This was the Straits Insurance Company, which was incorporated under the Indian Companies Act of 1866.

It had a paid-up capital of $3 million, and several British trading houses were listed as its major shareholders, one of which was Borneo Company. Straits Insurance offered insurance for marine risks in all parts of the world, but its business was mainly in the Straits Settlements, the Malay states, and Sumatra. There was, at this time, regular trade between Singapore and Penang with Sumatra. In 1886, the same shareholders formed a second company, the Straits Fire Insurance Company, with a paid-up capital of $2 million. Straits Fire Insurance, which provided cover for fire and general risks, performed well in the first few years. In 1892, it announced the setting up of a branch office in London and it purchased its own building in the Cornhill district of London.[4]

In February 1885, the Singapore Insurance Company, with British and some Chinese equity participation, was established. Among the British investors were the shipping agent Mansfield and Company and the trading houses of Borneo Company, Sarkie and Moses, and Gilfillan, Wood and Company. The most prominent of the Chinese in the company was Lim Eng Keng, who was one of the shareholders and directors.[5] Lim, Straits-born, took over his father's firm, the well-known Lim Lan and Company, in 1875. He later became a director of the Singapore Land Company and was a business partner of Syed Mohamed Alsagoff. Lim was a leader of the Singapore Hokkiens and besides being involved in the Singapore branch of the Straits Settlements Association, also served on the Municipal Board and the Chinese Advisory Board. Lim was therefore the first Straits Chinese involved in insurance.

It was also in 1885 that the first Chinese insurance company was set up. Formed in July of that year in Penang, Khean Guan Insurance Company Limited was largely Hokkien, and represented the first effort by local Chinese to organize insurance facilities. Mostly Penang Hokkiens, the early directors of Khean Guan were all connected with one another through trade. There were also marriage ties among families of the principal directors. The previous revenue syndicates now became a framework of the evolving business networks in the region. They adopted the limited company form and subsequently opened share subscription to the public.[6] Khean Guan relied on traditional links in modernizing Chinese business.[7]

---

4   "Statement of Accounts for Year Ending 1892, Straits Fire Insurance", *Post Magazine and Insurance Monitor* 54 (36), 9 September 1893.
5   "Report of Sixth Ordinary General Meeting of the Singapore Insurance Company Ltd, April 1890", Singapore.
6   Jennifer W Cushman, *Family and State: The Formation of a Sino-Thai Tin-mining Dynasty 1797–1932*, Singapore: Oxford University Press, pp 56–87.
7   Ibid, pp 79–80.

The early directors all had revenue farm background. Cheah Choo Yew was an opium farmer in Deli, Sumatra, for about 17 years, and later managed gambling farms in Siam, Hong Kong and Singapore.[8] Likewise, Ho Tiang Wan, Khaw Sim Bee, Khoo Thean Teik and Yeo Wee Gark were members of large revenue opium and gambling syndicates in Penang, Singapore and the Malay states.[9]

Many of the early Khean Guan directors also owned shipping companies and as these expanded, they needed insurance support. Cheah Choo Yew owned Eastern Shipping and Khaw Sim Bee headed Koe Guan Shipping. Koe Guan had extensive links with other Chinese shipping firms such as Wee Bin, then Singapore's largest local shipping line; Guan Lee Hin of Quah Beng Kee; and Ban Joo Hin, owned by Chang Pi-shih. Khaw Sim Bee also helped set up Eastern Shipping, which was important in the tin trade and was a major carrier of migrant labour from China to Southeast Asia. Another early director was Chuah Yu Kay of the Kong Hock Shipping Company.

The timing of Khean Guan's formation is of some significance. The Chinese shipping companies were, at this juncture, beginning to face serious competition from large British-owned companies. The most serious of the challengers was the Straits Steamship Company. The company was a merger of a number of Singapore Chinese and British shipping lines. Straits Steamship was linked to Straits Trading, the largest tin-smelting company in Malaya, as well as to an increasing number of Chinese miners. Furthermore, the Penang shippers would have noted that Straits Steamship enjoyed insurance facilities from British companies.

The first three local insurance companies did not, however, last long. Both the Straits Insurance Company and the Singapore Insurance Company experienced difficulties and were eventually bought over by the Commercial Union in June 1894. Khean Guan survived until 1914. It may be argued that Khean Guan operated in Penang, where the volume of international trade was small and, in fact, declining when compared with Singapore. Jennifer Cushman's study identified other factors as to why the business enterprise of the Khaw family went into decline. One was the unavailability of an institution within the group of companies to generate regular financing. Khean Guan was a general insurance company and the Khaw business enterprise did not have a life insurance company nor a bank. Indeed, there

---

8   *Malay Mail*, 10 February 1931.
9   Carl A Trocki, *Opium and Empire: Chinese Society in Colonial Singapore, 1800–1910*, Ithaca and London: Cornell University Press, 1990, pp 183–219.

was no bank in Penang until 1918, and by that time the Koe Guan group was already in decline. Another was the death of Khaw Sim Bee, which deprived the Khaw business conglomerate of strong leadership and management direction.

The decline of Koe Guan could also be due to its failure to establish links beyond the Chinese community. Koe Guan recruited some Europeans as managers and engineers. But it did not develop ties with Western business groups. Indeed, its Eastern Shipping group and Eastern Trading were formed to rival Straits Steamship and Straits Trading. And while the Khaw family enjoyed the trust of the Siamese court, it could not quite gain the acceptance of the colonial state. Eastern Shipping refused to allow its ships to be used by the authorities in World War I.

The men who were involved in Koe Guan were largely new immigrants and these successful businessmen were still drawn towards developments in what they still regarded as their homeland. Men such as Chang Pi-shih and Foo Choo Choon who were part of the Koe Guan group invested in their home provinces in south China. More than just profits, the railway building projects and the new industries they started there were an effort to help China modernize. It was this political orientation and the absence of connections with the colonial state and Western capital that may well explain why the Koe Guan group could not build a durable financial conglomerate.

Beginnings of the Great Eastern Assurance–OCBC Group

At a time of growing difficulties for Khean Guan, some Chinese merchants in Singapore decided to set up insurance companies and banks. The initiative came from a group of largely Straits Chinese from Malacca and Singapore whose vision was to develop what may later be described as the "OCBC conglomerate". The early core activities of this Straits Chinese group were trade and shipping. Through the process of modernizing their shipping business, the group greatly expanded and diversified into other sectors. They helped found the Great Eastern Life Assurance, the Eastern United Assurance, and the Overseas Assurance Corporation as well as banks. The OCBC group offers a contrast to the Koe Guan group.

The men whose early wealth helped start the Straits Chinese OCBC group of companies were traders, planters, tin miners, and shipowners. The founding members of this group were Hokkien. They were local-born, Malay-speaking and Western-educated, characteristics which caused them to be referred to as "Straits Chinese". There were also intermarriages among the families of its members which provided a further bond to the group. Many of them had work experience in Western firms. An important feature was their close links with the colonial authorities. Many were active in the Straits Settlements Association as well as the Straits Chinese British Association (SCBA).[10] Generally, they were politically acceptable to the colonial state and a number of them were appointed to representative bodies such as the Municipal Commission, the Legislative Council or the Chinese Advisory Board. But these Straits Chinese did not lose their links with traditional Chinese groups, and were active in, for instance, the Chinese Chambers of Commerce, Chinese school boards, and the guilds and associations. Subsequently, the group expanded to draw in other dialect groups, principally the Cantonese and the Teochew. Within a very short period, they skilfully combined their knowledge, connections and resources to modernize the management and technology of an increasingly diversified set of business ventures.

There were several key families and individuals who played a role in building up the OCBC. The figure who was perhaps the most influential was Dr Lim Boon Keng. Lim Boon Keng is today better remembered as a social reformer in his opposition to opium-smoking, participation in the queue-cutting campaign, and for his involvement in the Confucianist movement in Singapore.[11] He was the founder President of the SCBA. But Lim Boon Keng probably played just as important a role in encouraging Straits Chinese into modern commerce and industry.

Lim Boon Keng won the highly competitive Queen's scholarship to study medicine in Edinburgh University. He graduated in 1887 and after a period of research at Cambridge, he returned to Singapore in 1893. He set up his own medical practice and one of his partners was Dr SC Yin, who, besides supporting Lim's social causes, also joined him in his various business interests. Lim helped set up the SCBA and, together with Song Ong Siang, edited *Straits Chinese Magazine*, which promoted the association's ideas. Lim, although a Straits Chinese, came to be drawn to the political ferment in China. He first supported reformist Kang Yu-wei and came to accept the revival of Confucianism as a way to bring change to China. However, Lim also considered Western science and technology as necessary if China was to modernize and to strengthen itself. He, like

---

10 Memorandum and Articles of Association of the Eastern United Assurance Corporation Limited, Singapore: Kitts and Company, 1913.
11 Dick Wilson, *Solid as a Rock: the First Forty Years of the Oversea-Chinese Banking Corporation,* Singapore: OCBC, 1972, pp 29–33; *The Straits Times*, 7 January 1957.

other Straits Chinese, advocated modern education. Together with Khoo Seok Wan, he founded the Singapore Chinese Girls' School. When Khoo started *Thien Nan Shin Pao* in 1898, Lim was in charge of English editorial work. Lim published a Chinese newspaper, *Jit Sin Pau*, in 1899. In calling for social reforms, Lim and his colleagues distanced themselves from the older and more conservative Straits Chinese.

Lim distinguished himself by becoming one of the first Chinese to venture into Malaya's pioneering economic activities. He bought shares in Straits Trading, which became the largest tin-smelting company in Malaya and, later, a very large, diversified company in the region. Then when the commercially untested cultivation of rubber was introduced to the region, Lim encouraged Tan Chay Yan, another Straits Chinese, to start a plantation. In 1895 he risked his own investment in a joint venture in Malacca with Tan. The venture was successful. Lim later became a director of Singapore Rubber Limited.

It was in the finance sector that Lim was most influential. In 1912 he helped established the Chinese Commercial Bank, the first Hokkien bank in Singapore, becoming its founding chairman. He had a part in setting up two more Hokkien banks. Lim also saw the need for Chinese involvement in insurance. In 1914 he helped start the Eastern United Assurance Company. Tan Chay Yan, his rubber business partner, was the first chairman. Then in 1920, Lim was among those who formed the Overseas Assurance Corporation and became its founding chairman. In creating the beginnings of the OCBC conglomerate, Lim drew upon his links with the Straits Chinese, other Hokkiens, including those from Java, Chinese of other dialect groups, and British merchants and officials. He was one of the founders of the Singapore Chinese Chamber of Commerce and served as its president.

Another Straits Chinese who was important in helping to form the OCBC was Tan Cheng Lock. Tan was linked to Lim both in social affairs and in business. The great great grandfather of Tan Cheng Lock, Tan Hay Kwan, arrived in Malacca from China around 1771 and founded a flourishing junk trade that plied between Malacca, Riau, Banjermasin and Makassar. Tan Hay Kwan died in 1801, and his grandson Tan Choon Bock expanded the junk trade. Even though Malacca, as a port, was in decline, Choon Bock modernized his fleet by replacing his junks with steamers. He moved into agriculture and, while cultivating gambier, reportedly started the first tapioca plantation in the state. As in shipping, he introduced modern machinery in his tapioca estate at Pankalan Minyak, Jasin. Later, using his growing wealth, Choon Bock diversified into properties in Malacca and Singapore.

It was Tan Cheng Lock's uncle, Tan Keong Saik, who took over the family business and in 1890 merged his modernized shipping company with several others to form the Straits Steamship Company. He and his son-in-law, Lee Choon Chuan, sat on the board of Straits Steamship. The merger was significant because Straits Steamship became the leading shipping company in the region. Just as significant, it was an enterprise where local Chinese successfully teamed up with British businessmen. Keong Saik, with his English-language education and job experience in Borneo Company, ably worked out such a joint venture. Four years before taking his company into Straits Steamship, he served as one of five Municipal Commissioners. For several years, he was a director of Straits Steamship and, subsequently, became a director of the Singapore Slipway Company and the Tanjong Pagar Dock Company.

It was Tan Cheng Lock who, of all the Straits Chinese, emerged to be the most prominent in the rubber industry. When his grandfather, Tan Choon Bock, died, his father inherited nothing. Cheng Lock thereupon took up a teaching job at Raffles' Institution in Singapore. In his six years there, he established contact with other Straits Chinese leaders. Tan Cheng Lock was active in the Malacca SCBA.

In 1908, he returned to Malacca and worked for a while on the estate of his mother's cousin, Lee Chim Tuan, and, later, for Nyalas Rubber Estates Limited. In 1910, with the backing of Chan Kang Swi, a prominent businessman, and Lee Chim Tuan, he floated Malacca Pinda Rubber Estate, Ayer Molek Rubber Company, and United Malacca Rubber Estate. Through the years of the rubber boom, he built his wealth. In the years since then, he added Bukit Jelutong Estate, Bukit Katil Rubber Estate, Punggor Rubber Estate, Cathay Rubber Estate, Kew Rubber Estate, and Tong Watt Rubber Estate. He also became chairman of Nyalas Rubber Estates, with which he had worked. Over the years, Tan Cheng Lock shrewdly invested in several other companies, many of which had substantial British interest. Tan Cheng Lock was also a director of Straits Albion Press and of British Malaya Trustee and Executor Company, and the chairman of Chenglock Soohock and Company.[12] While Tan Cheng Lock sat on many boards of directors, he did not engage directly in the management. This allowed him time to take an active part in public affairs for which he came to be better known. It was Tan's involvement in rubber that later helped create a link between the OCBC and Sime Darby. Tan held shares in Sime Darby, an agency house involved in early rubber plantations in Malacca. The OCBC and Great

---

12 P Lim Pui Huen, *Tan Cheng Lock: A Descriptive List*, Singapore: ISEAS, 1989.

Eastern combined held the largest block of shares in Sime Darby. Tan and other OCBC directors sat on the board of Sime Darby. Tan joined Lim Boon Keng and Lim Peng Siang in forming Ho Hong Bank, the second of three Singapore Hokkien banks. In 1932 he agreed to merge the three Hokkien banks to form the OCBC, of which he was a director. Earlier in 1920 he had helped form the Overseas Assurance Company.

Another key Straits Chinese family was that of Lee Cheng Yan. His firm dealt in finance and property development. His son, Lee Choon Guan, started out by helping in the family company.[13] The younger Lee married the daughter of Tan Keong Saik and served for many years as a director of the Straits Steamship Company, probably representing the interests of the Tan family. But he was also a director of South British Insurance Company, a New Zealand firm, and was involved in several rubber, tin and industrial companies. He represented the Hokkiens on the Chinese Advisory Board and was a founding director of Eastern United Assurance.

The Tan Cheng Lock family was also close to another prominent Straits Chinese. He was Tan Jiak Kim of Kim Seng and Company and a good friend of Tan Keong Saik. Tan Kim Seng was from Malacca and was one of the first Chinese settlers in Singapore. His company was an import and export firm, and over the years built business relations with agency houses among which were Borneo Company and Boustead and Company. Tan Jiak Kim saw strategic reasons in participating in shipping and he became a director of Straits Steamship, where he served for over 25 years. Tan was an established leader of the Straits Chinese and was appointed to the Legislative Council at the age of 30.[14] He also joined the OCBC group, where he was very influential.

There were several other prominent Straits Chinese and among them were Lim Peng Siang, Tan Chay Yan, Tan Kheam Hock, Khoo Sian Tan and Ong Soon Tee. Lim Peng Siang owned the Ho Hong Steamship Company. It had a fleet of eight ocean-going liners and 22 smaller steamers. Lim Peng Siang floated a joint stock banking company, Ho Hong Bank, of which Lim Boon Keng became a shareholder and a director. Tan Chay Yan was a third-generation Malacca Chinese, and was educated at the Malacca High School. In 1892, at the age of 21, he was appointed to the Malacca Municipal Council. He also became active in the Straits Chinese British

---

13 Song Ong Siang, *One Hundred Years' History of the Chinese in Singapore*, Singapore: Oxford University Press, (reprint) 1967, p 111.

14 KG Tregonning, *Home Port Singapore: A History of Straits Steamship Company Limited 1890–1965*, Singapore: Oxford University Press, 1967, pp 8–9.

Association, and, through this, built a close relationship with Dr Lim Boon Keng. In 1895, in partnership with Lim Boon Keng, he planted a 43-acre estate at Bukit Lintang with rubber seedlings from the Singapore Botanic Gardens. Later, he helped float a Chinese syndicate called the Malacca Rubber and Tapioca Company to plant rubber on a 4,300-acre estate at Bukit Asahan, Malacca, thus becoming the first Asian to be involved in the industry.[15]

Tan Kheam Hock studied at the Penang Free School, and after working at the Mercantile Bank, was involved in a syndicate for the opium and spirit farms until 1906. He was active in the SCBA and on the Chinese Advisory Board. He succeeded Tan Chay Yan as chairman of Eastern United Assurance and was a director of a host of rubber, tin and industrial companies. Ong Soon Tee was one of the first pupils of the missionary-teacher W Oldham and was later active in the SCBA. He was also a director of Eastern United Assurance. Khoo Sian Tan was a Hai Cheng Hokkien, educated at the Penang Free School. He was involved in a Singapore revenue farm syndicate and held interests in various companies including the Sarawak Shipping Company and Thailand Mining Company. See Teong Wah, a founding director of Great Eastern, was educated at Singapore's St Joseph's Institution. He joined Hong Kong and Shanghai Banking Corporation (HSBC) as his father's assistant and, later, took over as comprador of the bank. See was made a Justice of Peace and served as Municipal Commissioner as well as President of both the Chinese Chamber of Commerce and the Hokkien Association.

The Insurance Companies

The start of Straits Chinese involvement in insurance was closely linked to two largely British companies, Straits Steamship and Straits Trading. These two companies, which were set up in the late 19th century, forged early business ties between the Straits Chinese and British merchants. The Straits Trading Company, established in 1887, was the largest tin-smelting and tin-trading company in the region. The Chinese presence was less evident in the early years. But even at its inception, the shareholders of Straits Trading included well-known Chinese such as Dr Lim Boon Keng, Loke Yew, Tan Jiak Kim and Looi Hoi Choon. In 1906, Loke Yew became a

---

15   JH Drabble, *Rubber in Malaya, 1876–1922: The Genesis of the Industry*, Kuala Lumpur: Oxford University Press, 1973, p 21; A Coates, *The Commerce in Rubber: The First 250 Years*, Singapore: Oxford University Press, 1987, pp 102–03.

member of the board of directors. Later his son, Loke Wan Tho, and Tan Chin Tuan were appointed to the board. A significant part of Straits Trading's transactions was with Chinese mining companies in the peninsula. Chinese miners supplied tin ore to be processed in the company's smelting works.[16]

It was in Straits Steamship that the developing Sino-British business collaboration was most visible. Straits Steamship was formed in 1890 following the merger of several local shipping companies, of which three were well-established Chinese firms. These included the shipping company of Tan Choon Bok of Malacca, which was represented on Straits Steamship's board of directors by Tan Keong Saik and later by Lee Choon Chuan. Straits Trading relied on Straits Steamship for the transportation of tin ore.[17]

It was the British and Chinese directors of Straits Trading and Straits Steamship who then started the Great Eastern Life Assurance. The founding chairman of Great Eastern was GA Derrick, who had served as an accountant in the Straits Trading Company. He acted as liquidator for the Singapore Insurance Company. Derrick must have been a key British businessman in this link with the Chinese merchants. His early interaction with the Chinese must have been through Straits Trading. Derrick was also a commanding officer of the Singapore Volunteers. Many members of the Singapore Volunteers were from the SCBA. Another director, FM Elliot, was a member of the Singapore Legislative Council and senior partner of a well-known law firm. He was also president of the exclusive Tanglin Club. AD Allan, another board member, was managing director of McAlister and Company. The Europeans associated with the Chinese were thus among the most influential members of the colonial society.[18]

Five of the first ten directors of Great Eastern were Straits Chinese linked to the Straits Steamship group. Four of them later helped found Eastern United Assurance. They and others in Eastern United Assurance also had stakes in the important Straits Trading Company.[19] Great Eastern, by concentrating on life insurance, differed from earlier local insurers in their efforts.

---

16 KG Tregonning, "Straits Tin: A brief account of the first seventy-five years of the Straits Trading Company Limited", *Journal of the Malayan Branch of the Royal Asiatic Society*, 36 (i), 1963: 79–152.

17 KG Tregonning, "The Origin of the Straits Steamship Company in 1890", *Journal of the Malayan Branch of the Royal Asiatic Society*, 38 (ii), 1965: 274–89.

18 Walter Makepeace et al, *One Hundred Years of Singapore*, reprint, Singapore: Oxford University Press, vol 1, pp 155, 200, 404; vol 2, pp 206, 226, 575; Report submitted to the 6th Ordinary General Meeting of the Great Eastern Life Assurance Company Ltd, 31 March 1913, Singapore.

19 Annual Report, The Great Eastern Life Assurance Company Ltd, 20 March 1913.

It was the experience in Great Eastern that the Straits Chinese brought with them in establishing Eastern United Assurance in 1913. Its founding chairman was Tan Chay Yan, and he served in that capacity until his death in March 1916.[20] Others involved in Eastern United Assurance were Tan Khean Hock, Quah Beng Kee and Ee Yew Kim. Lim Boon Keng was listed as a member of the Advisory Board.

Eastern United Assurance included the important Teochew and Cantonese dialect groups. In the early years, Seah Eng Lim, who was a director of the Teochew corporation Sze Hai Tong Banking and Insurance Company, and, later, of the Overseas Assurance Corporation, sat on the board of Eastern United. Significant Cantonese representation within Eastern United included Eu Tong Sen and Cheong Yoke Choy. Eu Tong Sen was a successful tin-miner from Perak who was first educated in China and then in Penang. He was the first Chinese on the Federal Council. Besides being involved in tin mining, he helped found Lee Wah Bank. Cheong Yoke Choy worked with Loke Yew in Selangor and became a wealthy tin miner and property owner. He co-founded the Kwong Yik Bank in Kuala Lumpur. It is likely that Cheong not only represented Cantonese interests but also Loke Yew's investment in Eastern United.

Perhaps the most important Cantonese was Wong Siew Qui, popularly referred to as SQ Wong. He was a son of Wong Ah Fook, a successful entrepreneur from Johor and founder of the Singapore Kwong Yik Bank. Wong Ah Fook held shares in Great Eastern and Eastern United. But while he took no active part in either company, his son, SQ Wong, a Middle Temple–trained lawyer and member of the Johor State Council, played an influential role in Eastern United, and later became its chairman.[21]

The founding of the Eastern United Assurance suggests that sections of the Chinese community were beginning to buy insurance protection against business risks. One founder-director of Eastern United was Chan Ngo Bee, who owned the Victoria Sawmill and Chop Seng Chiang Company. His company was also involved in an ice factory, and at one time, a shipping fleet. On one occasion, a major fire almost destroyed his sawmill and this event certainly impressed on him the need for insurance services. The early Chinese need for insurance was most evident in shipping.

---

20 Rene SK Young, "Malaysia", in *Insurance Markets of the World*, Zurich: Swiss Reinsurance Company, 1964, pp 476–84; A Wright and HA Cartwright, *Twentieth Century Impressions of British Malaya: Its History, People, Commerce, Industries and Resources,* London: Lloyd's Greater British Publishing Company, 1912, p 842.
21 Song Ong Siang, ibid, pp 354–55.

Then there were the new rubber factories. Risks were also high in the smoke-houses and storage places. Accidental fires could swiftly destroy whole consignments of sheet rubber awaiting shipment.

Eastern United also reflected the broader business linkages of the Straits Chinese business group. Its bankers were the Teochew Sze Hai Tong Bank and the Hokkien Chinese Commercial Bank. Two other banks that represented its Fire and Marine departments were the Chartered Bank and Hong Kong and Shanghai Bank. Banks and insurance companies required a customer base larger than that offered by the Hokkien community.

There was collaboration with Western groups. In 1920 Eastern United sold a stake to the South British Insurance Company, a New Zealand–incorporated company. With that, the New Zealand company had a representative on Eastern United's board of directors. Eastern United also employed European managers. HJ Fougere was appointed its first general manager and, a few years later, JW Harris became manager.

In 1920, the Straits Chinese group set up a third insurance company. This was the Overseas Assurance Corporation (OAC), started with a paid-up capital of $650,000 by Tan Cheng Lock, Dr Yin Suat Chuan and SQ Wong. Dr Lim Boon Keng was the OAC's first chairman. SQ Wong, by this time, was also a director of both Great Eastern and Eastern United. He and Dr Yin brought their insurance experience to the OAC. The OAC was a move backed by three Hokkien banks with which the OAC directors were associated.[22]

The role played by Song Ong Siang, a Straits Chinese and friend of Lim Boon Keng, is little noted. A Queen's scholar, Song completed his law studies in Britain and returned to set up a practice with James Aitken. Song did not appear to be involved in any of the business ventures of the Straits Chinese. But his firm was recorded as being the lawyers of the Eastern United Assurance.[23] Song and other Straits Chinese professionals must have been important in advising the Straits Chinese merchants as they negotiated deals with British merchants or when they set up banks and insurance companies. The Straits Chinese were able to consult Song when operating within a legal system which had served to advance their commercial interests.

---

22   Overseas Assurance Corporation, *The Overseas Assurance Corporation Limited, 1920–1980*, Singapore: Overseas Assurance Corporation, 1980.
23   Annual Report, The Eastern United Assurance Corporation Ltd, Singapore, 1914.

The Hokkien Banks

The Straits Chinese started banking at about the time they went into insurance. In 1912, Dr Lim Boon Keng headed a group to establish the Chinese Commercial Bank (CCB). He was its first chairman. He was joined by Lim Peng Siang of Ho Hong Company. All the directors of the CCB were Hokkien and in the early years, the bank mainly served the banking needs of that dialect group. It has been said that the CCB was among the first Chinese banks to popularize the use of current accounts among the Chinese.

Lim Peng Siang, together with Lim Boon Keng, then established a second Hokkien bank, the Ho Hong Bank, in 1917. Among the founder-shareholders of Ho Hong Bank were Lee Choon Chuan from the Straits Steamship and Tan Cheng Lock. Ho Hong Bank took the lead in opening branches all over Malaya. It even had branches in Burma and China. Lim Peng Siang relied on the bank to raise capital for his Ho Hong Company, which, at that time, was the largest local shipping concern in Singapore.

A third Hokkien bank, the Overseas Chinese Bank (OCB), was founded in 1919. On this occasion, Lim Boon Keng persuaded Oei Tiong Ham, the well-known Hokkien businessman from Java, to participate by taking up shares. Lim became the first chairman of the OCB. In all three banks, Lim played an influential role.[24]

All three banks flourished in the 1920s, especially in a period of rubber boom. But they ran into great difficulties during the Great Depression. The severe fall in the price of rubber resulted in depressed economic conditions. But it was also the sudden removal of the sterling from the gold standard which led to serious losses in foreign exchange that the banks were said to have speculated in. The banks also suffered losses because of political uncertainties in China at this time. A considerable amount of the banks' business had been the remittance of money from Southeast Asia to the various home provinces.

To overcome the crisis, the three banks merged in 1932 to form the Oversea-Chinese Banking Corporation. Control of the bank was handed over to a new set of directors. Lim was, by this time, too preoccupied with social issues and was not actively involved in the OCBC. However, Dr Yin, his medical partner, and Tan Cheng Lock were on the founding board of directors. Most of the directors came from the CCB.

---

24 Dick Wilson, *Solid as a Rock: The First Forty Years of the Oversea-Chinese Banking Corporation,* Singapore: OCBC, 1972.

A continuing strength of the OCBC group was its family and dialect ties. The new directors and those of the succeeding generation, such as Lee Kong Chian, Tan Cheng Lock, Tan Siew Sin, Lim Kho Leng and Tan Ean Kian, were all from founding families of the Hokkien banks. With a new generation, the bank embarked on a programme of modernization. Records were written and kept in English, and its exchange operations and control systems of branches modernized. It expanded regionally by opening branches in Bangkok and Jambi, as well as in all the towns in Malaya. Less than a decade after its establishment, the OCBC became the largest Chinese bank outside of China and owned almost three-quarters of the total assets of all Chinese banks in Malaya and Singapore.

The merger of the three banks thus greatly strengthened the banking position of the Straits Chinese business group. Since 1932, the OCBC had spearheaded the expansion and diversification of the Straits Chinese conglomerate. It continued to draw support from the three insurance companies it had been associated with—Great Eastern, Eastern United and the OAC. With this development, the Straits Chinese business network was firmly in place.

In this expansion and development, the Straits Chinese were helped by the fact that there were few regulatory rules governing the banking and insurance industries in Malaya and Singapore during the early years. In banking there were no regulations on minimum liquidity ratios, or on suspension of credit policies, periodic examination of accounts to prevent fraud, and the fixing of interest rates. It was not until the postwar period that there were central banks with supervisory roles. There was, likewise, in insurance a generally *laissez-faire* approach by the colonial state. Over the years, however, some regulations on life and general insurance companies were introduced. But there was no provision in the laws for the authorities to refuse permission to a company to commence insurance business. In Singapore, the colonial state placed few hindrances on banking and insurance as these were services seen as essential to commerce, upon which the island's economy depended. Furthermore, given the dominant position of British banks and insurers, the few Chinese banks and insurers could easily be tolerated.

Several other factors helped the OCBC group of banks and insurance companies at the time they started. First, there was a sharp rise in regional and international trade. The export trade grew with the development of the tin and rubber industries. This growing commerce benefited the Straits Chinese who were involved in the regional trade. The growing trade of Singapore and Malaya led to a demand for more shipping. Growing trade also required more funding and better credit facilities. It called for new insurance services. These were responded to by banks and insurance companies that included those of the OCBC group.

It was also a time of great social change. There was population growth and new urban centres had sprung up with the arrival of Chinese and Indian immigrants. There was also a sizeable class of European administrators and businessmen in these centres. And as the population became settled and there arose a distinct middle class, life insurance was sought for both security as well as a form of savings. General and life insurance were required when loans were taken to purchase homes or to start business. There were also changes in lifestyle with the coming of automobiles and trucks. In 1937, compulsory third-party insurance for all motor vehicles was gazetted. Earlier in 1933, workmen's compensation was introduced with the scheme underwritten by insurance companies. And the Chinese community had emerged to become a significant even though small insurance market.

The OCBC group did well in the early years because of business support from member companies within an emerging conglomerate and within the loose network of Chinese enterprises. The growing trade of the Straits Chinese and the increasing loan transactions of their banks gave business to the Straits Chinese insurance companies. Traders and shippers, for instance, required marine and fire insurance. And in a growing population, demand for business and personal loans grew. Bank loans required from customers coverage of insurance as security. The OAC was, as an example, the official insurer of the OCBC.

In turn, funds accumulated from savings and insurance premiums in Straits Chinese banks and insurance companies were invested in the developing business environment in Singapore and Malaya. Over the years, these funds bought into blue-chip companies. These not only brought good returns to the banks and insurance companies, but they created further business opportunities. The banking and insurance requirements of affiliated companies such as Straits Trading, Sime Darby Plantations, Fraser and Neave Ltd were passed on to the OCBC and its group of insurers. Through this was created a conglomerate which Koe Guan could not establish and which few other Chinese groups were able to match even in the later period.

Other Chinese Insurance Companies and Banks

Several other Chinese banks were also set up around the time of the creation of the three Hokkien banks. As with the OCBC group, these were dialect-based and served their respective dialect communities. The Cantonese started banking even before the Hokkiens when they opened the Kwong Yik Bank in 1903.

However, the bank failed in 1913. Despite this, a Cantonese bank using the name "Kwong Yik Bank" was opened in Kuala Lumpur in 1913 by Loke Yew and Cheong Yoke Choy.

The Teochews also had a bank earlier than the Straits Chinese. In 1907 they formed the Sze Hai Tong Bank and Insurance. Banking was the main business. At this time many Teochews were engaged in the growing trade, particularly in rice, between southern China and Thailand. The Sze Hai Tong Bank survived the Depression and continued to enjoy steady growth. It had branches in Bangkok and Hong Kong. The largest shareholder at the time of the Sze Hai Tong Bank's founding was Seah Eng Lim. Seah was a director of the Eastern United Assurance and this linked him to the Straits Chinese.

Linked, too, to the OCBC were founders of other new banks. Yeap Chor Ee, who founded the Ban Hin Lee Bank in Penang in 1918 (although the bank was incorporated only in 1935), was an original shareholder of the OCBC. In 1920, a Cantonese bank, Lee Wah Bank, was opened in Singapore and its founders were associated with the Straits Chinese. They were Cheong Yoke Choy, Eu Tong Sen and Lee Leung Ki. Cheong and Eu worked with the Straits Chinese in the Eastern United Assurance. An important part of Lee Wah Bank's business was the remittance of funds from Southeast Asia to southern China. This suggests that the Straits Chinese banks were also a response during this period to the growing trade between Singapore and Hong Kong.

The last bank to be established in Singapore in the prewar years was the United Chinese Bank (UCB). Set up in October 1935, it had a paid-up capital of $1 million. Its founding directors were Hokkiens. The UCB was to tap substantially into the experience of the OCBC. One of the founders of the UCB, Ong Piah Teng, had served as general manager of the OCBC. Ong became the UCB's first managing director. Tan Lark Sye, also a founding director of the UCB, was on the board of directors of the OCBC. Many of the early senior staff of the UCB such as accountants and managers were recruited from the OCBC. In the postwar period the UCB changed its name to United Overseas Bank (UOB).

An insurance company linked to the Cantonese was established in 1923. This was the Asia Insurance Company headed by Lee Leung Ki and several other Cantonese. Lee took a leading role in the setting up of Lee Wah Bank. Asia Insurance's paid-up capital of only $160,00 was small. Despite this, it survived the early difficult years as well as the 1932 Depression. It was able to do this through an alliance with three Hong Kong insurance companies. These were the Shanghai Fire and Marine

Insurance Company Limited, Lun Tai Mutual Fire and Marine Insurance Co Ltd, and Hong Nin Fire and Marine Insurance Co Ltd. In 1948 Asian Insurance also went into life insurance with the establishment of the Asia Union Life and Accident Assurance Society Ltd. Clearly then, the beginning of the OCBC group helped set the course for the Chinese in Malaya and Singapore in banking and insurance.

Competing against British Enterprises

The Chinese companies operated in a business environment where British banks and insurers were already well established. They managed to sustain early growth by serving fellow dialect members as well as others of the community. Dialect ties and personal links still counted in business during this early period. Many Chinese having difficulties or were uncomfortable with foreign banks or insurers turned to the Chinese companies.

It was in insurance that local companies felt most the competitive presence of foreign insurers. The large British companies, as did other European and American insurers, had agencies or branches in Malaya and Singapore. British companies, by their size and worldwide branches, remained dominant. With a comparatively bigger capital base, they were able to cope with large claims. British insurance companies enjoyed a better reputation of being secure and reliable. Indeed, the ability of British insurance companies to pay up all claims following the 1906 San Francisco earthquake, when so many others could not, greatly enhanced their reputation, both in the United States and elsewhere. And because of their worldwide branches, losses incurred in one region were covered by profits made elsewhere. Further, with the backing of larger assets, British companies could enter new areas by buying over existing small, local companies.

The incorporation of local insurance companies in Malaya and Singapore and the entry of European insurance companies persuaded British firms to seek a stronger presence in Malaya. Towards the end of the 19th century, German and Dutch insurance companies were expanding in Penang and Singapore through compatriot agency houses. Behn, Meyer and Company represented the North German Fire Insurance Company, while Katz Brothers Limited was the agent for Hamburg Bremen Fire Insurance Company and Aachen Munich Fire Insurance Company. Martijn and Company was acting on behalf of the Java Sea and Fire Insurance Company while GH Slot and Company represented the Netherlands Fire Insurance Company. Likewise, the Japanese Meiji Insurance Company had appointed

Mitsui Bussan Kaisha as agents in Singapore. The threat of the European companies was not only that they underwrote much of the insurance needs of compatriot companies but that they allegedly offered lower premium rates and higher coverage limits.

In Britain, large insurance companies belonging to the tariff cartel dealt with premium undercutting by buying up non-tariff companies where possible. In Malaya, in June 1894, the Commercial Union of London took over the Straits Fire Insurance Company. Started only in 1861, Commercial Union had expanded its overseas operations so rapidly that by the 1890s, it drew three-quarters of its premiums from abroad. Its total worldwide fire insurance income ranked second only to the Royal Insurance of Britain. After taking over Straits Fire Insurance, Commercial Union reorganized its business in Malaya. It registered a branch in Singapore to take over policies previously issued by Straits Fire Insurance.

Given the complexities of modern insurance and the dominance of British insurers, how did the Chinese companies compete? British companies had tremendous advantage and given their long years of experience had accumulated data on all classes of risks and had worked out appropriate tariffs. Premiums based on claims experience had been set so that they would not be too excessive as to invite undercutting, nor too low as to incur losses. Hence, the ratio of claims to premiums collected by the British companies in their overseas operations had always been favourable. The large insurance companies in Britain had formed the Fire Offices Association to set tariff rates, by which all member companies had to abide to avoid premium undercutting.

One way in which local Chinese insurers gained access to expertise, both in management and in acquiring tariff information, was to become members of the local Fire Offices Committees which were connected to the Fire Offices Association in London that ruled on insurance tariff.[25] They also recruited personnel from the large Western corporations or agency houses. Managers and officials, both expatriate and Chinese, who had gained experience and information were taken into Khean Guan, Great Eastern and Eastern United. Thus, one of the first directors of Khean Guan, for instance, was Goh Boon Keng. Born in Penang in 1872, Goh was educated at the Penang Free School. He was with the Mercantile Bank for three years before joining Behn, Meyer and Company. Behn, Meyer and Company

---

25 HAL Cockerell and E Green, *The British Insurance Business 1547–1970: An Introduction and Guide to Historical Records in the United Kingdom*, London: Heinemann Educational Books, 1976.

was a trading house representing a number of European insurance companies, mainly German.[26] Goh left the company to help establish the Khean Guan Insurance Company. Another director of Khean Guan was Quah Beng Kee, who was also from Penang Free School. He, too, had joined Behn, Meyer and Company. Another director, Tan Khean Hock, had worked in the Chartered Mercantile Bank of India, London and China for some eight years before moving to Khean Guan.

More important was prudent management. Local companies, even when they could get tariff information, sometimes offered lower rates in order to win business. But this simply exposed them to greater risks and to possible heavy losses. This indeed might have been a reason why some early local insurance firms encountered difficulties.[27] The subsequent Chinese insurance companies dealt with this problem by recruiting Western staff. Eastern United appointed a European, HJ Fougere, as its first general manager, and a few years later, JW Harris as its manager. Then in 1920 Eastern United sold a substantial block of shares to the South British Insurance Company and offered it a place on its board. For Eastern United, offering a stake to South British not only broadened its capital base but also gave itself added corporate value and international insurance connections.[28]

Reinsurance facilities was another major difficulty faced by local insurance companies when competing against large foreign ones. Through reinsurance, companies were able to hedge against a major risk. Without reinsurance facilities small local companies would either have to turn down large but hazardous risks or be exposed to ruinous claims. In Britain, members of the FOC were able to force out some small non-tariff companies by denying them reinsurance. In 1890 non-tariff companies managed to get reinsurance through Lloyd and later from non-British insurance companies. Likewise, Chinese companies in Malaya and Singapore were able to obtain reinsurance facilities from larger tariff and non-tariff members or from overseas companies. Or they combined to accept large risks.

---

26 Report of Campbell Davidson, October 1904, Guardian Assurance, Guildhall Library, London, Ms 16,209/22.
27 Marine Department, "Loss report book" giving names of vessels, details of insurance effected (interest and sum incurred, reinsurance if any), circumstances of loss, and details of final settlements of claim, 1881–1961, Commercial Union Assurance, Guildhall Library, London, Ms 23,710, 9 volumes; E Mensah, "Insurance in the Third World Countries with particular reference to Reinsurance", *Journal of the Insurance Institute,* vol 67, pp 62–70.
28 Report submitted to the 8th Annual General Meeting of the Eastern United Assurance Corporation Ltd, 27 October 1921, Singapore.

Post-Independence Period

In the postwar period and during the gathering pace of decolonization, the OCBC group took on an even larger corporate role and prominence. The Straits Chinese character, however, became less distinctive as it drew in other Chinese, particularly at the management level. But the people who held controlling interests were still from families that started the group or at least connected to them. Also significant was the expansion of other Chinese financial groups although the OCBC remained in the forefront and its influence continued to be evident.

In the first few months of the Japanese Occupation, all local and foreign banks in Malaya and Singapore were ordered closed. Liquidation proceedings were taken against major foreign banks and these included the Chartered Bank, the Hong Kong and Shanghai Bank and the Mercantile Bank. In April 1942, the OCBC and four other Chinese banks were allowed to reopen. But officers from the Japanese Military Administration closely supervised the operations.[29] Just before the fall of Singapore, a number of Chinese associated with the OCBC had managed to escape to Bombay, taking with them, it is said, important account books and records. They included Tan Cheng Lock and Tan Chin Tuan. Tan Chin Tuan registered the OCBC in India and maintained operations there as joint managing director.

In London, colonial planners and business groups discussed postwar recovery programmes. British planners recognized that banking and insurance were essential to the reconstruction of the economy and that when the war ended, these two services had to be restored very quickly. The resumption of financial services was expected to be difficult. One reason was that British agency houses, which had in the past handled much of the insurance services, would lack staff because of the war. Many had been evacuated before the war while a large number were interned by the Japanese. More pressing for the business community, which had suffered heavy losses during the war, were funds to restart their operations. It was estimated that some $475 million was needed to help in the recovery of the economy.

It was in such circumstances that banks, including local ones such as the OCBC, resumed business in Malaya and Singapore. The colonial authorities released all of the OCBC's prewar assets so that it could resume operations early. Tan Chin Tuan headed the recovery of the bank and it expanded its diversified operations and assets. Thus, with the end of the war, the OCBC and its group of insurance companies were well placed to resume operations.

---

29   Paul H Kratoska, *The Japanese Occupation of Malaya 1941–1945*, St Leonards, NSW: Allen and Unwin, 1998, pp 207–22.

A non-Straits Chinese who played a major postwar role in the OCBC was Lee Kong Chian. A first-generation immigrant from China, he had studied civil engineering. He first worked for Tan Kah Kee and eventually married Tan's daughter. Lee was involved in the Chinese Commercial Bank. He built up his rubber business and the Lee Rubber Company came to own a significant share of the OCBC. At the OCBC, he rose to become its chairman until 1966. Together with Tan Chin Tuan, he built OCBC into the conglomerate it is today.

Over the years, the OCBC increased its equity holdings in insurance and in other sectors of the economy. There were considerable cross-holdings of shares in all the companies held by the Straits Chinese. Thus, while the OCBC had controlling stakes in three insurance companies, all three, in turn, held sizeable blocks of shares in one another's companies as well as in the OCBC. The Overseas Assurance Corporation and Great Eastern Life Assurance, with steady growth in assets and business turnover, soon became the largest general and life insurers in the region. The OCBC also bought into a small Batu Pahat Bank established in 1919. SQ Wong became a director of the Batu Pahat Bank in 1923. The Batu Pahat Bank was later restructured to become the Pacific Bank. Separately, Great Eastern gained substantial stakes in several other large blue-chip companies both in Singapore and in Malaya. Many of these, such as Wearnes, Fraser and Neave and United Engineers, had started as British companies.[30]

The connection between the Straits Chinese group and Western entrepreneurs lasted well into the postwar period. The most significant of the Europeans was EMF Fergusson, who was a director of Straits Trading, as well as of Straits Steamship and Great Eastern. Others such as J Ford and FM Edmonds served in Great Eastern Life. NJ Davis was involved as director in five of the companies where the OCBC had bought stakes. The others who were associated with this group of companies were T Aiken, HW Moxon, and HB Roper Calbeck. Of the OCBC group of Chinese, SQ Wong, Lee Chim Tuan and Lee Kong Chian sat on boards where Europeans such as Fergusson, Ford and Edmonds were also members.

But the most important of the OCBC's links were with the old agency houses. Right at the start when the agency houses were just beginning to establish themselves in Malaya, the Straits Chinese decided to work with them. Through Tan Jiak Kim and Tan Cheng Lock, a connection was built with Borneo Company, Boustead and Company, and Sime Darby. Through Sime Darby and Straits Trading as well as the equities it held in Tronoh Mines Limited, the OCBC was linked to London Tin-Charter Consolidated.

---

30 *Facts and Figures of Malayan Companies*, Singapore: Fraser and Company, 1952.

London Tin, with eight Malaysian tin companies, was one of the world's largest tin concerns.

It was through links with agency houses and through its own acquisitions that the OCBC group gradually gained major and significant stakes in the finance, insurance, plantation, tin, trading and shipping sectors of the Malaysian and Singapore economies. As the old Western capital withdrew in the post-independence period, the OCBC group bought into Sime Darby. This agency house started in 1910 when Sime, a rubber planter, got together with Darby from the Hong Kong and Shanghai Bank to form the company. By the 1930s its issued capital was $1.8 million and its financial position was regarded as very sound by banks in England. By the 1950s it was managing and owning a large number of rubber estates. It extended its activities to shipping, insurance, general trading, manufacturing and processing. In 1958, Sime Darby Holdings Ltd was incorporated in London but was managed from Singapore. From its profits it built up portfolio investments in the United Kingdom, Australia and the United States. During the 1960s large-scale transfers of shares from Britain to Singapore and Malaysia took place. In the 1980s Sime Darby controlled over 40 companies, making it the largest conglomerate in Malaysia. These included companies in the tin, rubber, finance and management sectors. OCBC directors such as Tan Chin Tuan and Tan Cheng Lock sat on the board of Sime Darby. Following his retirement as Finance Minister, Tan Siew Sin, the son of Tan Cheng Lock, became its chairman.

Finally, the OCBC's part in helping the emergence of Chinese participation in the financial sector continued to be evident and may be seen in the career background of those who started new banks in Malaya. This was clear in the prewar period when founders of all the Chinese banks—Ban Hin Lee, Lee Wah and United Chinese—had links with the OCBC. In the postwar period, the men behind three major Malaysian banks were also from the OCBC. Khoo Teck Puat, who founded Malayan Banking, Malaysia's largest bank, was the son of Khoo Yang Tin, a founding shareholder of the OCBC. The younger Khoo himself joined the OCBC in 1933 as a clerk and rose to be deputy general manager in 1959. He left and helped found Malayan Banking in 1960. The founding chairman of Malayan Banking, Oei Tjong Le, was the son of Oei Tiong Ham of Indonesia, a founding shareholder of the OCBC. Two of Khoo Teck Puat's protégés at the OCBC, Khoo Kay Peng and Teh Hong Piow, also left to set up their own banks. Khoo Kay Peng set up the Malayan United Industries Bank in the 1970s. Teh Hong Piow set up the Public Bank in 1965. Today, it is regarded the best managed bank in Malaysia.

Conclusion

It has been suggested that Chinese entrepreneurs in 19th-century Southeast Asia were among the first Chinese capitalists. Even as China was seeking political and economic reforms in an effort to modernize itself, there were groups of Chinese in Malaya and Singapore who had already successfully moved into modern commerce and industry. Immigrants from China were freed from the cultural and bureaucratic constraints in China which are said to have hindered the development of modern Chinese entrepreneurship there. In Malaya and Singapore, the extension of British rule opened up economic opportunities for the Chinese. Amidst the political stability and predictable business environment, immigrant Chinese capital and labour were channelled into shipping, trading and large-scale tin mining.

By the 1880s the Chinese shipping groups were very much aware of the urgency to diversify and to modernize their enterprises. Firstly, the revenue farm system, which was a useful source of capital accumulation, was being phased out. The colonial state had developed a more regularized revenue collection system. Secondly, the traditional dialect and district associations that had provided support and mutual help to their members could no longer cope with new and more complex economic and social demands as these ties were beginning to be loosened. Finally, the Chinese saw serious competition with the entry of British capital into the region. British enterprises drew upon larger sources of capital and technology as well as modern management to give them a powerful competitive edge over the Chinese in the tin and rubber industries. With the use of new steamships by the Western shipping companies, Chinese shippers had also to replace their sailing junks. With ships becoming expensive to modernize and to maintain, marine insurance and banking became more necessary. Increased trade also required insurance protection. In the financial services, Western enterprises always held a pre-eminent position.

A key group in this transition to modern business was the Straits Chinese from Malacca and Singapore. It was a community that had a long tradition of trade in the region. They owned shipping companies that transported goods to all parts of the Southeast Asian region. They were linked to the large Hokkien trading community centred in Amoy that had been trading with Southeast Asia since early times. Both Koe Guan and the OCBC Group followed a similar course in diversifying and modernizing their business. They progressed from the key sectors of trading, tin mining and tin smelting to those of shipping, banking and insurance. Both used family ties and dialect networks to increase their resources and to expand. These business networks were shaped by shared social interests and linked through common dialect and educational background. They were also strengthened by marriage among the prominent families.

There were dissimilarities between the Koe Guan group and the Straits Chinese group. Whereas Koe Guan consisted largely of new immigrants, the Straits Chinese were an older community. But it was a new generation of entrepreneurs from within the Straits Chinese group which emerged at the end of the 19th century to play a key role in successfully leading the community into the modern sectors of banking and insurance. These Straits Chinese consolidated themselves within the Hokkien dialect group, connected the Hokkiens with other dialect communities, and linked themselves with the colonial state and Western capital. These new Chinese entrepreneurs were largely Western-educated. Straits Chinese such as Lim Boon Keng won scholarships to study in Western universities. They sought social reforms within their own society even as they showed concern about what was happening in China. They admired Western science and technology. The Straits Chinese were accepted by the colonial state and appointed to consultative bodies to represent the Chinese. Through such bodies, they came into contact with British officials and merchants. SQ Wong, associated with the Straits Chinese, served in the Johor state council for many years. The Straits Chinese, more than any other Chinese group, were able to establish links early with British merchants. They maintained their connections with the increasingly dominant agency houses and bought shares in emerging British companies.

Finally, the Straits Chinese possessed a more long-term and local business outlook when compared with the Koe Guan group. This may be explained by a political orientation they held which was distinguishable from that of some of their contemporaries who came as recent immigrants. Some merchants from the latter group regarded themselves as transient. But men such as Tan Chay Yan and Tan Cheng Lock were from families which had settled for generations in this region. They were among the first therefore to invest in rubber plantations, which required a longer time-frame for profitable returns. Likewise, they were prepared to have their assets tied up as they diversified into insurance companies and banks. Not surprisingly, it was men from this group, such as Tan Cheng Lock and Tan Chin Tuan, the dominant figures in postwar OCBC, who were beginning to articulate their vision of a political role for the Chinese in an independent Malaya. While in India during World War II, the two of them set up the Overseas Chinese Association as a forum.[31]

---

31   Yew Siew Sing, *Tan Cheng Lock: Straits Legislator and Chinese Leader*, Petaling Jaya: Pelanduk Publications, 1990; Lee Su Yin, "British Chinese Policy in Singapore, 1930s to mid-1950: with particular focus on the public service career of Tan Chin Tuan", MA thesis, NUS, 1995.

APPENDIX 1

The OCBC group and its share holdings in various companies (as of 1981)

Group member	With share holdings in
• **Eastern United Assurance Corporation Ltd**	British and Malayan Trustees Ltd Fraser and Neave Ltd
• **Great Eastern Life Assurance Co Ltd**	Cold Storage Holdings Ltd Fraser and Neave Ltd (13%) Gammon (Malaya) 1959 Ltd W Hammer and Co Ltd Hume Industries (Far East) Ltd William Jacks and Co (Malaya) Ltd Malayan Breweries Ltd Malayan Cement Ltd McAlister and Co Ltd The Metal Box Co of Malaya Ltd Overseas Assurance Corporation Ltd Overseas Chinese Banking Corporation (Fourth largest stakeholder) Robinson and Co Ltd Sime Darby Holdings Ltd Straits Steamship Co Ltd Straits Times Press (Malaya) Ltd Straits Trading Co Ltd United Engineers Ltd Wearne Brothers Ltd
• **Overseas Assurance Corporation Ltd**	Cold Storage Holdings Ltd Fraser and Neave Ltd Malayan Breweries Ltd Robinson and Co Ltd Straits Times Press (Malaya) Ltd Straits Trading Co Ltd Wearne Brothers Ltd

OCBC and its subsidiaries hold significant shares in and are represented on the boards of 38 core companies, some of which are:

1. Fraser and Neave Ltd
2. Malayan Breweries Ltd
3. Sime Darby Holdings Ltd
4. Straits Trading Co Ltd
5. United Engineers Ltd
6. Wearne Brothers Ltd
7. United Engineers (Malaysia)
8. Kempas (M) Bhd
9. Tractors Malaysia Bhd
10. Benta Plantations
11. Sime Darby Malaysia Bhd
12. Consolidated Plantations

Sime Darby

In 1974, Sime Darby controlled over 40 companies with a combined net asset of $715 million.

Its five subsidiaries

1. Benda Plantations
2. Consolidated Plantations
3. Kempas (M) Bhd
4. Tractors Malaysia Bhd
5. Sime Darby Holdings Ltd

Interlocked with

1. Dunlop Estates
2. Harrison and Crosfield
3. Highlands and Lowlands

APPENDIX 2

Insurance companies holding shares in Malayan publicly-listed companies, 1962

Insurance company	Holding shares in
• Atlas Insurance Co Ltd	Consolidated Tin Smelters Ltd
• American International Assurance Co Ltd	William Jacks and Co (Malaya) Ltd
• Asia Life Assurance Society Ltd	Fraser and Neave Ltd Malayan Breweries Ltd The Metal Box Company of Malaya Ltd Straits Times Press (Malaya) Ltd
• Britannic Assurance Co Ltd	Perak River Hydro Electric Co Ltd
• Eastern United Assurance Corporation Ltd	British and Malayan Trustees Ltd Fraser and Neave Ltd
• Great Eastern Life Assurance Co Ltd	Cold Storage Holdings Ltd Fraser and Neave Ltd Gammon (Malaya) 1959 Ltd W Hammer and Co Ltd Hume Industries (Far East) Ltd William Jacks and Co (Malaya) Ltd Malayan Breweries Ltd Malayan Cement Ltd McAlister and Co Ltd The Metal Box Company of Malaya Ltd Overseas Assurance Corporation Ltd Robinson and Co Ltd Sime Darby Holdings Ltd Straits Steamship Co Ltd Straits Times Press (Malaya) Ltd Straits Trading Co Ltd United Engineers Ltd Wearne Brothers Ltd
• London Assurance Co Ltd	Consolidated Tin Smelters Ltd
• London and Lancashire Insurance Ltd	Consolidated Tin Smelters Ltd

Insurance company	Holding shares in
• Medical Sickness Annuity Life Assurance Society Ltd	The Borneo Company Ltd
• Motor Assurance Co Ltd	Consolidated Tin Smelters Ltd
• Overseas Assurance Corporation Ltd	Cold Storage Holdings Ltd Fraser and Neave Ltd Malayan Breweries Ltd Robinson and Co Ltd Straits Times Press (Malaya) Ltd Straits Trading Co Ltd Wearne Brothers Ltd
• Pearl Assurance Co	Consolidated Tin Smelters Ltd
• Prudential Assurance Co Ltd	The Metal Box Company of Malaya Ltd British Borneo Petroleum Syndicate Ltd Consolidated Tin Smelters Ltd Perak River Hydro Electric Co Ltd
• Queensland Insurance Co Ltd	McAlister and Co Ltd
• Royal Exchange Assurance Co Ltd	Consolidated Tin Smelters Ltd

Source: *Facts and Figures of Malayan Companies,* Singapore: Fraser and Neave Company, 1962.

References

Ampalavanar Brown, Rajeswary. *Capital and Entrepreneurship in Southeast Asia*. Houndsmills, Basingstoke: The Macmillan Press, 1994.
_____, ed. *Chinese Business Enterprise in Asia*. New York: Routledge, 1995.
Butcher, JG. "The Demise of the Revenue Farm System in the Federated Malay States". *Modern Asian Studies,* vol 17, no 3 (1983): 387–412.
Chan, Wellington KK. *Merchants, Mandarins, and Modern Enterprise in Late Ch'ing China*. Cambridge, Mass: Harvard East Asian Research Center, 1977.
Chuleeporn, Pongsupath. "The Mercantile Community of Penang and the Changing Pattern of Trade, 1890–1941". PhD thesis submitted to London University, 1990.
Davenport, RPT, and G Jones, eds. *British Business in Asia since 1860*. Cambridge: Cambridge University Press, 1989.
Godley, Michael R. *The Mandarin-Capitalists from Nanyang: Overseas Chinese Enterprise in the Modernization of China 1893–1911*. Cambridge: Cambridge University Press, 1981.
Gomez, Edmund Terence. *Chinese Business in Malaysia: Accumulation, Accommodation and Ascendance*. Surrey: Curzon Press, 1999
Ho, Hwa Hiong. "Growth and Expansion of the Oversea-Chinese Banking Corporation Ltd". Graduation exercise, University of Malaya, 1980/81.
Khor, Eng Hee. "The Public Life of Dr Lim Boon Keng". Graduation exercise, University of Malaya in Singapore, 1958.
Lee, Edwin. *The British as Rulers: Governing Multiracial Singapore 1867–1914*. Singapore: University of Singapore Press, 1991.
Lee, Hock Lock, *The Insurance Industry in Malaysia: A Study in Financial Development and Regulation*. Kuala Lumpur: Oxford University Press, 1997.
Lee, Yoke Meng. *The Asia Insurance Story: A Celebration of Human Endeavour and Faith*. Singapore: The Asia Insurance Company Ltd, 1998.
Lim, Mah Hui. *Ownership and Control of the One Hundred Largest Corporations in Malaysia*. Kuala Lumpur: Oxford University Press, 1981.
Mackie, JAC. "Chinese Business Organizations". In *The Encyclopedia of the Chinese Overseas*, edited by Lynn Pan. Singapore: Archipelago Press, 1998, pp 91–93.
The Singapore and Straits Directory. (Various years)
Song, Ong Siang. *One Hundred Years' History of the Chinese in Singapore*. Singapore: Oxford University Press, reprint, 1967.
Sundaram, Jomo Kwame. *A Question of Class: Capital, the State, and Uneven Development in Malaya*. Singapore: Oxford University Press, 1988.
Tan, Boon Long. "Sime Darby: A Case Study of the Sime Darby Holdings Ltd—Guthrie Corp Ltd Takeover Bid". Graduation exercise, University of Malaya, 1967/68.

Tan, Chee Beng. *The Baba of Melaka*. Petaling Jaya: Pelanduk Publications, 1988.
Tan, Ee Leong. "The Chinese Banks Incorporated in Singapore and the Federation of Malaya". *Journal of the Malayan Branch of the Royal Asiatic Society* 42, 1 (1969).
Tan, Tat Wai. *Income Distribution and Determination in West Malaysia*. Kuala Lumpur: Oxford University Press, 1982.
Tregonning, KG. *Home Port Singapore: A History of the Straits Steamship Company Ltd, 1890–1965*. Singapore: Oxford University Press, 1967.
Wang, Gungwu. *China and the Chinese Overseas*. Singapore: Times Academic Press, 1991.
White, Nicholas J. *Business, Government, and the End of Empire: Malaya, 1942– 1957*. Kuala Lumpur: Oxford University Press, 1996.
Wilson, D. *Solid as a Rock: The First Forty Years of the Oversea-Chinese Banking Corporation*. Singapore: OCBC, 1972.
Yew, Siew Sing. *Tan Cheng Lock: Straits Legislator and Chinese Leader*. Petaling Jaya: Pelanduk Publications, 1990.
Yong, CF. *Tan Kah-kee: The Making of an Overseas Chinese Legend,* Singapore: Oxford University Press, 1987.
──────. *Growing with Singapore: United Overseas Bank*. Singapore: UOB Group, 1985.
──────. *The Overseas Assurance Corporation Limited: Sixty-Year Chronicle, 1920–1980*. Singapore, 1980.

Chapter 12

THE CHANGING ROLE OF ETHNIC CHINESE SMEs IN ECONOMIC RESTRUCTURING IN SINGAPORE: FROM "TWO-LEGGED" POLICY TO "THREE-LEGGED" STRATEGY

Ng Beoy Kui

Introduction

Since independence in 1965, Singapore has achieved remarkable economic development through several stages of economic restructuring. In the 1960s and early 1970s, the main focus of the economic restructuring was industrialization, with emphasis on labour-intensive industries. However, the remarkable success of industrialization had subsequently resulted in severe labour shortage. This prompted the government to switch gears towards capital-intensive industries in its economic restructuring strategy. In its eagerness to deliberately increase labour cost to wipe out labour-intensive activities and also ensure relatively cheaper capital goods through Singapore dollar appreciation, such policies caused a severe recession in 1985. The recession was a wake-up call for the government to realize the weakness arising from overdependence on multinational corporations (MNCs) and government-linked corporations (GLCs) as the "two legs" for economic development. The so-called "two-legged policy" was officially abandoned with the promulgation of the SME Master Plan in 1989. However, not much concerted effort was made on the part of the government to develop small and medium-sized enterprises or SMEs as another "pillar" of the national economy. With the emergence of the knowledge-based economy (KBE), or New Economy, since 1991, Singapore cannot continue with the past economic policies, despite their success, to sustain economic growth in the new setting. A new thrust in terms of policy direction and strategy has to be formulated so that Singapore, with no natural resources, can avoid the onslaught of threats and, at the same time, exploit any opportunities that may arise from the New Economy. With this background in mind, the Committee on Singapore's Competitiveness (CSC) came up with a report detailing the eight strategies that Singapore must adopt to achieve the vision of Singapore being an "advanced and globally competitive knowledge economy within the next decade" (MTI, 1998: 6–10). Unexpectedly, strengthening the base of SMEs was one of the eight key strategies recommended in the report. Previously, SMEs had either been totally neglected, as can be seen in the Strategic Economic Plan of 1979, or designated to play second fiddle to MNCs and GLCs in the national economy even after the SME Master Plan was instituted in 1989. Only in this CSC 1998 Report, and the plans that followed, were SMEs as a group given, for the first time, official recognition and prominence in various economic plans, policy directions and sectoral strategies.

In the light of these developments over the decades, the main purpose of this article is to trace the evolving role of ethnic Chinese SMEs in the economic restructuring process. The article will attempt to make some qualitative assessments on the new role of the ethnic Chinese SMEs in a knowledge-based economy (KBE). In the course of such assessment, the intention is to identify major problems and challenges likely to be encountered by ethnic Chinese SMEs in the decades ahead. In this article, the local SME is defined, as the Singapore Productivity and Standards Board (PSB) has done, as "a company with at least 30 per cent equity and less than $15 million in fixed productive assets, in terms of net book value of factory, machinery and equipment" (www.psb.gov.sg). As for a non-manufacturing company, it must have fewer than 200 employees.

This article is divided into five sections. After the Introduction, the next section aims to give a historical account of SMEs being left alone in the mainstream of the national economy. The third section attempts to provide reasons for the drastic change in government policy and attitude towards SMEs, while the fourth section deals further on the new role of SMEs in an era of the KBE. The concluding section assesses such new role and discusses major problems and challenges lying ahead for the SMEs in general and ethnic Chinese SMEs in particular.

Political Alienation: the "Two-Legged" Policy and Initial Engagement

In Singapore, SMEs as a group constitute almost 90 per cent of business establishments and contribute 50 per cent of the total employment. However, the SMEs account for only one-third of total value added. They are also less productive when compared with MNCs and GLCs and have only half the productivity of these counterparts. Most of the SMEs are involved in commerce, community, social and personal services, electronic contract manufacturing and precision engineering. Ethnic Chinese Singaporeans own most of the SMEs. For the purpose of this article, a typical ethnic Chinese SME is perceived as an enterprise owned and controlled mainly by a Chinese Singaporean. Among these enterprises, there are three distinct groups. The first group comprises traditional family business enterprises. The entrepreneurs are generally traditional in outlook and Chinese-educated. Familism is the cornerstone of this kind of enterprise. The second group differs from the former in terms of cultural traits, technical know-how, management style and educational background. The owners of the enterprises are from the new generation, and they prefer to call themselves "technopreneurs". The characteristics of family lineage and 'Chineseness' are less pronounced in these enterprises, their owners being generally cosmopolitan in outlook. In between these two groups of enterprises are those which have a strong foundation in the first group, but their owners are prepared to go beyond the traditional business areas covered by the first group, and break new ground. Most of these owners have inherited their business from their parents or grandparents and have attained tertiary education or professional degrees.

Political alienation and the "two-legged" policy

For the first ten years or so after independence in 1965, the PAP (People's Action Party) government's general attitude towards ethnic Chinese SMEs was non-interference and political alienation (Vasil, 1995; Rodan, 1989; Huff, 1994; Chan and Ng, 2001). This attitude arose from the conflict between the ruling PAP and the Chinese business community in general, represented by the Singapore Chinese Chamber of Commerce and Industry (SCCCI), specifically on Chinese language and educational issues prior to independence. The Chinese business community, which was assertive on these two aspects, considered the promotion of Chinese culture and education as part of its "social obligations", and less to do with vested commercial interests. In Wong's view (1997), these overseas Chinese merchants reluctantly filled the political vacuum left behind by the Kuomintang, and were serving as overseas "cultural heroes" after the "symbolic and sacred centre" in mainland China fell into the hands of Chinese Communists who opposed vehemently anything to do with Confucian values.[1] Such a political

---

1 The Great Proletarian Cultural Revolution, which lasted from 1966 to 1976, was anti-Confucianism.

stand, on Chinese education in general and the Nanyang University issue in particular, was in direct conflict with the objective of the PAP government to promote and forge a multiracial and multicultural society in a newly independent nation with a Chinese majority,[2] situated within the Malay Archipelago. The adoption of such a policy towards culture and education by the PAP government was, in fact, a direct response to, in the words of Vasil (1995: 34), "the internal ethnic imperatives as well as the regional geographical compulsions".

The political implication arising from such policy was to leave the Chinese business community outside the mainstream of national economic activities, especially the industrialization drive.[3] A "two-legged" policy then followed. Under this policy, the government actively encouraged MNCs to invest in Singapore, providing them with generous tax incentives. At the same time, GLCs such as the Development Bank of Singapore (DBS), INTRACO and the Jurong Town Corporation (JTC) were set up to participate in a wide range of economic activities. According to Huff (1994: 320), one of the reasons for the alienation of the Chinese business community was to "obviate any need for the PAP government to look to the Chinese-educated and China-oriented Chinese, who traditionally make up a majority of Singapore entrepreneurs, to drive its industrialization initiative". Accordingly, very little government assistance was offered to the local SMEs in the 1960s and the first half of the 1970s. They were indeed totally left alone. Such alienation and the deliberate promotion of MNCs and GLCs as the two main pillars of the national economy implied that local SMEs had little role to play in the ongoing economic restructuring process. When the economic restructuring switched its emphasis to economic diversification with the promotion of manufacturing, oil refining, financial services and tourism, the SMEs, which were mainly involved in entrepot trade and domestic commerce, were left out again. Understandably, they suffered a severe onslaught of the "crowding-out effect" arising from the rapid growth of MNCs and GLCs (Tan, 1996). The effect on the SMEs was particularly severe in terms of market competition, human resource recruitment and high labour cost *vis-à-vis* the MNCs and GLCs.

---

2   The ethnic Chinese constituted about 75% of the total population in Singapore, while Malays accounted for 15%, with other minority races forming the rest.
3   Another reason for such alienation was the view that ethnic Chinese SMEs, which were actively involved in the commerce and services sectors, were not interested in, as well as not capable of, involvement in manufacturing activities.

Initial engagement

However, from 1976 onwards, there was a slight change in government attitude towards the ethnic Chinese SMEs. Initial engagement of SMEs began with the introduction of the Small Industries Finance Scheme in 1976 to provide assistance for the modernization and diversification of small firms engaged in manufacturing and related activities. Other assistance schemes such as the Small Industries Technical Assistance Scheme and the institution of the Small Industry Advisory Committee under the Economic Development Board (EDB) as well as the Material Application Centre, which was under the purview of the Singapore Industrial Standards and Industrial Research (SISIR), were established to provide further support to SMEs. Such engagement was considered necessary at a time when the Singapore economy had to undergo a more drastic economic restructuring for further industrial upgrading.

After undergoing successful industrialization in the 1960s and 1970s, the Singapore economy, in the mid-1970s, began to feel severe pressure of labour shortage. In 1979, the government had no hesitation in introducing a "corrective wage policy", proposed by the National Wages Council (NWC) (Lim and associates, 1988). Under this policy, wages were deliberately allowed to increase with double-digit growth for the next three years. At the same time, employers' contributions to the Central Provident Fund (CPF) also rose from 15 per cent of each employee's wage or salary in 1976 to 25 per cent in 1984. Contributions to the Skills Development Fund (SDF) and a levy on foreign workers were also introduced to increase labour costs further. The purpose was to reflect relatively higher labour costs *vis-à-vis* the costs of capital goods. This was particularly so as the Monetary Authority of Singapore (MAS) had adopted a strong Singapore dollar policy since 1981 to reduce imported inflation (Ng, 1996). The strong Singapore dollar policy then implied a significant reduction in the prices of imported capital goods in Singapore dollar terms. Such a change in relative resource costs would then induce those labour-intensive industries to switch to more capital-intensive methods of production. The success of such economic restructuring required close co-operation on the part of the local SMEs, which used proportionately more labour than other types of enterprise. Only when the SMEs were restructured and upgraded successfully would more labour resources be released to other sectors for better resource allocation.

In the process of the economic restructuring, SMEs were expected to incur relatively higher adjustment costs, as compared with those of MNCs and GLCs. These might be translated into further political grievances among the SMEs, especially those of ethnic Chinese. These business enterprises somehow wielded significant political influence on constituents in the Housing and Development Board (HDB) heartland. Further political alienation of the ethnic Chinese SMEs would in the long run not be beneficial politically to the ruling PAP government as opposition parties might exploit such grievances to their advantage. However, the initial engagement was not successful partly because the SMEs could not adjust to the new circumstances as they lacked the required capital to enjoy scale economies, as well as the necessary technical know-how for the transformation. Secondly, the assistance provided by the government was not well received by the SMEs as application procedures for government assistance were too complex, and their eligibility criteria too stringent. Consequently, the government continued its "two-legged" policy with the SMEs still playing a marginal role in the national economy till the mid-1980s.

Economic Restructuring, Co-partnership and Regionalization

The "corrective wage policy" implemented since 1979 had resulted in "too rapid a restructuring programme which failed to co-ordinate the rate of phasing out of industries with that of establishing priority ones" (Lim and associates, 1988: 35). Specifically, infrastructure and manpower supports for high-technology industries were barely in place while local SMEs were not nurtured rigorously enough to have a place in the high-tech industries. Such misplacement was further accentuated by an erosion of international competitiveness through a sharp appreciation of the Singapore dollar against a basket of trading partners' currencies by 27.9 per cent in the period of 1980–85, as against an appreciation of only 7.1 per cent between 1974 and 1980 (Lim and associates, 1988: 36). This led to a deep recession in 1985 with a negative growth of 1.8 per cent, as compared with the double digit growth in the earlier 1970s and around 8 per cent in the late 1970s and early 1980s. The recession was so sudden that it caught the Singapore government by surprise.

Economic restructuring

To stimulate economic recovery, the government undertook a number of cost-cutting measures which included the imposition of a wage restraint for 1986 and 1987, and a cut of the employers' CPF contribution rate from 25 per cent to 10 per cent. The government also began to realize the importance of local SMEs to complement and supplement the bases of MNCs and GLCs to sustain economic growth and industrial upgrading. More specifically, local SMEs could be effective co-partners, suppliers and subcontractors to these large enterprises. Any upgrading and restructuring of these SMEs would also further release labour resources for more effective use in other sectors. This point was particularly relevant in the Singapore context, considering the fact that SMEs constituted about 90 per cent of total business establishments and 35 per cent of net value added. Yet they utilized 50 per cent of the nation's workforce. In addition, there was a dearth of entrepreneurial spirit among the younger generation. A policy change towards local SMEs would send a strong signal to these people that entrepreneurial spirit was much valued by the authorities. With this in mind, the government implemented several measures to strengthen the local enterprises, especially the SMEs. Among these was the establishment by the EDB of a $100 million Small Enterprises Development Bureau and a $100 million Venture Capital Fund. In addition, a Committee on Small Enterprises Policy was formed while the Small Industries Finance Scheme was also extended to companies in the services sector. On the whole, the government showed that it was serious about an eventual phasing out of the "two-legged" policy. In its place, a "three-legged" policy was expected to emerge eventually, to allow local SMEs to play a greater role in the national economy. However, the measures undertaken thus far to assist the SMEs were in general *ad hoc* in nature.

SME Master Plan and the "external wing"

By 1989, the government had firmed up its mind regarding the SMEs. In fact, the government was more ambitious than originally expected, and wanted to accord the SMEs a greater role to play. They were expected not just to be co-partners of MNCs and GLCs in the domestic economic arena, but also to have joint ventures with these counterparts in the regionalization drive. A more comprehensive SME Master Plan was thus announced in 1989, providing a large number of assistance schemes to upgrade and restructure SMEs. By 1998, 60 assistance schemes had been set up by the government to help nurture SMEs. A second board, called the Stock Exchange of Singapore Dealing and Automated Quotation (SESDAQ), with less stringent rules on listing was also set up to allow SMEs to raise the necessary capital for business expansion. More importantly, a regional co-operation scheme with neighbouring countries in the form of the Growth Triangle was conceived in late 1989. According to this concept, both local enterprises and MNCs were expected to set up labour-intensive production lines in either Johor State of Malaysia or Batam in Indonesia because of their abundant land and labour resources. Capital-intensive activities as well as research and development were expected to be centralized at regional headquarters in Singapore, which enjoys comparative advantages in human resource management and financial resources. The purpose was to exploit each region's respective comparative advantages especially in terms of land, labour and capital resources. The set-up of the Growth Triangle was also consistent with the continuing economic restructuring in that it encouraged the phasing out of labour-intensive industries from Singapore and reallocating these industries to the neighbouring countries.

The Singapore's drive to build an "external wing" was given a further boost when the Committee to Promote Enterprise Overseas was formally set up to encourage local enterprises to invest abroad. The strengthening of the "external wing" was not to limit ventures to the Southeast Asian region but also to extend them to Northeast Asia and South Asia. In North Asia, in particular China, local SMEs could exploit their management's Chinese educational background and extensive Chinese business networks. Geographical proximity and, more importantly, the advantages of familiarity and accessibility would give Singapore SMEs an edge over MNCs and GLCs in creating the "external wing" of the Singapore economy. Vasil (1995: 133) noted that "the fast-growing relationship and contact with China soon began to transform the Chineseness of Singapore from an unavoidable and unfortunate liability to an important and immensely profitable asset". In short, SMEs had a comparative advantage over MNCs and GLCs in investing in China as part of the establishment of an "external wing".[4] Singapore investors since then have become one of the largest groups of investors in China. In fact, China ranked first as the destination of Singapore investment overseas in 2001, overtaking Malaysia, the traditional destination for Singaporean investors, for the first time.

Globalization, New Economy and Technopreneurship

As early as 1991, the world underwent a drastic change when the US National Science Foundation privatized the Internet. The ensuing changes through globalization and digital revolution have transformed the world beyond recognition. In the economic sphere, such changes have brought about the 'third industrial revolution', which in turn has created the New Economy. The New Economy is vastly differently from the Old Economy in three noticeable characteristics (Tan, March 2000). The first is that the New

---

4   Such comparative advantage was later found to be illusory, see Chan and Ng, 2001, pp 44–48.

Economy is technologically based, especially on such fast-advancing technologies as infocommunications and life sciences. The second is the reliance on a risk-taking business culture for wealth creation, and the third is that the capital market values new ideas, concepts and knowledge as much as physical and financial assets.

Impact on the SMEs

Globalization and the digital revolution, which dominate in the New Economy, are expected to exert tremendous impact on SMEs in general and ethnic Chinese SMEs in particular. Unless the SMEs are able to adapt well in the new setting, they would not be able to compete and may be wiped out totally in the face of global competition. Unfortunately, a majority of the ethnic Chinese SMEs, with their conservatism and familism, are far more comfortable with the Old Economy. In the face of the new challenges, they may have no alternative but to change gear and upgrade themselves to survive because of significantly different characteristics and business practices, as well as new rules of the game in the New Economy (see Tables 1 and 2). However, the same new developments also provide vast opportunities to local SMEs for wealth creation (Chen, March 2001). Firstly, the threat arises mainly from the fact that in the New Economy, both the Internet and globalization have enabled consumers and users to make price and product comparisons directly and within a short period of time. As a consequence, consumers have more power and influence over suppliers in the market. They are in a better position to choose the supplier that provides the best and most competitive quotes. In addition, competitors overseas can readily offer their services and products without having to establish local offices or retail outlets in Singapore. In this respect, local SMEs, with relatively less geographical advantage, will now encounter more severe competition from competitors in both the domestic and overseas markets than ever before. However, the spread in the use of the Internet has also opened up new opportunities for SMEs. It is easier and cheaper now to do business and reach foreign markets and customers, and at lightning speed.

Secondly, threats may arise from a restructuring of value chain that may do away with traditional middlemen in the global market. Such disintermediation is possible because companies now have the ability to separate physical flows of goods and services from information management. For the majority of ethnic Chinese SMEs operating in the simple buy-sell model in their middlemen's role, the risk of disintermediation is indeed a real concern. However, there are also new opportunities for reintermediation by suppliers

Table 1: The New and the Old Economy: A comparison

Old Economy characteristics	New Economy characteristics
Business activities focused on domestic market	Business activities focused on region or globally
Risk averse	Greater appetite for risk
Adoption of pricing strategies or cost-saving processes to outperform	Engage in mergers and collaboration/alliances to gain market dominance
Having more branches or outlets	Restructuring to improve efficiency and reduce operating costs
Rigid management and emphasis on protocol and system	Younger, more flexible and dynamic CEOs or managers
Face-to-face business dealings	Transactions through e-business arrangements
"No urge to change something that is already good" attitude	Enterprise, innovation, creativity and capacity for change that should lead to continual improvement
Top-heavy, centralized management	Agile and flexible, decentralized management

Source: Adapted from *Chinese Enterprise*, June/July 2000, p 18.

Table 2: The New and the Old Economy: A comparison on human resource management

Old Economy characteristics	New Economy characteristics
Lifelong employment	Lifelong employability
Task specialization	Multitask undertaking
Local talent and tighter immigration policies	Augmentation of labour pool
Cash-based remuneration	Incentive-based remuneration
Fixed working hours and conditions	Flexible hours and conditions with greater emphasis on job satisfaction
Reactive, with little initiative, and unwilling to accept change	Proactive, enterprising and willing to accept new challenges

Source: Adapted from *Chinese Enterprise*, June/July 2000, p 19.

that can compile, refine, and add value to information before it is distributed finally to the consumers. SMEs have to think of various innovative ways to add value to their services and transactions so that they will rely less on the simple buy-sell model and continue to survive in the New Economy.

Thirdly, the New Economy also brings about increasing competition from new players with skills in information management. With the convergence of industries, particularly IT and telecommunications, management of information adds significant value to products and services. Any company which can master such skills will be able to exploit these opportunities and become a formidable competitor in the global market. Similarly, any company which fails to do so skilfully will be wiped out from the market in time to come. This is especially so for sectors like those of banking and finance, travel, retail and transportation in which ethnic Chinese SMEs tend to dominate. Moreover, the rapid convergence of information management industries, with a blurring of boundaries between telecommunications, computers and media, besides requiring new infrastructures, will stimulate new demand for information management services; and these will open up vast opportunities for SMEs and start-ups to serve the newly merged industry clusters.

Of no less importance is the increased presence of network externalities and technological interrelatedness in the New Economy. "Network externalities" refers to the increase in the value of a product arising from the increasing number of users of the product and other compatible products. For instance, the value of a software product such as Microsoft Word increases if the number of its users increases, and this is especially so if the product is equally compatible with different PCs. Likewise, "technological interrelatedness" implies that the value of a product is dependent on the supporting infrastructure of compatible technologies or products. For example, the value of a software product is greatly enhanced by the availability of operating systems, virus protection and compatibility with other different PCs. These network externalities and technological interrelatedness also pose both threats and opportunities to SMEs. The threats arise from free-rider problems that are common with any externality. The prevention of free-rider problems can be costly. In the same vein, both externalities and interrelatedness also allow SMEs an opportunity to free ride the existing market structure and infrastructure without incurring much cost.

Policy response, SME plans and assistance schemes

For the Singapore economy as a whole, the New Economy has changed significantly the rules of the game. It is clear that the ways Singapore used to compete in the international market as well as the successful economic policies it implemented in the past three and a half decades may no longer be appropriate in the New Economy context (Tan, March 2000). In particular, the reliance on MNCs and GLCs for entrepreneurship in the new environment will definitely be outmoded in the years ahead. Instead, the dynamic technopreneurship of SMEs will have to be the new thrust in sustaining economic growth. This is because the new breed of technopreneurs will be better able to cope more adequately with rapid technological developments, adapt readily to a risk-taking business culture and accept willingly innovations and creativity prevailing in the New Economy. These technopreneurs will therefore be able to tap the vast opportunities arising from globalization and the spread in the use of the Internet. Hence, for the Singapore economy to successfully enter such a new stage of economic development, further economic restructuring and upgrading become imperative to enhance international competitiveness. The pressure for such transformation becomes more urgent especially after the onslaught of the Asian financial crisis in 1997.

Against this background, the Committee on Singapore Competitiveness (CSC) was set up as early as November 1996 to map out restructuring strategies to meet challenges of the New Economy. After two years of review, the Committee produced a report which recommends the following eight strategies to prepare the Singapore economy to enter the New Economy (MTI, November 1998):

- Manufacturing and services as twin engines
- Strengthening the external wing
- Building world-class companies
- Strengthening the base of small and medium-sized local enterprises
- Human and intellectual capital as key competitive edge
- Leveraging on science, technology and innovation
- Optimizing resource management
- Government as business facilitator.

In the report, local SMEs are given formal recognition and prominence in the economic restructuring and upgrading. The government now considers SMEs seriously as another pillar of the national economy (Lee, SH, February 2001). In the various plans[5] it announced after the CSC report (especially the SME 21 and Technopreneurship 21, or T21), SMEs are expected to play an

---

5   After the publication of the Report of the Committee on Singapore Competitiveness, other plans with specific objectives or for certain sectors have also been formulated. So far, the plans include Public Service (PS) 21, Industry 21, Construction 21, Services 21, Retail 21, SME 21, Technopreneurship 21, Infocomm 21, Manpower 21, On-the-job Training 21 or OT21, and Productivity Action Plan 21 or Pro Act 21. All these plans would in one way or another involve SMEs directly or indirectly.

increasingly significant role in the New Economy and contribute to economic growth. The overall strategy of these plans is to remove any potential threats that may arise from globalization as these threats may seriously undermine the base of SMEs. The government strategy, therefore, is to strengthen the base of small- and medium-sized local enterprises by supporting them with more than 60 technical and financial assistance schemes. It is expected that the schemes would help local SMEs to restructure and adjust readily to the new environment so as to exploit any new opportunities that arise.

Previously, plans for SMEs were normally *ad hoc* in nature and not under any specific government agency's purview. The SMEs were in most cases treated as 'unwanted babies' which had been thrown around among various government departments and agencies, and had no definite 'caring mother' to look after their growth and welfare. However, with the announcement of SME 21 in January 2000, they are now officially under the purview of the PSB, with other government authorities required to provide all the necessary assistance to SMEs.

As noted in SME 21, SMEs in general have suffered from some notorious structural weaknesses, as follows: (www.psb.gov.sg/aboutus/plans/sme21.html):

- Weak entrepreneurial culture
- Insufficient management know-how and lack of professionalism
- Shortage of professional and technical manpower
- Insufficient use of technology
- Outmoded, unproductive methods of operation
- Limited ability to tap economies of scale
- Small domestic market.

Strengthening the base of local SMEs will help accordingly to remove the existing dualistic structure in the national economy arising partly from the past "two-legged" policy. The purpose of SME 21, therefore, is to create vibrant and resilient SMEs in the face of rapid technological changes, increasing globalization and changing patterns of market demand. These developments, as noted earlier, can be threats as well as vast opportunities for SMEs. In the light of these developments, local SMEs are designated in the SME 21 plan to be (www.psb.gov.sg/aboutus/plans/sme21.html):

- a source of entrepreneurship and innovation;
- a base of strong supporting industries and strategic partners for foreign SMEs and MNCs;
- manufacturers of high value-added products and global providers of professional services; and
- a robust domestic services sector enhancing the quality of life in Singapore.

Specifically, the three goals of SME 21 are doubling the productivity of the domestic services sector, trebling the number of SMEs with sales of at least $10 million each, and equipping one in three SMEs with e-commerce capability.

Apart from strengthening the existing base of the SMEs, the government is even keener on developing the technopreneurship sector to prepare Singapore to enter the knowledge-based economy. Technopreneurship 21, or T21, was formally announced in April 1999. This plan is an initiative involving both the government and the private sector in preparing and laying the foundation for the successful development of the technopreneurship sector. On the government side, a T21 Ministerial Committee headed by Deputy Prime Minister Dr Tony Tan was set up to oversee strategies in fostering the development of technology enterprises and to co-ordinate with the private sector to encourage local and foreign talent start-up and technology-intensive activities in Singapore. The Private Sector Committee, on the other hand, solicits views, provides feedback and suggests initiatives on the development of the technopreneurship sector. The Economic Development Board (EDB) is the lead government agency providing focus and direction of the technopreneurship drive.

Basically, T21 covers four main areas, namely, education, facilities, regulations and financing. In the area of education, universities and schools are currently under revamp to serve as an effective generator of trained manpower and also business opportunities. A Science Hub with world-class facilities is being planned to provide an intellectually stimulating and creative environment for technopreneurs. In addition, rules and regulations, which have been inhibiting the growth of technopreneurship, are being reviewed vigorously. In particular, rules on listing criteria (announced on 18 September 1999) and bankruptcy laws (effective from 3 July 1999) have been reviewed and liberalized to provide a more conducive environment for the development of the technopreneurship sector. As for financing, the government has set up in April 1999 a US$1 billion Technopreneurship Investment Fund to encourage and attract venture capital activities in Singapore.

With barely two years in operation, it is difficult at this point in time to assess how effective these plans are. However, one thing is for sure, the government is determined to go ahead with these plans. This is reflected in the amount of resources allocated, ongoing restructuring of government departments and agencies, and the setting up of various high level committees to implement the plans.

Role and strategies of ethnic Chinese SMEs

In the discussion above, it is noted that the SMEs are expected to play a more important role in the national economy. They are to form the foundation for the development of new products and processes as depicted in the well-known Japanese model of industrial structure with its three tiers of industries (CSC Report, 1998: 77). In this case, the SMEs as a group are expected to form the broad base of basic supporting industries. With rapid technological development, SMEs need to move up the technological ladder in tandem with their MNC and GLC customers to stay relevant as effective business suppliers and collaborators. Secondly, the SMEs are also expected to continue their role as an important contributor to the formation of an "external wing" of the Singapore economy. However, SMEs are now expected to go beyond the region to cover other parts of the world as well. They are also expected to invest overseas not only in traditional sectors such as trade, finance, hotels and real estates but also in new products and processes arising from the New Economy. In addition, SMEs are expected to be suppliers and collaborators of not only MNCs and GLCs but also foreign SMEs. In this respect, the government has decided to set up an SME Hub in Singapore to help strengthen the "external wing". Concurrently, the government also wants to transform a majority of SMEs into a new breed of technopreneurs to exploit opportunities that may arise from the New Economy. Of no less importance is the creation of a strong base to provide quality services for the domestic market.

Ethnic Chinese SMEs, especially the traditional ones, have been complaining that the government has not been assisting them adequately. In fact, most of them view the government's previous efforts in providing assistance schemes with suspicion. To them, promoting MNCs and GLCs preoccupied the government's main agenda of economic restructuring, and SMEs were only expected to play second fiddle to the former. With the launch of the CES Report and various plans in recent years, the SMEs should by now have no substantive complaints against the government, especially the government's intention and sincerity. What the SMEs should do now is to find ways to exploit to the fullest extent the assistance and facilities provided by the government to become more vibrant and resilient. Apart from the above, the SMEs' response to the new challenges should be to ensure that they are always ready to embrace new technology to stay competitive in the networking economy (Chen, March 2001). With the rapid pace of obsolescence, the SMEs must not end up becoming experts of a dying technology or product. They also need to increase connectivity with suppliers, customers and the general public through technology speedily.

And the focus should be on value creation. In addition, SMEs must always seek out and create new opportunities, such as outsourcing opportunities arising from the restructuring of value chains, especially from the semiconductor, telecommunication, IT and transport industries.

In order to achieve the above, the SMEs should upgrade themselves and send their employees for retraining. To increase connectivity with their clients, they have to introduce and expand e-commerce not just in B2B (business-to-business) but also B2C (business-to-customers). According to one study by the National University of Singapore (*Lianhe Zhaobao*, 8 March 2000), SMEs tend to be very conservative and too risk averse. They are, in general, reluctant to seek strategic alliance with competitors. They passively respond and adjust only after their competitors have made changes in strategy. They would not take a proactive strategy in the first place. In this study, of the 150 companies surveyed, only 15.2 per cent of these companies had websites for e-orders and only 8.6 per cent allowed payment through the Internet. However, a report by the government indicates that as at April 2001, some 17,000 SMEs were already leveraging on e-commerce to expand their customer reach. Likewise, SMEs have responded well to the government's call on the training of employees. According to the Skill Development Fund, the number of training places provided to employees reached 111,000 in 2000, compared with 63,720 in 1995. To enhance the human resource management of the SMEs, the government introduced on 17 April 2001 the Training Expertise and Assistance Management Programme (TEAM Programme). This programme is aimed at creating opportunities for the large companies with exemplary human resource development systems and programmes to share their expertise with the SMEs and to serve as their mentors.

SMEs are, in general, small in size in terms of value added, employment and profitability (CSC Report, 1998: 76) and these have prevented them from gaining access to technology, innovation, skilled professionals and management and marketing overseas. They also fail to enjoy economies of scale. One way to resolve these difficulties is to consolidate and pool resources to achieve synergy and improve competitiveness. In this respect, the government introduced the Business Fusion Programme in March 2000 to encourage SMEs of related industries or in the same value chain to come together to exchange information, share resources and enhance mutual co-operation (Tang, 29 March 2001). SMEs under the programme can better compete by leveraging on each other's resources and expertise. By pulling resources together, they are in a stronger position to venture into new markets. Since 2000, more than 200 SMEs have registered with the PSB to show their interest in the programme.

Of these, 97 have formed 30 fusion groups in industries such as automotive service and repair, industrial tool calibration, logistics, construction, silk screen printing, medical instrumentation and transportation.

Apart from collaboration with local partners, SMEs are also encouraged to collaborate with foreign partners. In this connection, the PSB launched the Business Connect Programme in 1997 to enable SMEs to seek new business opportunities outside Singapore and to explore the feasibility of business alliances with foreign partners (Yao, 30 April 2001). Since 1997, more than 30 inbound business-matching events have been held for delegates from Australia, Taiwan, Japan and several European countries. Almost 20 outbound business missions have also been organized. The Business Connect Programme has facilitated about 4,000 business meetings for some 5,800 companies. Besides these efforts, SingaporeConnect, a global business-matching service on the Internet, has attracted an average of 120 business collaboration interest queries each week and the website has been accessed more than eight million times.

With rapid changes in the new environment, the SMEs must also manage changes within their own set-up to bring about a smooth transition to the new setting. Globalization, the Internet, e-commerce and many other developments have totally changed the economic landscape and business relationships among various stakeholders. The SMEs cannot afford to be complacent because any lagging behind in this new business setting will not only end up in their losing business opportunities and also having to face the fate of being wiped out by new developments. Management of change in terms of changes in the management system, corporate culture, corporate governance, compensation and remuneration and many others becomes imperative in business management in the new environment. This is to facilitate a smooth transition to doing business in the New Economy as well as to exploit any opportunity that may arise. Of no less importance is the readiness to move away from familism. They must prepare to face the challenges arising from any change in family ownership structure in their business, either through merger or acquisition. Stock options for employees will be the order of the day, and this may further erode the traditional family ownership structure and control.

Conclusion

Ethnic Chinese SMEs with their sheer weight of numbers constitute the majority of traditional SMEs in Singapore; yet they were not in the mainstream of economic development in the country in the first three decades of its independence. Only from the mid-1990s, has the government accorded the SMEs an increasingly important role in the national economy. In the 1960s and 1970s, Singapore followed a "two-legged" policy, which emphasized the MNCs and GLCs as two main engines for economic development. Ethnic Chinese SMEs were totally left out of policy agendas on industrialization. This was in part due to the political alienation of these SMEs by the ruling PAP government as a result of their conflicting views on Chinese education and culture. The subsequent success of industrialization and economic diversification brought about severe labour shortage, which impeded the progress towards further industrial upgrading, especially economic restructuring towards establishing knowledge-intensive and capital-intensive industries. Such restructuring required the close co-operation of the more labour-intensive SMEs. With the onset of the economic recession in 1985, the government became more serious in restructuring SMEs into co-partners in economic development. An SME Master Plan was drawn up in 1989, together with a regionalization strategy to develop an "external wing" for the economy. Under these policies, the SMEs were expected to reallocate their labour-intensive plants in neighbouring countries and in the Asian region, especially China. However, despite the efforts of the Singapore government, the SMEs have not changed much in terms of their traditional characteristics, such as poor management and low productivity. After the Asian financial crisis in 1997, the government drew up the SME 21 and Technopreneurship 21 to provide a 'road map' for the SMEs and to nurture them into vibrant and resilient enterprises. It is expected that these enterprises will mature over time and be able to collaborate closely with MNCs and GLCs for further economic development. The ultimate goal is to develop the SMEs and the technopreneurship sector as the "third leg" of the Singapore economy.

The success in developing the "third leg" will hinge upon largely on the positive response of the ethnic Chinese SMEs to the government's policy initiatives. Of these SMEs, there are three distinct groups, and each of them could react differently to the policy initiatives. On the one hand, the SME sector is still dominated, albeit a diminishing trend, by the traditional ethnic Chinese SMEs which are unfortunately not well prepared to adjust to the new setting. On the other, there also exists an increasing number of new technopreneurial firms which are more receptive to changes and ready to ride on new technology. In between is the third group, which comprises former traditional family businesses that have transformed over time to take advantage of the new opportunities arising from the New Economy. The first group of SMEs are owned by the early entrepreneurs and, at most, the second generation of such entrepreneurs. Their mindset is still of the Old Economy. Despite government efforts, these enterprises still, for various reasons, shy away from government assistance schemes. They have not changed much over the decade and many of them do not even own a computer. Familism and paternalism are still prevalent in their management style. Naturally, they continue to encounter the same structural problems of human resource and technology. Most of the owners are Chinese-educated and their educational levels generally do not go beyond secondary school. They definitely are part of the HDB heartlanders. To them, unlike their forefathers, doing business is just to earn a decent living and not so much for wealth creation.

The second group of ethnic Chinese SMEs are more cosmopolitan in outlook. They are generally not characterized by family lineage ownership and are less 'Chinese'. A typical entrepreneur of this group, as depicted by Menkhoff (April 2001), is "a middle-aged (42.4 years), English-educated, male Chinese Singaporean with tertiary education and a specialization in engineering or management". They perceive themselves as opportunistic entrepreneurs who are achievement-oriented, adaptable to new environments and are willing to take risks. A significant number of these SMEs (about 45%) have utilized government assistance schemes and will continue to do so in the future.

The third group comprises mainly medium-size enterprises whose owners are highly educated either in Chinese or English. Most of these owners are bilingual and are generally the second generation of the earlier entrepreneurs. They have the backing of strong family financial resources to upgrade their traditional businesses, and are able to branch out into new businesses in the information technology sector. Their firms are the promising ones to become large enterprises. However, their success depends largely on successful adaptation to the New Economy, involvement in research and development, and ability to leverage on the knowledge and talents of their staff. In addition, they must also be prepared to share their wealth with their employees through the practice of stock options.

Apart from the different responses, the progress and transition in developing traditional SMEs and nurturing technopreneurship among new enterprises for the rest of this decade will not be without difficulties. Some of the impediments to the transition and the successful implementation of government policy initiatives, among others, include the following:

- Inertia and aversion to embracing new ideas and innovative ways of doing business
- Low tolerance for failure and aversion to new business risks
- Lack of drive and initiative in venturing abroad, especially beyond the Asian region

- Continued crowding-out effect by the MNCs and GLCs, especially on recruitment of talents and skilled employees
- Inertia in adapting to new environments arising from existing social and cultural barriers
- Lack of push factors to propel young individuals to seek to become technopreneurs as they have better job security in MNCs and GLCs
- Lack of intellectual pursuits and the desire to be involved in research and development.

To sum up, the Singapore economy in general and the SME sector in particular will be encountering the following three basic challenges in the next decade:

- How to overcome the impediments mentioned above with much less structural disruptions in the economy
- How to instil a desire for research and development and promote a technopreneurial culture among the young
- How to avoid being squeezed out in the "global brain war" between China, Taiwan and India on the one hand, and the United States and European countries on the other (*The Straits Times*, 5 June 2001).

And it is up to the people of Singapore in general, and the ethnic Chinese SMEs in particular, to take up these challenges courageously in the decades ahead.

References

Chan, Kwok Bun, and Ng Beoy Kui. "Singapore". In *Chinese Business in Southeast Asia: Contesting Cultural Explanations, Researching Entrepreneurship*, edited by ET Gomez and HH Hsiao. Surrey: Curzon, 2001, pp 38–61.

Chen, Peter. Speech by Peter Chen, Senior Minister of State, Trade and Industry and Education, at the launch of SME March at the Singapore International Convention Centre on 5 March 2001. <http://www.psb.gov.sg/smemarch/speech3.htm>

Huff, WG. *The Economic Growth of Singapore: Trade and Development in the Twentieth Century*. Cambridge: Cambridge University Press, 1994.

Lee, SH. Statement by Lee Suan Hiang, Chief Executive, Singapore Productivity and Standards Board, at the news briefing on SME March on 21 February 2001. <http://www.psb.gov.sg/smemarch/speech1.html>

Lianhe Zhaobao. "Local SMEs seldom involve in e-commerce", 8 March 2000, p 2.

Lim, Chong Yah, and associates. *Policy Options for the Singapore Economy*. Singapore: McGraw-Hill Book Co, 1988.

Menkhoff, Thomas. "Beyond the Asian Crisis—How Singapore's Small Entrepreneurs Manage Change". In *News Release by SCCCI and NUS: A Survey on Change Management Practices of Local SMEs*, 9 April 2001. Singapore: Singapore Chinese Chamber of Commerce and Industry, 2001.

Ministry of Trade and Industry (MTI), Singapore. *Committee on Singapore Competitiveness*. Singapore: Ministry of Trade and Industry, November 1998.

Ng, Beoy Kui. "Bank Liquidity Management and the Implementation of Exchange Rate Policy in Singapore". In *Economic Policy Management in Singapore*, edited by Lim Chong Yah. Singapore: Addison-Wesley, 1996, pp 253–73.

Rodan, G. *The Political Economy of Singapore's Industrialization: National State and International Capital*. Kuala Lumpur: Forum, 1989.

Singapore Chinese Chamber of Commerce and Industry (SCCCI). "Old Economy–New Economy: Crossing the Great Divide". *Chinese Enterprise*, June/July 2000: 18–20.

The Straits Times. "S'pore 'may lose out in global brain war'". Singapore, 5 June 2001.

Tan, Hock. "State Capitalism, Multinational Corporations and Chinese Entrepreneurship in Singapore". In *Asian Business Networks*, edited by Hamilton. Berlin: Walter de Gruter, 1996.

Tan, KY Tony. "Moving from the Old Economy to the New Economy: Implications for the Formulation of Public Policies". Speech at the Administrative Service Dinner and Promotion Ceremony held on 27 March 2000. <http://www.gov.sg/sprinter/>

Tang, GS. Speech by Tang Guan Seng, Senior Parliamentary Secretary for Trade and Industry, at the "SME March" ministerial visit to SMEs and opening of Trans-United Corporation Ltd on 29 March 2001. <http://www.psb.gov.sg/smemarch/speech7.html>

Vasil, R. *Asianising Singapore: The PAP's Management of Ethnicity*. Singapore: Heinemann Asia, 1995.

Wong, Siu-lun. "Chinese Entrepreneurs as Cultural Heroes". Public lecture for the East Asian Institute, National University of Singapore, 3 November 1997.

Yao, Matthias. Statement by Matthias Yao, Minister of State without Portfolio, Prime Minister's Office, at ministerial visit to Local Enterprises: Business Connect—Forging Business Partnerships Across Borders, 30 April 2001. <http://www.psb.gov.sg/smemarch/speech10.html>

Websites

<http://www.psb.gov.sg/aboutus/plans/sme21.html>
<http://www.psb.gov.sg/sme/definition/index.html>

Chapter 13

CHAMPIONS OF CHANGE OR PETTY DINOSAURS? A SURVEY OF ORGANIZATIONAL CHANGE MANAGEMENT PRACTICES OF CHINESE SMEs IN SINGAPORE

Thomas Menkhoff and Benjamin Loh

Introduction: Are Singapore's SMEs Ready for Change?

There is a general awareness of the importance of small and medium-sized enterprises (SMEs) for a country's economic growth, industrial development and employment generation. Economies are increasingly favouring smaller firms in an era of industrial and technological change and development (Bjerke, 1998: 252; Howard, 1991: 118–19; Toffler, 1991: 238–39) when the strategic resource of an economy is no longer based on financial capital, but on "people with drive, energy and willingness to start new business ventures and rejuvenate old ones" (Bjerke, 1998: 253). Especially with the changing economic landscape characterized by the growth of information and communication technologies, globalization and the changing patterns of market demand, the need for SME owners to make strategic responses towards the changing environment is crucial for sustaining success and survival (Pfeffer and Salancik, 1978; EIU and Andersen Consulting, 2000).

However, research on Singapore firms (eg, Menkhoff, Kay and Loh, 2002) suggests that the response of many family-owned SMEs to the new wave of economic and technological forces is insufficient. Many organizations fail to implement, for example, modern quality/productivity management concepts such as Total Quality Management (TQM) or Continuous Quality Improvement (CQI) owing to lack of management know-how, qualified staff and the organizational peculiarities of small family firms. Potential change targets such as strategy, people and/or technology (Leavitt, 1965) represent serious challenges for SME owners and are often systematically neglected. In addition, a recent survey (Chua, 2001) of 158 ethnic Chinese enterprises in Singapore showed that a relatively large proportion of these firms pay insufficient attention to IT skills upgrading, innovation as a source of competitiveness, product customization, customer satisfaction and e-commerce operations. Based on these indicators, the authors concluded that many SMEs in Singapore are not yet ready for the New Economy. Predictors and key ingredients of entrepreneurial "New Economy compliance", however, remain unclear.

SME policy-makers do hope that New Economy–related assistance schemes will motivate more local small entrepreneurs to embrace related changes proactively. To increase the online transaction capability of local SMEs and to encourage small entrepreneurs to adopt "ready-made" e-commerce solutions, both the then Singapore's Productivity and Standards Board (PSB, now the Standards, Productivity and Innovation Board) and the Infocomm Development Authority (IDA) have implemented various New Economy–related SME upgrading schemes in the past few years (see the subsection "Embracing e-commerce: The case of Far East Flora"). The characteristics of those small entrepreneurs who took up the challenge (and those who did not) have yet to be ascertained by empirical research.

Whether ethnic Chinese small enterprises in Singapore are "ready" for the New Economy is a hotly debated issue in the city state. Representative empirical data and sophisticated theoretical models, however, are hard to come by. With this in mind, our study was conducted in 1999/2000 to generate data on the change propensity of the local business community *vis-à-vis* the rapidly changing business environment and associated challenges such as the Asian crisis, the process of economic globalization and continuous technology development. The study was aimed at providing answers to the following questions:

- To what extent are the often heard "change or go bust slogans" in conjunction with local SMEs based on facts or imagination?
- What is really going on in local SMEs in terms of organizational change practices and management?
- How well do the CEOs of local SMEs manage change?
- To what extent do demographic variables and traits of owner-managers of SMEs predict the successful initiation of organizational change?
- To what extent are local small entrepreneurs willing to take risks? Are they receptive to change?
- What is their entrepreneurial orientation?
- What are the results and outcomes of change efforts at the firms' organizational level and their determinants?

This essay summarizes the main findings of the study which was jointly undertaken by researchers from the National University of Singapore and the Singapore Chinese Chamber of Commerce and Industry (SCCCI).

Background of research project

The project evolved in the context of the authors' consulting work as human resource development (HRD) advisors for SMEs in the region. During these assignments, it was realized that there are enormous barriers towards change not only amongst middle managers or lower-level employees but also amongst members of the firms' top management teams. This observation represented a puzzle in view of:

1   widespread theoretical pre-assumptions about the "strong" spirit of Chinese capitalism, "good" corporate governance and the premises of the Confucian ethics thesis as an explanatory framework for the "successful" economic behaviour of Chinese entrepreneurs which, however, ignore the down side of organizational behaviour in "Asian" (Chinese) firms such as alienation, resistance to authority or mismanagement (Redding, 1993; Backman, 2000);
2   the various external forces of change impacting on both small and big firms such as developments in technology and IT, changing customer needs and tastes, new legislation, increasing competitive pressures and so on; as well as
3   potentially disruptive internal forces of change in terms of customer complaints, reduced profits, outdated business strategies, low staff performance and morale, and inadequate skills and knowledge bases.

To crack this paradox, it was decided to conduct a baseline survey in order to generate empirical data on the change management practices of local SMEs and their owners. This area represents—despite all the "change or go bust slogans" put forward by consulting firms and other groups—a relatively poorly researched area. Other goals included the identification of organizational change drivers in local SMEs and the formulation of policy recommendations aimed at increasing the (presumably insufficient) receptiveness of the local SME community towards the supply of external management advisory services and utilization of proper change management concepts. The main research methods used included (1) semi-structured, qualitative interviews with management consultants and small entrepreneurs as well as (2) a quantitative survey of 101 SMEs.

Methodology and sample

Library and fieldwork were conducted in Singapore between April 1999 and December 2000. The methodologies employed included:

- semi-structured, qualitative expert interviews with management

- consultants and representatives of SME promotion bodies such as Singapore's Productivity and Standards Board (PSB);
- semi-structured, qualitative in-depth interviews with top executives, HR specialists and lower-level employees of SMEs;
- the administration of a questionnaire survey covering members (exclusively SMEs) of the Singapore Chinese Chamber of Commerce and Industry (SCCCI) from various sectors; and
- follow-up face-to-face and/or telephone interviews with about 50 entrepreneurs.

During the explorative stage of the study various qualitative interviews with management consultants (9) and small entrepreneurs (5) were conducted to develop hypotheses about the change management practices of local SME owners and to facilitate the development of the research model as well as the measuring instruments. These key informants were identified with the help of the SCCCI and Singapore's Institute of Management Consultants.

Subsequently, a SME survey was administered, together with the SCCCI, across industries and business types. The questionnaire included six sections: (a) demographics, (b) business characteristics, (c) organizational change, (d) personality traits, (e) firm performance and (f) external management consultants. It was intensively discussed, modified and pretested with various subject matter experts and selected small businessmen to ensure that all the questions were adequately formulated and properly understood.

The quantitative data were obtained from corporate members of the SCCCI, which has a total membership of about 3,000. In view of the generally poor response rate of mailed questionnaire surveys in Singapore, the questionnaire was faxed to those companies who are linked to the SCCCI via winfax (ie, 1,000 firms) in the summer of 2000. Due to complaints by some of SCCCI's members about this "lengthy procedure" and the "blocking of their fax machines", the Chamber subsequently decided to use e-mail instead of winfax to send out the questionnaire. Altogether, about 1,000 SCCCI members received the questionnaire via e-mail. In all, only 14 questionnaires were returned within the given time frame of two to three weeks. In view of this very poor response rate, it was decided to contact SCCCI members directly and to interview them face-to-face with the help of a team of four interviewers. At the same time, a second survey wave was initiated in October 2000, covering 500 members of the SCCCI. Sampled firms were selected at random from SCCCI's membership list. In all, 59 were returned.

The final sample was composed of 101 small and medium-sized firms (defined as firms with less than 200 employees) operating in different sectors, which included manufacturing (28.7%), trading (23.8%), professional services (20.8%), retailers (8.9%) and others. The key findings of the survey are presented in the next section.

Research Results: How Singapore's Small Entrepreneurs Manage Organizational Change

Business characteristics and entrepreneurial profile

The typical firm surveyed was a 100 per cent locally-owned, private limited company which had been established in the early 1990s by the respondent himself, who owned a substantial proportion of the business without any involvement of external parties, such as institutional and/or equity investors.

The average respondent turned out to be a middle-aged (42.4 years), English-educated, male Chinese Singaporean with tertiary education and a specialization in engineering or management. He had been in his current position for 10.5 years, with an average organizational tenure and total working experience of 13.3 years and 20.8 years respectively.

Most respondents perceived themselves as so-called "opportunistic entrepreneurs" (46.5%) who were achievement-oriented, effective in terms of adaptation, business planning and so forth, as well as willing to take risks (Carland et al, 1984; Bracker, Keats and Pearson, 1988). "Craftsman entrepreneurs", who are typified in entrepreneurship literature as relatively non-adaptive and more risk-averse persons aiming for a comfortable living rather than the highest possible level of performance (Smith, 1967; Filley and Aldag, 1978), made up 36.6 per cent of the sample. About 17 per cent of the respondents could not be categorized.

Emphasis was put on the measurement of two personality traits which have been identified as change drivers: "willingness to take risks" and "receptivity to change". Most local entrepreneurs (52.5%) classified themselves as risk-takers while 36.6 per cent appeared to be more risk-averse (ie, not willing to take risks); 10.9 per cent were neutral. With regard to the degree of change propensity, 76.2 per cent of the sampled entrepreneurs turned out to be receptive to change while 13.9 per cent were not (about 10% were neutral).

Contrary to the sometimes negative image of small entrepreneurs as being backward, risk-averse and static, survey data on the respondents' demographics suggest that the sampled small businessmen and women were flexible, adaptable individuals who—due to their personality traits—were open to the initiation of change and willing to take risks. This hypothesis is supported by data on the firms' change management practices.

Change management practices of local SMEs: Change targets

The survey suggests that the sampled Singaporean SME owners implemented organizational change measures on a routine basis. Changing the firm's strategic direction and technology, IT-related changes, and changes related to people and their task behaviours were the most frequently adopted measures (see Figure 1).

Figure 1: Most frequently adopted change measures

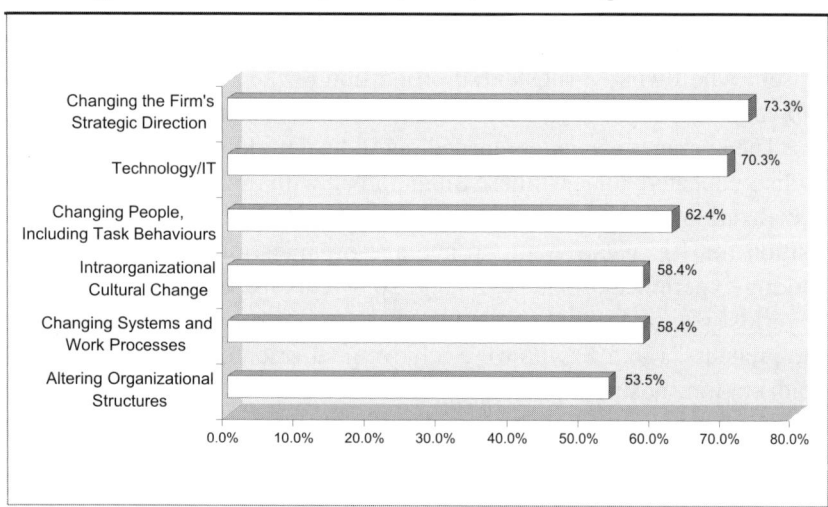

In terms of technology-related changes, Internet and e-commerce, purchase of new tools and equipment, and office automation and implementation of online procedures were classified as the three most important, major and critical change areas (see Figure 2). Significant people-related changes included the provision of employees with more company-related information, more consultation and more staff participation in decision-making processes (see Figure 3).

Figure 2: Major/Critical changes in technology-related areas

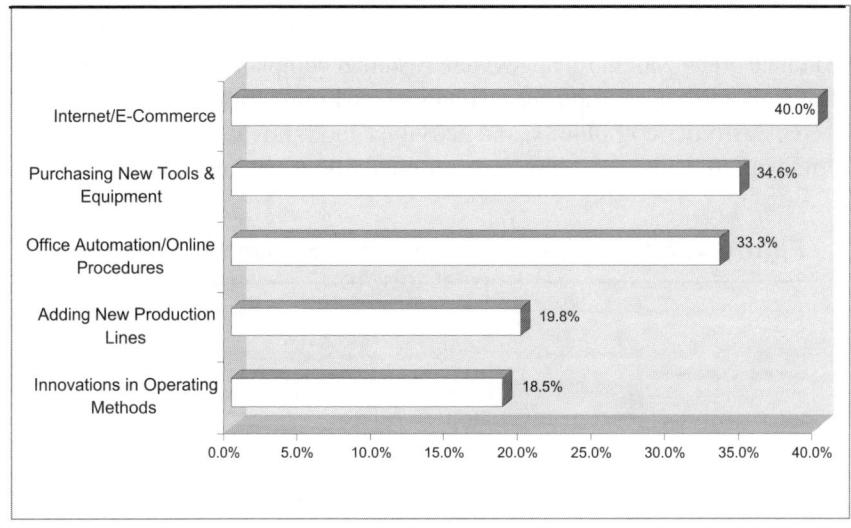

Figure 3: Major/Critical changes in people-related areas

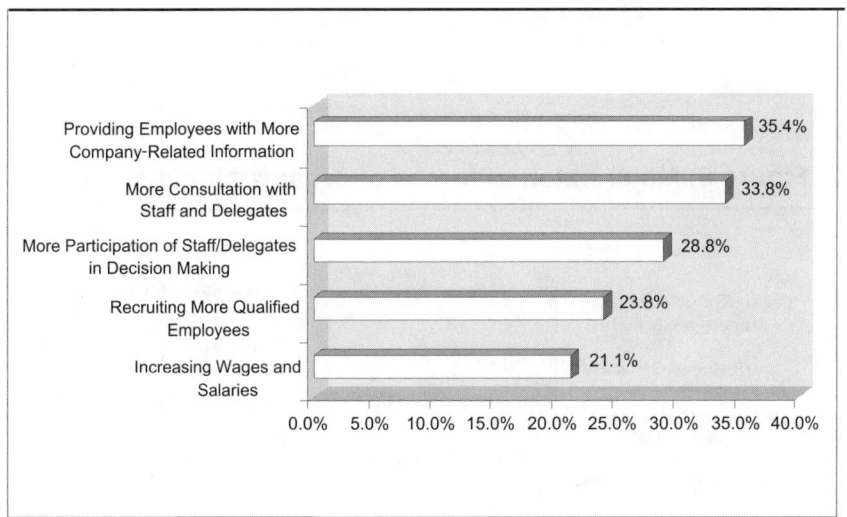

Forces of change

The three most important internal forces of change which motivated respondents to initiate organizational changes were customer complaints, outdated business strategies and a new emphasis on quality (see Figure 4). Changing customer needs, customer complaints, and activities and innovations of competitors turned out to be the most important external forces of change (see Figure 5).

Figure 4: Major internal forces of organizational change

Figure 5: Major external forces of organizational change

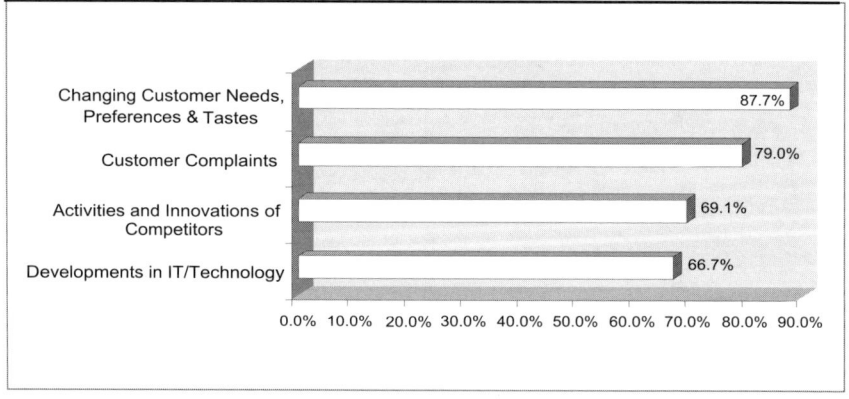

Type and extent of organizational change measures

Most respondents interpreted the nature of organizational change measures which had been initiated in their firms since mid-1997 as both reactive and proactive (58.8%); 27.5 per cent assessed the changes as reactive in nature. Only 13.8 per cent of all respondents had proactively implemented organizational change measures in anticipation of future difficulties, threats and opportunities.

The majority (66.3%) claimed that the adopted change measures were based on a detailed plan of action. Of the respondents, 46.3 per cent characterized the situation they had faced in their firms since mid-1997 as one of high urgency for change and low resistance towards change.

Those who had implemented sweeping, revolutionary changes throughout their firms made up only a small proportion of the survey participants (6.2%). About 17 per cent had initiated a radical redirection and restructuring of certain departments (see Figure 6). Most respondents characterized the extent of change which had occurred in their firms (eg, changes with regard to strategies, structures and/or management processes) since mid-1997 as either distinct (40.7%) or gradual (34.6%), for example, through improving work methods, policies and procedures in certain areas.

Outcome and impact of change measure(s)

More than half of all survey participants characterized the outcome of organizational change measures as successful (55.6%) and claimed that they had measured the effects of implemented organizational change

Figure 6: Extent of organizational changes initiated by respondents

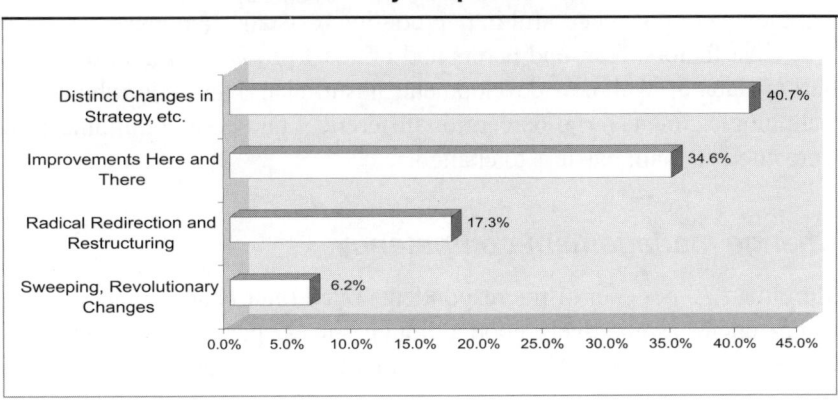

measures (75.3%). Improved job performance (60.5%) and retained business (60.5%), higher sales volume (59.2%) and fewer customer complaints/ higher customer satisfaction were cited as the three most important benefits of change initiatives (see Figure 7). Adverse administrative effects, increase in staff turnover and disruption of production were cited as the three most important negative consequences of implemented change measures.

Figure 7: Scale of benefits obtained by change measures

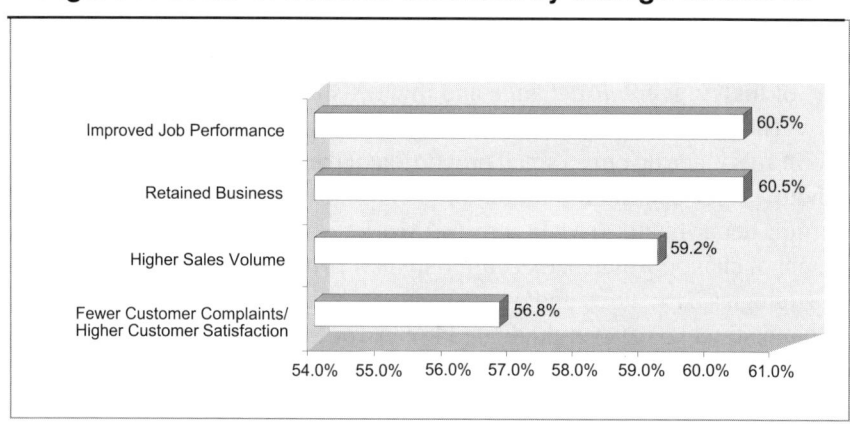

Resistance and barriers to change

All firms encountered resistance to change, particularly amongst non-executive employees but also amongst middle managers and top managers. Slightly more than half of the survey participants felt that they had been successful in tackling this problem (57.5%), 41.3 per cent interpreted themselves as somewhat successful while a small proportion (1.3%) felt that they were not successful in overcoming resistance amongst staff.

Cost factors, fear, bad habits and mindset problems, inability of old staff to catch up with new developments, insufficient knowledge about new technologies, managerial perception differences and poor communication were cited as main barriers to change.

Change management competency

More than 70 per cent of the respondents rated their change management competencies as good/very good although only 21 per cent had attended a relevant training course. About one third of all surveyed SME representatives

(31%) believed that they had a high/very high understanding of the change management concept.

Management consultancy services and SME assistance schemes

As expected about two-thirds of all survey participants (70.3%) had never utilized the services of external management consultants. Amongst those who had hired external expertise, general management, information management/computer applications and financial management turned out to be the most frequently received consulting inputs.

Of those who had utilized external expertise, 40.1 per cent acknowledged that the consultant(s) had a high impact on firm performance. Half of the respondents assessed the business impact of external management experts as moderate while 10.1 per cent rated it as low. The three most important reasons for not seeking external advice included the perception that external consulting inputs were costly, that many SME owners did not see the need to hire a consultant and that consultants did not fully understand the nature of the respective business (see Figure 8). Altogether, 45.1 per cent of the SMEs surveyed had utilized official SME assistance schemes provided by the government.

Figure 8: Reasons for not utilizing external consultancy services

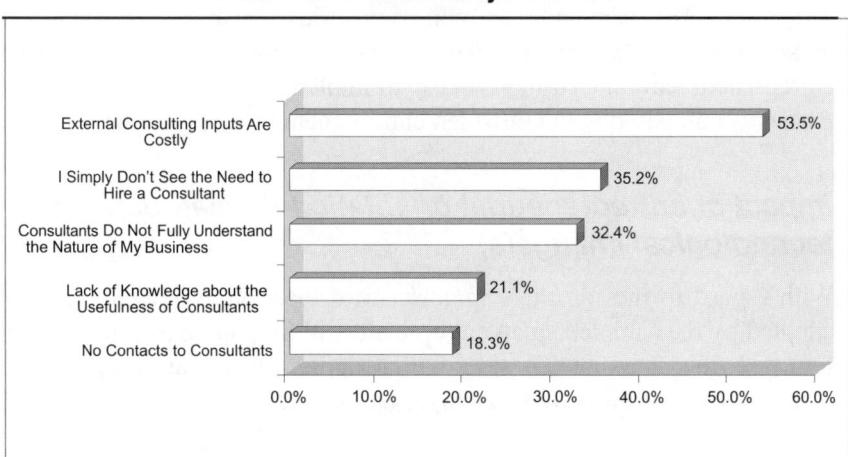

Research Results—How Singapore's Small Entrepreneurs Manage Technological Change

Technology has been identified as one of the most important factors behind the competitive advantage of successful SMEs (Simon, 1996). This might partly explain why technology/IT-related changes scored as the second most important/critical change target of the small entrepreneurs surveyed in the context of this study (see Figure 1), which indicates the great value local SMEs place on technological change measures. In view of the general paucity of data on the management of technological change in local (Chinese) SMEs, the following paragraph is aimed at examining potential differences between (1) craftsman entrepreneurs and (2) opportunistic entrepreneurs. Craftsman entrepreneurs who are typified in entrepreneurship literature as relatively non-adaptive and more risk-averse persons aiming for a comfortable living rather than the highest possible level of performance made up 36.6 per cent (37) of the sample. We would expect them to be less receptive to technological change than opportunistic entrepreneurs who are usually seen as (more) achievement-oriented, effective in terms of adaptation, business planning and so forth as well as willing to take risks. Opportunistic entrepreneurs made up 46 per cent (47) of the sample.

Impact of entrepreneurial orientation on initiation of technological change(s)

The various cross-tabulations and non-parametric tests which were conducted as part of our initial exploratory data analysis work indicate that opportunistic entrepreneurs are indeed more likely to implement technological change measures compared with craftsman entrepreneurs (see Figure 9).

Impact of entrepreneurial orientation on major/critical technological change(s)

With regard to the top three major/critical technology-related changes adopted by the sampled small entrepreneurs in Singapore as illustrated in Figure 2, the data analysis reveals that opportunistic entrepreneurs are comparatively more active in implementing Internet and e-commerce initiatives (Figure 10), purchasing new tools and equipment (Figure 11) and automating their offices as well as operating procedures (Figure 12) than craftsman entrepreneurs.

Figure 9: Initiation of technological changes by entrepreneurial orientation

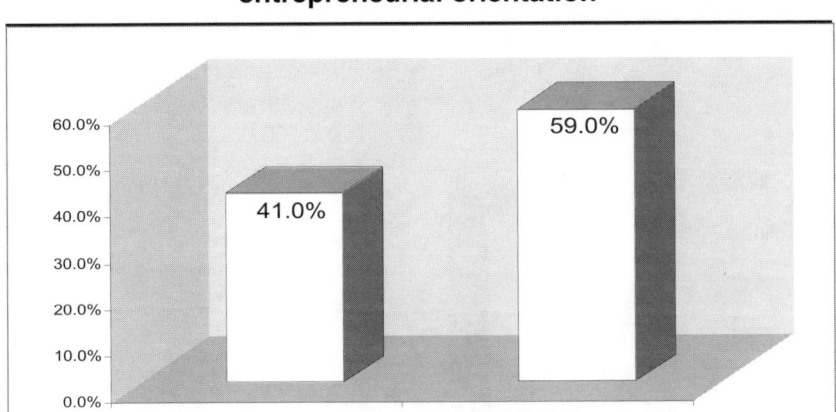

Figure 10: Implementation of Internet/e-commerce-related technological changes by entrepreneurial orientation

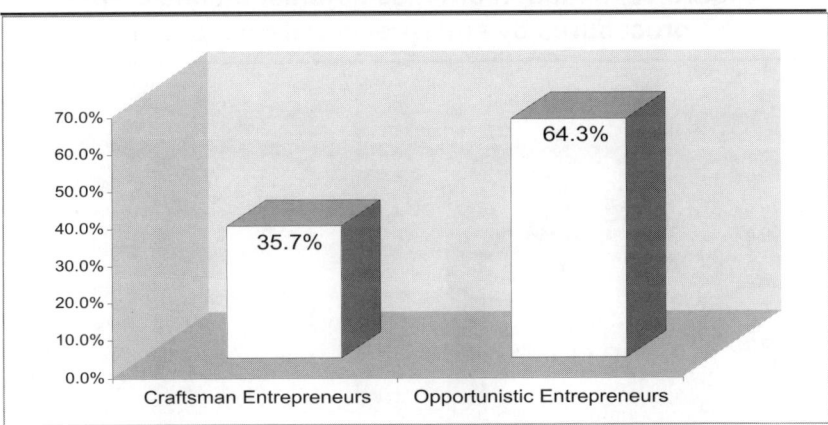

Critical internal forces of technological change(s)

The five most important/critical internal forces of change which motivated respondents to initiate technological changes were customer complaints, outdated business strategies, ineffective management strategies, reduced profit and a new emphasis on quality (see Figure 13).

Figure 11: Purchase of new tools and equipment by entrepreneurial orientation

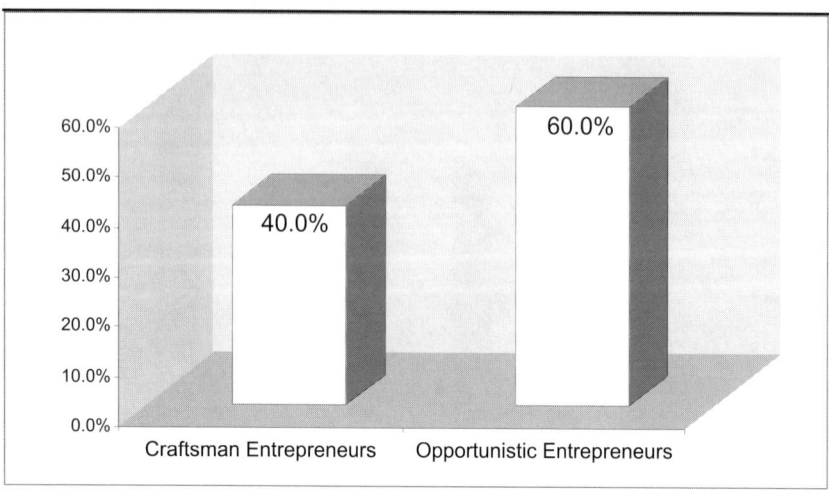

Figure 12: Initiation of office automation and online procedures by entrepreneurial orientation

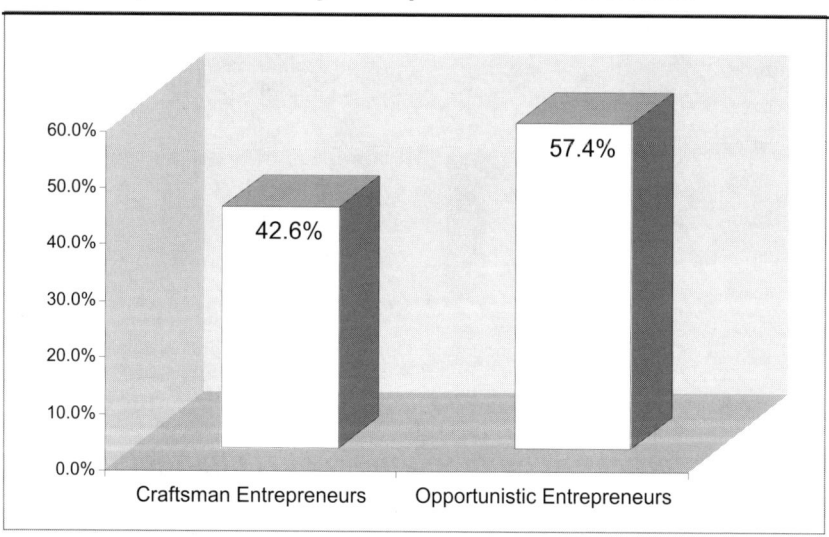

Figure 13: Important/Critical internal forces of technological changes

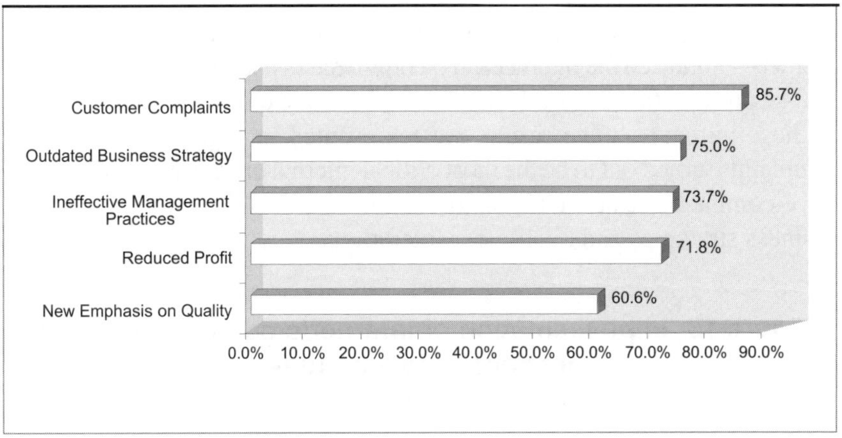

- Customer Complaints: 85.7%
- Outdated Business Strategy: 75.0%
- Ineffective Management Practices: 73.7%
- Reduced Profit: 71.8%
- New Emphasis on Quality: 60.6%

Critical external forces of technological change(s)

Changing customer needs, preferences and tastes, customer complaints, and activities and innovations of competitors turned out to be the most important external forces of change triggering technological change measures, followed by developments in new technology and the Asian crisis (see Figure 14).

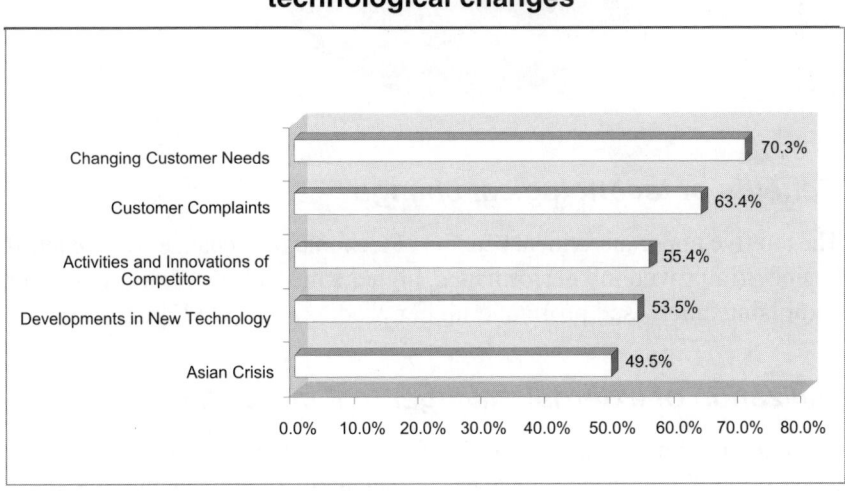

Figure 14: Important/Critical external forces of technological changes

- Changing Customer Needs: 70.3%
- Customer Complaints: 63.4%
- Activities and Innovations of Competitors: 55.4%
- Developments in New Technology: 53.5%
- Asian Crisis: 49.5%

Critical internal forces of Internet and e-commerce-related technology change(s)

In view of the relatively large number of respondents who had—in one way or another—embraced the Internet and e-commerce as part of their technological change projects (see Figure 15), it was decided to explore the internal forces of these initiatives. The results are represented in Figure 16. Customer complaints turned out to be the most critical internal driving force of Internet and e-commerce-related technology change measures, followed by outdated business strategies and quality considerations.

Figure 15: Implementation of Internet/e-commerce-related technological changes

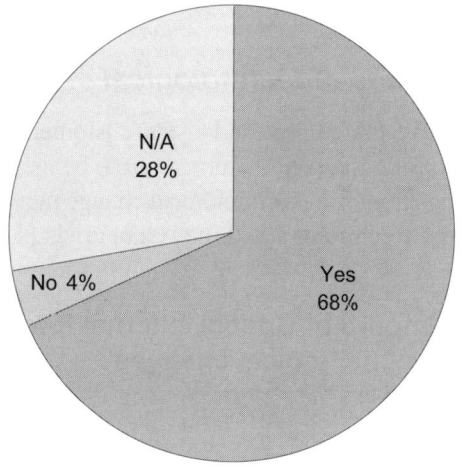

Benefits of technological change

The top five important/critical benefits of technological change were retained business/improved job performance, higher sales volume, fewer customer complaints, increased profit and higher productivity (see Figure 17).

Utilization of external management consultants

As stated earlier, about two-thirds of all survey participants (70.3%) had never utilized the services of external management consultants. Are there

Figure 16: Important/Critical internal forces of Internet/e-commerce-related technological changes

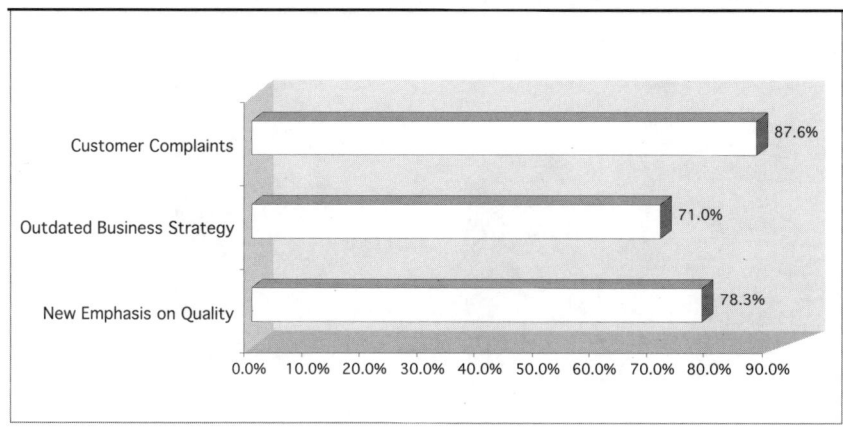

Figure 17: Important/Critical benefits of technological change

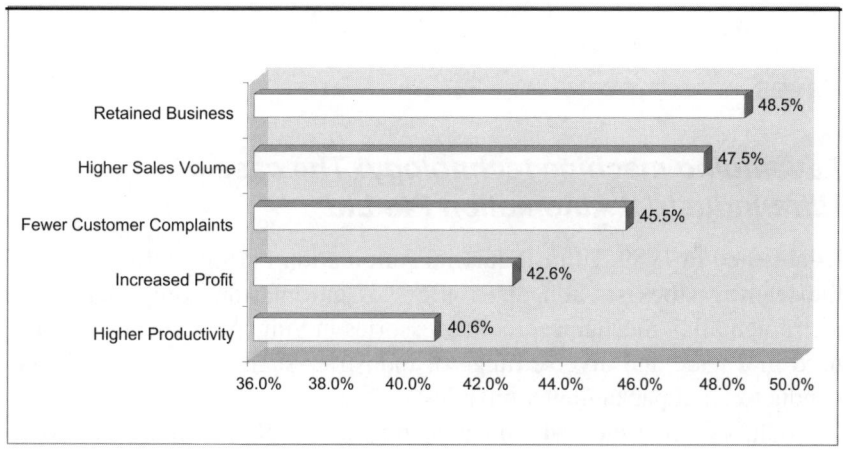

any differences between the two types of entrepreneurs introduced earlier in this respect? As indicated by Figure 18, opportunistic entrepreneurs are more likely to utilize the services of external management consultants than craftsman entrepreneurs. While 34 per cent of the opportunistic small businessmen surveyed had done so, the respective percentage of craftsman entrepreneurs was about 24 per cent.

Figure 18: Utilization of external management consultants by entrepreneurial orientation

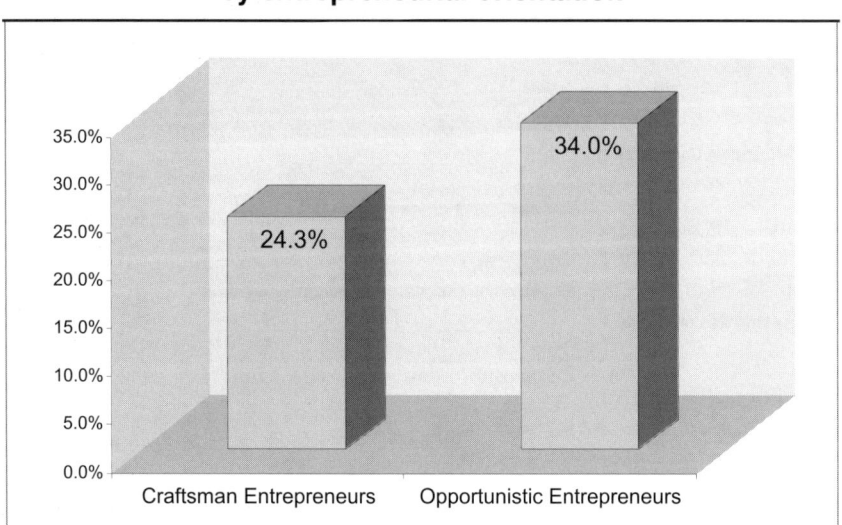

Cases

Leveraging machine technology: The case of Ultra-Industrial Automation Pte Ltd

Established in 1989, Ultra-Industrial Automation Pte Ltd (UIA) is one of the leading stockists and distributors of automation components and instrumentation mechanical tool accessories in Singapore. Its products are used in a wide and diverse range of industries such as disk drive, semiconductor, and packaging companies.

Chris Chan is the co-founder and director of UIA. He holds a diploma in electrical engineering. He was responsible for initiating technological changes within his company in response to the increasing competition from and innovation of rival companies in the automation components industry. At that time, Chan was convinced that in order to keep his clients and increase his market share in the industry, he had to cut cost of components by 10 to 30 per cent.

Hence, in 1994, UIA diversified its operations to include the manufacture of its own Modular Aluminium Profile Structure (MAPS), which is a safety enclosure for machine structures. Its low-cost product was priced 20 to 30 per cent lower than those of its existing foreign-based rivals, and this change led the company to achieve a turnover of over $1 million that year.

However, the implementation of this technological change was not smooth-sailing from the start. The raw materials for MAPS had to be sourced from overseas suppliers initially, and this resulted in problems concerning the quantity of orders and delay in lead times. This was solved in late 1998 when Chan forged a business alliance with a local supplier which was able to produce the materials that could meet the specific requirements of the manufacture of MAPS. This move has since cut down inventory costs and lead time, and allowed longer payment terms than overseas suppliers did, as well as better profit margins. Besides the manufacture of MAPS, Chan also introduced new products such as "Stepper" and "Servo Drive", which are controller and positioning systems for his products.

In addition to a highly focused product range, Chan feels that another factor in UIA's competitive edge is its ability to conduct specialized after-sales training for its customers. Through specialized and regular professional support, UIA has helped its customers to cope with their present as well as future technical requirements. UIA's engineers are trained in conducting seminars and are also constantly updated on the latest innovations through regular attachment with overseas companies. Chan has also invested in a machine shop to add value to his products. The introduction of this service provides end-users with a one-stop shop for the servicing and finishing of all the product's component parts. This gives him a further edge over his competitors as none of them provides such an intensive machining capability. With the technological innovation of and increase in his product range, Chan needs a bigger market place to sell his products. He feels that his products have to enter the global market beyond his existing Southeast Asian base. Hence, from the end of 1997, he has exported his products to Taiwan, South Africa, China, Mexico and the USA. His next target is the European market.

Chan expects Southeast Asia to experience robust industrial development in the 21st century and is gearing up his company to seize the tremendous growth opportunities that will be available. Already in the pipeline are plans to extend the company's manufacturing arms to neighbouring countries like Indonesia, Malaysia and China. And with an overall annual turnover of more than $13 million, UIA is well positioned to be a leading player in its specialized market.

Embracing e-commerce: The case of Far East Flora Pte Ltd

Far East Flora was founded by the Cheok brothers in 1965. At that time, the three brothers operated their retail flower business from the back of their van. Their first flowers and gifts department was formed in 1978 to complement and improve the company's product line and services. Since then, Far East Flora has expanded and now sells over 2,000 freshly cut flowers and other gift items in its garden "supermarket". As a member of Interflora, it has embarked on an e-marketplace platform to sell and deliver its products to over 60 countries in the world. Today, Far East Flora is a major importer, exporter and wholesaler of freshly cut flowers, enjoying a turnover of S$22 million last year.

Far East Flora Pte Ltd is an SME which has taken advantage of government assistance schemes to reinvent itself for the New Economy. To assist the SME sector to keep pace with changing environmental demands, the Singapore government offers over 60 assistance schemes to ensure that SMEs survive and remain competitive. One such scheme is the "Jumpstart Programme", which is offered by the Standards, Productivity and Innovation Board (SPRING Singapore). The scheme aims to accelerate the online transaction capability of SMEs by helping them adopt "ready-made" e-commerce solutions. About 17,000 SMEs have taken advantage of this scheme. Another 1,500 SMEs have also made use of the e-Business Industry Development Scheme, which is jointly offered by SPRING Singapore and the Infocomm Development Authority (IDA). This scheme allows SMEs to join an e-marketplace that is customized to meet the needs of suppliers and customers in the various industry sectors.

Conclusion

Contrary to popular belief that local SME entrepreneurs are risk-averse, unprogressive and rigid, our study reveals that the majority of the respondents (53%) saw themselves as risk-takers. Three in four respondents (76%) characterized themselves as receptive to change. The data collated show that local entrepreneurs have the gusto to take up risks, and that they are flexible and responsive to both internal and external forces of change. Our pioneering research on change management practices of SMEs in Singapore relates the pattern of organizational changes engaged by local SME owner-managers, as well as the drivers, barriers and types of respective adaptation processes, in the midst of challenges and developments occurring in a never static business environment.

Survey data indicate that the demographic characteristics of small entrepreneurs in terms of age, organizational tenure, educational level and specialization as well as the cognitive perspectives of SME owners are decisive when it comes to an understanding of the propensity to change, proactive change management and improved firm performance.

The study clearly shows that Singapore's small entrepreneurs place great value on new technology adoption and respective change projects. After strategy, technology is the second most important change target of the sampled Singaporean (Chinese) small entrepreneurs. Case companies have proactively embraced the Internet and e-commerce and invested in the modernization and automation of tools, equipment, operating procedures and offices. Besides internal and external forces of change such as customer complaints and outdated business strategies, entrepreneurial orientation and demographic traits are important predictors of one's receptivity to technological change. Entrepreneurs with an opportunistic orientation, tertiary education and a specialization in either engineering or management are more likely to be technological change masters compared with craftsman entrepreneurs who put significantly lesser emphasis on technology change.

To sum up, the data clearly show that more local small and medium-sized companies have come to accept the importance and benefits of organizational change and external change advocates such as management consultants and official SME incentive schemes. However, to further propagate the change management concept as a sort of New Economy survival tool kit, relevant skills upgrading and awareness building measures are necessary to turn more local SME owner-managers into change masters.

References

Backman, M. *Asian Eclipse—Exposing the Dark Side of Business in Asia*. Singapore: John Wiley, 2000.

Bjerke, B. "Entrepreneurship and SMEs in the Singaporean Context". In *Competitiveness of the Singapore Economy: A Strategic Perspective*, edited by MH Toh and KY Tan. Singapore: Singapore University Press, 1998.

Bracker, J, B Keats and J Pearson. "Planning and Financial Performance among Small Firms in a Growth Industry". *Strategic Management Journal* 9 (1988): 591–603.

Carland, JW, F Hoy, WR Boulton and JAC Carland. "Differentiating Entrepreneurs from Small Business Owners: A Conceptualization". *Academy of Management Review* 9 (1984): 354–59.

Chua, Soo Ee. "The New Economy and Chinese Enterprises in Singapore". Unpublished MS. Faculty of Business Administration, National University of Singapore, 2001.

Economist Intelligence Unit, and Andersen Consulting. *Beyond the Bamboo Network: Successful Strategies for Change in Asia*. Hong Kong: Economist Intelligence Unit, 2000.

Filley, AC, and RJ Aldag. "Characteristics and Measurement of an Organizational Typology". *Academy of Management Journal* 21 (4) (1978): 578–91.

Howard, R. "Can Small Businesses Help Countries Compete?" In *Entrepreneurship: Creativity at Work*. Boston: Harvard Business School Press, 1991.

Leavitt, HJ. "Applied Organizational Change in Industry: Structural, Technical and Human Approach". In *New Perspectives in Organizational Research*, edited by WW Cooper, HJ Leavitt and MW Shelly II. New York: John Wiley, 1965.

Menkhoff, T, L Kay and B Loh. "Worlds Apart? Reflections on the Relationship between Small Entrepreneurs and External Change Advocates in Singapore". *Journal of Asian Business* 18 (1) (2002).

Pfeffer, J, and GR Salancik. *The External Control of Organizations: A Resource Dependency Perspective*. New York: Harper and Row, 1978.

Redding, SG. *The Spirit of Chinese Capitalism*. Berlin: De Gruyter, 1993.

Simon, H. *Hidden Champions: Lessons from 500 of the World's Best Unknown Companies*. Boston, MA: Harvard Business School Press, 1996.

Smith, N. *The Entrepreneur and His Firm: The Relationship between Type of Man and Type of Company*. East Lansing, Mich: Michigan State University, 1967.

Toffler, A. *Power Shift*. London: Bantam Books, 1991.

Part IV

Religion

Chapter 14

MALAYSIAN CHINESE RELIGIOUS CULTURE: PAST AND PRESENT*

Jean DeBernardi

When Chinese from southeastern China immigrated into the Straits Settlements and Malaya, they encountered a heterogenous, cosmopolitan community whose development had been fostered by the growth of global capitalist trade networks. In this social environment, the Chinese immigrants reproduced the social structures and practices of the popular religious culture of their native country, which blended ancestor worship with cosmological and ethical frameworks derived from Daoism, Buddhism and Confucianism. At the same time, however, participation in the "global ecumene" and interaction with the social forms of modernity promoted the local reworking of religious forms and practices. In the dialectic with colonialism, globalization, modernization and nationalism, Chinese "traditional" culture developed new forms and meanings.[1]

In this article, I investigate the ways in which the Chinese have reworked their religious culture in both colonial and contemporary Malaysia. In considering Chinese religious culture from this perspective, I focus on the political and social dimensions of that culture. In particular, I explore the way that religion both defines the boundaries of community in the idiom

---

* I conducted the historical research on which this article is based at Cornell University's Wason Collection, the Public Records Office in London, the Singapore National Archives, the National University of Singapore Library, and the Echoes of Service archive in Bath, England. I completed the first phase of the research with support from a Luce Fellowship at the Center for Southeast Asian Studies at Cornell University, and research grants from the American Philosophical Society and the Southeast Asian Council of the Association for Asian Studies. I have taken the opportunity afforded by subsequent research trips to continue this archival research, and would like to thank the Canada ASEAN Centre, the Social Science and Humanities Research Council of Canada, the Wenner-Gren Foundation for Anthropological Research, the University of Alberta Central Research Fund, and the Faculty of Arts Support for the Advancement of Scholarship Committee, for their research support.

1   Aihwa Ong and Donald Nonini also note that persistent and apparently "timeless" features" of Chinese culture often disguise new social arrangements (Ong and Nonini, 1997: 8).

of the sacred, and constructs a public face for the Chinese community and its subcultural groupings.

The Early Modern Period

The cities of colonial Malaya were nodes in the global networks of capitalism that drew immigrants from India, Southeast Asia and China (as well as European sojourners). While they were predominantly Chinese, the populations of cities like Penang and Malacca were class stratified and diverse. Moreover, the Chinese community itself was highly heterogenous, including speakers of dialects of three different Chinese languages—Southern Min, Yue (or Cantonese) and Hakka. Freed from their localized communities of kin, many Chinese who immigrated into Southeast Asia encountered a diversity of ideas and ways of life, and a cosmopolitan urban life.

Although many scholars have disparaged Chinese popular religious culture both as a superstitious folk religion and the epitome of "traditional Chinese culture", I conclude instead that Chinese community temples and sworn brotherhoods were social forms that the immigrants refashioned in the social contexts of early modernity. In the colonial Straits Settlements, the Chinese community's prosperity gave it the means to build communal temples, to design institutions of self-government, and to claim social honour through extravagant, rivalrous feasts and festival displays. At the same time, its sworn brotherhoods used traditional materials—spirit possession, invulnerability magic, a legendary history and the blood oath—to ritually seal a social contract for urban immigrants who no longer lived in a mono-ethnic, kinship-based social world.

Although I focus on the political dimension of popular religious organizations, it is important to recall that temples and sworn brotherhoods also offered spiritual protection and even salvation to participants. Chinese immigrants who left their native territories for foreign lands found themselves lacking the localized spiritual protection of their traditional territorial gods and ancestors. In colonial Malaya, they learned to placate new territorial gods—*Nadogong* (那督公, whom they imagined as having Malay ethnicity), but also prayed to their demon-expelling *Wangye* (王爷, or divine kings) to protect them from plague and conflict. The Chinese in Malaya also worshipped universal saviours like Guanyin (观音), a Bodhisattva who turned back from nirvana in order to save all humans.[2]

---

2   In Penang, Guanyin also is popularly known as the "Goddess of Mercy".

Universal salvation religions like Pure Land Buddhism that emphasize voluntary (rather than ascriptive) association and individual salvation, would appear to be especially well suited to the social contexts of early modernity, which freed individuals from their territorial and kinship structures to roam the global ecumene (with all its perils).

While the Chinese built religious institutions to serve their community's spiritual needs, nonetheless these temples and sworn brotherhoods also existed in an intercultural contact zone, as a point of conjuncture between Chinese and non-Chinese communities. In what Marshall Sahlins has labelled the "structure of the conjuncture", we find "the alliances that cross ethnic boundaries and correlate oppositions within the colonial society to political differences among the local people" (Sahlins, 1994: 385).

As John and Jean Comaroff have noted, ethnic consciousness developed in the structure of the conjuncture as the consequence of "encounters between peoples who signif[ied] their differences and inequalities—in power, economic position, political ambitions, and historical imaginings—by cultural means" (Comaroff and Comaroff, 1997: 388). Precisely because the Chinese in the Straits Settlements lived in a complex, multi-ethnic society, their religious practices developed into symbols of community and subculture. Moreover, in the colonial context Chinese religious practices were imbricated with the exercise of authority, the expression of economic power, and the construction of a uniquely Chinese past that formed the basis for a historical sense of identity.

The Baba Chinese, for example, used cultural forms to maintain their distinctiveness in a situation of cultural contact and change. In the early years of migration to Southeast Asia, the Baba creolized Chinese and Malay languages and lifestyles, while they continued to observe the cultural and social practices of Chinese religious culture (Purcell, 1967 [1948]; Shellabear, 1977 [1913]; Tan, 1988). Later, the Straits Chinese creolized Baba and English culture, and educated Straits Chinese like Lim Boon Keng turned to a rationalized form of Confucianism as a form of racial pride (DeBernardi, 1995).

Thus the Straits Chinese participated in the early stages of what Marshall Sahlins has termed the "modern culture movement". Sahlins proposes that this movement is part of a larger process of structural transformation, in which globalization results in the syncretism of traditional with modern elements. At the same time, however, we also find local communities selecting and developing traditional cultural practices—the potlatch or *chingay*, to give two examples—as signs of their difference and uniqueness. He concludes that the process of transformation has resulted in "the formation of a world *system* of cultures, a Culture of cultures—with all the characteristics of a structure of differences" (Sahlins, 1994: 389). We find precisely this kind of systematization of difference in the colonial Straits Settlements.

Indirect rule and the structure of the conjuncture: The Guanyin Temple

How, then, did religious differences become allied to political and ethnic differences in the period of early modernity? To consider this question, we must examine the structure of the conjuncture between the Chinese community and ethnic others. In multi-ethnic communities, colonial rulers often adopted a policy of indirect rule that empowered community leaders to govern their communities according to their own norms. Consequently, in Chinese diaspora communities in Southeast Asia, the leaders of Chinese sworn brotherhoods and community temples often acted as the "headmen" of their communities (Wong, 1963). For example, under Dutch jurisdiction, Malacca's Cheng Hoon Teng (青云亭) temple became the headquarters for the leaders of the Chinese community known as "Kapitans". Although the British later abolished this office, the president of the temple continued to serve as the head of the Malaccan Chinese community (Tan, 1949: 5–6).

The leadership of the Guanyin Temple played a similar role in Penang. Indeed, the Penang community temple was founded by Chinese immigrants from Malacca, and modelled not upon a temple in China, but rather on the Malaccan temple. Penang Chinese originally named the Guanyin Temple the Cantonese-Hokkien Temple (Kong Hok Kiong; Guangfugong,广富宫), and it served both as a temple and as a community tribunal and council for these two sub-ethnic groups until the 1880s (Khoo, 1993: 150). At that time, Chinese leaders established a new Chinese Town Hall beside the temple to carry out these administrative functions, and worked together to build the current temple, wholly religious in its functions (Poh, 1978: 35). The two still stand side by side as symbols of Penang's Chinese community— the one antique and numinous, the other modern and secular.

While Chinese community leaders were informally linked to the colonial bureaucracy, they also used their popular religious temples to maintain vertical links with members of their ethnic communities. Penang's elite provided financial support to build community institutions like the Guanyin Temple and the Temple of Paradise, a magnificent Buddhist monastery that gained Imperial patronage. Through communal institutions like Penang's Heaven and Earth sworn brotherhood, they also provided leadership and support for the building of public hospitals for lepers and the poor. In supporting these religious and charitable organizations, the Chinese elite translated their wealth into the social capital of honour and face (Weber, 1946: 188–90).

As many have described it, the Chinese in 19th century colonial Malaya engaged in extravagant ritual displays. They did so, however, in a multi-ethnic setting in which sub-ethnic groups defined the boundaries of their social groups through ritualized performances, while displaying the sacrality, affluence, and power of their community to ethnic others. Penang's Guanyin Temple (观音亭) and Singapore's Thian Hock Keng (天福宫) Temple, for example, were the sites for ceremonial occasions on which the Chinese elite displayed signs of its high rank. Jonas Daniel Vaughan noted that these occasions were both "gorgeous" and expensive, and wondered "that such a practical people, whose whole time is devoted to the acquisition of wealth should waste their money upon such absurdities". He concluded, however, that these temple processions were no different from political spectacles of "civilized London", adding that "[t]he writer witnessed the Lord Mayor's show in 1874 and was much struck by its strong resemblance to the Chinese procession in the Straits" (Vaughan, 1971 [1879]: 49).

While the British policy of indirect rule may have enhanced the authority of Chinese community leaders, conflict sharpened awareness of ethnic differences and political inequalities. Take, for example, the Penang riots of 1856, which were sparked when the police tried to dismantle the stage at the Guanyin Temple during a temple festival. Both the Chinese and British communities had built their sacred community centres near the waterfront of central Georgetown, each claiming centrality for its members through the definition of sacred space. But the proximity between the church and the temple led the British Anglicans to complain about the "extraordinary disturbance caused by the Chinese crackers and bombs", which distracted them from their Sunday worship (*Pinang Gazette*, 1863). The Chinese compromised by refraining from celebrating their festivals on Sunday, but since the British also worshipped on other days of the week, the British complaints continued.

In 1856, a new police act empowered the local police to impose restrictions on Chinese celebration of their temple festivals. The police first refused a licence for a popular festival at the Guanyin Temple, then issued a licence for Saturday and Monday (but not Sunday). On Saturday evening, the police demanded that the stage at the Guanyin Temple be dismantled (intending to prevent a stage show performance on Sunday). Since the stage was built on the temple grounds, and not in public space, however, the Chinese refused.

Despite warnings from the leaders of the Cantonese and Hokkien communities, the police insisted on dismantling the stage themselves, and the Chinese fought against this attack on their temple precincts.

The following day, all Chinese shops closed, and the leaders of the Chinese community protested this provocative police action to the colonial Governor. When he refused to investigate their grievances against the police, the leaders, assisted by their lawyer, Jonas Richard Logan, successfully appealed to the Governor-General in India, who rebuked Governor Blundell for his mishandling of the problem. While the local government did impose new restrictions on the performance of Chinese festivals, they proved difficult to enforce.[3]

While the policy of indirect rule empowered the Chinese community, conflicts like these sharpened the identification between ethnicity and religious culture. In 1875, for example, a Chinese Brethren evangelist reported that when he sought to preach on the temple grounds of "the great idol temple of Penang called Koan-im teng" someone associated with the temple attempted to prevent him from teaching the "foreigner's doctrine", arguing that "This ground is the idol's ground, and not the ground of the governor or of the public" (Chiam, 1875: 168). The Chinese evangelist successfully claimed the identity of an ethnic insider to assert his right to remain on this sacred ground (which he argued had been built with donations from the Chinese community). This suggests that race (rather than religion) provided the more profound claim to defining identity. But as a consequence of the Penang riots, the temple precinct came to symbolize an autonomous zone of sacred Chinese space (by contrast with the public space controlled by the British), and further represented a religiously defined division between ethnic insiders and outsiders.[4]

While religious organizations often were formed on a basis of sub-ethnic identity, we also find in these diaspora communities new forms of inter-ethnic collaboration and co-operation. One intriguing example was

---

3   S.S.R. DD33 Annual Report of the Police Force of P W Island and Province Wellesley for 1860–1861. See also S.S.R R32 Governor to Government of India, 21 April 1857 and 28 September 1857; Land grant from the East India Company to the Trustees of the Chinese Temple, 29 December 1838; copy in S.S.R. S25, Item 1170, Government of India to Blundell, 31 July 1857. Historian CM Turnbull concludes that as a consequence of this conflict, many members of the unofficial community began to actively support transfer of control from the Government of India to the Colonial Office in London (1958).

4   For a contemporary study of the history of Penang's Guanyin Temple, see Ong Seng Huat (1999).

the celebration of the Shi'ite festival of Muharram, which was known in Penang as *boria*. In this festival, Malay and Tamil participants wearing mourning dress commemorated the tragic death of their founder, Hussain. Groups enacting the conflict between Sunni and Shi'ite Muslims often would clash in what some regarded as a recreation of the fundamental schism through which the group was formed. But in Penang, the festival performances included not only Shi'ites in "masquerade", but also multi-ethnic groups of "dancers" (who performed competitive "games" in the streets, including one called "Dragon"). In 1859, the dancers included 60 teams of dancers, whom police registration records identified as Bengali, Malay, Hindu, "Kling", Burmese, Portuguese and Chinese. The Chinese contributed two *singha* or lion dance teams of 15 to 20 men, whose stylized cultural performance today represents the quintessence of "Chinese culture" at multicultural festivals worldwide.[5] The Malay dancers performed the *ronggeng*. While we may discern a foreshadowing of contemporary multicultural displays in the Muharram procession, the British found the event alarming, and after restricting its performances in 1861, they prohibited it altogether.

This festival demonstrates, however, that within this ten-day religious event, groups representing different cultural traditions co-operated to display their differences (although sometimes these roving teams of dancers would encounter each other on the streets, and rather than playing games, would fight). In joining these teams of dancers, the young male dancers (many of whom were members of what the British police termed "societies") engaged in displays of their strength and prowess. Indeed, the Penang celebration of Muharram resembles nothing so much as contemporary athletic events in which teams from different countries come together to compete in games (having first agreed upon a common set of rules).

Ritual, cosmology and power:
The Chinese sworn brotherhoods

Let me now discuss another group that used elements from popular religious culture in its ritual practice—Chinese sworn brotherhoods. The immigrant Chinese formed branches of the Heaven and Earth (or Triad)–style groups in the colonial Straits Settlements, but also improvised new forms of sworn brotherhood in the situation of diaspora. In 1844, for example, Straits-born

---

5   S.S.R. DD38 Penang: Letters to the Governor, May 1863–December 1863: 127 (NL604).

Hokkien Chinese who broke away from the Ghee Hin organized the God of Prosperity (Toa Pek Kong; Dabogong,大伯公) or Kien Tek (Jiande,建德) sworn brotherhood (Penang Riots Enquiry, Vol III: 20; Blythe, 1969: 75). Like the leadership of community temples, the leaders of the sworn brotherhoods were held responsible by the Europeans to control their followers, and often acted as colonial agents (see, for example, Trocki, 1990).

The sworn brotherhoods initiated new members (usually recent immigrants to the Straits Settlements) with an impressive, lengthy ritual performance that introduced the initiates to the group's authority structure, symbols, social rules and secret signs of recognition.[6] According to the founders of Penang's God of Prosperity sworn brotherhood, in writing down their shared code of conduct—which their leaders enforced in a temple courtroom—they imitated "the mode, by which an Emperor would regulate an Empire".[7] The inventors of their ritual process appropriated symbols of imperial authority to sacralize their social contract and to claim divinely sanctioned authority for their leaders (see also DeBernardi, 1993; 2003).

At the same time that the sworn brotherhoods defined strict boundaries between insiders and outsiders, these groups also existed in the structure of the conjuncture with ethnic others. Moreover, like European Freemasonry, the Chinese sworn brotherhoods were groups formed in the early modern period—a period of globalization, sojourning, and increasing contact with ethnic others that led many to propose new forms of cosmopolitanism.

For example, European Freemasonry initially brought together three of Great Britain's ethnic groups—English, Irish and Scots.[8] But in the early 19th century, the Masons "de-Christianized" their ritual practices and membership rules to allow a broader base for membership in the global networks of capitalism. The Masons required potential members to practise a religion with a monotheistic basis, and initiates took the group's membership oath on the sacred book of their religious tradition. In the Straits Settlements, Muslims and Parsis (who practised the Zoroastrian religion) were early members, but Buddhists were excluded as a consequence of their apparent

---

6   Nineteenth-century descriptions of the Heaven and Earth Society ritual of initiation include Abdullah, 1852; 1970 [1849]; Milne, 1845 [1826]; Newbold and Wilson ,1840–41; Pickering, 1878b; 1879; Schlegel, 1991 [1866]; Vaughan, 1971 [1879]; Ward and Stirling, 1977 [1925]; Williams, 1849). See also Blythe, 1969.

7   Penang Riots Enquiry, Volume III. *Minutes of Evidence Taken Before the Commissioners Under the Penang Riots Enquiry Act of 1867*: 23 (abbreviated below as "PRE").

8   For overviews of European Freemasonry, see Margaret Jacob (1981; 1991) and Steven C Bullock (1996).

"atheism" (Haffner, 1988 [1977]: 72). European authors like Gustave Schlegel noted, however, that members of the Heaven and Earth Society worshipped the Lord of Heaven without the mediation of the emperor, and consequently concluded that they were monotheists (Schlegel, 1991 [1866]: 5). Hints in the historical record suggest that European Masons recognized the Ghee Hin as a Masonic group, and on that basis allowed Ghee Hin leaders the privilege of visiting their lodge.[9]

Like European Masons, the Chinese sworn brotherhoods also allowed non-Chinese to join their groups (although membership appears to have been confined to Asians). Indeed, many early reports of the groups came from Muslims who took lightly their oath of secrecy since it was sworn before Chinese gods, and several Malays shared details of the sworn brotherhood's ritual process with curious European friends.[10] Moreover, although the Heaven and Earth Society was deeply Chinese in its symbolic practice, the groups sometimes recruited non-Chinese members on the basis of residence. For example, one Indian whom the police interrogated after the Penang riots of 1857, reported that members invited him to join the Ghee Hin after he had been robbed, promoting it as a more effective form of protection than the local police could offer. He underwent the lengthy ritual of initiation, and while he understood little of the ritual Master's performance, he comprehended the social and financial commitments that he undertook by joining.

Moreover, like the European Masons, the Chinese apparently encouraged Malays and Indians to form their own sworn brotherhoods, with ritual practices based upon their own cultural traditions. This ensured that the oath would have sacrality and binding force for Muslim initiates, just as an oath before Chinese deities did for Chinese initiates. William G Stirling reports, for example, that:

---

9   One missionary noted that "[t]he English, instead of destroying these secret societies, have tried to introduce Masonic elements among the Chinese freemasonry; and many respectable merchants among them generally frequent the lodge of the place where they are" (Pickering, 1878a: 21). This suggests that in the Straits Settlements Freemasons might have encouraged Chinese to form Masonic lodges, or to 'improve' existing sworn brotherhoods with Masonic elements, and then invited the leaders (the so-called 'respectable' Chinese) to visit their lodges. Similar practices are well attested in North America, where some Freemasons recognized Chinese sworn brotherhoods as kindred Masonic lodges. As a consequence, Chinese in North America adopted the name "Freemasons" and even used the Masonic symbol on the exterior of their lodges (Lyman, 1964).
10 See, for example, Vaughan (1971 [1879]).

> In swearing in Malays, the Koran was placed on the candidate's head and with the arms held aloft he repeated the following oath, "If I betray the secrets of this Society, may the Koran devour my entrails." A cup of blood from the drops taken from candidates' fingers was sometimes mixed with milk, as emblematic of mother's milk and foster brotherhood (Stirling, 1925: 60).

In answer to the question, "Who is your mother?", members were to answer "The Red Flag Society" (Stirling, 1925: 58). In translating their ritual practices into Malay religious and cultural forms, the sworn brotherhoods used the same approach as the British did in their courts of law and their Masonic lodges, in which they ensured truthfulness by having the individual swear an oath on the sacred book of his own religious tradition.

The long period of tolerance of the sworn brotherhoods came to an end in 1890, when the British government outlawed the groups, fearing that the sworn brotherhoods had become an "empire within the empire". In their defence, Penang Ghee Hin members argued in a memorial (presented to the British government as a petition) that the Ghee Hin's role was as much a product of British policy as Chinese inclination:

> Your memorialists venture to call attention to the fact that if under the former Registration acts certain control was allowed to the headmen of these Societies the exercise of which might have given rise to the allegations that they claimed an "imperium in imperio"; on the other hand grave responsibility was cast on them—a responsibility as to the use and exercise of which they appeal with confidence to the fact, and which has been successfully used in the preservations of order and the safety of the State.[11]

The headmen of the sworn brotherhoods may have used "traditional" Chinese materials to construct their authority, but they also reinvented their institutions to serve the needs of a multi-ethnic diaspora community in the colonial contact zone.

The Temple of Paradise

Perhaps coincidentally, in the same period in which the sworn brotherhoods were outlawed, the Chinese community in Penang launched two building projects—construction of a Chinese Town Hall next to the Guanyin Temple, and the building of the Temple of Paradise. Completion of the monumental Buddhist Temple of Paradise (Hokkien: Kek Lok Si, 极乐寺) in Penang in

---

11 CO 273/159 (March–April 1889) No. 10582 ("Societies Ordinance"), "Memorial from the Trustees and Headmen of the Ghee Hin Society in Penang and Province Wellesley and other residents in the Settlements regarding the Societies Ordinance": 570.

1904 unquestionably expressed the growing affluence and modernity of this diaspora community. In sacralizing the landscape with this impressive religious architecture, the wealthy Chinese elite created a new centre of symbolic power that merged the religious and the political (Cartier, 1997: 566).

This temple was so extraordinary an architectural achievement that the Chinese government invited the temple's chief monk to Beijing, and he returned with an Imperial gift of 7,000 volumes of Buddhist "psalms" and other sacred works. He also brought back an Imperial edict that constituted "the Chinese Temple at Air Etam the Head of all Chinese Temples in Penang", and which conferred upon him the "dignity of Chief Priest of Penang" (*Straits Echo Mail Edition*, 1905). The Chinese community celebrated the event with a grand-scale procession that proceeded from the Chinese Town Hall in Georgetown to the Temple of Paradise in Ayer Itam. Participants carried the Imperial warrant in a sedan chair, and transported the Buddhist sutras and scriptures in eight pony-drawn carriages. Also present were Penang's prominent citizens, who wore Mandarin costume for the occasion.

The Temple of Paradise dazzled the European community, whose members had tended to disparage Chinese popular religious culture as messy and superstitious idol worship. One journalist described the temple as "beautiful and unique", adding that "[i]t has cost a great deal of money, chiefly subscribed by the Penang and Straits Chinese, to whom it is a distinct credit" (*Straits Echo*, 18 February 1904). And in 1927 a missionary noted:

> Sad is the sight of a Chinese Buddhist town temple. ... How different is this city temple from the great Kek Lok Si Monastery at Ayer Itam, Penang, where all is clean and orderly, where visitors are requested to "compose yourselves like gentlemen," and are reminded of the priests' vow of poverty. Here in Singapore everything is dirty and the beauties of the place are marred by tawdry decorations and paper images scattered among the bronze and marble works of art. ... (Semple, 1927: 37–38; cited in Purcell, 1967 [1948]: 140).

This lavish construction undoubtedly elevated the status of Chinese religion in the eyes of ethnic others who had tended to decry it as superstitious and idolatrous, at the same time that it won the highest level of recognition for the community and its religious leadership from the Imperial government. And here we find another significant dimension to the "structure of the conjunction" that still informs social action in Malaysia—the use of monumental architecture in rivalrous communal display.

The Modern Period

In 20th-century Malaysia, modernity became linked with the post-colonial development of the nation-state, and the reinvention of traditions (rather than their demise). In the modern period, religious structures and practices often have provided traditional containers for new social and ideological contents, including most conspicuously nationalist and ethnic identities that are so prominent a feature of the contemporary world (Eisenstadt and Schluchter, 1998).

In the modern Malaysian state, ethnic nationalism—enacted through constitutional guarantees and government policies—has significantly informed the relationship between Malaysia's diverse ethnic groups. Both the Malaysian constitution and the *Rukunegara* (Rule of Law) blend together elements of two distinct forms of nationalism that Anthony D Smith describes as "territorial" and "ethnic". A territorial nation is defined by "a definite, compact territorial homeland; common legal codes and the equality of all members before the law; the social and political rights of citizenship; and a shared 'civic religion' and mass, public culture" (Smith, 1999: 190). The fourth principle of the *Rukunegara* affirms the equality of all citizens, while the fifth principle ("Good Behaviour and Morality") suggests that citizenship should transcend communal identity.

The *Rukunegara* also emphatically affirms, however, the principle of ethnic nationalism, describing the nation as a community of culture and history whose bonds are almost familial. In promulgating the *Rukunegara* in 1970, the government stressed that the Constitution upholds the special position of "the Rulers, the position of Islam as the official religion, and the position of Malays and other Natives". While the *Rukunegara* also affirms "the legitimate interest of other communities" whose members are now citizens in the new nation-state, nonetheless Malay language, culture and religion (rather than a shared civic religion) define the nation.[12]

In the new nationalistic structure of the conjuncture, many Malaysian Chinese feared that they would not be able to transmit their language, culture, and religious traditions to future generations (see DeBernardi, 2003). After the racial violence of the 1969 May 13th Crisis and the subsequent enactment of the 1970 National Economic Policy—a programme of affirmative action for the Malay population that disadvantaged the Chinese—some Chinese leaders sought strategies by which to "bring Chinese ideas inside" the ruling Barisan Nasional government. In the early 1970s, Penang Chinese leaders'

---

12 See also Gordon Means, 1976 [1970]: 401–03.

strategies included the launching of a social movement with the slogan *huaren datuanjie* (华人大团结, or "Chinese great unity"). While Penang's Chief Minister Lim Chong Eu—a Gerakan party leader—played an important role in this movement, its organizers sought to subordinate political party divisions to the need for greater unity.[13]

Consequently, Penang's leaders sought to develop a spirit of shared purpose among the Chinese by raising funds in support of local community projects, including the renovation of a rural Chinese school, the development of a private Chinese hospital, and, most importantly, the building of a new Chinese Town Hall, which one fundraiser described as "the leading community centre for the Penang Chinese, and a symbol of our unity". In 1983, the new Town Hall hosted its first major event—the pan-Malaysian Chinese conference of Chinese guilds and associations to endorse a Joint Memorandum on National Culture that they presented to the government later that year. In that memorandum, the authors challenged the government's policy of basing Malaysian national culture on Malay culture alone, arguing that national culture should instead be based on the "culture of all ethnic groups" (*Joint Memorandum on National Culture*, reprinted in Kua, 1990: 210–11).[14]

As one means to co-ordinate fundraising for community projects (including the Chinese Town Hall), Penang's Chinese leadership turned to a popular religious "grass roots" organization—the Daoist Central (or "Hungry Ghosts") Festival. In its traditional form, this festival divided the Penang Chinese into a number of distinct market areas and neighbourhoods, each celebrating the event on a rotating basis throughout the seventh lunar month. In 1973 and 1974, however, the organizers proposed drawing together the diverse local festival committees to form a new "Penang Central Festival Representative Committee". In 1975, the organizers produced a set of bylaws that stipulated that the co-ordinating committee would consist of 30 elected representatives drawn from the approximately 130 participating street and area committees.[15] As one of

---

13 Interview with Chang Yong Mee (5 July 2001). Raj Vasil reported that in 1971, a Chinese Unity Movement emerged with the goal to "instil the spirit of unity among Malaysian Chinese so that they can play their role effectively in nation-building" (*The Straits Times*, 17 April 1971, cited in Vasil, 1980: 203; see also Loh, 1982, for an analysis of the politics of Chinese unity in the early 1970s focusing on the Malaysian Chinese Association).
14 See also the report of this event in a 1983 commemorative volume published by the Penang Chinese Town Hall, entitled "Quanguo Huaren Wenhua Dahui"(All-Malaysia Chinese Culture General Meeting).
15 *Binjou Qingzan Zhongyuanjie Weiyuanhui Zhangcheng* (Bylaws of the Representative Committee for Penang's Celebration of the Central Festival), enacted in 1975.

the group's patrons described it, the new Representative Committee "collected" local-level organizations into a "large, united, leading organization" that brought together members of all social classes in support of charitable goals and Chinese education (Lin, 1979). In creating this centralized structure, the modernist organizers hoped to refocus the meaning of the event from the ritual placation of ghosts to the support of collective charitable goals.

The Central Festival Representative Committee raised funds for these projects during the annual street celebrations as they unfolded throughout Penang during the seventh lunar month, but, more importantly, at the banquets that concluded the festivities. The festival co-ordinators invited politicians and wealthy members of the community to attend these banquets as guests of honour, calling upon them to sing Mandarin songs, make speeches, and publicly donate a contribution to that year's fundraising effort. One of the advisors to the Central Festival Representative Committee, State Assemblyman Khor Gark Kim (also a member of Gerakan), noted that the "excellence" of the event lay not in its Daoist religious aspect (with its "undesirable, rustic customs and the superstitious placation of ghosts"), but rather in its structure as a "territorial organization to which the people have entrusted their souls". He concluded that Penangites had "poured new life into this local organization", generating an "active" form of unity that brought together people of all social classes and political parties in support of concrete goals (Khor, 1979).[16]

While the reorganized Central Festival used a traditional popular religious structure to tap Penangites' public-spirited generosity (and promote Chinese unity), rivalry between Chinese and Malay communities played out in the idiom of monumental religious symbols. In the late 1970s, for example, the government appropriated land from a Chinese-medium school in order to build an elegant new State Mosque in a centrally located and highly visible location at the junction of the road leading to the Temple of Paradise. Penang Chinese often complained about this expropriation, but would add that the Chinese were raising funds to build a monumental 1.2 million dollar statue of the Goddess of Mercy on a hillside above the Temple of Paradise. They invariably added the fact that this new statue would be "taller than the new State Mosque", and someone spread the rumour that Muslims praying in the new Mosque would face the Goddess of Mercy statue when they prayed towards Mecca (a rumour that proved to be false). Finally, Penang's Municipal

---

16 Khor Gark Kim noted in an interview, however, that while their fundraising efforts had been very successful, they had not succeeded in convincing Penangites to spend less on ritual offerings and the performance of costly rites of passage like marriage and funerals (interview, 1 June 1980).

Council objected to its construction, and the statue (which already was partly built) was shortened (Kua, 1992: 77). Consequently, while the Guanyin statue was an imposing presence on the hillside above the Buddhist Temple, the statue was *not* taller than the State Mosque.[17]

More recently, Vision 2020 proposes new secular symbols of social unity that promise to mute the nationalist agenda that has informed Malaysian politics since independence. The opening ceremonies of the 1998 Commonwealth Games, for example, presented a dramatic interpretation of Malaysia's history that climaxed with futuristic images of Vision 2020. The first vignette in this dance-drama described the Malay peoples as "peaceful but not united", but sharing traditional community ties and culture. The beautifully costumed dancers demonstrated their cultural harmony in diversity in the performance of five traditional dances (including the *ronggeng*). The second vignette presented Malaysian history after the 16th century as a period of turmoil and disruption. Huge, menacing dragons towered over the dancers, and the narration identified these dragons as representing Dutch, Portuguese, British and Japanese imperialism. Curiously, although the dragons evoked China rather than Europe, the narration did not mention Chinese (or Indian) immigration into Malaysia in the colonial period. With independence, Malaysians (now wearing silver overalls and red sequined caps) drove the dragons away. In the final vignette, the dancers celebrated technology and Malaysia's plans for a Multimedia Supercorridor wearing futuristic costumes, while the narration announced that "development was the key to unity and progress". While the dance drama represented a desire for "unity and progress", its creators also muted ethnic differences in order to represent Malaysia to the rest of the world as a unified (rather than multicultural) society.

This visionary image presents a "future" that the government is seeking to promote in the present. The government encourages Malaysians to celebrate public holidays like Chinese New Year and Hari Raya with open houses and street parties that are ethnically inclusive, which suggests a retreat from communal agendas (Carstens, 1999). For example in 1999, the Penang State Government organized a secular, multicultural "street party" that gathered 10,000 participants in Georgetown's heritage area to celebrate Chinese New Year (Suthakar, 1998; *Utusan Express*, 1998).

---

17 Because the structure began to disintegrate, the statue built in the 1980s has now been replaced with a much grander new statue. For a history of Kek Lok Si that includes discussion of more recent developments like the construction of the Guanyin statue, see the commemorative volume published in 1993. See Ji Le Si (1993).

The Malaysian government also pursues the goal of "unity and progress" through forms of social engineering. For example, non-Islamic religious organizations complain that the government severely restricts the construction of new religious buildings, while conspicuously sponsoring the construction of mosques and extravagant monuments to modernity like the Petronas Towers and the new Shah Alam Airport. As a consequence of these policies, few non-Islamic religious groups are permitted to build in newer areas of development. As I discuss elsewhere, the festival events of Penang Chinese local religious culture structure an experience of community in the symbolic media of space, time and social memory (DeBernardi, 1992; 2003). Without access to land on which to build new temples, the Chinese can no longer easily reproduce traditionally constructed neighbourhoods using the symbolic idioms and ritual practices of Chinese local religious culture.[18] In progressive, multi-cultural Malaysia, however, these traditionally constructed neighbourhoods have receded in importance, replaced by modern housing estates and urban high-rise apartments. At the same time, a new generation of educated Chinese often elect modern, rationalized forms of religious practice over the more localized forms of popular religious culture. Consequently, many now join modernized world religions like Mahayana Buddhism or evangelical Christianity that link them into networks with global scope.[19]

In response to these challenges, Daoists now seek to rationalize their image and promote their religion. For example, the United General Assembly of Malaysian Daoist Organizations now sponsors a Religious Culture Research Centre that produces and distributes Mandarin publications on Daoism and popular religious culture. The authors of these books and pamphlets seek to demonstrate Daoism's systematic, logical nature while exploring Daoism and popular religious culture's deep historical roots in China.[20] At the same

---

18 With the liberalization of government policy in the mid-1990s, this situation appears to be changing. For instance, with the support of the MCA, Chinese in Bagan Jermal were able to draw on government funding to construct a new Nine Emperor Gods Temple (*The Star*, 24 November 1999).

19 For analysis of the appeal of world religions like Buddhism and Christianity for contemporary Malaysian Chinese, see Judith Nagata, 1991; 1995; 1999. Other studies of the modernization of these world religions in contemporary Malaysia include Raymond LM Lee and Susan Ackerman, 1997; and Ackerman, 1984; 1993.

20 See, for example, current Religious Culture Research Centre director Ong Seng Huat's study of the worship of Xuantian Dadi, which explains the historical origins of worship of the popular saint (nd), and his recent book on Chinese popular festivals (Ong, 2001). See also Chen Yao Ting's pamphlet-length studies of Daoist history, gods and immortals (nd).

time, members of popular religious temples increasingly demonstrate pride in their history and heritage through the publication of handsomely produced commemorative volumes.[21]

Conclusion

In contemporary Malaysia, religion has provided a fulcrum for identity formation in a modern nation-state whose majority ethnic population defines its identity in religious terms. Religious practices mark boundaries between insiders and outsiders in the idiom of the sacred, but they also link members of this diaspora community with the form and content of Chinese civilization. Most strikingly, Chinese temples provide sites of cultural authentication for members of a complex community who often derive a sense of identity from their history and their relationship to the prestigious forms of Chinese culture.

While popular temples may provide signs of traditional Chinese culture for members of this cultural hybrid diaspora community, the sacred spaces, ritual practices and narratives of popular religious culture also localize the Chinese, transmitting the social memory of their experiences in Malaysia. For example, Malaysian Chinese still recall their community's conflict with China's last ruling dynasty when they worship the Lord of Heaven, but they also transmit the social memory of competition with the British for the control of public space, and the racial violence of the May 13th riots. Their stories interpret the "structure of the conjuncture" not as historical events, however, but rather in archetypally constructed narratives that explain the outcome of events in light of geomantic forces, spiritual warfare magic and divine preferment.

In Penang, for example, one spirit medium recalled conflict between British and Chinese communities over the control of space, claiming that

---

21 For example, on the occasion of their centenary, Poh Hok Seah (the temple that once housed the God of Prosperity sworn brotherhood that the British outlawed in 1890) documented their history and ritual practices in a handsome bilingual commemorative volume (*Poh Hock Seah Centenary 1890–1990*), while the Penang Guanyin Temple recently published a book tracing their history [Ong 1999]). The Penang Heritage Trust—a group that seeks to protect Penang's cultural heritage and to win UNESCO recognition for Penang as a World Heritage Site—also sponsors activities and conferences that sometimes lend synergistic support to the Chinese community's commitment to the preservation of its popular religious culture. For a detailed consideration of the Penang Heritage Movement, see Nagata 2001.

the British attacked the geomancy of the Guanyin Temple by building a well (an attack on earth) and a clock tower (an attack on heaven). Construction of the well killed the stone lions in front of the temple—they could no longer run to the seaside to play. But Guanyin took care of the clock—it failed to block her prescient view of the sea (and never struck the hour correctly). The inventor of this story translated Chinese struggles with the British for control of public space (which took many forms over many decades) into a single archetypal narrative, a narrative that interprets this conflict as a battle for geomantic control of Penang's landscape.[22] While participation in world religions may have greater appeal for many contemporary Malaysian Chinese, nonetheless popular religious culture continues to transmit social memory in the aesthetically compelling forms of architecture, icon and story.

In this article, I have considered the way that Chinese religion has existed in the structure of the conjuncture between community insiders and outsiders. In the context of diaspora, Chinese sacred sites became sites that defined cultural authenticity and autonomy, and symbols of "traditional China" for a community undergoing social change. At present, the antiquity of Malaysian Chinese temples offers tangible proof of the depth of Chinese roots that stand against the stereotype that they are merely sojourners and birds of passage.

References

Official records

Records of the Government of the Straits Settlements. Singapore: National Library.

Indian Administration—Straits Settlements Records (SSR)

Series DD Letters from Resident Councillor of Penang to Governor, 1833–1866.
Series R Governor's Despatches to Bengal, 1831–1867.
Series S Bengal Letters to Governor, 1830–1866.

Straits Settlements Government, Miscellaneous

Minutes of Evidence Taken Before the Commissioners under the Penang Riots Enquiry Act of 1867, sitting in the Office of the Public Works Department, Beach Street, George Town, Penang, Monday, 26 August 1867 [abbreviated PRE].

---

22 For a detailed analysis of some of these conflicts as they developed in Singapore, see Brenda Yeoh, 1996.

Colonial Office Records. London: Public Record Office.
CO 273 Series. Straits Settlements, Original Correspondence.

Books and articles

Abdullah bin Abdul Kadir. "Concerning the Tan Tae Hoey in Singapore". Translated by T Braddell. *Journal of the Indian Archipelago and Eastern Asia* 6 (1852): 545–55.

_____. *The Hikayat Abdullah: An annotated translation*. Translated by AH Hill. Kuala Lumpur: Oxford University Press, 1970 [1849].

Ackerman, Susan E. "Experimentation and Renewal among Malaysian Christians: The Charismatic Movement in Kuala Lumpur and Petaling Jaya". *The Southeast Asian Journal of Social Science* 12 (1) (1984): 35–48.

_____. "Rebuilding Sacred Worlds: Lay-oriented Buddhism and Catholic Reformism in Malaysia". *Sojourn* 8 (1) (1993): 128–52.

Binjou Gejiequ Qingzan Zhongyuanjie wei Hanmin Huaxiao Choumu Zhongjian Jijin Weixinlu (槟州各街区庆赞中元节为汉民华小筹募重建基金微信录, Penang All-Locations Celebrating the Central Festival on behalf of Hanmin Chinese Elementary School Donation Fund Small Commemorative Publication). Penang, 1979.

Binjou Qingzan Zhongyuanjie Weiyuanhui Zhangcheng (槟州庆赞中元节委员会章程, Bylaws of the Representative Committee for Penang's Celebration of the Central Festival). Penang, 1975.

Blythe, Wilfred L. *The Impact of Chinese Secret Societies in Malaya: A Historical Study*. Kuala Lumpur: Oxford University Press, 1969.

Bullock, Steven C. "Review Essay: Initiating the Enlightenment? Recent Scholarship on European Freemasonry". *Eighteenth-Century Life* 20 (1) (1996): 80–92. <http://muse.jhu.edu/demo/ecl/20.1er_stevenson.html>

Carstens, Sharon. "Dancing Lions and Disappearing History: The National Culture Debates and Chinese Malaysian Culture". *Crossroads: An Interdisciplinary Journal of Southeast Asian Studies* 13 (1) (1999): 11–64.

Cartier, Carolyn L. "The Dead, Place/Space, and Social Activism: Constructing the Nationscape in Historic Melaka". *Environment and Planning D: Society and Space* 15 (1997): 555–86.

Chen, Yao Ting (陈耀庭). *Daojiao Jianshi ji qi Shenxian Xitong* (道教简史及其神仙系统, A Brief History of the Daoist Religion Including the System of Gods and Immortals). Kuala Lumpur: Malaixiya Daojiao Zuzhi Lianhe Zonghui/Zongjiao Wenhua Yanjiu Zhongxin, nd.

Chiam, Kim Kak. "Letter from Penang". *Echoes of Service*, December 1875.

Comaroff, John, and Jean Comaroff. *Of Revelation and Evolution: The Dialectics of Modernity on a South African Frontier* (vol II). Chicago: University of Chicago Press, 1997.

DeBernardi, Jean. "Space and Time in Chinese Religious Culture". *History of Religions* 31 (3) (1992): 247–68.

    ―――. "Epilogue: Ritual Process Reconsidered". In *"Secret Societies" Reconsidered: Perspectives on the Social History of Modern South China and Southeast Asia*, edited by David Ownby and Mary Somers Heidhues, pp 212–33. Armonck, New York: ME Sharpe, 1993.

    ―――. "Lim Boon Keng and the Invention of Cosmopolitanism". In *Managing Change in Southeast Asia: Local Identities, Global Connections* (CCSEAS XXI), edited by Jean DeBernardi, Gregory Forth and Sandra Niessen, pp 173–87. Edmonton: Canadian Council for Southeast Asian Studies, 1995.

    ―――. *Penang Chinese Religion: Memory, Modernity, and the Politics of Unity under Empire and Nation-State*. Stanford: Stanford University Press, 2003.

Eisenstadt, Shmuel N, and Wolfgang Schluchter. "Introduction: Paths to Early Modernities—A Comparative View". *Daedalus* 127 (3) (1998): 1–18.

Haffner, Christopher. *The Craft in the East*. Hong Kong: District Grand Lodge of Hong Kong and the Far East, 1988 [1977].

Jacob, Margaret C. *The Radical Enlightenment: Pantheists, Freemasons and Republicans*. London: George Allen and Unwin, 1981.

    ―――. *Living the Enlightenment: Freemasonry and Politics in Eighteenth-Century Europe*. New York: Oxford University Press, 1991.

Ji Le Si Qingzu Kaishan Yilingyi Zhounian (极乐寺庆祝开山一零一周年, or Kek Lok Si Celebrates the One Hundred and First Anniversary of Its Cutting into the Mountain). Penang: Ji Le Si, 1993.

Khoo, Su Nin. *Streets of Georgetown, Penang: An Illustrated Guide to Penang's City Streets and Historic Attractions*. Penang: Janus Print and Resources, 1993.

Khor, Gark Kim (许岳金). "Congratulatory Address". In *Binjou Gejiequ Qingzan Zhongyuanjie Weixinlu* (Penang All-Locations Celebrating the Central Festival Small Commemorative Publication). Penang, 1979.

Kua, Kia Soong, ed. *Malaysian Cultural Policy and Democracy*. First published in 1985 as *National Culture and Democracy*. Kuala Lumpur: The Resource and Research Centre, Selangor Assembly Hall, 1990.

    ―――. *Malaysian Political Realities*. Petaling Jaya: Oriengroup, 1992.

Lee, Raymond LM, and Susan E Ackerman. *Sacred Tensions: Modernity and Religious Transformation in Malaysia*. Columbia: University of South Carolina Press, 1997.

Lin, Qingjin (林庆金). "Congratulatory Address". In *Binjou Gejie Qingzan Zhongyuanjie wei Hanmin Xiaoxue Choumu Zhongjian Jijin Weixinlu* (Penang All-Locations Celebrating the Central Festival on behalf of Hanmin Chinese Elementary School Donation Fund Small Commemorative Publication). Penang, 1979.

Loh, Kok Wah. *The Politics of Chinese Unity in Malaysia: Reform and Conflict in the Malaysian Chinese Association, 1971–73*. Singapore: Maruzen Asia, 1982.

Lyman, Stanford M. "Chinese Secret Societies in the Occident: Notes and Suggestions for Research in the Sociology of Secrecy". *Canadian Review of Sociology and Anthropology* 1 (2) (1964): 79–102.

Means, Gordon. *Malaysian Politics*. London: Hodder and Stoughton, 1976 [1970].

Milne, William C. "Some Account of a Secret Society in China Entitled 'The Triad Society'". *Transactions of the Royal Asiatic Society* 1 (1826): 240–50, reprinted in *The Chinese Repository* 14 (2) (Feb 1845): 59–69.

Nagata, Judith. "Local and International Networks among Overseas Chinese in Southeast Asia and Canada". In *The Quality of Life in Southeast Asia: Transforming Social, Political and Natural Environments* (CCSEAS XX), edited by Bruce Matthews, pp 225–81. Montreal: Canadian Council for Southeast Asian Studies, 1991.

———. "Continuity and Change in World Religious Traditions: The Intersection of the Global and Parochial in Malaysian Buddhism". In *Managing Change in Southeast Asia: Local Identities, Global Connections* (CCSEAS XXI), edited by Jean DeBernardi, Gregory Forth and Sandra Niessen. Edmonton: Canadian Council for Southeast Asian Studies, 1995.

———. "The Globalization of Buddhism and the Emergence of Religious Civil Society: The Case of the Taiwanese Fo Kuang Shan Movement in Asia and the West". *Communal/Plural* 7 (2) (1999): 231–48.

———. "Heritage as a Human Right: A New Style and Language of Civil and Community Activism in Penang, Malaysia". Paper prepared for the Annual Meeting of the Association for Asian Studies, March 2001.

Newbold, Lieutenant, and Major-General Wilson. "The Chinese Secret Triad Society of the Tian-ti-huih". *The Journal of the Royal Asiatic Society of Great Britain and Ireland* 6 (1840–41): 120–58.

Ong, Aihwa, and Donald Nonini, eds. *Ungrounded Empires: The Cultural Politics of Modern Chinese Transnationalism*. New York: Routledge, 1997.

Ong, Seng Huat (王琛发). *Huaren Minjian Jieri Yanjiu* (华人民间节日研究, Investigation into Chinese Popular Festivals). Petaling Jaya: Nilai Memorial Park (NS) Sdn Bhd, 2001.

———. *Guangfugong Lishi yu Zhuanqi* (广富宫历史与传奇, History and Biographies of the Cantonese and Hokkien Temple [Kong Hock Keong]). Penang: Xiecheng Yinwu Gongsi (协成印务公司), 1999.

———. *Xuantian Shangdi Xinyang de Yanbian* (玄天上帝信仰的演变, The Development of Belief in the Emperor of the Dark Heavens). Kuala Lumpur: Malaixiya Daojiao Zuzhi Lianhe Zonghui/Zongjiao Wenhua Yanjiu Zhongxin (马来西亚道教组织联合总会／宗教文化研究中心), nd.

———. *Cong Beidou Zhenjun dao Jiuhuang Dadi* (从北斗真君到九皇大帝, From the Perfected Lords of the Northern Bushel to the Nine Emperor Gods). Kuala Lumpur: Malaixiya Daojiao Zuzhi Lianhe Zonghui/Zongjiao Wenhua Yanjiu Zhongxin, nd.

Pickering, WA. 1878a. "Annual Report of the Protector of Chinese for the Year 1878". Published as paper 24 in the *Proceedings of the Legislative Council of the Straits Settlements (with Appendices) for 1880*.

———. 1878b. "The Chinese Secret Societies and Their Origin", Part I. *Journal of the Straits Branch of the Royal Asiatic Society* 1: 63–84.

———. 1879. "The Chinese Secret Societies and Their Origin", Part II. *Journal of the Straits Branch of the Royal Asiatic Society* 3: 1–18.

Pinang Gazette. Notices. 7 March 1863.

Poh, T. *Chinese Temples in Penang*. Penang: Forda, 1978.

Poh Hock Seah Centenary 1890–1990 (宝福社百周年). Penang: Poh Hock Seah, 1990.

Purcell, Victor WWS. *The Chinese in Malaya*. Kuala Lumpur: Oxford University Press, 1967 [1948].

"Quanguo Huaren Wenhua Dahui" (全国华人文化大会, All-Malaysia Chinese Culture General Meeting). In *Binzhou Huaren Dahuitang Qingzhu Chengli Yibai Zhounian: Xinxia Luocheng Kaimu Jinian Tekan* (槟州华人大会堂庆祝成立一百周年:新厦落成开幕纪念特刊, Commemorative Publication of Centenary Celebrations and Inauguration of New Building Penang Chinese Town Hall), pp 320–29. Penang: The Phoenix Press Sdn Bhd, 1983.

Sahlins, Marshall. "Goodbye to Tristes Tropes: Ethnography in the Context of Modern World History". In *Assessing Cultural Anthropology*, edited by Robert Borofsky, pp 377–94. New York: McGraw-Hill, 1994.

Schlegel, Gustave. *Thian Ti Hwui The Hung-League or Heaven-Earth-League: A Secret Society with the Chinese in China and India*. Scotland: Tynron Press, 1991 [1866].

Shellabear, WG. "Baba Malay". In *A Centenary Volume, 1877–1977. Malayan Branch of the Royal Asiatic Society Reprint Number Four,* 36–59. Singapore: Times Printers Sdn Bhd, 1977 [1913].

Smith, Anthony D. *Myths and Memories of the Nation*. Oxford: Oxford University Press, 1999.

Stirling, William G. "The Red and White Flag Societies". *Journal of the Malayan Branch of the Royal Asiatic Society* 3 (1) (April 1925): 57–61.

Straits Echo. 18 February 1904.

Straits Echo Mail Edition. "Air Etam Temple". 20 January 1905: 42.

Suthakar, K. "Penang to hold Feb 22 street party for 10,000". *The Star*, 21 December 1998.

Tan, Chee Beng. *The Baba of Melaka: Culture and Identity of a Chinese Peranakan Community in Malaysia*. Petaling Jaya: Pelanduk Publications, 1988.

Tan, Cheng Lock. "Cheng Hoon Teng Temple". Reprinted from *The Straits Times* of 31 August 1949.

Trocki, Carl A. *Opium and Empire: Chinese Society in Colonial Singapore*. Ithaca: Cornell University Press, 1990.

Turnbull, CM. "Communal Disturbances in the Straits Settlements in 1857". *Journal of the Malayan Branch of the Royal Asiatic Society* 31 (1) (1958): 94–144.

Utusan Express. "Further Enhance Unity during the Chinese New Year Celebrations". 28 January 1998. <http://www.utusan.com.my/archives>

Vasil, Raj. *Politics in a Plural Society: A Study of Non-Communal Political Parties in West Malaysia.* Kuala Lumpur: Oxford University Press, 1971.

Vaughan, Jonas Daniel. "Notes on the Chinese of Pinang". *Journal of the Indian Archipelago* 8 (1854): 1–27.

———. *The Manners and Customs of the Chinese of the Straits Settlements.* Kuala Lumpur: Oxford University Press, 1971 [1879].

Ward, John Sebastian Marlo, and William G Stirling. *The Hung Society, or the Society of Heaven and Earth,* vol I. Taipei, Republic of China: Southern Materials Center, 1977 [1925].

Weber, Max. "Class, Status, Power". In *From Max Weber: Essays in Sociology,* translated, edited, and with an introduction by HH Gerth and C Wright Mills, pp 180–95. New York: Oxford University Press, 1946.

Williams, W Wells (with the assistance of Johann Hoffman). "Oath Taken by Members of the Triad Society, and Notices of Its Origins". *Chinese Repository* 18 (1849): 281–95.

Wong, Choon San. *A Gallery of Chinese Kapitans.* Singapore: Dewan Bahasa Dan Kebudayaan Kebangsaan/Ministry of Culture, 1963.

Yeoh, Brenda SA. *Contesting Space: Power Relations and the Urban Build Environment in Colonial Singapore.* Kuala Lumpur: Oxford University Press, 1996.

Chapter 15

RELIGIOUS COMPOSITION OF THE CHINESE IN SINGAPORE: SOME COMMENTS ON THE CENSUS 2000

Choong Chee Pang

Introduction

The Singapore government has conducted a census of population which includes religion every ten years since 1980. The seriousness with which the government takes religion in this multireligious nation is clearly indicated in the fact that in August 1987, the Ministry of Community Development took a rather unusual action to commission a research team from the National University of Singapore (NUS) to do a research project on "religion and religious revivalism in Singapore". The NUS team consisted of Assoc Prof Eddie CY Kuo, Head of the Sociology Department, Assoc Prof Jon ST Quah, Acting Director of the Institute of Policy Studies, and Dr Tong Chee Kiong, Sub Dean and Lecturer in the Faculty of Arts and Social Sciences. Prof Kuo was the Project Coordinator. The major objectives of the Project were as follows:[1]

A   To identify the religious trends in Singapore.

B   To describe the characteristics of those persons who have been attracted to Christianity, and to find out, among the new converts, the reasons for and the process of their conversion.

C   To explore and discuss the extent and nature of religious revivalism and the relevance of anomie as an explanatory factor for religious revivalism in Singapore.

D   To analyse the present status of Taoism and Buddhism, and the category of those persons who claim to have "no religion", and to project their future positions in Singapore.

---

1   See Eddie CY Kuo, Jon ST Quah and Tong Chee Kiong, *Religion and Religious Revivalism in Singapore* (Singapore: Ministry of Community Development, October 1988), pp 2–3.

E   To discuss the social and political implications of the changing religious composition and increased religious revivalism in Singapore.

F   To make recommendations for policy consideration on issues relating to religion in Singapore.

It must be noted that objectives B and E were of particular significance and importance especially because of the perceived "growth" and "revivalism" of Christianity in the 1980s as well as the alleged involvement of some Christian activists in sociopolitical matters. In May 1987, 16 people were arrested for being involved in a "Marxist conspiracy". It was also in this context that the then Prime Minister, Lee Kuan Yew, in his 1987 National Day Rally speech warned religious leaders against mixing religion with politics because "no government was going to stand by and not defend itself when religious groups started to venture into its turf" (*The Straits Times*, 17 August 1987). It is also in the same light that the "timing" of the commissioning of the NUS research team by the Ministry of Community Development in August 1987 is to be perceived.

The yearlong research covered, among others, a literature review,[2] an analysis of the 1980 census data,[3] a case study on trends in traditional Chinese religion,[4] and a national survey.[5] The final report of the research team, *Religion and Religious Revivalism in Singapore*, was published by the Ministry of Community Development in October 1988.

Major Findings of Prof Kuo's 1987–88 Research Team

The following is a summary of the major findings:[6]

1   There has been an impressive growth in the number of Christians since the 1950s, especially among charismatic churches which are attracting

---

2   See Jon ST Quah, *Religion and Religious Conversion in Singapore: A Review of the Literature* (Singapore: Ministry of Community Development, December 1987).
3   See Eddie CY Kuo, *Religion in Singapore: An Analysis of the 1980 Census Data* (Singapore: Ministry of Community Development, December 1987).
4   See Tong Chee Kiong, *Trends in Traditional Chinese in Singapore* (Singapore: Ministry of Community Development, 1988).
5   See Kuo and Quah, *Religion in Singapore: Report of a National Survey* (Singapore: Ministry of Community Development, August 1988).
6   For details see Kuo, Quah and Tong, *Religion and Religious Revivalism in Singapore*, pp 4–9.

a substantial number of young and fervent "born again" converts and they are mostly English-educated.

2   There seems to be a parallel increase in the number of people who belong to the category of "No Religion". They come from both English and Chinese language streams.

3   Concomitantly, followers of the traditional Chinese religion have declined in number, although they still form the largest religious category in Singapore. The term "traditional Chinese religion" was used in the Research Project to refer to the combined categories of "Taoism" and "Buddhism", as defined by the census authority. It is therefore necessary to refer to relevant materials and statistics which indicate that while the number and proportion of Taoists have decreased significantly since 1980, Buddhism seems to be able to hold its ground. The inclusion of Buddhism in the moral/religious education course, among other factors, has facilitated its promotion and drawn attention to it. The fast-growing Buddhist sects such as the Nichiren Shoshu group are clearly another source of Buddhist influence.

It is clear from the above major findings that in the last couple of decades, the three major religious categories which have undergone rapid changes are "Christianity", "No Religion" and "traditional Chinese religion" ("Taoism" and "Buddhism"). In the final report these three categories are also given separate treatment in the form of three case studies. The highlight is obviously that of Christianity.[7]

In the case of Christianity, the Christians and Christian converts are recognized as (1) younger in age, (2) better educated, (3) of higher socio-economic status in terms of occupation, income and housing type, (4) those who have attended mission schools, (5) those who have received an English-stream education, and (6) those who speak English as the dominant home language. In the Report, the researchers note in particular that most, if not all, of these factors also characterize the emergent generation of Singaporeans in general.[8] However, they consider that "the expansion of Christianity will reach a saturation point to be counter-checked by other religious categories such as No Religion and Buddhism". Mr Lee Kuan Yew is quoted as saying that "Singapore is too Asian to become a Christian society".[9]

---

7   Ibid, pp 9–18.
8   Ibid, p 10.
9   Ibid, pp 10–11.

The researchers show particular concern about the "social and political consequences" of the growing trend in Christianity, especially since Christians are already thought to have been "exerting an influence, politically, socially and economically, far greater than the number they represent in the population".[10]

In the case of No Religion, they observe that the non-religionists share some characteristics with the Christians; that is, in age, education and socioeconomic background, as compared with followers of other religions, although when compared with the Christians, the non-religionists are slightly lower in educational level and socioeconomic status. Moreover, the non-religionists also differ from their Christian counterparts in the following aspects: (1) they belong to both the Chinese and English language streams, while the Christians are mostly English-educated; (2) consequently, they are from both Mandarin-speaking and English-speaking families, while the Christians are mostly from English-speaking households, very much unlike the Taoists, who belong mostly to dialect-speaking families; and (3) they are almost exclusively Chinese, while Christian converts are found in all ethnic groups except perhaps the Malay.[11] The researchers believe that those non-religionists who are actually not hard-core atheists or anti-religious "are likely to shift or 'drift' to accept a certain religion (more likely Buddhism) when the psychological need for religious solace is strong (such as at a time of personal crisis)".[12]

In the case of the traditional Chinese religion, the researchers found that recently there has been a trend towards a clearer distinction between Taoism and Buddhism. It was therefore important and necessary to analyse the two separately, following the official categories of the census authority. Latest statistics indicate that there has been a decline in the number and percentage of Taoists in Singapore. The Taoists here are practically all Chinese and they are typically (1) older in age, (2) with relatively low levels of formal education, (3) dialect-speaking and (4) of relatively lower socioeconomic status, when compared with the followers of other religions. They represent the old generation.[13] The Taoists have rituals and traditional practices but not systematic theology and well-structured organization.

The Research Team discovered that unlike Taoism, Buddhism in Singapore has been able to retain its position and grow in the last decade. Its trend towards "intellectualization" has led to a renewed interest in the religion

---

10   Ibid, p 11.
11   Ibid, p 20.
12   Ibid, p 12.
13   Ibid, p 25.

and made it more attractive to the better-educated Chinese. In comparison with Christianity, No Religion and Taoism, there seems to be no significant association between Buddhism and certain demographic variables such as age, educational level and social status. It is therefore a religion for a segment of Chinese of all ages, of different educational levels and from various socioeconomic strata. Well-run meditation courses and talks, systematic and philosophical approach to Buddhist beliefs as well as the inclusion of Buddhism in the Religious Knowledge programme in schools are thought to have contributed significantly to the renewal and growth of Buddhism in recent years.[14] Buddhists have also been increasingly more active in voluntary welfare, social and charitable services, much the same way as their Christian counterparts have been. Young and fervent Buddhists in particular are also far more active now in sharing the faith with their peers and associates. Buddhist students are also consistently engaged in propagating their religion on campuses. Prof Kuo's Research Team thinks that "in the long run, Buddhism may well provide a viable alternative to those young Chinese who find themselves 'too Chinese' to convert to Christianity".[15]

Recommendations of Prof Kuo's Research Team

In view of the rapid changes in the religious composition of the population of Singapore, especially among the Chinese, in the last couple of decades, the final report registers several of the Research Team's concerns. The major concern is obviously the perceived "rapid growth in Christianity" which may affect "the longtime delicate equilibrium of all religions in Singapore".[16] In the case of Christianity, it is not just the numerical and percentage growth that causes concern, but also its "politically-oriented social actions" which are inspired by radical Christian thinking such the Liberation Theology.[17] The Team feels strongly that this and other concerns call for "careful monitoring and handling" and consequently recommends "the creation of an Inter-Religious Council (IRC) to monitor the relations between the different religious groups in Singapore and to minimize friction between them".[18]

It is important to note that although the Team has clearly and repeatedly pointed out the "revival of Buddhism" in its findings, this reality never

---

14   Ibid, p 28.
15   Ibid.
16   Ibid, p 31.
17   Ibid, p 32.
18   Ibid.

seems to be one of its concerns. Moreover, in regard to the traditional Chinese religion, especially Taoism, the Team commends the "timely" effort of the Singapore Federation of Chinese Clan Associations for preparing a manual on Chinese rites and customs and suggests that "greater effort should be directed at promoting Chinese cultural heritage among school students. Chinese traditions can act as a buffer against growing Westernization".[19] As far as the Team is concerned, the perceived expansion of Christianity in Singapore is undoubtedly part of the "growing Westernization" process.

Finally, for "further research" the Team suggests that the effects of the Religious Knowledge programme in schools should be systematically studied and that more data on religion should be gathered in the approaching 1990 population census.[20]

Census of Population, 1990

Following their own suggestions for further research in the October 1988 report, Prof Eddie CY Kuo and Dr Tong Chee Kiong jointly wrote a monograph on the religions of Singapore based on the 1990 census of population. The monograph was published in 1995.

The monograph basically confirms the major findings and reiterates the main concerns of the 1987–88 study, such as the growth and revival of Christianity and Buddhism and the decline of Taoism. Rather predictably, the expansion of Christianity as a "proselytizing religion" continues to be of major concern and is highlighted in the "Summary and Discussion" of the monograph, which concludes with the following statement:

> The findings from the 1990 census on religion show clearly that the religious scene is quickly changing in Singapore. As a result, there are already increasingly more frequent inter-religious contacts between followers of various religions. While the number of converts remains moderate, such religious switching concentrates with the Protestant Christian group. The conversion trend implies shifting of religious boundaries at the societal level. Given the potent force of religion, it is important that the religious issue is handled with sensitivity, at both the individual and the institutional level. Religious harmony is vital to the continuous stability and indeed survival of Singapore, as in all multireligious societies.[21]

---

19   Ibid, pp 41–42.
20   Ibid, pp 44–45.
21   Ibid, p 59.

Religious Composition of the Chinese in Singapore: Some Comments on the Census 2000

In writing this article, I am greatly indebted to Prof Eddie CY Kuo and his fellow researchers for the studies they have made on the religions of Singapore in the 1980s and early 1990s. Some of their major findings, suggestions and recommendations are not only most relevant but also indispensable to this article's comments on the Census 2000. This is because the present article is meant to do nothing much more than simply picking up some of Prof Kuo and his team-mates' major findings and concerns and comparing them with what the data of the Census 2000 show, to see to what extent the religious scene of the Chinese in Singapore has changed, if at all, since the late 1980s. That is why a much larger proportion of the article is devoted to the research of Prof Kuo and his associates rather than to comments on the Census 2000.

The present article's data on the religious composition of the Chinese in Singapore are largely based on the contents of the "Singapore Census of Population, 2000: Advance Data Release No 2 (Religion)", which was published by the Census of Population Office, Singapore Department of Statistics, in November 2000. Here are some comments:

A   Table 1: Resident population aged 15 and over, by religion

	Number			Per cent		
	1980	1990	2000	1980	1990	2000
Total	1,640,078	2,078,842	2,494,630	100.0	100.0	100.0
Christianity	165,586	264,881	364,087	10.1	12.7	14.6
Buddhism	443,517	647,859	1,060,662	27.0	31.2	42.5
Taoism	492,044	465,150	212.344	30.0	22.4	8.5
Islam	258,122	317,937	371,660	15.7	15.3	14.9
Hinduism	58,917	77,789	99,904	3.6	3.7	4.0
Other Religions	8,971	11,604	15,879	0.5	0.6	0.6
No Religion	212,921	293,622	370,094	13.0	14.1	14.8

This table simply gives an overall picture of the religious composition of the whole population from 1980 to 2000, which is not the particular concern of this article except to take note of the fact that Islam and Hinduism have remained rather stable since 1980 and that significant changes have taken place among the Chinese alone, especially in Taoism and Buddhism, and to a lesser degree, in Christianity.

B   **Table 2: Resident population aged 15 years and over, by ethnic group and religion**

Ethnic group/Religion	Per cent		
	1980	1990	2000
Chinese	100.0	100.0	100.0
Christianity	10.9	14.3	16.5
Buddhism	34.3	39.4	53.6
Taoism	38.2	28.4	10.8
Other Religions	0.2	0.3	0.5
No Religion	16.4	17.7	18.6

The first section on the Chinese in Table 2 is the main concern of the paper. The main shift were obviously from Taoism and Buddhism, and not as Prof Kuo and his fellow researchers had earlier anticipated, from Christianity, although they had correctly predicted the continuous decline of Taoism and continuous growth of Buddhism, largely at the expense of the former. Although the shift towards Christianity continued, the growth in proportion of Christians was rather gradual—from 10.9 per cent in 1980 to 14.3 per cent in 1990 and 16.5 per cent in 2000. Table 2 also shows very clearly that the shift towards No Religion was not very significant. When Taoism and Buddhism were taken as a whole and regarded as "the traditional Chinese religion", the proportion of Chinese who followed either Taoism or Buddhism or who made no clear distinction between the two, in fact, declined from 73.5 per cent in 1980 to 67.8 per cent in 1990 and 64.4 per cent in 2000. Reasons and factors for the growth or decline of these religions (and No Religion) remained largely the same in the last two decades or so.

C   *Age and religion*

The 2000 Census quite clearly shows that for the Chinese, the level of religious affiliation was "positively correlated with age: the higher the age, the higher was the level of religious affiliation. Conversely, the younger the age, the higher is the proportion reporting No Religion".[22]

---

22 *Advance Data Release No 2*, p 4.

For example, the Census data indicate that among the Chinese aged 55 and over, about 12 per cent reported No Religion. In contrast, among the younger Chinese aged 15 to 24 years, a higher proportion of 23 per cent reported No Religion. It is also significant that from 1990 to 2000, the proportion of the Chinese reporting No Religion increased across all age groups, with the middle age groups showing the largest increase. For example, for the Chinese aged 35 to 54, those who claimed No Religion increased from 31.4 per cent in 1990 to 35.8 per cent in 2000. This is something that the earlier research of Prof Kuo's Team had not quite expected.

D   *Christianity as the second most important religion of the Chinese*

As Taoism fell to 10.8 per cent among the Chinese according to the Census 2000, Christianity, with 16.5 per cent, replaced Taoism to become the second most important religion of the Chinese in Singapore, although in terms of both percentage and actual number it was very much far behind Buddhism, which claimed 53.6 per cent of the whole Chinese population aged 15 and over (Table 2).

E   *Spread of Buddhism among the better-educated*

This was already anticipated by Prof Kuo's Research Team, which was particularly impressed by the process of "intellectualization" that had taken place, among others, in Buddhism in Singapore. On the other hand, Christianity, which continued to attract some of the better-educated in competition with the category of No Religion, and to a lesser degree, with Buddhism in recent years, actually showed clear signs of decline nationally within each educational group of the adult residents with secondary and higher qualifications.

It is very important to point out that while Christians still form the largest religious group among university graduates, their percentage declined from 39.3 per cent in 1990 to 33.5 per cent in 2000. By a marked contrast, Buddhist graduates very impressively jumped from 15.1 per cent to 23.6 per cent in the same period. In absolute terms, the number of Buddhists actually increased by four times in the last decade, compared with an increase of just about 1.7 times for the Christian graduates. This was also another phenomenon which Prof Kuo's Team seemed not to have expected although it was keenly aware of the potentials which renascent Buddhism in Singapore had in attracting university students and graduates, in competition with Christianity and No Religion.

Table 3: Resident population aged 15 years and over, by religion and highest qualification attained

Religion	Total		Full-time students		Below secondary		Secondary		Post-secondary		University	
	1990	2000	1990	2000	1990	2000	1990	2000	1990	2000	1990	2000
Total	100.0	100.0	100.0	100.0	100.0	100.0	100.0	100.0	100.0	100.0	100.0	100.0
Christianity	12.7	14.6	17.1	14.3	6.3	6.4	16.1	14.6	24.7	20.8	39.3	33.5
Buddhism	31.2	42.5	29.0	37.3	34.1	51.5	30.3	41.6	25.7	38.3	15.1	23.6
Taoism	22.4	8.5	18.2	8.5	29.4	13.2	14.8	5.8	13.0	5.5	7.4	2.7
Islam	15.3	14.9	12.0	16.2	17.1	17.2	17.3	18.9	8.5	11.2	2.6	3.5
Hinduism	3.7	4.0	2.9	3.6	3.9	3.5	3.9	4.1	3.1	3.5	3.5	6.9
Other Religions	0.6	0.6	0.5	0.7	0.5	0.5	0.7	0.7	0.7	0.7	0.9	0.9
No Religion	14.1	14.8	20.3	19.3	8.7	7.7	16.9	14.3	24.4	20.0	31.1	28.9

F *Correlation between religion and language*

Table 4: Resident population aged 15 years and over, by religion and language most frequently spoken at home

Religion	English		Mandarin		Chinese Dialects		Malay		Tamil		Others	
	1990	2000	1990	2000	1990	2000	1990	2000	1990	2000	1990	2000
Total	100.0	100.0	100.0	100.0	100.0	100.0	100.0	100.0	100.0	100.0	100.0	100.0
Christianity	39.2	39.8	8.2	8.3	8.2	9.9	0.7	0.7	8.2	6.7	11.1	11.1
Buddhism	21.2	24.8	43.1	60.0	43.2	1.0	0.4	0.2	0.1	0.1	3.7	10.3
Taoism	7.2	2.2	26.7	11.2	36.0	15.5	0.2	0.0	0.0	0.0	0.1	0.5
Islam	6.1	7.1	0.0	0.0	0.0	0.0	98.2	98.8	16.5	17.9	15.2	16.3
Hinduism	5.3	5.4	0.0	0.0	0.0	0.0	0.2	0.1	74.7	75.0	38.9	43.6
Other Religions	1.4	1.5	0.1	0.2	0.1	0.2	0.0	0.0	0.2	0.1	26.1	14.7
No Religion	19.5	19.2	21.8	20.3	12.5	13.3	0.3	0.1	0.3	0.2	4.9	3.5

Strong correlation between religion and language in Singapore has long been acknowledged by people who are interested in the religion of Singapore, including Prof Kuo's Research Team. The 2000 Census simply confirms this indisputable observation. The latest Census shows clearly that Christians still form the largest group among the English-speaking population nationally while Taoism and Buddhism, the traditional Chinese religions, remain the main religions of the Mandarin- and dialect-speaking populations.

G *Religious affiliation and socioeconomic strata*

Prof Kuo's Research Team has already rightly noted the correlation between religious affiliation and socioeconomic strata. The 2000 Census data quite clearly show that Christians and people of No Religion seem to belong to the higher socioeconomic strata, judging from the types of housing they occupy (Table 5).

Table 5: Resident population aged 15 years and over, by religion and type of dwelling

Religion	HDB 1–2 rooms		HDB 3 rooms		HDB 4 rooms		HDB 5 rooms or executive		Private flats & houses	
	1990	2000	1990	2000	1990	2000	1990	2000	1990	2000
Total	100.0	100.0	100.0	100.0	100.0	100.0	100.0	100.0	100.0	100.0
Christianity	5.5	6.8	8.0	9.7	10.0	10.2	20.3	17.4	30.0	34.3
Buddhism	27.8	41.8	32.2	46.3	34.1	46.3	29.4	39.5	26.1	30.1
Taoism	32.7	11.8	25.1	10.5	23.2	9.8	15.3	6.4	13.2	4.2
Islam	16.1	23.7	19.9	16.7	16.2	17.4	11.9	14.3	3.3	2.8
Hinduism	4.7	5.2	3.3	3.9	3.7	3.9	4.0	4.2	3.7	3.6
Other Religions	0.3	0.4	0.4	0.5	0.6	0.5	0.7	0.8	0.9	0.9
No Religion	12.8	10.5	11.1	12.5	12.2	11.9	18.4	17.4	22.9	24.2

Again, it is significant to point out that in terms of percentage, the number of Christians, Buddhists, and people of No Religion who occupy private flats and houses have *all* increased, and not just the Christians alone. It looks as if these three categories of people will continue to 'compete' in this as well as in other areas.

Conclusion

The religious composition of the Chinese in Singapore is a very complex issue. The 2000 Census data on religion have yet to be more thoroughly and critically examined. The scope of this article is admittedly very limited since it is largely based on the information that comes from *Advance Data Release No 2*. The focus of Prof Kuo's Research Team was clearly on Christianity, which is very understandable given the particular sociopolitical context of the 1980s. It is therefore not at all surprising that the team specially highlighted the "social and political implications" of the perceived expansion of Christianity. But that was some 12 years ago. In the 2000 Census, the focus was, or should have been, on the phenomenal growth and the great potential of Buddhism in Singapore, which currently claims 42.5 per cent of the total population aged 15 years and over, or 53.6 per cent of the Chinese aged 15 years and over. Its sheer number alone deserves serious recognition. A fair and legitimate question to raise is: Is this reality likely to cause serious concern for scholars and the government alike, in the way/ways that Christianity in the 1980s obviously caused? If not, why not? Is it because Buddhism is usually perceived to be sociopolitically less active and therefore less threatening to the stability of the society? As Buddhism in Singapore is becoming increasingly involved with society through its concerted efforts in social services and other related activities, its overall influence on the Singapore society as a whole evidently should not be overlooked. Nor should the kind of "down-to-earth" or "this worldly" Buddhism (Ren Jian Fo Jiao), which originated in Taiwan and which has become increasingly influential and powerful not only in Taiwan, but in other places be bypassed. One of the most powerful Taiwanese monk, Xing Yun Fa Shi, is commonly called a "political monk", and quite rightly so. Lastly, as Prof Kuo's team clearly noted, the Nichiren Shoshu Buddhist Association, which represents the largest of the Japanese New Religion, has been attracting a significant number of young Chinese with its very effective outreach programmes and grass-roots activities and network. It has already gained access to major national and social events such as National Day Parade which have gained them considerable public recognition and legitimacy. Has the Association been adequately understood sociopolitically, including its Japanese origin and background? More relevant and related issues could perhaps be raised about the future of Buddhism in Singapore.

Chapter 16

THE MOSES OF CHINA: HUANG NAISHANG AND THE CHINESE CHRISTIAN COMMUNE IN SIBU

Philip Yuen-sang Leung

Introduction

> These Chinese people came from the Fuzhou (Foochow) area in the province of Fujian. They came in hundreds and in thousands; they spoke a distinct dialect, and they seemed to know each other so well here and back home in China. Their migration was planned, controlled and well organized!

The above passage does not refer to the illegal Chinese immigrants from Fuzhou in recent years who have flooded the Chinatown and neighbouring areas in New York City. The description, however, applies to a similar group of Chinese immigrants from Fuzhou (福州) who migrated in a well-organized manner to the Sibu area in Sarawak about a century ago.

These Chinese immigrants who came primarily from the Fuzhou area in northern and northeastern Fujian (福建) were called "Hokchiu", and they left China in several batches from 1901 to 1903, settling down in the Rajang River delta in the present-day Third Division of Sarawak, East Malaysia. The colony they founded was called "New Fuzhou" (New Foochow, 新福州), which is Sibu today.

Three distinct characteristics defined the Sibu community from its formation in the early 20th century.

First, *sub-ethnicity*. The settlement was dominated by the Fuzhou people (Hokchiu) from northern Fujian. This was rather unique because among the hundreds of Chinese settlements in Southeast Asia, only the Sibu community was and still is predominantly Hokchiu. In most other Chinese communities, the most dominant sub-ethnic groups were either Teochew (Chaozhou, 潮州, people from East Guangdong, 广东) or Hokkien (people from southern Fujian). The Cantonese and Hakkas also became the largest groups in several communities. But the Hokchiu from Fuzhou, among the sub-ethnic or dialect groups in coastal China, were not the group most likely to migrate, and Sibu was the only community that witnessed their dominance throughout the formation and development of the community.

Secondly, *planned and organized migration*. The early immigrants from Fuzhou came to Sibu through a well-crafted plan developed by the leader of the migration, Huang Naishang (Wong Nai Siong, 黄乃裳, 1849–1924), through a patiently negotiated deal with the local ruler of Sarawak, Rajah Charles Brooke. Thus the migration was very different from those recruited and organized by coolie traders and brokers, or those who migrated voluntarily seeking job opportunities and family reunions.

Third, in the migration and development of the Sibu community, *religion* (in this case, *Christianity*, particularly the Methodist church) played an extremely important role by providing leadership, vision, plans, organizational and financial assistance to the immigrants.

In fact, this article will examine and analyse the migration of the Fuzhou people, the formation of the Sibu settlement, and the development of the community, along the lines of the theme in the previous chapter which focuses on the role of religion.

The Land of Egypt: Northern Fujian in the Late 19th Century

The southern section of Fujian province has been an emigrant society in China since the 17th century. People from Xiamen (厦门), Zhangzhou (漳州), Quanzhou (泉州), Tong'an (同安), Jinjiang (晋江) and adjacent areas had many external connections and these ties could be traced back to the early or medieval periods. In the records of Southeast Asian countries, these people from southern Fujian were generally known as "Hokkiens" and they emigrated from China for political, economic and family reasons. They formed the largest dialect group in many Chinese communities throughout Southeast Asia, including Singapore, Penang, Malacca and Manila. In other overseas Chinese communities, it was the Chaozhou (Teochew) group or the Cantonese who made up the largest sub-ethnic group.

In the 19th century, when Chinese emigration became phenomenal, the people from northern Fujian also joined the movement. However, they left their country not in massive waves like the people of Guangdong and southern Fujian, but in 'twinkles' until the turn of the century when Huang Naishang organized a migration movement that involved more than thousands of people. To the fellow countrymen who had long preferred a settled life in Confucian China, the enormous migration was like an exodus, causing a lot of attention in the region.

Like the Jewish exodus from the land of Egypt, the Fuzhou people left China for the same reasons: natural disasters and economic hardship and despotic rule.

In his research on calamities in modern China, Li Wenhai (李文海) and his co-workers have singled out ten most disastrous natural calamities in China in the last two centuries.[1] But none of them occurred in northern Fujian. Compared with the people living in late 19th-century Shanxi (山西) who were hit hard by the drought and famine of the 1870s and 1880s, or those who lived in South China where disastrous floods visited so frequently, Fuzhou and its neighbouring areas seemed to be relatively calm. However, a more careful investigation into local history reveals that in the second half of the 19th century, Fuzhou was no safe haven in the era of calamities. During the 19th century and the early half of the 20th, the area was hit repeatedly by floods, fires, typhoons, earthquakes and plagues.

To the local people, floods and storms were the frequent harassers. In 1848, the year Huang Naishang was born, the Fuzhou area recorded one of the most disastrous floods in its local history. Two years after, there was a widespread famine after flooding.[2] Ling Xiao (凌霄), in his *Yishi suibi* (一士随笔), reported that in the summer of 1876 there were torrential rains and huge floods in Fuzhou which caused numerous deaths and rendered hundreds of thousands homeless.[3] There were several more disastrous floods before the end of the century and this problem continued to plague northern Fujian in the Republican period. Wang Zhenzhong (王振忠), in a recent study, points out that fire also contributed to the social unrest and economic hardship of the Fuzhou society. The main reasons for the frequent outbreak of fires, he says, were twofold: high temperature in the summer and local houses built of wood. Fire broke out frequently in autumn when the weather became dry while the summer heat lingered. A local slogan declared, "Fuzhou is a city wrapped in paper" (*zhibiao Fuzhou cheng*, 纸裱福州城),

---

1 Li Wenhai (李文海) et al, *Zhongguo jindai shida zaihuang* (中国近代十大灾荒) (Shanghai: Shanghai renmin chubenshe, 1994); also see Li Wenhai and Zhou Yuan (周源), *Zaihuang yu jijin, 1840–1919* (灾荒与饥馑) (Beijing: Gaodeng jiaoyu chubenshe, 1991).
2 Zhan Guanqun (詹冠群), *Huang Naishang zhuan* (黄乃裳传) (Fuzhou: Fujian renmin chubenshe, 1992), p 4.
3 Wang Zhenzhong (王振忠), *Jin liubai nian lai ziran zaihai yu Fuzhou shehui* (近六百年来自然灾害与福州社会) (Fuzhou: Fujian renmin chubenshe, 1996), pp 8–9.

meaning the city was prone to fire. In addition to the paper lanterns, the wooden houses were the primary cause of the disastrous fires in the city.[4]

Then came the plagues. In the late 1880s and early 1890s, bubonic plague visited northern Fujian several times, killing tens of thousands of people in the area, notably in 1890, then in 1894 and 1896.[5]

Moreover, there were droughts, hail storms, and even earthquakes, all conjuring up images in the minds of the Fuzhou Christians of the ten calamities Moses imposed upon the land of Eygpt before the pharaoh let the Jewish people go.[6] Indeed, it was a difficult time for most Chinese Christians in Fuzhou or elsewhere in China. Unlike Xiamen in the south and Shanghai in the north, Fuzhou, since its opening in 1843, had been uncomfortable and uneasy with the presence of foreigners and were relatively hostile to Christianity. Two missionary couples from the Methodist Mission, Judson Dwight Collins and Moses White and their wives, were sent there in 1847, following the missionaries from the London Missionary Society, Lyman B Peet and Stephen Johnson, who arrived in Fuzhou in the early part of the year.[7] They encountered a lot of resistance and did not make substantive progress, and the first decade of Christian mission was quite uneventful, followed by the disruption of the Taiping rebellion.[8] But after the Beijing Convention, which allowed missionaries to venture into the neighbouring villages for religious propagation, the church grew rapidly with new leadership provided by the energetic Nathan Sites (1830–95) and the help of local Chinese colporteurs. However, the growth of the church also aroused suspicion from the official-gentry class and resulted in frequent confrontations and legal disputes. For example, in the early 1890s, there were series of protests against mission work in Changding (长汀), Liancheng (连城), Ninghua (宁化), Qingliu (清流) and Guihua (归化) in the mountainous region in northwestern Fujian, and "in 1895, in Pingnan (屏南) and Tangkou (棠口), the masses drove the foreign missionaries out

---

4   Wang Zhenzhong, *op cit*, pp 10–11, 14.
5   Ibid, p 23.
6   For the conditions of the Jews in Egypt, see the Book of Exodus in the Old Testament, chapter three.
7   Ellsworth C Carlson, *The Foochow Missionaries, 1847–1880*. (Cambridge: Harvard University East Asian Research Center, 1974), pp 5–6; also Zhan Guanqun, *op cit*, p 10.
8   The initial response of the Fuzhou people towards the arrival of foreign missionaries is discussed in Ellsworth C Carlson's book, *The Foochow Missionaries, 1847–1880*, pp 18–19; also see Chen Zhiping (陈支平), *Fujian zongjiaoshi* (福建宗教史), pp 421–25. Ng Chin-keong, in his recent article, also discussed the tension between foreign missionaries and local gentry in Fuzhou in mid-19th century.

of their town".⁹ In fact, Fuzhou and the northeastern region of Fujian had the highest rate of "missionary cases" (*jiao'an*, 教案) in the late Qing period. Between 1862 and 1881, 67.6 per cent of these cases in the province of Fujian occurred in this area.¹⁰ Compared with other treaty-ports such as Xiamen, Ningbo (宁波) and Shanghai (上海), Fuzhou was special in the sense that it was a political and cultural centre in the province, with a high concentration of mandarins in the city, including the governor-general of Fujian and Zhejiang (*Min-Zhe zongdu*, 闽浙总督), the governor (Fujian *xunfu*, 福建巡抚), the general (Fuzhou *jiangjun*, 福州将军), the provincial treasurer (*buzhengshi*, 布政使), the provincial judge (*anchashi*, 按察使), and all other major officials. The presence of a mandarin tradition in Fuzhou was not conducive, if not inhibiting, to the expansion of business and foreign trade. With the exception of tea, export trade at Fuzhou actually declined in the second half of the 19th century.¹¹ Moreover, there was a collective memory of and a sense of pride in the famous Confucian scholars the region had produced since the Song period. Ellsworth Carlson describes Fuzhou thus: "It was the site of the annual examinations for the first (*hsiu-ts'ai/ xiucai*, 秀才) degree and of examinations, held twice in five years, for the second (*chu-jen/juren*, 举人) degree. Within the walled city large numbers of men of property and learning resided; they were referred to by the missionaries as the 'literati' or the 'gentry'." This literati or gentry class also contributed to the resistance to Christianity and to the anti-Christian movement although foreign trade, especially in tea export from Fuzhou, was developed in mid-century by Cantonese compradors.¹² The tea trade quickly became the labour-intensive driving force of the economy of the locality, involving farmers, pickers, and brokers and distributors. However, according to Robert Gardella, the tea economy of northern Fujian suffered a sharp decline at the end of the 19th century owing to keen competition from Japan, Taiwan and South Asia. In 1882, a total of 60,656,000 pounds

---

9   Chen Zhiping, *Fujian zongjiaoshi,* pp 424–25.
10 See Li Jinqiang (Lee Kam Keung, 李金强), "Qingji aiguo jidutu Huang Naishang zhi yanjiu" (清季爱国基督徒黄乃裳之研究) in *Jindai Zhongguo lishi renwu lunwenji* (近代中国历史人物论文集) (Taipei: Institute of Modern History, Academia Sinica, 1993), p 828; also see Jones Kirby, Jr, "The Foochow Anti-missionary Riot", *Journal of Asian Studies* 25, 4 (1966): 665–79.
11 Lan Daju (蓝达居), *Xuannao di haishi: Mindongnan gangshi xingshuai yu haiyangrenwen (*喧闹的海市:闽东南港市兴衰与海洋人文*)* (Nanchang: Jiangxi gaoxiao chubenshe, 1999), pp 23–24.
12 Robert Gardella, *Harvesting Mountains: Fujian and the China Tea Trade, 1757–1937.* (Berkeley and Los Angeles: University of California Press, 1994), p 50.

of tea left Fuzhou for Great Britain, comprising 67 per cent of the port's foreign exports in that year. And in 1890, only 23,135,616 pounds went to Britain, only 40 per cent of the port's exports.[13] Between 1850 and 1870s, a picul (133 lbs) of tea was sold for more than 20 taels, but the price was reduced to three to five taels in the 1880s and after, a 75–85 per cent loss in value.[14] This not only caused economic hardship for the tea farmers, but also affected tea sellers, pickers, and the entire economy of Minbei (闽北, in northern Fijian) which was so dependent on one cash crop. One report of that time said, "Those [who] opened *chazhuang* (茶庄) and the tea-chest makers went broke, and many producers could no longer rely on tea [for income]. Those with fields recultivated them, and the ones without land cut brushwood for a living. How lamentable that people who laboured to plant tea received so much bitterness from it! Only those cultivating land for food can continue to have tea gardens ... People without food let the tea mountains return to wasteland—they cannot [afford] to look after them."[15]

All these contributed towards intensifying economic hardship and a widespread sense of despair in the region. To the Christians, it was doubly hard, especially in the 1890s, when the anti-Christian movement picked up fuel and momentum in coastal China, first along the Lower Yangzi and then in Shandong (山东). Soon these culminated into the life-threatening movement led by the Boxers. Fujian was also affected by the Boxer movement. The persecution of missionaries and Christians began in 1899 and it aroused fear and panic in many cities including Fuzhou.[16]

It was against this background that the migration movement of the Fuzhou Christians to Sarawak occurred. Organized by a church leader of the Methodist Mission, Huang Naishang, about 1,500 Fuzhou people, most of them Christians, left their homes in Fuzhou in 1901–02 for a "promised land" in a remote island far beyond the borders of their home country, and they called this place the "New Fuzhou", implying it was their new home or "new Jerusalem".

The Chinese Moses: Huang Naishang (Wong Nai Siong)

Huang Naishang was born into a farmer's home on the 25th of July in 1849 in a village called Liudu (六都) in the Fuzhou prefecture. Like other farming

---

13　Ibid, p 112.
14　Ibid.
15　Ibid.
16　See Zheng Zhenwen (郑真文) in *Fuzhou wenshi ziliao xuanji* (福州文史资料选辑), vol 2, 1983.

families in northern Fujian, he grew up in the village working on the fields and studying the Confucian classics. When Nathan Sites began his itinerant preaching of the Christian gospel in the area, Huang was attracted to this new religion. Together with his uncle Huang Fuju (黄福居), he became interested in Christianity and finally was baptized into the Methodist church in 1866 at the age of 18. He then went on to the city of Fuzhou to study theology under the tutelage of Sites and other missionaries, becoming a full-time preacher of the Methodist Episcopal Church after training.[17] A Methodist pastor or preacher was assigned to a circuit (*lianhuan,* 连环) which encompassed a very large area with a number of churches or mission stations with or without pastors. The preacher travelled from one station to another, taking charge of Sunday services and visiting Christian communities regularly. The stations were usually located in rural towns and transportation between them was not convenient and usually quite difficult. It was a demanding and challenging task to most missionaries and Chinese preachers. Physically, Huang was not up to the routine of grind and travel, and he felt ill after a couple of years. Later, he had to give up the travelling and settled down to a secretarial position at the Methodist Mission headquarters in Fuzhou. During those years he probably picked up some English working with foreign missionaries and compiling the annual reports for the mission. He collaborated with Mrs SL Baldwin, Myron Wilcox and others in translating several English works into Chinese, including the *Five Essays on Abolition of Footbinding* (with Mrs Baldwin) and *History of the United States* (with Wilcox). Huang showed increasing concern and sympathy over the plight of the Chinese people and began to advocate reform in China. It was probably due to the translation projects and the new knowledge gained from them that Huang went beyond evangelism and spiritual quest to become a social activist and supporter of the reform movement led by Kang Youwei and Liang Qichao.

In order to become a respected intellectual in traditional China, Huang took a step backwards into the Confucian world by taking the civil service examination in 1876. He successfully passed the examinations earning a *xiucai* degree which would give him a good standing among the Confucian elite and within the official-gentry class.[18]

Huang became an active promoter of social and educational reform in the last two decades of the 19th century. He wrote dozens of essays advocating reform, first in a Christian monthly published by the Methodist

---

17 See Li Jinqiang (李金强, Lee Kam Keung), *op cit*, p 816.
18 Zhan Guanqun, *op cit*, p 18.

church, the *Xunshan shizhe* (郇山使者), and later in a local Chinese daily he founded in 1896, the *Fu Bao* (福报).[19]

Huang went to the national capital of Beijing in 1894 for another attempt at the civil service examination in which Kang Youwei and Liang Qichao also took part. They all failed in the endeavour, but they all joined the massive protest movement against Japanese aggression in China during the Sino-Japanese War later that year. After the protest, Kang and Liang went down to Shanghai and promoted their reformist ideas in the *Qiangxue Bao* (强学报), while Huang returned to Fuzhou and began to promote similar ideas through the *Fu Bao*.

In 1898, the "Hundred Days Reform" was initiated by the young emperor Guangxu (光绪) in Beijing, with the support of Kang Youwei, Liang Qichao and others. Early that year in January Huang Naishang also went to the capital with his son Jingdai (景岱) for another attempt at the civil service examination. During their sojourn in Beijing, he and his son were staying at the Fujian Huiguan (福建会馆), where they came to know one of the reform activists from Fujian, Lin Xu (林旭), who then introduced them to many reformers in the government. Reformism was in the air in the capital and all major reformers were gathering around the young emperor offering their suggestions and ideas. Huang was in close touch with some of them, including the so-called "six gentlemen" (*liu junzi*, 六君子) who later became the "six martyrs" in the abortive reform movement.[20] Huang also befriended WAP Martin, Alexander Williamson, Timothy Richard and other missionaries, and visited Li Hongzhang (李鸿章), Wang Xifang (王锡蕃) and other *yangwu* (洋务, officials) who had no direct involvement in the reform movement.

Huang was implicated after the Hundred Days Reform failed. He was warned by his friends early enough to leave the capital. In the autumn of 1899, he and his son left Tianjin on a British steamer, returning to Fuzhou via Shanghai. Worried about persecution, he and his entire family left China for the Nanyang (南洋, South Seas, ie, Southeast Asia) in September, taking refuge in the home of his daughter and son-in-law, Mr and Mrs Lin Wenqing (Lim Boon Keng, 林文庆). In Singapore, upon the recommendation of Lim Boon Keng, Huang took up the editorship of a local Chinese newspaper, the *Rixin Bao* (日新报). He became acquainted with some reform-minded

---

19 Ibid, pp 17, 33.
20 For Huang's reminiscences, see "Fucheng qishi zixu (绂丞七十自叙)" in Liu Zizheng (刘子政), *Huang Naishang yu xinfuzhou* (黄乃裳与新福州) (Singapore: Nanyang xuehui, 1979), pp 79–98; also see Zhan Guanqun, *op cit*, 43–44.

Chinese in the local community, notably Qiu Shuyuan (Ku Seok Wan, 邱菽园), and continued to advocate reform for China in his newspaper. Ku and Lim were well known for their support of Kang Youwei and the Reform movement in China. However, Huang also met some young Singaporean Chinese who were contemplating a more radical option—which was to join Sun Yat-sen's revolution. These young men from the local community included Chen Chunan (陈楚楠, Tan Chor Nam) and Zhang Yongfu (张永福, Teo Eng Hock), who later became the most active revolutionaries in the Southeast Asian region.[21] Teo recalled their days in Singapore thus: "(Huang, Tan) Chor Nam ... we were close and often together ... When we talked about the suffering experience of living under a foreign regime, we felt that we were like the Negro slaves (in America). When we talked about the national shame that was yet to be avenged, we pulled out our swords and brandished, forgetting our difference in age (Wong [sic] Huang) was then fifty-six, I was thirty, Chor Nam was eighteen, and (Lim) Nee Soon twenty)."[22]

The idea of an organized migration of fellow Christians from Fuzhou for development and colonization overseas was probably born during this period of Huang's sojourn in the British colony. As editor and reporter for *Rixin Bao* (*Jit Shin Pao*, 日新报), he had to write essays concerning both China and the Chinese communities in the local region. He therefore made several trips to the neighbouring areas in Southeast Asia, and during a trip to Sarawak, he discovered that the Rajang River delta with its uninhabited plains, fertile soil, tropical weather, rich timber and vegetation was an ideal place for plantation and settlement. He then negotiated with the White Rajah of Sarawak, Charles Brooke, and secured a contract to bring in new immigrants from China for the development of the area. With the agreement signed by Huang and Brooke, with Lim Boon Keng as witness, now an organized migration movement began.[23]

Did Huang have the biblical story of exodus from Eygpt in mind when he organized the emigration of his people from Fuzhou? Did he see the Rajang delta as a "promised land" of "flowing milk and honey"?

There is nothing in his writings to suggest such an allusion. Yet we are sure that Huang as a preacher and church secretary was familiar with the Old Testament and the story of Moses. He also read about the pilgrims

---

21　Zhan Guanqun, *op cit,* p 62.
22　Leung Yuen Sang, "Religion and Revolution: Response of the Singapore Christians toward the Revolutionary Movement in China", in *The 1911 Revolution: The Chinese in British Southeast Asia,* edited by Lee Lai-to (Singapore: Heinemann Asia, 1987), p 76.
23　For the agreement between Huang and Charles Brooke, see Appendix I in John M Chin, *The Sarawak Chinese* (Kuala Lumpur: Oxford University Press, 1981) pp 136–39.

who travelled a great distance from Europe to America for a better life and religious freedom. These must have been images and frames of reference, if not motivating forces, in his mind before his own migration movement took shape.

In reality, however, Huang Naishang could be said to possess several personality traits of Moses, the leader of the Jewish exodus movement from ancient Egypt. First, in both men there was a strong sense of group identity and inter-group tension contributed to the exodus. When Moses came to realize his Jewish identity, he developed a commitment and a mentality that was guided by racial concerns. For example, when he saw another Jew suffering from maltreatment in the hands of an Egyptian, his temper flared and he was driven by rage to punish and kill the Egyptian. Leaving, therefore, became one way of solving the race problem. In the case of Huang Naishang, the issue of race or group relations was even more complicated. In the final decade of the 19th century, the racial tension between the Han Chinese and Manchu rulers seemed to intensify and at times erupted into open conflicts in South China. Huang was certainly aware of the growing tension between the Chinese and the Manchus, and by the early years of the 20th century he had become an anti-Manchu revolutionary. But before 1900 the issue of race did not seem to be the key issue in his mind because he was an ardent supporter of the Hundred Days Reform movement led by Emperor Guangxu, based on Manchu-Chinese collaboration in reforming China. The more immediate concern for him, in the context of intergroup relations, was not race relations but the growing tension between the Chinese Christians and other groups in the community. Huang felt that the Chinese Christians in Fujian were under extreme pressure from the government and the environment they lived in and they were desperately in need of help and relief. They were despised and considered heretical by the Confucian scholar-gentry class; they suffered from cultural and social discrimination in the community; and in the wake of the Boxer uprising, they were harassed and persecuted. Like Moses, who saw exodus from Egypt as a way out of bondage and suffering, Huang thought leaving China for a new land a possible solution to the problems of fellow Christians who were persecuted in Fujian. In both cases, it was a strong identification of group/race and their commitment to liberate their group/race from suppression that drove them to action, that is, organizing an emigration movement for their own people.

Secondly, both Moses and Huang were leaders who had had a bicultural education. Moses grew up in the palace of the Pharaoh and had an elitist education in Egypt, while Huang managed to receive a good

Confucian education and earn a degree in the Chinese civil service examination. Moses was Egyptian-educated but thoroughly Jewish, and Huang was Confucian-educated but nonetheless a staunch Christian. In both cases the bicultural training helped them in challenging the *status quo* and pursuing new options. And in both cases, biculturality was a leadership quality that helped in the organization of the two migration movements.

Lastly, there was in both men a belief in divine intrusion and assistance in their endeavour, as they believed firmly that there was a "paradise" on earth awaiting them and that they would build a new community according to God's plan. In other words, religious conviction was a strong motivating force behind both migration movements. Religion not only served as an impetus for exodus, it also helped in the organization of the migration. To this aspect we now turn.

The Exodus: Church and Organized Migration

Huang Naishang began planning for the migration of Fuzhou people in 1900, immediately after his visit to the Rajang River delta in Sarawak. He went from Singapore to Kuching as the editor of the *Rixin Bao*, reporting on the conditions of the Chinese who were scattered around Southeast Asia. He met in Kuching a successful Fujianese merchant and local leader, Wang Changshui (Ong Tiang Swee, 王长水, 1864–1950), whose family originally came from southern Fujian.[24] Wang had extensive business connections with the Singapore Chinese community and was a close friend of Ku Seok Wan and Lim Boon Keng. He learnt about Huang and his plans from Lim Boon Keng, Huang's son-in-law, and was interested in Huang Naishang's idea of importing Chinese labour for development in colonial Southeast Asia. He introduced Huang to the "White Rajah" of Sarawak, Charles Brooke, who also favoured Chinese immigrant labour. Huang travelled from Kuching to the Rajang River delta area and was impressed by the fertility of the soil, the heavy vegetation and the weather. He described the place as a land of great potential and resources though he did not use the biblical phrase "the land of milk and honey". At the end of this inspection

---

24 Ong Tiang Swee or Wang Changshui was born in Sarawak, son of Ong Ewe Hai (Wang Youhai,王友海, 1818–89), who came from Tongan, Fujian, via Singapore to settle down in Kuching in 1846. The Ong family became the most influential traders and leaders of the Chinese community in Kuching in the second half of the 19th century. See John M Chin, *The Sarawak Chinese,* pp 41–46.

tour, he returned to Kuching and negotiated a contract with Charles Brooke to bring in 1,000 Chinese adult and 300 child labourers for the development of the Rajang delta. The Sarawak government would give to individual labourers a loan of $30 for each adult and $10 for each child to facilitate their migration from China to Sarawak. The loan was to be paid back in instalments within six years.[25] The 17-clause contract was signed on 27 July 1900 between Huang Naishang and Charles Brooke, with Ku Seok Wan and Lim Boon Keng as guarantors. Huang also asked for a loan of $30,000 from the Sarawak government to clear the place and make preparations for the arrival of the immigrants, including the construction of six "long houses".[26]

The recruitment of labourers began in mid-August at the height of the Boxer movement in 1900, when the siege of foreigners in Beijing culminated in a joint expedition of foreign forces into the national capital. But in the provinces, anti-Christian sentiment and rumours of massive killings were still prevalent. Huang and his assistant, Li Chang (Lek Chiang, 力昌, or Lek Ngee Seng, 力义生), went separately in two directions in northern Fujian to recruit the labourers for their project. Huang returned to his home district Min Qing (闽清), and visited neighbouring Gu Tian (古田) and Min Hou (闽侯) for recruitment, while Li Chang went southwards from Fuzhou to Yong Tai (永泰), Chang Le (长乐) and Long Xi (龙溪) for the same purpose. However, their recruiting efforts had very different results: Huang was successful in signing up hundreds of volunteers while Li Chang could recruit only a handful of labourers.

The secret for Huang's successful recruitment was church networking. Huang was able to sign up emigrants through church organizations and with the assistance of church pastors such as the Reverend Chen Changhui (陈长惠) of Gu Tian. In Min Qing, most of the labourers recruited belonged to the Methodist church of which Huang was a member. The role of the church was apparent in this endeavour. Li Chang, a native of Yong Tai and not a Christian, relied on kinship and clan ties in the recruitment campaign but failed miserably. Unlike the people of southern Fujian, Fuzhou villagers at this time were still quite suspicious of coolie brokerage and deception by overseas businessmen. In Yong Tai and Long Xi, Li Chang could sign up only a small group after months of promotion. On the other hand, Huang, a member of the Methodist church with gentry-scholar status, was able to win the trust of his fellow villagers in Min Qing. In Gu Tian, a large number of the emigrant

---

25 Zhan Guanqun, *op cit,* pp 77–79.
26 Ibid, p 81.

labourers signed up because of the support of Rev Chen Changhui. Chen Guandou (陈观斗), the pastor's son, also joined the emigrants as a leader of the first batch of Fuzhou emigrants to arrive in Sibu.[27]

All in all, about 1,500 labourers were recruited, 90 per cent of whom were members of the Methodist church. They were sent in three batches to the port of Fuzhou for transportation by junk to Singapore and then to Sarawak. The Christian connection was also clearly seen in the transportation network. The company that arranged the junks for departure from Fuzhou was headed by the Rev Chen Changhui. In Singapore, the person who handled the reception and accommodation of these emigrants was also a Chinese Christian whose two sons were educated at the Anglo-Chinese College in Fuzhou.[28] The ships also made a stopover at Xiamen or Amoy, but we have not enough evidence to show any church involvement during the brief stay. Upon arrival in Sibu, the Anglican church in Sarawak and the Methodist Mission from China and Singapore also contributed financially and spiritually to the early development of the settlement. The first thing after their arrival, according to a Methodist church leader, was the construction of a chapel called "Xin'an Tang" (新安堂, Hall of New Peace) for Sunday service and worship.[29]

At any rate, it is not an exaggeration to say that the Christian church played a key role in organizing the migration of these Fuzhou labourers from their homeland to Sarawak, providing religious as well as practical assistance during the voyage and throughout the entire project and subsequent development of the community.

The "Promised Land": The Christian Commune of "New Fouzhou"

The first batch of 91 Fuzhou immigrants, led by Li Chang and Chen Guandou, left Fuzhou in December 1900 and only 72 arrived in Sibu in January 1901. Some of them had left the group while stopping over in Singapore either because they were suspicious of the project or because they were persuaded by others to stay in Singapore. The second batch of 535 arrived two months

---

27 Ibid, p 83.
28 Ibid, p 86.
29 Yao Qiaoqin (姚峭嶔), "Jidujiao Weili gonghui zhi yailue" (基督教卫理公会之崖略), in *Shiwu Fuzhou Kenchang wushi zhounian jinian kan* (诗巫福州垦场五十周年纪念刊) (Sibu, 1951), p 83.

later, this time under the leadership and supervision of Huang Naishang. The last batch of 511, also led by Huang himself, arrived in Sibu around June the following year, in 1902.

The Fuzhou Christian colony in Sibu in many ways is a unique case in the history of overseas Chinese settlements. The composition of the settlers, organization of the migration, and the central role played by the church were all elements not commonly found in other overseas Chinese communities.

First, its *composition*. We have mentioned earlier that they came primarily from the northern region of Fujian, in the neighbourhood areas of Fuzhou. They spoke a distinct dialect among themselves and many of them were related because of kin ties and church connections. In other words, linguistically and culturally it was a very cohesive community. But more importantly, the "New Fuzhou" settlement in Sibu comprised not only male labourers, as was the case with many other overseas Chinese communities, especially newly established ones, but also women and children. In fact, almost one-third of the Fuzhou labourers in Sibu brought along their wives and children from the very beginning. Approximately, there were some 130 families in the three batches. This unusual fact indicates that the immigrants were probably influenced by the stories of the pilgrims who colonized America and the Jewish exodus from Egypt. In both those cases, the immigrants/emigrants brought along their families with the intention to settle down for a long period (if not permanently) in the new colony and not just a brief sojourn. In other words, taking women and children along reveals a "settler" mentality.

Secondly, the *nature* of the Fuzhou community in Sibu deserves more attention and scrutiny. It was organized almost like a "commune" in the People's Republic of China in the late 1950s and early 1960s. In many overseas Chinese communities in Southeast Asia and "Chinatowns" in America, power and politics within the community often evolved around two groups of people: merchants and gangsters. The merchants had their trade guilds but their social influence was usually channelled through the *hui-guan* (会馆). Headmen of the secret societies (*tang*, 堂, or *tang-hui*, 堂会) controlled gambling, opium sale and prostitution which formed an important part of the economic and social life of the "Chinatown" and they often appeared as businessmen and community leaders. In the Fuzhou community in Sibu, however, there was a conspicuous absence of both the *hui-guan* and the *tang*. Instead, the church or church organizations played a central role in regulating social life and even in economic activities. A *hui-guan* for the Fuzhou people in Sibu, the "Fuzhou gonghui" (福州公会,

Foochow Association), for example, was not established until 1930, almost 30 years later than the Xin'an church and other churches in Sibu.[30] Another organization established for the purpose of organizing social welfare and other communal activities in Sibu was the Guangyuan she (光远社), in 1909, which later changed its name to Guangyuan Cishan she (光远慈善社) in 1924, its main responsibilities being charity and welfare.[31]

References

Baker, Richard T. *Ten Thousand Years: The Story of Methodism's First Century in China*. New York: Board of Missions and Church Extension, the Methodist Church, 1947.
Carlson, Ellsworth C. *The Foochow Missionaries, 1847–1880*. Cambridge, MA: East Asian Research Center, Harvard University, 1974.
Chen, Zhiping (陈支平). *Fujian zongjiaoshi* (福建宗教史). Fuzhou: Fujian jiaoyu chubenshe, 1996.
Chin, John M. *The Sarawak Chinese*. Kuala Lumpur: Oxford University Press, 1981.
Gardella, Robert. *Harvesting Mountains: Fujian and the China Tea Trade, 1757–1937*. Berkeley: University of California Press, 1994.
He, Guiqing (何桂清). *Fuqing xianzhi* (福清县志). Fuzhou, 1989.
Lan, Daju (蓝达居). *Xuanao di haishi* (喧闹的海市). Nanchang: Jiangxi gaoxiao chubenshe, 1999.
Li, Jinqiang (Lee Kam Keung, 李金强). "Qingji aiguo jidutu Huang Naishang zhi yanjiu" (清季爱国基督徒黄乃裳之研究). In *Jindai Zhongguo lishi renwu lunwenji* (近代中国历史人物论文集). Taipei: Institute of Modern History, Academia Sinica, 1993, pp 813–32.
Li, Wenhai (李文海) et al. *Zhongguo jindai shida zaihuang* (中国近代十大灾荒). Shanghai: Shanghai renmin chubenshe, 1994.
Li, Wenhai, and Zhou Yuan (周源). *Zaihuang yu jijin, 1840–1919* (灾荒与饥馑). Beijing: Gaodeng jiaoyu chubenshe, 1991.
Liu, Zizheng (刘子政). *Huang Naishang yu xin fuzhou* (黄乃裳与新福州). Singapore: Nanyang Xuehui, 1979.
———. *Huang Naishang yu Shiwu* (黄乃裳与诗巫). Beijing: Zhongguo huaqiao tushu gongsi, 1991.

---

30 See John M Chin, *The Sarawak Chinese,* p 83.
31 Liu Zizheng (刘子政), *Huang Naishang yu Shiwu* (黄乃裳与诗巫) (Beijing: Zhongguo huaqiao chuben gongsi, 1991), p 39.

Liu, Zizheng, and Liu Yongzhi (刘詠芝). "Shiwu jin liushi nian lai dashi ji" (诗巫近六十年来大事记). In *Pengcheng Liushi qianzhi Shiwu zupu* (彭城刘氏迁殖诗巫族谱). Sibu, Sarawak: 华英印务公司,1958, pp 13–26.

Sng, Bobby EK. *In His Good Time: The Story of the Church in Singapore, 1819–1978*. Singapore: Graduates' Christian Fellowship, 1980.

Tian, Nong (田农). *Shalaoyue huazu shehui jiegou yu xingtai* (沙捞越华族社会结构与形态). Singapore: Lianhe wenxue chubenshe, 1977.

Wang, Zhenzhong (王振忠). *Jin liubai nianlai ziran zaihai yu Fuzhou shehui* (近六百年来自然灾害与福州社会). Fuzhou: Fujian renmin chubenshe, 1996.

Yao, Qiaoqin (姚峭嶔). "Jidujiao weili gonghui zhi yailue" (基督教卫理公会之崖略). In *Shiwu Fuzhou kenchang wushi zhounian jinian kan* (诗巫福州垦场五十周年纪念刊). Sibu, Sarawak: Shiwu Fuzhou kenchang wushi zhounian jinian kan bianji weiyuanhui, 1951.

Yong, Paul. *A Dream of Freedom*. Selangor Darul Ehsan, Malaysia: Pelanduk Publications, 1991.

Zhan, Guanqun (詹冠群). *Huang Naishang zhuan* (黄乃裳传). Fuzhou: Fujian renmin chubenshe, 1992.

 Part V

Literature

Chapter 17

TRADITION AND MODERNITY IN THE FICTION OF LEE KOK LIANG AND CATHERINE LIM: MALAYSIAN AND SINGAPOREAN CHINESE PERSPECTIVES

Koh Tai Ann

> Forget your ambivalent attitude in the use of languages. You are born a hybrid and you must remain one to be true to yourself. You must think of humanity only—not words. You want to show Ah Kow as a man with hope and despair trudging along and you want everyone to share your concern for him—despite the words used.
>
> Despite the words.
> Despite the cauldron boiling inside you.
> Despite yourself.
>
> — *Lee Kok Liang, 1989* [1]

> I described myself as an English-educated Chinese writer writing in English about English-educated and uneducated Chinese in situations strongly coloured by my temperament derived in part from my traditional Chinese and Catholic background for English-educated Chinese, Malay, Indian and other readers in Singapore.
>
> What greater cultural anomaly could there be?'
>
> — *Catherine Lim, 1991* [2]

When Catherine Lim described herself, an "English-educated Chinese writer writing in English", as a "cultural anomaly", that is, someone who is something

---

[1] "The Somnambulist Careening around the Crater", in *Perceiving Other Worlds*, edited by Edwin Thumboo (Singapore: Times Academic Press for Unipress, 1991), p 324. (An address originally delivered at the symposium on "Literature in Asia and the Pacific Region: Perceiving Other Worlds" held in Singapore, November 1989.)

[2] "The Writer as Cultural Anomaly", in *Perceiving Other Worlds*, edited by Edwin Thumboo (Singapore: Times Academic Press for Unipress, 1991), p 375. (An address originally delivered at the symposium on "Literature in Asia and the Pacific Region: Perceiving Other Worlds" held in Singapore, November 1989.)

of a contradiction or paradox, and when the late Lee Kok Liang at that same symposium (on "Literature in Asia and the Pacific Region: Perceiving Other Worlds", held in Singapore in 1989) declared of himself, "You are born a hybrid and you must remain one to be true to yourself", both writers implied that their cultural identities as Chinese were contrary to an implicit norm because while being Chinese who lived in Chinese-language environments, they spoke and wrote best, or chose to write, only in English and not in Chinese.

Paradoxically it is their hybrid and "anomalous" cultural identities as English-educated, Westernized, former colonials writing in English, but who are at the same time, descendants of immigrant Chinese who live in the multicultural environment of Malaysia and Singapore, that have enabled Lee and Lim to write the kind of fiction that they have. Both Lee and Lim are, moreover, familiar with a Chinese language (whether a dialect, Hokkien, or Mandarin. Lee, furthermore, despite being Baba or Straits-born Chinese, also attended Chinese schools).[3] To be English-educated, for their generation, is to belong to a professional middle class which has grown up inside the community and thereby intimately knows it and its culture. But by being outside it through a Westernizing, 'foreign' education, they are able to depict the community and "Ah Kow" with sympathetic yet critical insight for local English-educated Chinese audiences much like themselves, and also for the English-educated of other ethnic communities, and reach, besides, a global audience of English readers. Being highly educated in a world language like English, which they both possess with the native speaker's inwardness, gives them access, as well, to other cultures and literatures, and to different models and modern perspectives, such that, as was once said of Lee, he is able to depict "sensitively" the culturally complex Malaysian world that he inhabits "with an outsider's detachment and an insider's understanding".[4]

Lee and Lim are thus embodiments of a kind of modern hybrid Chinese cultural identity, the familiar products of overseas immigrant Chinese

---

3 Lee Kok Liang was a fifth generation Straits-born Chinese (whose mother was "a saronged woman, quick-tempered, with a mixture of Siamese, Chinese and Malay culture"), yet "not the typical Baba in the Straits Chinese environment". He attended both English and Chinese schools for his primary and secondary education, while his home language was "a patois of Malayan Hokkien dialect compounded with Siamese phrases and Malay expressions" (Kedah being near the Siamese border). During the Japanese Occupation, he went "to school with four language books—Siamese, Japanese, Malay and Chinese", and because of such a background and education, could "read in Chinese, write in English and speak in Malay" ("The Somnambulist Careening around the Crater", in *Perceiving Other Worlds,* p 320).

4 "Speaking for the Mute", The *Asiaweek* Literary Review, *Asiaweek,* 1 February 1985, p 50.

culture, British colonial and post-colonial circumstances in Malaya, Malaysia and Singapore, incorporating multiple and diverse identities which are not as anomalous as Lim believes—except to those with purist concepts as to what constitutes a "true blue" Chinese. Their personal histories illustrate that such hybrid identities are becoming, rather, the norm in the diverse multicultural and multi-ethnic societies of Malaysia and Singapore, especially among the Chinese. As the Malaysian academic Tan Chee Beng has argued, there is "no global Chinese identity", but "there are different models of Chinese culture and there are different Chinese identities".[5]

The first local writer and first short story writer to have become a best-selling author in Singapore, Catherine Lim (b 1942) is so much regarded as a Singaporean, that most Singaporeans, and even Malaysians, might be surprised to learn that she was also, like Lee Kok Liang (1927–92), born and raised in Kedah. (She took Singaporean citizenship only after her marriage to a Singaporean.) Like Lee, she is Hokkien (Fujian) Chinese, but unlike him, she is not Baba, but had an English-educated father, hers being an accountant. Both attended the Penang Free School, but while he was Buddhist and attended English as well as Chinese schools, despite being Baba, he has declared that unlike the other Baba he did not regard England as the "homeland" although his father was a "stern follower of the British Raj". Lee's Westernized education was reinforced when he went abroad to study law and arts at the University of Melbourne. It was there that he developed his love of writing and published his early efforts in a literary journal that he also edited. He proceeded afterwards to Lincoln's Inn, where he qualified for the bar, but at the same time, worked assiduously at honing his skills as a fiction writer, securing a commission to write a short story (the essay-like "Return to Malaya") for one of the renowned London magazines, *Encounter*, before returning in 1954 to the then Malaya. Apart from practising law, he also found time to be active in local politics as a member of the short-lived Socialist Front (defunct in 1969), a state assemblyman (1959–63) and a municipal councillor (1958–63), following a family tradition of prominent service in local government, his paternal grandfather having been Chinese Secretary of the Kedah Sultanate, and his maternal grandfather, a Chinese Kapitan to the Malay Sultan of Kedah.[6]

---

5   Tan Chee Beng, "People of Chinese Descent: Language, Nationality and Identity", in *The Chinese Diaspora: Selected Essays*, vol 1, edited by Wang Ling-chi and Wang Gungwu, Singapore: Times Academic Press, 1998, p 41.
6   Quotes and source of information: Syd Harrex, "In Memory of Lee Kok Liang (1927–1992)" in *Skoob Pacifica Anthology No 1: Southeast Asia Writes Back!*, edited by CY Loh and Ike Ong (London: Skoob Books Publishing, 1993), p ix.

His own interest in politics was probably one with the kind of political engagement to be found in his short stories.

On her part, Lim is a convent-school, solely English-educated Catholic who used to be a self-confessed Anglophile. Not surprisingly, she did her degree in English Literature and obtained a Diploma in Education in 1964 at the University of Malaya, taught in Kuantan for three years, and upon marrying a Singaporean businessman, moved in 1970 to Singapore, where she continued teaching and worked for her doctorate in Applied Linguistics from the National University of Singapore. Unlike Lee, Lim, having for the most part lived a quiet life as wife, mother and teacher, seems to have been an accidental author, jotting down her stories in an old exercise book which by chance came to light, and she was encouraged to publish them. This first collection was *Little Ironies*, subtitled *Stories of Singapore* (1978), although much of the material was mined from her experience growing up in a small town in Kedah, Malaya.

Although Lee Kok Liang, perhaps thinking of his own multicultural society and an international audience, would have liked to get beyond language to focus on "humanity only—not words" such that readers would recognize, beyond language, their common humanity with "Ah Kow", his representative of humanity is still an obviously local Chinese with the Hokkien or Cantonese name, Ah Kow, who inhabits a fictional universe imbued with Chinese traditional cultural beliefs which underpin a particular world outlook. In Lee's and Lim's earlier fiction, it is also a particular kind of Chinese social class very specific to Malaysia and Singapore. Lynn Pan's description of "'Chinese' culture in Singapore" (made in a context dismissive of claims that it is "Confucian") seems to me aptly applicable to the fictional Chinese cultural world of Lee's and Lim's stories. She notes (quoting a Western sociologist who has lived and worked in Singapore) that it consists of "an amalgam of many bits of tradition ... some more Malayan than Chinese, and very few any longer practised in China, the whole thing held together by a rather vague ideological model of what Chinese culture *should* be". She adds that

> the "many bits of tradition" may include a cleaving to Confucian values, but in Singapore these values come mixed with elements of popular religion, Taoist and Buddhist superstitions, and folk cults and beliefs which, so far from being Confucian, would make a true-blue Confucian wince.[7]

---

7   Lynn Pan, *Sons of the Yellow Emperor: The Story of the Overseas Chinese* (1990), (London: Mandarin Paperbacks, 1991), p 264.

This description is as applicable to the beliefs underpinning the funeral ceremonies and rites narrated in Lee's short stories "Death is a Ceremony" and "Dumb, Dumb by a Bee Stung", as it is to the beliefs and practices of the mother-in-law of Lim's short story "Or Else, the Lightning God". It is less the sophisticated "high culture" of the educated Chinese and mandarins than the "folk culture" of the uneducated immigrant Chinese.

In Lee's and Lim's short stories, this eclectic compound of "Confucian" values, superstitions, folk customs, Buddhist and Taoist religious practices, forms a "Chinese traditional culture" that dictates how most of the largely immigrant Chinese characters order or live their lives as narrated in authentic detail through their thoughts, behaviour and actions. Both Lee and Lim are interested in the tyranny of custom or traditional beliefs which vest power in authority figures who more often than not abuse it: the domestic tyranny of fathers, mothers-in-law, and elders in general who traditionally exercise authority; and a generally callous treatment of weak individuals or subordinates, encouraging a culture of bullying on the one hand and self-abnegating servility on the other, by oppressed individuals who, in turn, fiercely wait for their chance to rebel and to exact revenge. They also depict the oppressiveness or irrelevance of customary forms, whether social or religious, especially when merely followed in form, in the absence of substance or spirit.

At the same time, as the traditional authority of the older folk weakens in relation to the economic power of their modern, often English-educated descendants and family members, they find that the traditions that they have brought over from old China are soon discarded, and both they and their customs no longer enjoy the respect that used to be their due. Thus a recurrent image in Lim's stories, such as in the aptly titled "Family", is the mother-in-law's or grandmother's possessions being regarded as "rubbish" or junk. In a symbolic trashing and abandonment of old traditions, the "rubbish" is cleared out, whatever its value to the elderly owner, destroyed on modern grounds of orderliness, lack of space, and uselessness—in this case, on the perfectly rational and practical ground that the old lady's prayer candles could set the "rubbish" alight and make the family flat a "fire trap". But the "rubbish" burnt in "Family" is richly symbolic of ancestral family pieties and bonds, testifying to the importance placed on continuities of the generations and milestones in family life. Such sentiments are, however, beyond the comprehension or beneath the concern of the old mother's modern descendants. The "rubbish" includes "umbilical cords" saved from the births of her many children, "each tied with blessed yellow thread and wrapped in lucky red paper", but which have never been presented to the adult children, as should have been the traditional practice, because the old mother knew that being "modern", they would have been repelled by these "worms". Another item burnt is what the children perceive to be an "old ugly tablet with the red paint peeling off". They do not know, nor would they have cared, that it is an "ancestral tablet".[8] In *The Serpent's Tooth*, the daughter-in-law is repelled by her old mother-in-law's old-fashioned, ornate, and begrimed four-poster bed, and refuses to have it in her modern furnished house—until she discovers that the "junk" piece of furniture, when properly cleaned and restored, is thereby transformed into an expensive and fashionable traditional Chinese "antique" bed which she could use, show off, and keep as a valuable investment for future sale. The materialistic values of the marketplace ironically earn such items appreciation, in every sense of the word, as traditional "heritage" cultural goods.

Above all, both writers expose on the part of virtually all their Chinese characters, an obsessively materialistic spirit and a highly calculating mentality, which might have been understandable in an immigrant society struggling for survival and determined to make good (a spirit which indeed defines the immigrant), but in contemporary circumstances of material comfort, the continuance of such a spirit and mentality reflects a vacuum at the heart of society. Lee's Buddhist outlook leads him to cast a searching eye on the motivating material spirit within Chinese immigrant culture in his ironically titled story "Ami To Fu". The prayers to Buddha by the grandmother which are meant to cleanse the mind of all worldly desires, are unconsciously mixed up with dreams of wealth. Her family members are shown hiding in and sharing a cave, each person's space selfishly and warily demarcated, to wait out the war. One of the sisters and her husband seem to pay great affectionate attention to their baby, while the other sister, in seemingly friendly fashion, keeps on visiting the couple's part of the cave. It slowly emerges that the frequent attention to the baby is actually a constant surreptitious checking to see that the gold nuggets secretly wrapped round the baby are safe both from the knowledge of, and thus theft by, other members of the family. Theft is a real possibility when we note that the other sister, under the guise of being nice to her sister, is surreptitiously digging about the sandy floor, trying to discover where the nuggets are hidden.

Meanwhile, oblivious of the intense drama of acquisitive struggle around her, the old mother chants her prayers. But her prayers, too, drift towards thoughts of gold, of

---

8   "Family", *Deadline for Love and Other Stories* (Singapore: Heinemann Asia, 1992), pp 27–29.

riches coming in showers dig dig for riches in far-off lands the junk rolls through waves of gold children in sarung-wombs money is modern modern money death is nothing sarung everything the junk rolls into womb of gold ami to fu ... modern can never be without gold sleep is nothing gold is everything wake up wake up the beginning of man wake up wake up.[9]

But if one reads the above story as also being symbolic of the ruthless acquisitive forces behind modern capitalism and the material want which drove the immigrant to these shores, then it is apparent that Lee's stories also embody wider social or political themes.

In many of his stories, Lee implicitly perceives the role of the writer to be the representation of the marginalized and the voiceless victimized. The mute or dumb character is a recurrent figure in his short stories, such as the victims in the short story which provides the title of his first collection, *The Mutes in the Sun*: the humpback urchin in "Dumb, Dumb By a Bee Stung" who represents the neglected poor, but whose persistent presence the rich family ignore in their superstitious obsession with ensuring that the funeral procession takes a propitious "lucky" route for the family's continuing prosperity; and the temple servant, the mute Ah Lan, in his novel *Flowers in the Sky*.

In *The Mutes in the Sun*, parents pervert traditional family values (or traditional beliefs are themselves seen to be perverting and corrupting) and abuse their power for material gain, or they use money to buy others off without concern for the victims. A wealthy Chinese father and pillar of the community uses his influence to ensure his son Met's success in school, but he, more sinisterly, also pays off the uncle of his son's friend and classmate, Kee Huat, to cause the teenager's disappearance. The father does this out of lust for Kee Huat's girlfriend, Gaik Lang, also a classmate. On her part, Gaik Lang's mother, a prostitute, sells her daughter to him, while Gaik Lang, in agreeing to marry the wealthy man, betrays her boyfriend and classmate. The son's feelings are never considered and he is therefore not informed about the coming wedding. On the wedding day, Gaik Lang insists on following customary form by setting up an altar table to the man's late wife as if adhering to mere custom would right matters. Her action and his remarriage are further contaminated by an ominous suggestion that his late wife's death had been caused by his abuse. Distress at his friend Kee Huat's mysterious disappearance and the memory of his dead mother drive the son, in a fit of sudden madness, to kill Gaik Lang at

---

9 "Ami To Fu", *The Mutes in the Sun and Other Stories* (Singapore: Heinemann Educational Books, 1974), p 142.

the wedding. Estranged from his father, he thereafter lives among the town's abandoned poor, where he meets Kee Huat, who has been forced to become a vagrant, too. Together they set fire to his father's sawmill, the source of the *towkay's* wealth, and thus his power and influence, symbolizing at the same time, the exploitative forces of industrial capitalism: "a long building … a grey formless achievement of the industrial man". Having achieved psychic satisfaction by this destructive, but cathartic act, the anarchic outsiders and subversives "strode up the street like two buccaneers adventuring into the unknown".[10]

A kind of conflict between the traditional and the modern in Lim's novels, which is not found in Lee's stories, is that enacted between the women—the tradition-bound, uneducated mother-in-law or "old mother" and the modern, English-educated daughter-in-law. The "old mother", imbued with all the cultural and folk beliefs brought over from old China, insisting on its forms and on her traditional authority, is bound to clash with her daughter-in-law, who is a product of Westernization and women's liberation. This conflict is most sharply represented in Lim's stories such as "Or Else, the Lightning God" (1980); in her first novel, *The Serpent's Tooth* (1982) and in her latest novel, *Following the Wrong God Home* (2001). However, the English-educated daughter-in-law, unlike her counterparts in the past, is hardly the victimized. She is usually depicted as being also a product of a parvenu, hard-driving and driven society which breeds the kind of "kiasuism" (of being afraid to lose out to others) rooted in the traditional Chinese fear of "loss of face". This fear of being a "loser" is intensified in the modern competitive, acquisitive, mercilessly "meritocratic" society of Singapore, resulting in that same immigrant lust for wealth and status, for "making it" as a winner. The newly middle-class, English-educated women as a type are frighteningly recognizable, if not also sometimes ridiculous. They are house-proud, efficient, ambitious Singaporean wives and mothers or career women, usually with English Christian names (such as "Angela"), obsessed with their also similarly foreign-named children's performance at school, who exercise all their powers to further their own and their husbands' careers (becoming a government minister is the highest ambition), but are impatient with their superstitious, tradition-bound mothers-in-law. It is ultimately, as always, about power, for they, too, not unlike the uneducated slave mistresses of old with their bondmaids, exercise tyrannical power over their maidservants.

---

10 *The Mutes in the Sun and Other Stories* (1963) (Singapore: Heinemann Educational Books, 1974), pp 127, 128.

Yet, even as these modern English-educated women outwardly show a supreme confidence that they are all doing the right things, they are revealed to be at heart, spiritually impoverished and adrift. The traditions, customs and beliefs of the older generation will not serve contemporary circumstances nor their modern needs; but they cannot find anything to replace these and are left only with the immigrants' driving spirit, which is basically an all-consuming culture of materialism. Yet their materialism is not driven by the need for economic survival, but for display, power-play and status. Generalizing more broadly, the personal pathology of these women could be said to mirror a general insecurity, intrinsic to the well-known "survival mentality" of Singapore as a whole where the only valid arguments are the economic. In these conflicts, Lim's sympathies are obviously with the older generation:

> I feel sorry for these poor people on the edges, for example, the old man, the old woman, the mother-in-law, the uneducated mother-in-law, the child especially. I seem particularly unsympathetic towards women like myself—the so-called confident women, who straddle two worlds, English-speaking women who are successful professionally, who are probably insecure spiritually, morally.[11]

While clear about whose side she is on, Lim has little to offer these modern women, apart from the age-old advice to do your "duty" and "endure with a sob"—which is the theme of her collection *The Woman's Book of Superlatives* (1993)[12] and of stories such as "The Bell Jar". If they choose not to "endure" and do their "duty" they must pay the consequences, and this tends to be the theme of her later work, as in her latest novel, *Following the Wrong God Home* (2001), where the heroine tries to break free and follow romantically the urgings of the heart, shaking off the constraints of duty and of society's and her family's expectations. Traditional Chinese culture, while exhorting self-cultivation and discipline, does not really encourage—is even hostile to—individualism. The individual is constantly exhorted to put society above self, obey authority whether in the form of parents or other authority figures, and adhere to norms of propriety often designed to put the individual in his or her proper place. Self-cultivation and self-discipline, within a system of reciprocity of duties or responsibilities to ensure harmony, must mean varying degrees of repression of the self

---

11   Lim Li-En, "An Interview With Catherine Lim", in *Women in Bondage: The Stories of Catherine Lim* (Singapore: Times Books International, 1999), p 69.
12   Lim, "Prologue: Images", in *The Woman's Book of Superlatives* (Singapore: Times Editions, 1993), p 4.

and consequently, stifling its desire for self-fulfilment, self-identity and self-actualization or—in Lee Kok Liang's words—"to be true to yourself" (as quoted above, in the epigraph to this article). The demands for rectitude and propriety, coexisting with the focus on material success that permeates a Chinese community of recent immigrants, can exact a heavy psychic cost on individuals, especially women. In Lim's fiction, they are either single-mindedly in tune with the prevailing cultural environment and focus on achieving material comfort and socially-defined success, even to the extent of suppressing their own humanity and real emotional needs, or they find romantic escape in rebellion and rejection of the current social norms, but usually to their own ultimate damnation and destruction.

Romantic idealism and love, because they cater to individual desire, seem to be one response to the constraints of society even if the satisfaction of individual desire might be disruptive of family and the social order. Romance is a very European concept, and, in fact, the Romantic movement—both in its philosophy and artistic, including literary, expression in the 19th century—was a reaction against rationality, order and, consequently, self-repression of the preceding neoclassical period. In 18th-century Europe, societal values were similarly emphasized in opposition to the desires and passions of the self. What reined in the unruly fires of desire were rationality and restraint. The Romantics also valued idealism—that fineness of the soul that is uncalculating—over cold rationality and practical worldliness, unique, original self-expression over conformity. In short, they placed pursuit of the heart's desires and a passionate engagement with life against repression, constraint, calculation and caution, poetry over prose. The Romantic poet Blake famously declared and summed up this spirit in a line rich with ambiguity: "Damn braces; bless relaxes".

In Lee's stories, therefore, and increasingly in Lim's later fiction, we see represented characters who desire to break the bounds, want more individual freedom and expansion of the spirit, more song, more poetry, less crass materialism. In Lee's "Death is a Ceremony", we discover that the silent eldest son had left home long ago, returning only for his mother's funeral. The costly elaborate rituals and ceremonies (motivated as much by superstition as by "face", and described in authenticating detail by Lee) leave him unmoved. Noticing his silence at the wake, a sociable neighbour attempts conversation, remarking upon the many material changes to "the old place—many new buildings", expansion plans, increase in "big motorcars", but

> The silence continued. In the silence he heard the songs of his mind, repeating the poems he had read, and he felt a great loneliness among these people

who talked about rice, cars, and praying for great wealth from the gods. His mother had dreamt of gathering the world's gold for him and started showing him her collected jewelry, one of which he remembered distinctly as a lovely brooch with embedded diamonds, her prized possession, and told him she would give this to his wife when he married. She was caging and suffocating him with her love for wealth and she was so damned superstitious about it— the wealth, that is, lighting joss-sticks after joss-sticks to the gods, until he could take it no more and went off one day. And he had felt very clean.[13]

Nonetheless, he quietly retrieves the "lovely" diamond brooch, which has been superstitiously cast on the burning coffin by his aunt, now a fire-damaged thing "shining like some ugly oily beetle", looking like the mere object that it is, and gives it to his sister's son, the oldest male grandchild. It is an ironic gesture because he thereby recognizes the next male heir and the continuity of a tradition he is helpless to change. He reflects, "things haven't really changed", and decides to go away for ever. To the end, his mother is seen as having cared more for wealth, for the transient material things of this world, not love or charity, concerned only to maintain tradition by keeping the useless, merely decorative expensive objects within the family. Even in death, her treasured brooch, not finding a recipient in her son and heir, who had left the family home years ago, was thrown on her burning coffin to follow her to the netherworld. Her physical death was thus no more than merely "a ceremony", the real death—of the relationship with her son and heir, and of her spirit—having happened long ago.

Similarly, the young, soft-hearted English-educated woman character, Yi Ling, in Lim's *Following the Wrong God Home*, is defined by her love of poetry and a corresponding dislike for her hard-headed materialistic, manipulative and controlling wealthy mother-in-law, and her over-achieving autocratic prig of a Singaporean husband, Vincent Chee, with his ambition of becoming a government minister and always keeping close to the centres of control and power. As the title suggests, which god should an individual follow? Should her choice be dictated by head or heart? How is she to know which is the right or wrong god?

Yi Ling's loving, sensitive nature is expressed in her tenderness for the poor and helpless (eg, rather melodramatically picking up a dead baby she sees on the street on the way to her own wedding, soiling her wedding dress in the process with its dried blood). She is lovingly protective of her elderly servant despite the latter's old-fashioned, traditional ways and eccentric treasuring of a god brought with her from China for whom she

---

13   *Death is a Ceremony and Other Stories* (Singapore: Federal Publications, 1992), p 4.

hopes to find a home in Singapore. In fact, Yi Ling loves this servant, Ah Heng Cheh, who has brought her up, more than her own tight-lipped, cold mother. Her personal dilemma turns on the fact that she dutifully marries Vincent and gives up her American lover, Ben Gallagher, an expatriate university lecturer, for the sake of providing a home for this servant, who would also get the expensive medical care she needs from her wealthy in-laws. The lover is depicted as a contrast to the Singaporean husband. He is a foreigner, an American with liberal political opinions which she shares, and who maintains his personal integrity even at the risk of his job. In the novel, he obviously symbolizes Western liberal and democratic values as well as the uncalculating fearless spirit of a freely acting, autonomous individual. He appreciates her poetry, they are both romantically in love, and because he seems to hold out the hope to her of individual fulfilment and happiness, she follows her heart, abandoning her marriage and family, including her only son.

Yet before the end, Yi Ling realizes that "The god of love left incomparable joy, but also an indescribable mess", and wistfully clings on to the hope, not only for herself but for all women caught in similar circumstances, that perhaps "love and duty" were not, after all, "irreconcilable", that she could have it all: "that one day, not too far off, she would be holding the man she loved with one arm and the little son she had left for him with the other."[14] But this was never to be.

As if to remind Yi Ling of her Chinese heritage and urge upon her its moral imperatives of duty, fidelity and propriety, Lim has the lovers frequently meet at Sai Haw Villa (Haw Par Villa, thinly disguised) with its vulgar, folk interpretations of Confucian teachings such as stone images of filial piety like the old man being given suck by his filial daughter at the expense of her own crying baby, and the Halls of Hell with their horrendous, sadistic punishment of wrongdoers—such as adulteresses. Lim lays on the symbolism even thicker, by having the couple being often accompanied by the old servant Ah Heng Cheh, who is also looking for a place to deposit her ugly-looking god. The old servant thus also conveniently provides her with a cover for her illicit trysts with her lover.

It occurs to this reader, that Ah Heng Cheh's god would have fitted very well into the Sai Haw/Haw Par Villa, which, as a detractor accurately describes it, consists of "grotto after grotto, panel after panel, clot after clot of gaudily coloured statuary arranged in scenes from folklore and mythology—the Monkey God clashing with Red Baby, white rabbits fighting black rats,

---

14 *Following the Wrong God Home* (London: Orion, 2001), p 302.

men being cut into little pieces and boiled in a pot",[15] and so forth. The old servant strikes me as an instance of the recurrent type of all those uneducated ancient Chinese female figures in Lim's stories with their superstitions, folk religion and vulgarized Chinese customs. This is the type (mother-in-law, old mother, old aunt) whom Lim portrays as embodying the traditional Chinese culture with which she is most familiar in the world of small town Malaysia; Chinatown, Singapore; and the HDB "heartland" of one-room and two-room flats—largely inhabited today by the uneducated aged poor and their families, those immigrants who had not "made it" in Singapore's fast-paced, generally English-educated, modern society. It is significant that after her old servant's death, Yi Ling, according to her wishes, brings her ashes and the old god back to the ancestral village temple, as if both its reinstatement in its original Chinese "homeland" and her own journey to the shrine are vicarious fulfilment of the old woman's dashed hopes of a homecoming during her own lifetime. This was, indeed, the universal dream of members of the first generation of older immigrant Chinese, especially of those faithful old Chinese "amahs" or maidservants such as Ah Heng Cheh ("Cheh" meaning "Sister", as amahs were thus often addressed), a breed that is now no more. Yi Ling herself never returns home to Singapore as her plane crashes on the way back. Does this mean that her true cultural identity is, willy-nilly, tied to that of the old China of the old servant and her ancient god, and that her plans to marry Ben, destroyed by the crash, would have been a travesty of her "Chinese" inheritance?

The situation of Yi Ling seems to be one of many attempts in Lim's later fiction to explore the following questions:

> But what of the chaos that inhabits us? What of the inner moral struggles in a seemingly placid society? What of the alleged discontents and passions that are said to inhabit the inner world of the Singaporean as he moves about in his totally secure world, well fed, well shod, well housed?[16]

Yi Ling's is one resolution, albeit romantically and destructively escapist.

In deliberate contrast to Yi Ling's choices, are Mona's, the heroine of one of Lim's better-crafted and finely observed stories, "The Bell Jar". Recent reports in the papers of an increasing percentage of marriages in Singapore breaking up because of the woman's rather than—as is more usually the case—the man's adultery, make this story prophetic of a trend, and despite its depiction of a stock situation, not the less true. A successful

---

15 *Sons of the Yellow Emperor: The Story of the Overseas Chinese* (1990) (London: Mandarin Paperbacks, 1991), p 177.
16 "The Writer as Cultural Anomaly", p 374.

40-year-old graduate and professional woman, Mona—with the regulation Singaporean "graduate husband", two children, like herself with English names, an inconvenient old, uneducated mother, a Filipino maid, a dog called Spike, nice house and two cars—yet desperately needs to escape from it all. With a sense of relief, she goes on a ten-day conference:

> "I need to get away," she thought desperately. "I'm under this bell jar and I want to run away and breathe."
>
> She realized, with a feeling of mounting panic, that she would always be inside this huge silent invisible dome: home, office, the society itself, each with its share of hard rules and claims, to bind and suffocate. Each day she drove from home with its querulous incessant demands, to the office with its ironclad correctness, propriety and bureaucratic small-mindedness and back home through the impeccable roads, with the impeccable crowds marching always to the impeccable Government slogans.[17]

At the conference, she meets and has an intensely romantic affair with an American, Burt, that is invested with an almost religious aura, like a spiritual experience. His invitation is described thus: "its sheer audacity of total disregard for convention, propriety, logic, its bold bid to partake of the divine authority of that call to the fishermen washing their nets by the sea: 'Come with Me.'"[18] They have common interests, he is eligible, a younger man and so on—in fact, everything her awful Singaporean Chinese husband is not, and all that she has ever dreamed she wants as lover and partner.

But, unlike Yi Ling, and despite the bouquet of flowers which arrives upon her return home, with another invitation, she understands the power of the bell jar: "it made those who breathed its air and moved within its enclosed spaces feel safe, folding their wings upon themselves and never daring to spread them out in the gusts and storms outside." She finds herself thinking of her children, her husband, her mother, whether her daughter passes her piano examination, worries that her son might "be brooding and getting poor grades in school", and so on. "For such is the fearful power of women's bell jars: come back and do your duty."[19]

The incidental references in this story to the stress induced by "the impeccable Government slogans", "hard rules and claims, to bind and suffocate" and "ironclad correctness, propriety" reveal a growing tendency in Lim's later fiction to suggest the powerful presence of the Singapore

---

17 "The Bell Jar", *Deadline for Love and Other Stories* (Singapore: Heinemann Asia, 1992), pp 137–38.
18 Ibid, p 140.
19 Ibid, pp 144–45.

government and its pervasive emphasis on repressive "Confucian values" in the lives of the people which are translated into the form of pressures and stresses felt by characters in her fiction. For instance, in *Following the Wrong God Home,* the stress is felt by Yi Ling through the effect the authority figures of her husband and his mother have on her. It is also the first of her novels to be overtly "political". The Ben Gallagher character seems based on a real-life expatriate lecturer employed by a local university who had similar liberal political views, but got into trouble with the authorities and was forced to leave the university in a hurry—except that in his case, unlike in the novel, there had been no love affair with a local woman with similar liberal views. The triumph of pragmatic hard-headedness and materialism over altruistic and passionately engaged soft-heartedness and idealism that Lim depicts in her later fiction, mirrors what she sees in modern Singapore.

In 1994, Lim, in the first of two newspaper articles, theorized on the "Great Affective Divide" that she believed existed between an authoritarian government and the people—that despite all the material benefits it had achieved for the people, it had not gained the latter's affection; in the second article, using as an example, the large salary increases for government ministers, she chided the Prime Minister for this "final retreat of [his] earlier ideals" and the Senior Minister for lending the weight of his authority to intervene on behalf of "the new worldly materialism of the times" and "put forward this proposal of a new calculus of leadership", thus placing a crass "monetary worth" on what should be fundamentally noble, altruistic public service on the part of government leaders. This self-interested salary rise, she believed, would "cause a widening of the 'Great Affective Divide'". In conclusion, she warned that while the people pragmatically "will vote with their heads", "the heart is a dangerously volatile and unpredictable instrument and no one can say at what precise point it takes over from the head".[20] Yi Ling's rebellious abandonment of material security and escape from an authoritarian husband and her family to the destruction of her own interests and self, and to the detriment of theirs, seem to be Lim's fictional enactment of what happens when the "dangerously volatile and unpredictable" heart "takes over from the head". Do the Yi Lings of Singapore have a choice?

But her treatment of the theme of repression and its consequences can be less tragic and more comic. Repression and its effect on behaviour and mental health are hilariously described, not without a satirical sting and

---

20 Catherine Lim, "One Government, Two Styles", *The Straits Times*, 20 November 1994, p 12.

some basic truth, in two stories found in her collection *O Singapore! Stories in Celebration* (1989).

"The Malady and the Cure" satirizes public campaigns, the overall effect of which is to emphasize order and conformity and a return to traditional values. Its main character, the servile Mr Sai Koh Phan (ie, sycophant), a civil servant and principal of a "well-run, well-disciplined" primary school, properly grateful to the government for the prosperity and comfort he enjoys, unwaveringly adheres to every state-initiated campaign: he "wears a crew-cut" and ensures his pupils too are "neatly cropped" when long hair is forbidden; has two children when told to "Stop at two" as part of the state family planning campaign, but goes on to have four when the slogan changes to "Have three—or more, if you can afford"; immediately changes his name into *hanyu pinyin* to conform to the "Speak Mandarin, Avoid Dialects" campaign, forcing his sons to give up "the Western names that they have given themselves", which he believes is "evidence of the harmful moral influences from the West"—despite their protests that they "will not be known by the new names which they find difficult to pronounce". He even goes so far as to force his children to change all their pets' "Western names" to Chinese names spelt in unfamiliar *hanyu pinyin*.

However, his body signals that all such conformity is against nature, and eventually reacts by going into painful knots simply at the thought of the long list of Dos (eat more wheat, plant a tree, keep hair short, be courteous, stop at two, etc) and Don'ts (spit, dirty toilets, litter, stop at two, etc). The malady is only cured when his doctor advises him to join the thousands of Singaporean civil servants who, being "sons of the soil" (pun intended) cannot sully their own backyard, but are encouraged to travel abroad to do it, on foreign soil leased from the Malaysian government—to spit, litter, use foul language and generally being their natural untrammelled selves. They let themselves go in exuberant self-expression until "the constrictions and knots and tightnesses disappear".[21]

Similarly afflicted by repression is the Vice-Consul, "quintessence of moral uprightness, the ideal Confucian product", in the story "Sorry … Temporary Aberrations". Like the civil servant, he, too, cannot help himself from "temporary aberrations" in speech and action although they embarrassingly contradict his image as a "Confucian gentleman". In a speech to the Society for the Promotion of Confucian Values, "in order to correct the wrongful impression that Confucius was prejudiced against

---

21 *O Singapore! Stories in Celebration* (Singapore: Times Books International, 1989), pp 23–24.

women and the adoption of Confucian values will mean pushing Singapore's women back to where their mothers and grandmothers were", he "begins to rage against the possible feminists in the audience", but unintentionally says something which has a most un-Confucian, obscene and sexist, double meaning—which, tellingly, subverts his own argument.[22]

When we come to such short stories, including the more recent collections mentioned above, and her recent novel, *Following the Wrong God Home*, the world of Lim's fiction has already begun to diverge from that of Lee's two collections of short stories. Despite there being almost a difference of a generation between them, Lee being born before the war, the earlier published short stories of both writers tended to be set in the fifties and early sixties, when the immigrant Chinese rural and urban linguistic and cultural environment in Malaya and Singapore shared more similarities than they do now. As recent a novel as Lim's *The Teardrop Story Woman* (1998) is still set in the fifties against the background of the Malayan Emergency. For the then already adult lawyer, Lee, newly returned from study overseas in 1954, the Malayan Emergency, anti-Communist years of the New Villages, of rural poverty and small town casualties and economic desperation described in his "Return to Malaya" and other stories, were very present and real. For the child Catherine, eighth in a family of 14 children, the fifties of her childhood were filled with adult stories and observation of the life around her neighbourhood, living in a shophouse amongst a large extended family in the small town of Kulim, located near plantations and jungle. It was a time spent listening avidly and illicitly to small town gossip and adult conversations, to "the myriad Chinese legends told [her] by an endless stream of elderly relatives and neighbours", and regular visits to open-air Chinese *wayang* (outdoor theatre) with the family servant. These "voices from childhood" were to inspire the 17 short stories of her first volume, *Little Ironies*, albeit subtitled *Stories of Singapore*,[23] as well as a much later novel, *The Bondmaid* (1995). It is a measure of the Chineseness of these stories (only one, "Miss Pereira", is about a non-Chinese) and the divergent social, political and economic development of Singapore and Malaysia in the late seventies, that one cannot imagine them being called "Stories of Malaysia". And yet, as she herself notes:

> It is so difficult to say that my characters are Malaysians or Singaporeans. They are people we meet from all walks of life. You do actually meet them in Singapore, like the Singapore heartlanders, although the very poor people I

---

22 *O Singapore! Stories in Celebration*, p 27.
23 "The Writer as Cultural Anomaly", pp 370, 371.

write about in *Little Ironies* probably no longer exist in affluent Singapore. So, the difference is perhaps degree of affluence. But the basic Chinese character, the superstitiousness, the conflicts between mother-in-law and educated daughter-in-law must be the same in Malaysia and Singapore as in *Or Else, the Lightning God*, for example.[24]

While *Following the Wrong God Home* could be said to be Lim's most Singaporean among her more recently published novels (both *The Bondmaid* and *The Teardrop Story Woman* being set in Malaysia of the fifties, the former obviously influenced by Chinese popular *wayang* and film stories), Lee's best work and only novel, *Flowers in the Sky* (1981), is uniquely Malaysian in spirit and provenance in its multicultural concerns. Among its major themes is also repression, but the result of a religious conflict between spirituality and materialism, especially the corruption of spiritual values by the worldly values of the latter, as well as the struggle between the desires of the flesh and the imperatives of the spirit. While the novel is about, as one critic has put it, "the corruption that accompanies transplantation of cultural traditions in a new environment",[25] as importantly, it examines how the limitations of one's own cultural traditions and spiritual values can be shown up, through implicit contrast and comparison with other cultural traditions and beliefs. Lee's liberal capacity to cross boundaries, to inhabit his inherited culture, yet transcend it, is best illustrated in what is often rightly regarded as one of the most thoughtful and best Malaysian novels in English. In its way, it is about the Chinese community, about tradition and modernity, and yet it is also the expression of a multicultural perspective. Ultimately, even while conveying regret at corruption from the Buddhist point of view, the novel also suggests that the nature of truth and rightness of belief and action might simply be a function of one's faith and religious perspective. The technique of juxtaposition of different stories in the novel, without authorial comment, enables each human situation to be seen in the light of other beliefs and faiths, and evaluated at the same time, by being seen from the different perspectives of other human situations governed by these different faiths and beliefs coexisting in time and space in Malaysia. Harmony and peace might, indeed, be achieved by the individual by adaptation and compromise, even if the

---

24 Lim Li–En, "An Interview With Catherine Lim", in *Women in Bondage: The Stories of Catherine Lim* (Singapore: Times Books International, 1999), p 61.

25 Syd Harrex, "Scalpel, Scar, Icon: Lee Kok Liang's *Flowers in the Sky*", in *The Writer's Sense of the Contemporary: Papers in Southeast Asian and Australian Literature*, edited by Bruce Bennett, Ee Tiang Hong and Ron Shepherd (Nedlands: The Centre for Studies in Australian Literature, University of Western Australia, 1982), p 40.

bliss or happiness may be illusory, like the "flowers in the sky", experienced not through pure spirituality, but is a sense of wellbeing rendered possible by means of a modern anaesthetic drug administered through the body. What then of the Ven Hung's preoccupation with "purifying" himself from the sensuality of the flesh, thus causing himself to suffer the agonies of frustrated desire, when another coexisting religion, Hinduism, seems to allow that spirituality can be obtained through the experience of pure sensuality, as in the case of the Hindu Gopal with his *sakti*?

Flowers in the Sky is thus unique in the context of both Lee's and Lim's works in that it has a complex multicultural texture to its fictional fabric, features a truly multiracial cast of characters, and is multireligious in reference and perspective even while it apparently focuses on Buddhism, and one of its major characters is a Chinese Buddhist monk. The Chinese Buddhist monk, the Venerable Hung, is not Malaysian, but a missionary sent from mainland China, and his experiences and surgery form one of the two interlocking main stories. The other main story features Mr K, the Tamil Christian surgeon who operates on and cures him and who is not Malaysian either, but, like his wife, is of Sri Lankan origin. One of the two minor stories revolves around another patient of Mr K, the Chinese Miss Looi who is terminally ill with cancer, suffering the corruption of the flesh and eventually dying of it. In apparently deliberate contrast to both her story and that of the monk's spiritual agonies, is the story of the Tamil Hindu police inspector Gopal who is searching for his *sakti* or ideal lover/wife. He happily discovers her in the form of a Tamil Indian servant girl working in Mr K's household, blissfully finding a fulfilment in the flesh with her that is both intensely sensual and yet spiritual, and he gives up his job to become a Hindu priest.

The Malay police inspector Hashim, trained in Japan, is an expert in riot control, and plays a minor but important role in maintaining harmony between the crowd which has turned up to claim a statue of the Hindu elephant god, Ganesh, who has washed up on Mr K's property, and the much annoyed Mrs K, who wishes to drive them off her land. Being Christian, she does not share the Hindu believers' sense of the sacredness of the event or of the god, Ganesh, believed to be the remover of obstacles. The pervasive, dominant Malay presence and power are more subtly suggested by the way Ven Hung's attempts to meditate are frequently interrupted by "the call of the muezzin [wafting] down, muted but still distracting",[26] implying the difficulty of practising one's own faith or beliefs without being aware of the faiths of others in multicultural Malaysia.

---

26 *Flowers in the Sky* (Singapore: Heinemann Educational Books [Asia], 1981) p 147.

The issues that confront Ven Hung as a Chinese Buddhist monk are firstly personal and religious: his struggle to suppress and overcome the desires of the flesh, especially sexual desire, to achieve peace and, ultimately, nirvana. Secondly, his very attempts to spread his faith entail the corruption of the enterprise and the purity of his spiritual mission. His mission in Malaysia being to attract more devotees, he soon discovers that he will not succeed unless he manages to build his own temple first. However, to achieve this he has to cultivate the favour of the local merchants. Gradually, he is himself drawn into their materialistic universe. In an indictment of the materialistic, wealth-driven, status-conscious world of the Chinese immigrant community, Lee has the Ven Hung confide in a letter to his abbot in China, that to begin with, there are not many devotees because they are all preoccupied with making a living on the farms and at their businesses. Then they are unimpressed by the unobtrusive smallness of the Buddha statue he has brought with him and take it upon themselves to buy bigger and more statues to donate to the temple, whereas he wishes that "he could find at least one with whom he could talk about the Great Doctrine". In order to be able to send more money to the abbot, he "has to please the merchants and make the temple more decorative". Moreover, he even has had to give equal space in his temple to other gods:

> They were keen to have Kuang Kong, the God of War, on the main altar with the World-Honoured One. Resistance against them seemed to displease the powerful merchants and your humble one's temple stands on a piece of land over which these merchants have control. The laws of this country are strange. Land donated to the temple must be held by a committee. The temple as such cannot be the owner on the rolls.

He then reports the installation and his blessing of Kuang Kong: "The people here like sounds: chants, ringing of bells, cymbals and drums impress them. Silence they ignore like a falling leaf."[27] We then later learn of the Ven Hung's dislike of the look of the most un-Buddhist God of War who grasps a "vicious-looking halberd" in one hand, while his "right leg trod fiercely on the figure of a scrawny and emaciated human being. The entire expression was one of utter aggression". Moreover, it was not even well crafted and "had obviously been carved by a rough hand. For all he knew, it might have been made by a coffin maker". But it did draw a big crowd of "devotees".[28]

---

27 *Flowers in the Sky*, p 110.
28 Ibid, p 111.

At the end of the novel, when he leaves Dr K's clinic after his operation, we are given a vivid illustration of the radically differing value given to things by different religions from contrasting perspectives. One man's belief is another's superstition; what one culture may regard as abhorrent, another may see as being quite propitious. As he leaves the clinic, the doctor notices with amusement, the "tiny" monk getting into a chauffeur-driven Mercedes car with the number plate 666, which a Christian like himself recognizes as "the number of the beast" (Book of Revelations, chapter 13). He doubts whether his pastor would ride in one with that number. But, what Mr K does not know is that 666 "sounded like 'Joy, Joy, Joy' in Cantonese. And the monk is very proud of the numbers and has used considerable influence upon the Registrar and Inspector of Motor Vehicles to get them".[29]

The episode also illustrates how the worldly materialism and superstitions of the Chinese mercantile community have finally had their effect on the monk, despite all his earlier scruples, caught as he is between the unworldly spiritual ideals of his religion and his worldly desire to see his temple's and his own influence spread in the local Chinese community. Material wealth has not only put a prestigious Mercedes car at his disposal, enabled him to have a successful operation at an expensive private clinic, thereby regaining his physical health and wellbeing, even given him an albeit drug-induced glimpse of that utter bliss that seems like an experience of nirvana, but has also given him his temple and the land on it, status to his religion (Kuang Kong and those impressively large, ostentatious Buddhist statues) as well to himself, and multiplied his congregation of "devotees". He has finally achieved joy of a kind through compromise, and that compromise seems to form the basis of "joy" in the imperfect world depicted in Lee's novel, where "joy" is happiness based on material wealth, the dream of the immigrant Chinese (including this monk) who had found their way to these shores.

---

29 *Flowers in the Sky*, p 157.

Bibliography of Works by Lee Kok Liang and Catherine Lim

Lee, Kok Liang (1927–92)

Death is a Ceremony and Other Short Stories. 1992. Singapore: Federal Publications. 201 pages.
Flowers in the Sky. 1981. Kuala Lumpur: Heinemann Educational Books (Asia). 161 pages.
The Mutes in the Sun and Other Stories. 1963. Kuala Lumpur: Rayirath (Raybooks). 229 pages.

Lim, Catherine (1942–)

Following the Wrong God Home. 2001. London: Orion Books. 328 pages.
The Howling Silence: Tales of the Dead and Their Return. 1999. Singapore: Horizon Books. 128 pages.
The Teardrop Story Woman. 1998. London: Orion Books. 329 pages.
The Bondmaid. 1997. London: Orion Books (Oriel Paperback). 342 pages. (1995. Singapore: C Lim Pub. 382 pages.)
Kampong Amber. Unpublished playscript. 1994. 64 leaves.
Meet Me on the Queen Elizabeth 2! 1993. Singapore: Heinemann Asia. vii, 210 pages.
The Woman's Book of Superlatives. 1993. Singapore: Times Books International. 144 pages, illustrated.
The Best of Catherine Lim. 1993. Writing in Asia series. Singapore: Heinemann Asia. 189 pages.
Deadline for Love and Other Stories. 1992. Writing in Asia series. Singapore: Heinemann Asia. vii, 145 pages.
Love's Lonely Impulses (collection of poems). 1992. Writing in Asia series. Singapore: Heinemann Asia. vii, 71 pages.
O Singapore! Stories in Celebration. 1990. Singapore: Times Books International. 128 pages.
The Shadow of a Shadow of a Dream. 1987. Writing in Asia series. Singapore: Heinemann Asia. 211 pages.
They Do Return. 1983. Singapore: Times Books International. 109 pages.
The Serpent's Tooth. 1982. Singapore: Times Books International. 184 pages.
Or Else, the Lightning God and Other Stories. 1980. Writing in Asia series. Singapore: Heinemann Educational Books (Asia). 194 pages.
Little Ironies: Stories of Singapore. 1978. Writing in Asia Series. Singapore: Heinemann Educational Books (Asia). 97 pages.

Chapter 18

EVOLVING MULTILINGUAL THEATRE IN SINGAPORE: THE CASE OF KUO PAO KUN

Quah Sy Ren

In this article, I intend to present the case of Kuo Pao Kun, a Singaporean playwright/director on whom the term "doyen" is exclusively used by the local English media. In the Chinese press, he is the only dramatist to be described as *dashi* (master). The leading status of Kuo in Singapore theatre is now "beyond any reasonable dispute" (Sasitharan, 2000: 10) in both Mandarin- and English-speaking communities. Today, he is not only a dramatist of Singapore, but often perceived as a representative of Singapore (regardless of race and language) in the global arena of cultural and intellectual exchanges. In the context of language and performance politics, Kuo Pao Kun and his practice of multilingual theatre are worthy research subjects. In my following discussion, however, I do not intend to place the focus so much on the politics, but to present an account of the position of Kuo in Singapore theatre since the 1960s, of which many readers may not be aware—as Singaporeans are generally more familiar with the Kuo Pao Kun since the 1980s.

Where Did Kuo Pao Kun Come from?

Let me begin with the Australian academic David Birch, whose account of the history of Singapore English-language theatre excludes Kuo Pao Kun. Such an exclusion is most telling of Kuo's position in Singapore theatre.

Birch is generally perceived as one of the leading researchers in this field.[1] In the late 1980s, Birch wrote a series of articles under a general title

---

1   For example, in the "Introduction" to *Interlogue: Studies in Singapore Literature, Volume 3: Drama*, editor Kirpal Singh listed Birch with "notable writers" Max le Blond, KK Seet and Robert Yeo (Singh, 2000: 11). In Krishnan (1997), Birch's "Singapore English Drama: A Historical Overview 1958–1985" is published as the "Prologue", and thus treated as one providing a general context in which the more specific discussions by the other essays are carried out.

"The Life and Times of Singapore English Drama", published in the now defunct journal *Performing Arts*. The period covered in his three articles was from 1958 to 1986. Ten years later, Birch published an "updated version" of those earlier articles in *9 Lives: 10 Years of Singapore Theatre*. The period of study stated in this later, revised article was "1958–1985" (Birch, 1997). Curiously enough, this period was one year short compared with the previous period: the year 1986 was missing.

It might seem trivial to single out the fact that a year was left out in Birch's later article. However, if we revisit the development of Singapore theatre in the 1980s and earlier, there is something worth a second thought.

Before the 1980s, Singapore theatre was noticeably divided into different language streams, namely, Chinese, English, Malay and Tamil. Critics generally recognized such a division—not only in theatre but in all segments of Singapore's society—as the result of the colonial governing authorities' "separate-and-rule" policy, resulting in a situation which sociologist Kwok Kian Woon described as "compartmentalization". In the case of theatre, practitioners strove along their own courses and their works bore different characteristics—all well within their respective communities. For example, English-language theatre was dominated by expatriates. The search for Singaporean identity did not actually find a workable way until the 1970s. English-language theatre, as perceived by Singaporean academic/director Max le Blond, was "shackled by a colonial consciousness and a colonial view of reality" (le Blond, 1986: 115). In contrast, Chinese-language theatre had always been active—especially vibrant during the postwar-pre-independence period of the 1950s, and from the late 1960s to the early 1970s—with a strong social and political consciousness partly inherited from the Chinese May Fourth political and cultural movement of the early 20th century.[2]

Practitioners and audiences of different language streams, however, were normally interested in and confined to their own community. They went in search of a national identity in their own separate ways. As such, before the 1980s, the development of theatre within each community was generally not known to members of the other communities. An English-language writer, in an article published in 1971 attempting to provide an

---

[2] English materials on Singapore Chinese-language theatre are scarce except occasional journalistic reports published in local English-language newspapers like *The Straits Times*. This is apparently a situation closely related to the forementioned "compartmentalization" of different communities. For a detailed description and analysis of the Singapore Chinese-language theatre in the post–World War II period, readers have to be able to access Chinese materials such as Zhan (2001) and Han (2000).

overview of Singapore's arts scene, on the one hand, despicably commented that (traditional) Chinese theatre was "a moribund imitation of the former glories of the imperial Chinese stage—down-at-heel, tawdry, without the smallest spark of inventiveness", and on the other, astoundingly demonstrated his absolute ignorance of the vibrant Chinese spoken drama scene since the late 1960s (Moore, 1971).

Let us return to Birch's articles. In his account of Singapore English-language theatre of the 1980s, Birch singled out Stella Kon's *Emily of Emerald Hill*, together with the establishment of professional theatre companies such as ACT 3 and TheatreWorks, and deemed 1985 as "[t]he turning point of Singapore English theatre" (Birch, 1997: 41–42). His observation is valid in so far as the above instances are concerned. The production of *Emily of Emerald Hill* has indeed set a new paradigm with its representation of localized language and themes. However, there is no mention in his article of another play produced in the same year, which is now acknowledged as equally significant and internationally acclaimed: Kuo Pao Kun's *The Coffin Is Too Big for the Hole*.

It could possibly be argued that Birch did not consider Kuo's *The Coffin* as a "genuine" English-language play as it was first performed in Mandarin in July 1985 and restaged in English in December of the same year. (As a matter of fact—and already accounted for in several articles—*The Coffin* was first written in English and its debut was the translated and revised Mandarin version.) The same argument, however, would be invalid for Kuo's second monodrama, *No Parking on Odd Days*, which was written and produced in English in June 1986, performed by Lim Kay Tong, a well-known actor in the English theatre circle. It is still not known why Birch left out such an important event in the development of Singapore theatre in his earlier article (Birch, 1989). But from what has been presented so far, could it be that Birch's later dropping the year 1986 from his period of study was due to the fact that he was unfamiliar with Kuo and his works? Or was it because Birch did not perceive Kuo, with his deep-rooted Chinese background, as a "true" member of the English-language theatre?

The fact revealed through Birch's articles may not be as simple and trivial as it appears. It blatantly illustrates the reality that Singapore society was a clearly divided one until as recent as the 1980s. Most members within each community used their own language; they did not need to understand, and were inaccessible for direct and accurate information by the other communities. Kuo's significance in establishing a Singaporean theatre beyond the usual language boundaries began to receive recognition only when his works were performed for English-speaking audiences and were accepted by them after the mid-1980s. Being a bilingual playwright/director with exposure to a world which was not restrained by one language medium, however, Kuo started to contribute by constructing a multilingual theatre and in imagining a multicultural Singapore way before the English-language community came to realize his existence.

Kuo's Pluralistic Background

When he returned from Australia after his tertiary theatre education at Sydney's National Institute of Dramatic Art in 1965, Kuo set up the Singapore Performing Arts School (SPAS) with his dancer/choreographer wife Goh Lay Kuan. Besides providing intense and specialized training, SPAS was successful in staging dance and drama productions from its establishment. At a time when expatriates dominated the English-language theatre, language used and issues represented on stage were generally remote from the reality of local society. In contrast, SPAS was avant-garde both in its artistic representation and thematic exploration. Kuo was a pioneer in introducing unconventional theatrical modes. When naturalistic settings were still the accepted convention, Kuo's stage designs were unusually simple and symbolic, breaking the stage illusion normally expected by the audience. Being the first to introduce the German dramatist Bertolt Brecht's works to Singapore's Chinese-language theatregoers, Kuo himself was also influenced by Brecht's non-naturalistic style. A writer observed that his first full-length play *Hey, Wake Up!* (1968) resembled Brechtian theatre with the employment of chorus reciting and singing.[3]

Before *Hey, Wake Up!* was staged in 1968, Kuo translated and directed three Western-language plays in two years for SPAS's production: *The One Day of the Year* by Australian Alan Seymour (in 1966), *A Raisin in the Sun* by African-American Lorraine Hansberry and *The Caucasian Chalk Circle* by Brecht (both in 1967). Well informed in dramatic works and theatre development of the world, Kuo did not confine himself to naturalistic conventions or plays written in Chinese. Since the 1980s, he has continued to direct plays from a broad selection of countries, including the United States, South Africa, Malaysia, Switzerland and Hong Kong.[4] His wide-

---

3 *Nanyang Siang Pau*, 17 November 1968.
4 The plays are: *Sorry, Wrong Number* by American Louise Fletcher (1981), *Sizwe Banzi Is Dead* by South African Athol Fugard (1982), *Atap Genting Atap Rembia* by Malaysian Kala Dewata (1982), *The Island* by Fugard (1985), *The Fire Raiser* by Swiss Max Frisch (1987) and *Fishing Eagles* by Hong Kong playwright Chen Zhihua (1994).

ranging interests provides him with inspiration from various sources, as well as an open mindset in the construction of a pluralistic theatre.

Early on, SPAS was also determined to represent issues that were familiar to Singaporeans and their indigenous life. Significantly, Kuo and Goh dealt with multicultural themes as early as in SPAS's first public performance in October 1965. A dance piece entitled "Ali and Ah Li" depicting the relationship between a Malay and a Chinese was included in the programme. It was reported that the dance highlighted the noble quality of mutual help and friendship among different races, and fully reflected the life of local society.[5] In addition, the anchor item of that performance, a piece with dance, song and poetry recitation, "The Story of the Sea", had been created with inspiration from a short verse written by a Malay poet. A critic commented that the piece should be perceived as a milestone in the creation of a Singaporean culture as it was imbued with indigenous feelings, and it manifested indigenous spirit.[6] These pieces were undoubtedly early attempts to create artistic representation of Singapore's multicultural reality. It also demonstrated Kuo and Goh's awareness and interest in multiculturalism as early as in the mid-1960s.

At a time when Singapore had just attained self-rule and later independence, the building of national identity—first Malaysian and then Singaporean—was apparently one of the pressing issues on the political agenda and in discourse. Creative arts were seen as a possible means for achieving such a goal. Lee Khoon Choy, then Political Secretary to the Prime Minister, once asserted that the arts could be used to promote national identity and racial unity. And that, he stressed, should be the artists' foremost mission.[7] The government's vision of a future Singaporean culture, at the time, was constructed on the basis of communication among and integration of the different races. Although Singapore had never succeeded in the realization of such an imagined integrated multiracial culture, with or without the government's call and intervention, Singaporeans had been attempting to creatively imagine their own versions of multiculturalism.

As we can see from SPAS's earlier experience, highly stylized and symbolic artistic forms such as dance and music were easier for the manifestation of multicultural themes. The programme booklets of SPAS's dance and music performances during the early days were printed in both Chinese and English. It was obvious that SPAS wanted to reach out to non-

---

5   *Nanyang Siang Pau*, 11 October 1965.
6   *Nanyang Siang Pau*, 24 October 1965.
7   *Nanyang Siang Pau*, 19 November 1964.

Mandarin-speaking audiences, demonstrating its ambition to expand its audienceship. When it came to language, however, the problem was not only with how various languages were represented on stage, but how the performance in different languages would be received by a linguistically and culturally diversified audience. It seemed to be mission impossible in the 1960s when cross-community interaction was uncommon and theatre was usually produced for the audience from a generally homogeneous background.

It was difficult to imagine a multilingual theatre. Another problem was that, in both the English- and the Chinese-language theatre, purity in language was considered the apparent and approved choice. As late as the early 1980s, the general perception was still that standard British English was the only acceptable language on stage, and actors were uncomfortable speaking local-accent English (le Blond, 1986: 117). Similarly, although various Chinese dialects and Mandarin were simultaneously used in some commercial skits, employment of mixed languages would not escape attacks from "serious" theatre audience and practitioners. It is interesting to note that, in recent years, the debate on language purity has re-emerged in a different playing field and is carried out in a wider politico-economic context. This time, criticism is from politicians while most artists defend the legitimacy of a local-style language (Singlish), stressing the relationship between such language and the sense of belonging, which points to how a people's version of national identity could be conceived. It would be observed in the following discussion that the evolution of multilingual theatre since the mid-1980s is not only a result of innovative artistic representation, but it should also be perceived as a critical part of an identity searching process.

One would then ask: why didn't Kuo Pao Kun, being an effectively bilingual playwright/director, cross over to the English-language theatre from the very beginning of his professional career? The answer is obvious. Besides the active expatriate theatre, the local English-language theatre scene of Singapore in the 1960s was far from promising in providing a favourable environment for artistic creativity. In addition, its audience was small, as compared with the dynamic modern Chinese-language theatre since the 1950s. Kuo admitted that he did not begin working in the English-language theatre as it was then limited in scope (Klein, 2001: 118). In contrast, the Chinese-language theatre in Singapore had a history which could be traced back to at least the early 1920s. Furthermore, the historical fact that practitioners in the Chinese-language theatre had since the 1930s begun to emphasize the production of locally written plays as an imperative form of engaging local society and building local consciousness,[8] was certainly more appealing to the young and enthusiastic Kuo.

Crossing the Linguistic Boundaries

When Kuo returned to the theatre scene in the 1980s, the social and cultural climate was very different from that prevalent until the mid-1970s.[9] In 1982, Kuo was invited by 14 Chinese drama groups to write and direct *The Little White Sailing Boat*. It was the first time in the 1980s when theatre companies started a series of collaborative efforts, hoping to revitalize the Chinese-language theatre scene, which had been gravely struck when, in the first half of the 1970s, many artists were alleged to be involved in leftist, political activities, and detained. *The Little White Sailing Boat*, in critic Yu Yun's view, was not a "new beginning" as it appeared to be, but "a full stop, a conclusion, a swan song" (Yu, 2000: 23). It was of course only in retrospect that such a remark could be made—and, more importantly, from the viewpoint of the development of the Chinese-language theatre. Ironically, the "full stop" of the Chinese-language theatre also marked the beginning of Kuo's new career with his debut on the English-language theatre scene soon after.

By the early 1980s, the situation of the Chinese-language theatre was similar to that of all other societal sectors which used the Chinese language. English being made *lingua franca* (in the name of "administrative language" but not "national language") among Singaporeans from different racial backgrounds was one main factor. English being granted a status higher than all other languages marginalized the latter, including Malay, Tamil and other Indian languages, and, of course, Mandarin and Chinese dialects. Decisions made during that period, which resulted in the eventual disappearance of Chinese-language education, are now generally recognized as another major cause of the steep decline in Chinese-language standard

---

8 Although Chinese-language theatre seemed more related to political struggle (as Kuo himself contended in an interview, see Klein, 2001: 115), I would argue that the practitioners/activists' interest in local society and people demonstrated a strong sense of belonging to the place, and this inevitably led them to a reflection of their identity.

9 Kuo was detained without trial from March 1976 to October 1980 for, in his words, "treading too close to politics" and that it "was a time when it was easy to get implicated in political activities". He talked about his experience as a political detainee for the first time—exactly 20 years after his release—in an interview with Klein (see Klein, 2001: 110–14).

and the shrinking of all fields related to the language. Most drama groups which had been very active in the past, such as the Singapore Amateur Players, I-Lien Dramatic Society and Southern Arts Society, were faced with problems of dwindling attendance and lack of artistic talent. The founding of Practice Theatre Ensemble (PTE) in 1986 by Kuo Pao Kun, which was much hoped for, did not accurately reflect the bleak future ahead of Chinese-language theatre groups but should be seen more as the actualization of Kuo's personal idealism to establish a professional Chinese-language theatre company. It was yet another irony that PTE was established at a time when the general environment appeared gloomy. That being said, PTE's survival and leading role were not incidental. It was because, among other factors, PTE clearly indicated its direction, from the very beginning, in bilingualism.

Kuo first crossed the linguistic boundaries when he wrote his first English play, a monodrama entitled *The Coffin Is Too Big for the Hole*, in 1983. He was a newcomer on the English-language theatre scene. Until then, Kuo was perceived as an artist of the Mandarin-speaking community. It is interesting to note how Krishen Jit, a reputable critic of Kuo's theatre, neatly divided Kuo's works into two seemingly distinctive and non-overlapping stages. In his "Introduction" to Kuo's first collection of plays, the only two subheadings in his article were: "Kuo Pao Kun and Modern Chinese Theatre of Singapore" and "Kuo and Contemporary Theatre in Singapore" (Krishen, 1990: 18). From its English debut in November 1985, *The Coffin* was very well received by the English-speaking audience. The full text of the play was later published in *The Straits Times*, Singapore's only English morning paper.[10] *The Coffin*, together with Kuo's other monodrama, *No Parking on Odd Days*, marked his entry into Singapore's English-language theatrical world.

At this stage of his creative life, Kuo expanded his space with writing and directing in both Chinese and English. In the real situation, there was no other playwright who was able to write effectively and creatively in two languages, and took playwriting as a serious profession.[11] Bilingual playwrights of a younger generation such as Kok Heng Leun and Goh Boon Teck—products of the post-1970s bilingual education—only emerged later in the 1990s.[12] Since then, all Kuo's plays have been produced in both Mandarin and English, except one, *Kopitiam* (*The Coffeeshop*), which was first staged

---

10 *The Straits Times*, 7 December 1985.
11 Of course, there were other amateur playwrights like Li Lien Fung, who writes in both Chinese and English.
12 Kok and Goh are bilingual in Chinese and English. There are also playwrights who are bilingual in other language combinations, for example, Alfian Sa'at in English and Malay, and Elangovan in English and Tamil.

in 1986 by 23 Mandarin drama groups. And, of course, there were the multilingual theatre productions which did not fall into the conventional categorization of language streams.

From Bilingual to Multilingual Theatre

The next stage of Kuo's creativity was his venture into multilingualism. The first multilingual play which left the audience with a profound and unforgettable impression was *Mama Looking for Her Cat* (1988). Before *Mama* made its phenomenal impact, one should be reminded that theatrical representation of different races and languages had been on Kuo's creative agenda as early as the 1960s, and persisted through to the 1980s. Such effort was sometimes demonstrated in a subtler manner. For example, *Kopitiam*, a play written and directed in Mandarin (with occasional instances of the use of Chinese dialects) for Mandarin-speaking audiences, includes an Indian character and dialogue in Malay. A non-Chinese critic like Krishen Jit had no difficulty in pointing out the intention of "multicultural representation" in the Chinese-language production. In Kuo's own directorial version of *Lao Jiu—The Ninth Born* (performed predominantly in Mandarin, 1993), there was also an Indian character, who spoke mostly in English and occasionally in Mandarin.[13] It should be noted that for these productions, the primary audience were Mandarin-speakers. The composition of audience was critical to Kuo's usage and treatment of languages, as can be seen in his later works, the target audience of which became predominantly English-speakers.

Beginning with *Mama Looking for Her Cat*, which some critics perceived as groundbreaking multilingual theatre, Kuo began a stage of experimentation in which he did not show much concern whether the lines were fully intelligible to the audience. Another piece with similar linguistic characteristics is *0Zero01* (1991). Despite the fact that the two plays vastly vary in their thematic exploration, their use of a wide spectrum of different languages placed the audience in an uneasy position which they had not experienced hitherto. In *Mama*, there were several languages spoken during the performance, including Mandarin, English, Tamil, Hokkien, Cantonese and Teochew. In *0Zero01*,

---

13 The use of different languages is only captured in the Chinese edition of Kuo's plays collection, in which English dialogues are printed in the original form in the play text, with Chinese translation in the footnotes. In the English edition, all other languages are translated and printed in English in the main text. For this part of dialogue in *Lao Jiu*, see Guo, 1995: 163–264.

English, Malay, Teochew and Hainanese were used during the first staging. These two plays are very different in the sense that the former is a critical reflection of the social reality while the latter is a search for personal history and identity. *Mama* is a true reflection of Singapore's reality of language division among races as well as between generations, represented by the incommunicability of people using different languages. *0Zero01* is a process in which individuals search into their inner spirituality, hence the use of the language with which they could most spontaneously and naturally express their feelings.

The use of different languages on stage without providing any kind of translation for the audience was a bold and untried experimentation. Kuo must have deliberated on the effects of alienating the audience and inviting antagonistic responses. Paradoxically, it was also the same elements of theatrical representation of how languages divided the society in reality that brought issues with social, cultural and political significance into the artistic realm. Multilingual representation proved to be closer to the audience's heart; it struck a cord with the audience's search for social and cultural identity.

As we can see from exemplifications in Kuo's multilingual theatre, the representation and treatment of multilingualism are closely associated with the artist's reflections on his position in a society where some members of various language, racial and cultural backgrounds are continuously attempting to find a way to communicate and integrate. It is apparent that Kuo's interest in multilingual theatre is not only related to his role as a dramatist with strong sense of experimentation, but that it inevitably evolved from his proclaimed social position at the "margins". Such an intellectual awareness within Kuo is demonstrated through his consistent effort in representing the pluralism of Singapore society. With his provoking experimentation as a beginning, we have come to see more artistic representations of multilingualism and multiculturalism since the late 1980s, especially in the works of similarly socially-conscious and intellectually-inclined theatre practitioners from companies such as The Necessary Stage and Drama Box.

The more recent multilingual plays by Kuo have different characteristics. They are more audience-oriented. These works include *Geylang People in the Net* (1997), *Sunset Rise* (1999) and *One Hundred Years in Waiting* (2001, co-written with Haresh Sharma and Chong Tze Chien).[14] These plays are more realist and socially conscious, as compared with the abstract and soul-searching *Mama* and *0Zero01*. Kuo has created a different model for multilingual theatre.

---

14 While all other productions of Kuo's plays discussed in this article were produced by his own company, *One Hundred Years in Waiting* was co-produced by PTE and The

First, these later plays bluntly reflect the reality in Singapore that different languages are used in a specific physical space (community). As a member of this society, people do not necessarily understand each and every word they hear. Such a multilingual representation is therefore more realistic than the pursuit of purity in language in the past (as mentioned earlier in this article).

Second, it is apparent that Kuo is more aware of the audience's presence and that the audience of these plays comprises primarily English-speakers. Kuo does not show particular concern of whether his ideas get across with a language that the audience understands in his earlier multilingual works. Taking a closer look at the staging of his later plays, however, we would realize that the most important ideas are usually repeated in English by the same or another performer, if they are expressed in languages other than English. It is most obvious in the performance of *One Hundred Years in Waiting*, during which English subtitles are provided when Mandarin is spoken. In this production, there is no doubt that the target audience is exclusively English-speaking.

The opening paragraph of Sasitharan's Introduction to the most recent edition of Kuo Pao Kun's collection of plays reads: "That Kuo Pao Kun is the most important dramatist working in Singapore theatre since independence is now beyond any reasonable dispute. Indeed this judgement would, arguably, still be true if the survey was rolled back to the early 1920s, when reliable historical records of indigenous modern theatre practice in the country first began" (Sasitharan, 2000: 10). At this juncture, I wonder: Had Pao Kun not written any play in English and entered the English-language theatre scene, would he be only perceived as a dramatist of the Chinese-language theatre, or, more sadly, would he be totally left out of the history of "Singapore theatre"? It is indeed impossible to answer these questions retrospectively, but they starkly remind me of how Singapore English-language theatre has been presented in David Birch's articles.

Necessary Stage, a theatre company which produces mainly English-language plays. It should also be noted that quite a few plays written by Kuo have been produced in English by another major English-language theatre company, TheatreWorks, and directed by Ong Keng Sen. The collaboration between Kuo and theatre practitioners from other language streams is another topic which deserves further research.

References

Birch, David. "The Life and Times of Singapore English Drama: Loosening the Chains 1958–1963". *Performing Arts* 3 (1986): 28–32.

──────. "The Life and Times of Singapore English Drama: Searching for a Voice (1965–1969)". *Performing Arts* 4 (1987): 48–53.

──────. "The Life and Times of Singapore English Drama: Images of Singapore (1970–1986)". *Performing Arts* 5 (1989): 1–12.

──────. "Singapore English Drama: A Historical Overview 1958–1985". In Krishnan (1997), pp 22–53.

Guo, Baokun (郭宝昆, Kuo Pao Kun). *Bianyuan yixiang: Guo Baokun xiju zuopin ji (1983–1992)* (边缘意象：郭宝昆戏剧作品集, Images at the Margins: A Collection of Kuo Pao Kun's Dramatic Works [1983–1992]). Singapore: Shibao, 1995.

Jit, Krishen. "Introduction". In Kuo, *The Coffin Is Too Big for the Hole and Other Plays* (1990), pp 7–28.

Klein, Ronald D, ed. *Interlogue: Studies in Singapore Literature, Volume 4: Interviews*. Singapore: Ethos Books, 2001.

Krishnan, Sanjay, ed. *9 Lives: 10 Years of Singapore Theatre*. Singapore: The Necessary Stage, 1997.

Kuo, Pao Kun. *The Coffin Is Too Big for the Hole and Other Plays*. Singapore: Times, 1990.

──────. *Images at the Margins: A Collection of Kuo Pao Kun's Plays*. Singapore: Times, 2000.

Le Blond, Max. "Drama in Singapore: Towards an English Language Theatre". In *Discharging the Canon: Cross-Cultural Readings in Literature*, edited by Peter Hyland. Singapore: Singapore University Press, 1986, pp 112–24.

Moore, Donald. "The State of the Arts in Singapore". *The New Nation*, 24 July 1971.

Han, Yong Hong (韩咏红). *Xinjiapo duli hou de Huayu xiju yanjiu (1965–1978)* (新加坡独立后的华语戏剧研究, A Study of Chinese Theatre in Post-Independent Singapore [1965–1978]). MA dissertation, National University of Singapore, 2000.

Sasitharan, T. "Kuo Pao Kun and the Theatre of Tensions". In Kuo, *Images at the Margins*, 2000, pp 10–16.

Singh, Kirpal, ed. *Interlogue: Studies in Singapore Literature, Volume 3: Drama*. Singapore: Ethos Books, 2000.

Yu, Yun. "The Soil of Life and the Tree of Art: A Study of Kuo Pao Kun's Cultural Individuality through His Playwriting". In Kuo, *Images at the Margins*, 2000, pp 18–59.

Zhan, Daoyu (詹道玉). *Zhanhou chuqi de Xinjiapo Huawen xiju (1945–1959)* (战后初期的新加坡华文戏剧, Singapore Chinese-Language Theatre in the Early Postwar Period [1945–1959]). Singapore: Xinjiapo guoli daxue zhongwenxi, Bafang wenhua, 2001.

Chapter 19

SINGAPORE POETRY IN ENGLISH AND CHINESE: A COMPARISON BETWEEN SIMON TAY AND CHIA HWEE PHENG

Koh Hock Kiat

Poetry has always been a very important form of artistic expression. In Singapore's multilingual environment, poetry has been playing the role of the initiator and leader in the different languages of literary creation, taking centre stage in Singapore literature creation regardless of the language medium. The prestige status of poetry is demonstrated through the abundance of its publications, high probability of winning awards as well as the strong support of the Singapore government. The popularity of poetry in Singapore can be seen from the publication of *Rhythms: A Singaporean Millennial Anthology of Poetry* by the National Arts Council as well as the addition of a poetry award in the Golden Point Award 2001 in four different languages.[1]

In the 1980s, many outstanding poets emerged on both the English and the Chinese literary scene. They demonstrate originality in their styles, topics as well as techniques of writing, using different languages. The selection of topics and life experiences for their poetry presents characteristics which are uniquely Singaporean. Simon Tay (b 1961)[2] and Chia Hwee Pheng (谢惠平, b 1957)[3] are

---

1 Kirpal Singh and Wong Yoon Wah, *Rhythms: A Singaporean Millennial Anthology of Poetry* (Singapore: National Arts Council, 2001).
2 Simon Tay teaches international and constitutional law at the Faculty of Law, National University of Singapore. He has written five books of poems, stories and essays: *Prism* (1980), *5* (1985), *Stand Alone* (1991), *Over Singapore* (1993) and *Alien Asian* (1997). He has twice been an International Writer at the University of Iowa and, in 1991, *Stand Alone* was short-listed for the Commonwealth Prize (Asia-Pacific). In 1996, the National Arts Council named him a Singapore Young Artist of the Year. He currently serves as a Nominated Member of Parliament.
3 Chia Hwee Pheng writes under the pen name of Xi Nier. His literary publications include *To Kidnap The Time* (poems, 1989), *Trustworthiness* (poems, 2001), *The Unbearable Heaviness of Life* (short story, 1992) and *The Serious Mask* (short story, 1999). He has won the Golden Lion Literary Awards for fiction (1982) and poetry (1992) and was awarded the NBDCS Book Award in 1990 and 1994.

two of these outstanding poets who continuously examine the changes of Singapore and search for subject matter in literary creation as they express their thoughts, emotions and views through their poems. The readers can feel their love, passion and worries for the society. The poets do not become impulsive because of their passion for the people and society. Instead, they express their thoughts and passions in a calm, objective and subtle manner. Most of their poems were created based on their real-life experiences in Singapore, with the objective of improving the quality of life.

The concern of my article is not with the reasons for the relative popularity of poetry in comparison with other forms of literature creation, nor is it with the situation of multimedia literature creation in Singapore. The aim of this article is to seek an in-depth understanding of the two poets' concern for their society by comparing and contrasting their themes, styles as well as techniques.

Tay and Chia are only four years apart in terms of age. Tay uses English as his writing medium, whereas Chia uses Chinese. They are like two clouds floating in the blue sky, moving in different directions but both producing silver linings. Both started their literary creation in the early 1980s. They have written both poems and short stories and have been working persistently at their literary creation for nearly 20 years, producing numerous excellent poems. In addition to the publication of numerous literary works, they have also received important literature awards, making them prominent in Singapore's English and Chinese literature world respectively.

Some say that Singapore society is one that is highly organized but restrictive in terms of creativity or thought. However, from Tay's and Chia's poems, we realize that Singapore society actually is an open and free society in which poets can freely choose their themes, language medium as well as wording to express their views about and hopes for their society.

Both Tay and Chia were born and bred in the same environment but they have produced literary works with different styles and themes. Apart from the differences in creative direction, there are significant differences in their personal characteristics. In this article, the author intends to study their literary creations in three main areas: innovation, artistic value and choice of themes. From this study, the author hopes to discover how the two poets with different cultural backgrounds and using different language media express their concern for Singapore society through the deployment of language, style and techniques in their poems.

As mentioned above, Tay and Chia both started their poetry writing in the 1980s. Then, as later, the content and theme of their literary works were closely related to the country's development and nation-building.

Singapore was already an advanced international city in the 1980s. The country was actively preparing itself for globalization, and the roots of cosmopolitanism were becoming apparent during this period. According to the Oxford dictionary, "cosmopolitan" means "belonging to all parts of the world, not restricted to any country or its inhabitants". In the midst of accepting new concepts and discarding old baggage, contradictions between tradition and modernization occurred. In this environment, the poets sought to capture both the resistance to and acceptance of foreign culture in their literary creations.

Most of Tay's literary works are found in the two collections of poems *Prism* and *5*, which consist of about 70 poems, created mostly in the early eighties. The majority of Tay's poems have their themes reflecting Singapore's life and society, based on traditional Asian values, with their emphasis on the value of life and the upgrading of its quality. In these poems, Tay uses different techniques, ranging from simple description to one expressing sarcasm, to raise the meaning of the poem to a higher level. He is capable of, and very effective in, injecting his emotions, sharp observations and persistent ideas into the limited lines of his poems, capturing the beauty of insights which might otherwise be gone in a flash.

Chia writes under the pen name of Xi Nier (希尼尔). Most of his literary creations are collected in his two poetry publications: *To Kidnap The Time* (绑架岁月) and *Trustworthiness* (轻信莫疑). Chia's poems capture his life experiences, the realization of the art of beauty as well as the underlying philosophical meanings. The format and content of the poems are well defined and have originality and creativity. Chia graduated from a Chinese secondary school's technical stream. He then proceeded to a polytechnic and earned his engineering diploma. While holding a job, Chia undertook self-study in classical literature in his leisure hours and continued with his literary creation. His poems were published in the newspapers regularly in the eighties. He tried to seek a balance in his poems, defending Chinese culture and the desire to preserve traditions. He had seen the diminishing of Chinese schools, the difficult situations they were in as well as the declining standards of the Chinese language. As a result, he wished to put forward his views on the changes in Singapore society through his poems and help in stabilizing Singapore society.

Tay was nurtured in a Westernized environment, with English as his only language. He had his secondary school education at Anglo-Chinese School, which has traditionally been an English-medium school. Hence, in his childhood and youth, he was never in close contact with his mother tongue or culture. Tay has said that the language in which he communicated with his mother then was English. In Singapore's multiracial society, he had never viewed himself as a Chinese. After graduating from the National University of Singapore with a degree in law, he proceeded to Harvard University for his higher degree. He experienced a cultural shock when the people in the United States of America treated him as a foreigner. He discovered that he had more Asian characteristics and tried to learn Chinese while he was at Harvard although he gave up after a few months.[4]

Tay started his literary creation using English as the writing medium when he was an undergraduate. His early literary works seemed mostly in search of creativity in format as well as imagination in content. Tay preferred classical literature and his creative purpose then was "art for art's sake". His poetry creation was in tune with the globalization of Singapore and he seemed to be more balanced than Chia in the process of accepting new changes and discarding old baggage.

Tay emphasized freedom in creativity. For example, in "Opinions on a Block of Glass", he says:

> Sits at the table,
> Awaits work,
> Reformation.
> Able hands
> To mould aimless images
> Into reflection.
>
> "Cut it clean,
> Make edges plain,
> Focused for every eye."
>   You advise.
>   Should I?
>
> This block of glass
> Is mine
> And I prefer to craft
> A prism;
> Three or more sides,
> Three or more times
> Reflection,
> Its corners framed
> By passing rainbows,
> Splintered light.

---

4   Simon Tay, *Alien Asian: A Singaporean in America* (Singapore: Landmark Books, 1997).

In this poem, we can see that technique is the key factor in that transmutation of a poet's experience into the singular, self-contained life of a poem.[5] Tay uses the technique of question and answer in his poem, doubting if he should follow instructions and advice. He points out strongly that, that is his glass and he can only finish the creation that he most desires if he crafts it personally. The glass mirror's reflection and rainbows images in the poem are an important symbolic language. The poem is written in simple language, which gives the reader a wider expanse to stretch their thoughts, and provides them with strong stimulation.

In the poem "On the Changi Airport Construction", Tay says:

Tractors shovel earth over my laughing memories
Of sand and sand castles.
They build as I had,
But they for jumbo planes, oiled machines;
I, for morning dreams.

The lorry runs along the seascape
The scaur I used to run.
But they on Boeing errands;
I, sea-soaked, swimming-trunked,
Ran in Saturday-velvet-joy.

I understanding Boeing,
His lorries, men.
Only regret they must build
Skyways to mar the earth and sand
Over unborn smiles of jumping-running
Boys.

Here, Simon shows his happiness and eagerness in looking forward to the new airport. He describes the feeling of looking forward as a dream in the morning that is full of hope and enthusiasm. This is very different from that of Chia's poetry.

Chia's poetic compositions were significantly influenced by Taiwanese modern poems. In the early eighties, most of Singapore's poets who used Chinese as a writing medium wrote their poems from the view of a foreign traveller with very strong emotions towards their hometown. Chia's early literary creations generally presented the reality of local society. This was due mainly to the influence of the changes in the society and its educational

---

5   Foreword by Professor Edwin Thumboo to Simon Tay's *Prism*, Singapore, 1980, p 3.

system. He frequently questioned the issues brought about by the changes in the society.

For example, in his poem "Shi Ji Qing Huai" (世纪情怀, Centennial Reflections), which is about the fountain in memory of Mr Tan Kim Seng, he sarcastically says:

> When the sea breeze slips by on either side of you
> And the crowds depart in haste before you
> Then allow me to stand by your side
> And enjoy a little sweet water of a hundred years old
> The water supply does not flow of itself
> It lacks your capacity
> For a hundred years, your life's work flows without ceasing
> Towards every household
> On a certain evening, a drop of tear without display
> Flows into my heart
> Then I turn around
> And vanish into the crowd …
> My happiness this evening is paid for with cash
> Your loneliness each night is recorded by flowing water
> A sea breeze ruffles the hair of lovers
> The sea voices stir up the sorrow of change
> Outside the Kang Le Pavilion, a whiff of smoke
> Causes me to cough
> And causes your tears to flow

The changes in society have been so great that not many people can still remember Mr Tan, who was instrumental in bringing about the supply of clean tap water. On the day of the 106th anniversary of the Tan Kim Seng Fountain's completion, Chia came to the Fountain and was shocked to discover that it had stopped operating. Today, as we enjoy such excellent water supply, the fountain which commemorates our patron, has ironically run dry.

Another poem of Chia's, "Du Lie Shi" (读烈士) is about Mr Lim Bo Seng. He makes a good contrast between the cold and the ignorance of the people who are taking photographs. His descriptions in the poem, from the smart statue, the focus of the camera, to the strangers and ruthlessness of time, from the hero to mere history, are all aimed at giving the reader a feeling of coldness.

From a portion of the poems in Tay's two poetry collections, *Prism* and *5*, we can see that they demonstrate his carefree manner and his emphasis on format and technique. Tay puts himself in the position of an observer, emphasizing personal entertainment and happiness, observing the changes in Singapore and the world. Although he cares about the society, he seldom writes about politics. To him, poetry is only a source of entertainment and its purpose is not to change society. He observes the changes in the society, showering his country with his love. He communicates his pride in being a Singaporean through such poems as "By the Sea", " Watching the Sunset", "Night Walk Marine Parade", "Responses to the Children" and "The Aged Park Speaks". In all these poems, Tay shows his love and care for his country as a young Singaporean poet, just as he does in his poem "Singapore Night Songs":

> if you can not learn to love
> (yes love) this city
> you have no other

Singapore uses English as a common language, and Mandarin has become the language for linkage with the mother tongue culture. In a multilingual and multicultural society, most of us agree that English is, and should continue to be, the working language. In Singapore, understanding the different ethnic groups can often be achieved through English as our common language. It is the unifying language in our multilingual nation and it is also the language for scientific advancement and economic prosperity. Clearly Singapore culture is affected by similar issues of late, of capitalism, information technology and globalization. But for multi-ethnic Singapore, for emotional and cultural reasons, we have to ensure that we keep our cultural values in the creative literary works in Tamil, Malay, Chinese and English alive as part of Singapore's heritage.[6]

The learning of English and Mandarin for the Chinese was made compulsory at the primary level in schools from 1960 and at the secondary

---

6 In the International Chinese Language Teaching Seminar held in December 1989, the former Prime Minister, Mr Lee Kuan Yew, pointed out that Chinese Singaporeans would and must continue to speak, read and write their language. This is a basic need for their self-identity and self-respect, especially in a world dominated by the English language and American culture through the print and electronic media. To Mr Lee, learning the language (mother tongue) is learning of a cultural value system. He said: "One of the strongest factors for Singapore's success was the cultural values of the generation of the 1950s–70s. That generation had been brought up to accept the need for sacrifice by the individual for the sake of family and society. They also believed in hard work, thrift and honouring of one's obligations. These cultural values contributed to our success. Because this is my experience, I have placed great store on maintaining these cultural values in Chinese Singaporeans." (Excerpt of speech at the dinner organized by the Singapore Federation of Chinese Clan Associations and the Singapore Chinese Chamber of Commerce and Industry on 17 February 1991.)

level from 1966. From 1971, students of different ethnic groups have sat for a common examination, the Singapore-Cambridge General Certificate of Education.[7] The bilingual policy ensures that each child is proficient in his/her mother tongue and aware of his/her cultural heritage. On the surface, this situation would benefit poets who write in the English medium too.

In his poem "Speaking English", Tay says:

> Load the ship.
> Unload the ship.
> The word you taught
> Beyond the nod of a head
> Was, "slave".
> And how the King spoke only of sceptre,
> Lance and whip.
>
> My quiet peoples took many years
> Under the strap of sun and rain
> To learn more words,
> To chant before your face and
> Behind your back.
> To spell you away.
> Your words remained
> In preparing our new lands
> We were not concerned in what language
> Preparations were made.
> Even those who picked your words up,
> Brandishing their symmetry under a sun all ours,
> Little knew how the grammar
> Possessed.
>
> Load the ship.
> Unload the ship.
> Few words we learnt
> Bent to our using
> O my people, who will learn new rituals,
> To invent magic's and sentences?
> Tie a knot of red hair to fingers
> And prepare spells against the devils
> And the devils speaking within us;
> Or else the sun and rain beat down.

---

7   Reported in *The Straits Times*, 1 July 1970.

However, in reality, English is an administrative and business language and in literature creation, it has not been given the emphasis. On the contrary, the situation has caused anxiety in the poets who use Chinese as a creation medium and that has motivated them to create. Because of the rapid changes in technology and society, most people are also in the state of change and some feel that some things of value would be lost, such as traditional culture, values, old buildings, streets and so forth.

In Chia's poem, we vividly see a poet who is busy bidding farewell to tradition. In "Impressions of the Land" (土地印象), he says:

> Unexpectedly, I have lost my bearings
> In this familiar land
>
> A kind of chilling sorrow
> Seeps into my breast
>
> A stain of desolation
> Spreads along the former streets of hometown
> The years like a passing stream
> Decades carried on its back
> A life-like
> Painting
>
> Whoever was it
> While life was nodding
> Sold it for his modern scene,
> This desolation
>
> Someone forgot
> To add with his brush
> The banyan tree of the story-teller

The poet talks about the impressions of the land, especially old buildings and people. He shows his worry and sadness for the loss of tradition. He has captured the changing scenes of different corners of the Lion City. We can also find such feelings in the poems "Of the Dragon Tribe" (或者龙族), "Two Generations Lantern Festival" (两代中秋) and "Visit to River Kallang" (寻访故河加冷). Chia has tried to capture the tears and laughter amidst the flicking lights. From his memories of tapioca, frangipani flowers, rambutans, jackfruit and potato leaves, visit to the lily pond, clouds and flying birds, he creates a beautiful scene of the countryside.

Reading Chia's poems is a big project in which the reader may frequently wander between "understanding" and "not understanding". The poet is like a Norman hiding in the forest of the city, using the fast changing language of the poem, playing musical notes repeatedly. In "Misty Ponggol" (雾榜鹅) and "Window View" (窗外即景), he uses a technique which comprises an intermittent mixture of realism and imagination, reflecting the showdowns of the change period and unclearness of history. The impressions of coldness and forgetfulness introduce some shadows to the reader's view.

In comparing Tay's and Chia's literary works, the author has discovered that there are differences in their content and theme creation. Tay is more optimistic and he cares more about the new look after changes. Chia is more pessimistic. He is worried about the losses after changes. In terms of artistic value, Tay emphasizes more on the value of personal beauty, bringing up the value of life, upgrading of individual life quality as well as beautifying of one's life. Chia emphasizes the artistic view. He cares about the loss of Chinese culture and his artistic style is based on that of traditional Chinese creation structure. In terms of creation techniques, Tay places more emphasis on rhythm, whereas Chia stresses the symbolic representation of language and the poem's theme.

From their poems, we can boldly say that the content and style of Singapore's Chinese and English poems are unique. Integral to the poems are Singapore's culture and history; the poems are an earnest voice and record. When we connect the 'dots and lines' of these literary creations, examining the words carefully, we will see the history, culture, time and so on, all revealed from within the words, which can be tested for precision, expression of meaning, tone, sound, rhythm and space. Reading these poems we will experience a sense of participation in the historical events and this stimulates our minds and adds to our knowledge.

References

Kwan-Terry, John. "Ulysses Circling the Merlion: The Invention of Identity in *Singapore Poetry in English and Chinese*". In *Perceiving Worlds*, edited by Edwin Thumboo. Singapore: Times Academic Press, 1991, pp 115–38.

Lee, Tzu Pheng. "Introduction, Singapore Poetry in English". In *Anthology of ASEAN Literature: The Poetry of Singapore*, edited by Edwin Thumboo. Singapore: Singapore ASEAN Committee on Culture and Information, 1985.

Singh, Kirpal, and Wong Yoon Wah (eds). *Rhythms: A Singaporean Millennial Anthology of Poetry*. Singapore: National Arts Council, 2001.

Tay, Simon. *Prism*. Singapore: SH Tay, 1980.

———. *5*. Singapore: Department of English Language and Literature, National University of Singapore, 1985.

———. *Stand Alone*. Singapore: Landmark Books, 1991.

———. *Over Singapore*. Singapore: Archipelago Press, 1993.

———. *Alien Asian*. Singapore: Landmark Books, 1997.

Thumboo, Edwin (ed). *Anthology of ASEAN Literature: The Poetry of Singapore*. Singapore: ASEAN Committee on Culture and Information, 1985.

Xi Nier (希尼尔, Chia Hwee Pheng). *To Kidnap the Time* (绑架岁月). Singapore: May Poetry Club, 1989.

———. *The Unbearable Heaviness of Life* (生命里难以承受的重). Singapore: Qi Yang Publishing, 1992.

———. *The Serious Mask* (认真面具). Singapore: SNP Publishing, 1998.

———. *Trustworthiness* (轻信莫疑). Singapore: Singapore Association of Writers, 2001.

Index

A
Aachen Munich Fire Insurance Co, 241
Adnan Saidi, 126
Aik Ho, 177
Aiken, T, 245
Aitken, James, 236
Aldag, RJ, 281
Aliens Bill, 96
Allan, AD, 234
Allport, Gordon, 36
Amalgamated Steel Corp (Amsteel), 176, 190
Amazon.com, 39, 40
Amoy University, 99
Anderson, Benedict, 124
Anderson Consulting, 277
ASEAN, 5
Asia Insurance Co, 240
Asia Union Life and Accident Assurance Society Ltd, 241
Asiatic Development, 179
Aw Boon Haw, 176, 177, 180, 191

B
Backman, M, 279
Baldwin, SL, 343
Ban Chye Ho Club, 215
Ban Hin Lee Bank, 240, 246
Ban Joo Hin, 227
Ban Kah Choon, 111
Barisan Nasional (BN), 144-148, 150, 152, 153
Barisan Sosialis, 143, 154
Batu Pahat Bank, 245
Behn, Meyer and Co, 241, 242, 243
Beijing Convention, 340
Birch, David, 377, 378, 379, 387
Bjerke, B, 277
Blundell, Governor, 306
Blythe, Wilfred, 90
Bolt, Paul J, 129, 130
Borneo Co, 223, 226, 231, 232, 245
Boustead and Co, 223, 232, 245
Bracker, J, 281
Brecht, Bertolt, 380
British Malaya Trustee and Executor Co, 231
Brooke, Charles, 338, 345, 347, 348
Builders' Guild of Selangor, 203
Butcher, John, 184

C
Carland, JW, 281
Carlson, Ellsworth, 341
Carstens, Sharon, 315
Celestial Reasoning Society, 93, 94
Census 2000 (Singapore), 331-336
Central Provident Fund, 259, 260
Chan, Chris, 294, 295
Chan Kang Swi, 231
Chan, KE, 56, 59
Chan Kong Choy, 82
Chan Kwok Bun, 113, 176, 178, 182, 183, 192, 257
Chan Ngo Bee, 235
Chan, SJ, 96
Chandra, R, 58
Chang Pi-shih, 208, 227, 228
Chang, Queeny, 74, 79
Chartered Bank, 223, 225, 236, 244
Chayang Association, 88
Cheah Choo Yew, 227
Cheang Hong Lim, 87, 89
Cheang Sam Teo, 89
Chen Changhui, Reverend, 348, 349
Chen Chunan, 345
Chen Delun, 203
Chen Guandou, 349
Chen, Peter, 263, 269
Chen Sheng Tang, 72
Cheng Heng Jem, William, 176
Cheng Hoon Teng, 304
Cheng Kee Hean Club, 215
Cheng, William, 190
Chenglock Soohock and Co, 231
Cheong Yoke Choy, 235, 240
Chew Hean Swee, 99
Chia, Felix, 74
Chia Hwee Pheng, xv, xvi, 389-398
Chiam Kim Kak, 306
Chiang, Claire, 176, 178, 182, 183, 192
Chiang Kai-shek, 104
Chiew Seen Kong, ix, x, 34, 35
Chiew Yoke, 184
China CCP, 98
China Press, 154
Chinese Advisory Board, 91
Chinese Affairs Department, 99
Chinese Chambers of Commerce, 77, 80, 95, 143, 229
Chinese Commercial Bank, 230, 236, 237,

245
Chinese Guilds and Associations (CGA), 150, 151
Chinese Heritage Centre, 129
Chinese Merchants General Chamber of Commerce (CMGCC), 97
Chinese Philomatic Society, 94
Chinese Town Council, 80
Chng, David KY, 86, 213
Chong Tze Chien, 386
Choon Guan Hock Club, 215
Choong Chee Pang, xiv, 325
Chop Seng Chiang Co, 235
Chow Mun Seong, 185
Chua Jui Ming, 82
Chua Moh Choon, 90
Chua Soo Ee, 277
Chuah Yu Kay, 227
Chui Huai Lim Club, 215
Chung Ho T'ang, 94, 95, 106
Chung Hwa Confucian School, 155
Chung Keng Kwee, 176, 191
Citizens' Consultative Committees (CCCs), 113
Clementi Smith, Sir Cecil, 91, 93, 96, 98
Coca-Cola, 22, 39, 40
Cohen, Myron, 181
Collins, Judson Dwight, 340
Comaroff, John and Jean, 303
Comintern, 98
Commercial Bank of China, 219
Commercial Union, 227, 242
Committee on Singapore's Competitiveness, 255, 266
Committee to Promote Enterprise Overseas, 262
Community Centre Management Committees (CCMCs), 113
Companies Act 1866 (India), 225
Cultural Revolution, 40
Cushman, Jennifer, 227

D
Davis, NJ, 245
Davos World Economic Forum, 121
DeBernardi, Jean, xiv, 301, 303, 308, 312, 316
Dell, 41
Democratic Action Party (DAP), 138, 143, 145, 146, 149-152
Democratic Party, 105
Deng Xiaoping, 115, 130
Derrick, GA, 234
Development Bank of Singapore (DBS), 258
Dongjiaozong, 157, 160, 164, 165

Drama Box, 386

E
East India Company, 86
Eastern Shipping, 227, 228
Eastern Trading, 228
Eastern United Assurance Co, 228, 230, 232-236, 238, 240, 242, 243
Eber, John, 103
Economic Development Board (EDB), 259, 261, 268
Economist Intelligence Unit, 277
Edmonds, FM, 245
Education Act 1961 (Malaysia), 158, 159, 163, 168
Education Ordinance 1995 (Malaysia), 159, 168
Ee Hoe Hean Club, 99, 215, 216
Ee Yew Kim, 235
Eisenstadt, SN, 312
Elliot, FM, 234
Emperor Guangxu, 344, 346
Eu Tong Sen, 191, 235, 240

F
Far East Flora Pte Ltd, 278, 296
Federation of Chinese Associations, Malaysia, 150
Federation of the Selangor Chinese Guilds, 208
Fergusson, EMF, 245
Filley, AC, 281
Foo Chee Choon, 208
Foo Choo Choon, 176, 191, 228
Foot, Rosemary, 129
Ford, 40
Ford, J, 245
Fougere, HJ, 236, 243
Fraser and Neave Ltd, 239, 245
Freedman, Maurice, 89
Friedland, Jonathan, 190

G
Gan Eng Seng, 215
Gan Eng Seng School, 167
Gardella, Robert, 341
Genting, 176, 178, 188
George, Cherian, 118, 132
Gerakan Rakyat Malaysia, 138, 143, 148, 149, 151, 154, 313, 314
GH Slot and Co, 241
Ghee Hin, 87, 88, 184
Ghee Hok, 87, 89, 90
Ghee Kiat Society, 212

Gidlund, Janerik, 130
Gilfillan, Wood and Co, 226
Gillis, John R, 126
Goh Boon Keng, 242
Goh Boon Teck, 384
Goh Chok Tong, 119, 122-124, 132
Goh Keng Swee, 120
Goh Lay Kuan, 380, 381
Golas, Peter J, 201
Gomez, Terence, 179, 188, 189, 190
Great Eastern Life Assurance (GE), xiii, 220, 228, 231, 233-236, 238, 242, 245
Guan Lee Hin, 227
Guild of Chinese Medicines of Singapore, 206
Gunong Sayang Association (Singapore), 79

H
Hack, Karl, 112
Haffner, Christopher, 309
Hamburg Bremen Fire Insurance Co, 241
Hamid, Arshat, 58
Hansberry, Lorraine, 380
Harper, TN, 112
Harris, JW, 236, 243
Harrison and Crosfield, 223
Hau Say Huan, 99
Hean Yean Guild, 198
Heng Pang Kiat, 203, 208
Heng Pek Koon, 190
Hill, Michael, 119
Hiscock, Geoff, 190
Ho Eng Seng, 69
Ho Hong Bank, 232, 237
Ho Hong Co, 236
Ho Hong Steamship Co, 232
Ho Khai Leong, xii, 137
Ho Tiang Wan, 227
Hoalim, Philip, 103
Hobsbawm, Eric, 124
Honda, 176, 188
Hong Kong and Shanghai Banking Corp (HSBC), 223, 225, 233, 236, 244, 246
Hong Nin Fire and Marine Insurance Co, 241
Housing and Development Board (HDB), 18, 19, 260
Howard, R, 277
Huang Fuju, 343
Huang Jianli, 112, 114
Huang Jingdai, 344
Huang Naishang, xv, 338, 342, 343, 344, 345, 346, 347, 348, 350
Huff, WG, 113, 257, 258
Hui Hsien She, 92
Hujung Goldsmith Group, 198

I
I Ching, 210
I-Lien Dramatic Society, 384
Infocomm Development Authority (IDA), 278, 296
Institute of Management Consultants, 280
Institute of Political Studies, 110
INTRACO, 258

J
Java Sea and Fire Insurance Co, 241
Jek Yeun Thong, 114
Jit Shin Pao, 230, 344, 345, 347
Jit, Krishen, 384, 385
Johnson, Stephen, 340
Jordan, AB, 99
Jurong Town Corp (JTC), 258
Justice Party, 153

K
K'ang Yu-wei, 93-95, 210, 229, 343, 344, 345
Kao, John, 127
Karniol, Robert, 130
Katz Brothers Ltd, 241
Kay, L, 277
Keats, B, 281
Khaw Sim Bee, 227, 228
Khean Guan Insurance, 221, 226, 227, 228, 242, 243
Kheng Leong Society, 212
Kheng Teck Society, 212, 213, 214
Khoo Joo Ee, 74, 79, 80
Khoo Kay Peng, 246
Khoo Seok Wan, 93, 95, 230
Khoo Sian Tan, 232, 233
Khoo Su Nin, 304
Khoo Teck Puat, 246
Khoo Thean Teik, 227
Khoo Yang Tin, 246
Khor Gark Kim, 314
Kim Ban Choon Club, 215
Kim Seng and Co, 232
King An, 86
Klein, Ronald D, 382
Ko Teck Kin, 105
Koe Guan Group, 221, 228, 239, 247, 248
Koe Guan Shipping, 227
Koh Hock Kiat, xv, 389

Koh Tai Ann, xv, xvi, 355
Kok Heng Leun, 384
Kon, Stella, 379
Kong Hock Shipping, 227
Kong Hok Kiong, 304
Ku Seok Wan, 347, 348
Kua Kia Soong, 313, 315
Kuo Pao Kun, xvi, 377-387
Kuo, Eddie CY, 115, 325, 326, 329-336
Kuok, Robert, xiii, 176, 178-180, 188, 189, 191, 193
Kuomintang (KMT), xi, 77, 95, 97, 98-100, 102, 104-106, 142, 257
Kwok Kian Woon, 118, 378
Kwong Yik Bank, 185, 221, 235, 239, 240

L

Labour Party, 143
Lai Teck, 102
Lam Aik Company, 188
Lat Poh, 186
le Blond, Max, 378, 382
Leavitt, HJ, 277
Lee Cheng Tee, 89
Lee Cheng Yan, 215, 232
Lee Chim Tuan, 231, 245
Lee Chin Tian, 99
Lee Choon Chuan, 231, 234, 237
Lee Choon Guan, 232
Lee Group, 186, 187
Lee Hsien Loong, 116, 117
Lee Kam Hing, xiii, 185, 219
Lee Khoon Choy, 114, 381
Lee Kok Liang, xv, 355-375
Lee Kong Chian, xiii, 105, 176-178, 180, 183, 185-189, 191-193, 238, 245
Lee Kuan Yew, 13, 101, 102, 105, 111, 112, 114, 118, 121, 125, 130, 326, 327
Lee Leung Ki, 240
Lee Loy Seng, 192
Lee Rubber Co, 177, 185-187, 245
Lee San Soon, 82
Lee, SH, 266
Lee Wah Bank, 235, 240, 246
Leete, R, 56
Leifer, Michael, 111
Leung, Philip, xv, 337
Li Chang, 348, 349
Li Hongzhang, 344
Li Wenhai, 339
Liang Qichao, 343, 344
Lien Ying Chow, 105
Lim Ah Lek, 82

Lim Bo Seng, 126, 394
Lim Boon Keng, 91, 93, 94, 97, 229, 230, 232, 233, 235-237, 248, 303, 344, 345, 347, 348
Lim, Catherine, xv, 355-375
Lim Chong Eu, 149, 313
Lim Chong Yah, 259, 260
Lim Giok Lan, Shirley, 74, 79
Lim Goh Tong, xiii, 176, 178, 188, 189
Lim Ho Puah, 215
Lim Hong Bee, 102
Lim How Seng, 213
Lim Kay Tong, 379
Lim Kho Leng, 238
Lim Kit Siang, 149, 150
Lim Lan and Co, 226
Lim Mah Hui, 220
Lim Nee Soon, 94, 97, 345
Lim Peng Siang, 215, 232, 237
Lim Yew Hock, 106
Lin Qingjin, 314
Lin Wenqing, 344
Lin Xu, 344
Ling Liong Sik, 82
Ling Xiao, 339
Lion Group, 176, 190
Liu, Hong, 129
Logan, JR, 306
Loh, Benjamin, xiv, 277
Loh Boon Siew, xiii, 176, 188, 189, 190
Loke Wan Tho, 234
Loke Yew, xiii, 176, 183-185, 191, 233, 235, 240
London Missionary Society, 340
London Tin-Charter Consolidated, 245
Looi Hoi Choon, 233
Lun Tai Mutual Fire and Marine Insurance Co, 241
Lynch, Daniel C, 130

M

MacDonald, Malcolm, 103
Mackie, Jamie, xii, 175
Mahathir Mohamad, 153
Malacca Rubber and Tapioca Co, 233
Malay Nationalist Party (MNP), 101
Malayan Banking, 246
Malayan Chinese Association (MCA), 101, 138, 141-143, 145-151, 154, 221
Malayan Civil Service (MCS), 97
Malayan Collieries, 185
Malayan Communist Party (MCP), xi, 77, 95, 98-104, 142, 157

Index 405

Malayan Constitution, 139
Malayan Democratic Union (MDU), 101, 103
Malayan General Labour Union, 98
Malayan Indian Congress (MIC), 101, 141
Malayan People's Anti-Japanese Army (MPAJA), 101
Malayan Planning Unit, 100
Malayan Singapore Committee for Premier Chiang's Birthday Aeroplane Fund, 99
Malayan United Industries Bank, 246
Malaysian Chinese Association (MCA), 61, 82
Mansfield and Co, 226
Mao Tse-tung, 104
Marshall, David, 106
Martijn and Co, 241
Martin, WAP, 344
Material Application Centre, 259
McAlister and Co, 234
McDonald's, 22, 39
McKeown, Adam, 127
Meiji Insurance Co, 241
Menkhoff, Thomas, xiv, 273, 277
Mercantile Bank, 225, 242, 244
Merdeka University, 165
Microsoft Word, 39, 265
Ministry of Community Development, 325, 326
Ministry of Trade and Industry, 25
Mirzan Mahathir, 190
Mitsui Bussan Kaisha, 242
Monetary Authority of Singapore (MAS), 259
Moore, Donald, 379
Moxon, HW, 245
Munro, William Bennett, 137
Munshi Abdullah, 70

N
Nanyang Press, 154
Nanyang University, 114, 115, 131, 156, 208, 258
National Chinese Internet Programme, 129
National Front, 61
National Library Board, 129
National Product Company, 186
National University of Singapore, 115, 278, 325
National Wages Council (NWC), 259
Necessary Stage, 386
Netherlands Fire Insurance Co, 241

Ng Beoy Kui, xiii, 113, 255, 257, 259
Ng Kong Beng, 188
Nichiren Shoshu Buddhist Association, 336
Ning Yang Association, 88, 199
North City Guild, 198-202
North German Fire Insurance Co, 241
North Nu Guild, 198
Nu Ban, 198, 199
Nu City Guild, 198
Nyalas Rubber Estates Ltd, 231

O
Oei Tiong Ham, 237, 246
Oei Tjong Le, 246
Oldham, W, 233
Olympic Games, 128
Ong Aihwa, 124
Ong Pang Boon, 114
Ong Piah Teng, 240
Ong Soon Tee, 232, 233
Ong Teng Cheong, 120
Ong Tiang Swee, 347
Ooi, Diana, 78
Ooi Giok Ling, 111
Ordinance to amend the Law relating to Societies, 91
Oriental Holdings, 176, 188
Ormsby-Gore, 180
Oversea-Chinese Banking Corporation (OCBC), xiii, 180, 185, 187, 219, 220-222, 228, 230-232, 237-241, 244-247
Overseas Assurance Corporation (OAC), 220, 228, 230, 232, 235, 236, 238, 239, 245
Overseas Chinese Association, 248
Overseas Chinese Bank, 237

P
Pacific Bank, 245
Pahang Motorcar Service Co, 185
Palm, 39, 40
Pan Malayan Islamic Party, 149
Pao Huang Hui, 93-95, 106
Pearson, J, 281
Peet, Lyman B, 340
Penang Central Festival Representative Committee, 313, 314
Penang General Merchants' Association, 211
People's Action Party (PAP), xi, 102, 105, 106, 111-114, 118, 119, 143, 257, 258, 260, 272

People's Association, 113
Peranakan Association of Singapore, 79, 83
Persatuan Peranakan Cina Kelantan, 79, 83
Persatuan Peranakan Cina Melaka, 79, 83
Persatuan Peranakan Cina Pulau Pinang, 79, 80
Petronas Towers, 316
Pfeffer, J, 277
Pickering, WA, 89, 90
PMCJA (Pan-Malayan Council of Joint Action)-PUTERA (Pusat Tenaga Ra'ayat), 103
Png Poh Seng, 74
Poh, T, 304
Practice Theatre Ensemble (PTE), xvi, 384
Pranger, Robert J, 137
Public Bank, 246
Purcell, Victor, 303, 311

Q
Qiu Shuyuan, 345
Quah Beng Kee, 227, 235, 243
Quah Sy Ren, xvi, 377
Quah, Jon ST, 325

R
Raffles College, 189
Raffles, Stamford, 12
Rajaratnam, 37
Ranger, Terence, 124
Rawang Electric Supply Co, 185
Redding, SG, 279
Restaurateurs' Guild of Selangor, 203
Restaurateurs' Guild of Singapore, 202
Richard, Timothy, 344
Rixin Bao, 344, 345, 347
Rodan, G, 257
Roper Calbeck, HB, 245
Royal Insurance, 242
Rubber Traders Association, 186
Rudolph, Jurgen, 69

S
Sahlins, Marshall, 303, 304
Sai Siew Min, 112, 114
Salancik, GR, 277
Sarawak Shipping Co, 233
Sarkie and Moses, 226
Sasitharan, T, 377, 387
Saw, Swee Hock, 46
Schlegel, Gustave, 309

Schluchter, Wolfgang, 312
Seah Eng Lim, 235, 240
Searle, Peter, 179, 189
See Teong Wah, 233
Selangor Chinese Medicinal Merchants' Guild, 207
Selangor Grocers' Guild, 203
Selangor Wine and Spirit Dealers' Association, 203
Semple, 311
Serendak Hydraulic Co, 185
Seymour, Alan, 380
Shah Alam Airport, 316
Shanghai Fire and Marine Insurance Co, 240
Shanghai Yihe Gongsi Baoxian Hang, 219
Shantung Relief Fund, 99
Sharma, Haresh, 386
Shellabear, WG, 303
Shih Chung Branch School, 161
Shulin Yuan Club, 215
Sime Darby, 220, 223, 231, 232, 239, 245, 246
Simon, H, 288
Singapore Amateur Players, 384
Singapore Botanic Gardens, 233
Singapore China Relief Fund, 99
Singapore Chinese Chamber of Commerce, 102, 105, 230
Singapore Chinese Chamber of Commerce and Industry (SCCCI), 113, 129, 257, 278, 280
Singapore Chinese Girls' School, 230
Singapore Chinese High School, 99
Singapore Chinese Mobilization Council, 99
Singapore Chinese Peranakan Association, 73, 79
Singapore Citizenship Ordinance 1957, 105
Singapore City Committee, 104
Singapore City Council, 105
Singapore Federation of Chinese Clan Associations, 129, 330
Singapore Grocers' Guild, 203, 204, 211
Singapore Industrial Standards and Industrial Research (SISIR), 259
Singapore Insurance Co, 227, 234
Singapore Land Co, 226
Singapore Performing Arts School (SPAS), xvi, 380, 381
Singapore Piece Goods Traders' Guild, 202, 203, 205
Singapore Productivity and Standards

Board (PSB), 256, 267, 270, 271, 278, 280
Singapore Progressive Party (SPP), 101
Singapore Rubber Limited, 230
Singapore Slipway Co, 231
Singapore Textile Dealers' Friendly Association, 205
Singapore Volunteer Corps, 102
Singapore-Malaya Chinese Textile Merchants' Association, 205
Sino-Japanese War, 93, 98
Sites, Nathan, 340, 343
Skills Development Fund, 259
Small Enterprises Development Bureau, 261
Small Industry Advisory Committee, 259
Smith, Anthony D, 312
Smith, N, 281
Sng Choon Yee, 99
Song Ong Siang, 91, 92, 94, 96, 215, 229, 236
Soon Peng Yam, 105
South British Insurance Co, 232, 236, 243
Southern Arts Society, 384
Southseas China Relief Fund Union, 99, 104
Standards, Productivity and Innovation Board, 278, 296
State Chinese (P) Association (SCA), 80, 83
State Chinese (Penang) Association, 76
Stirling, William G, 310
Stock Exchange of Singapore Dealing and Automated Quotation (SESDAQ), 261
Straits Albion Press, 231
Straits Chinese British Association (SCBA), xi, 73, 76, 77, 79, 80, 83, 94-97, 100, 102, 106, 142, 229, 231-234
Straits Chinese Magazine, 94, 229
Straits Fire Insurance Co, 226, 242
Straits Insurance Co, 223, 225, 226, 227
Straits Settlements, 3, 69, 72, 73, 75, 76, 86, 92, 93, 180
Straits Settlements Association, 226, 229
Straits Settlements Legal, Medical and Civil Services, 97
Straits Steamship Co, xiii, 185, 228, 231, 232, 233, 234, 237, 245
Straits Trading Co, xiii, 185, 228, 230, 233, 234, 239, 245
Sun Yat-sen, 5, 94, 125, 126, 345
Suryadinata, Leo, viii, x, xvi, 69

Suthakar, K, 315
Suzhou Industrial Park, 130
Suzuki, 190
Swatch, 22
Syed Mohamed Alsagoff, 226
Sze Hai Tong Bank, 220, 235, 236, 240

T
T'ung Meng Hui, 94, 95, 97, 106
Tan, BA, 56
Tan Beng Swee, 89
Tan Boo Liat, 97
Tan Chay Yan, 97, 192, 230, 232, 233, 235, 248
Tan Chee Beng, 69, 73, 75, 303
Tan Cheng Lock, 82, 96, 221, 230, 231, 232, 236, 237, 238, 244-246, 248, 304
Tan Cheng Siong, 215
Tan Chin Tuan, 105, 215, 234, 244, 245, 246, 248
Tan Choon Bock, 230, 231, 234
Tan Chor Nam, 94, 97, 345
Tan Ean Kian, 238
Tan Eng Joo, 177, 188
Tan Ern Ser, 35, 111
Tan, Eugene, xi, 109
Tan Hay Kwan, 230
Tan Hock, 258
Tan How Seng, 86
Tan Jiak Kim, 232, 233, 245
Tan Kah Kee, 95, 98-100, 102, 104, 106, 176, 177, 180, 182, 185, 186, 188, 193, 216, 245
Tan Keong Choon, 105
Tan Keong Saik, 231, 232, 234
Tan Kheam Hock, 232, 233, 235, 243
Tan Kia Hong, 178
Tan Kim Cheng, 87
Tan Kim Seng, 87, 89, 232, 394
Tan Koon Suan, 82
Tan KY, Tony, 262, 266
Tan Lark Sye, 105, 177, 240
Tan Liok Ee, xii, 155
Tan Seng Poh, 215
Tan Seng Tong, 72
Tan Siew Sin, 82, 221, 238, 246
Tan Sri Noah Omar, 179
Tan Teck Lun, 203
Tan Tock Seng, 87, 89
Tan, Tony, 268
Tang Liang Hong, 118
Tanglin Club, 234
Tanjong Pagar Dock Co, 231

Tank Jiak Kim, 215
Tay, Simon, xv, xvi, 389-398
Technopreneurship Investment Fund, 268
Teh Hong Piow, 246
Teo Eng Hock, 94, 97, 345
Tey Nai Peng, x, 45, 56, 58, 59
Thailand Mining Co, 233
Thien Nan Shin Pao, 94, 230
Thoe Lam Jit Poh, 94
Tian Chua, 153
Tien Ti Hui, 87
Tiger Balm, 176
Toffler, A, 277
Tokong, 89
Tong Chee Kiong, 325, 330
Triad, 87, 89, 90
Trocki, Carl A, 86, 308
Tronoh Mines Ltd, 245
Truman, President, 104
Tso Ping Lung, 92, 93
Tun Husein Onn, 179
Tun Razak, 179
Tunku Abdul Rahman, 178
Turnbull, CM, 91

U

Ultra-Industrial Automation Pte Ltd, 294, 295
United Chinese Bank, 240, 246
United Chinese School Committees' Association, 150
United Chinese School Teachers' Association, 150
United Democratic Party, 143
United Engineers, 245
United General Assembly of Malaysian Daoist Organizations, 316
United Malays National Organisation (UMNO), 101, 138, 140, 141, 143, 145, 148, 151, 153, 154, 160, 179, 190
United Overseas Bank (UOB), 240
US National Science Foundation, 262

V

Vasil, Raj K, 114, 131, 257, 258, 262
Vaughan, JD, 73, 89, 198, 305
Venture Capital Fund, 261
Verchere, Ian, 190
Victoria Sawmill, 235
Vision 2020, 315

W

Wang Bangjie, 203, 208
Wang Changshui, 347

Wang Gungwu, ix, xvi, 1, 101
Wang Xifang, 344
Wang Zhenzhong, 339
Wearnes, 245
Weber, Max, 305
Wee Bin, 227
White Paper on Singapore's Shared Values, 121
White, Moses, 340
Wilcox, Myron, 343
Williamson, Alexander, 344
Wilson, Dick, 187
Wong Ah Fook, 235
Wong Choon San, 304
Wong Kan Seng, 175, 183
Wong Lin Ken, 86
Wong Nai Siong. *See* HUANG NAISHANG
Wong Siew Qui, 235, 236, 245, 248
Wong Siu-lun, 257
Workers' Party, 118
World Chinese Business Network, 129
World Chinese Entrepreneurs Convention, 129
World Trade Organization, 128
World War I, 228
World War II, 5, 45, 49, 77, 96, 248
Wynne, ML, 89

X

Xiao Tao Yuan Club, 215
Xing Yun Fa Shi, 336

Y

Yap Ah Loy, 208
Yeap Chor Ee, 240
Yen Ching-hwang, xiii, 195
Yeo, George, 125
Yeo Hiap Seng, 38
Yeo Wee Gark, 227
Yin Suat Chuan, 97, 229, 236, 237
Yong, CF, xi, 85, 113, 180, 182
Yu Lieh, 94
Yu Yun, 383

Z

Zhang Yongfu, 345